McGraw-Hill Education

3 MCAT Practice Tests

THIRD EDITION

McGraw-Hill Education
3 MCAT Practice Tests

THIRD EDITION

George J. Hademenos, PhD

Candice McCloskey Campbell, PhD

Shaun Murphree, PhD

Amy B. Wachholtz, PhD

Jennifer M. Warner, PhD

Kathy A. Zahler, MS

Thomas A. Evangelist, MA   Contributor

New Yo   drid
Mexico   nto

1 2 3 4 5 6 7 8 9   LOV   21 20 19 18 17 16

ISBN   978-1-259-85962-5
MHID   1-259-85962-2

e-ISBN   978-1-259-85963-2
e-MHID   1-259-85963-0

MCAT is a registered trademark of the Association of American Medical Colleges, which was not involved in the production of, and does not endorse, this product.

McGraw-Hill Education products are available at special quantity discounts to use as premiums and sales promotions or for use in corporate training programs. To contact a representative, please visit the Contact Us pages at www.mhprofessional.com.

Amy B. Wachholtz, PhD, would like to thank Christopher Ayala, MA, for assistance with fact checking and editing the behavioral and social sciences material in this volume.

Contents

MCAT Basics | The Computerized Test Format | Where and When to Take the
MCAT | How to Register for the MCAT | Taking the MCAT More Than Once |
Your MCAT Scores | How Medical Schools Use MCAT Scores | Reporting
Scores to Medical Schools | For Further Information | The Format of
the Test | What Is Tested in the Science Sections | What Is Tested in Critical
Analysis and Reasoning Skills | General Test-Taking Strategies

MCAT PRACTICE TEST 3

About the Authors

George J. Hademenos, PhD, is a former Visiting Assistant Professor of Physics at the University of Dallas. He received his BS from Angelo State University, received his MS and PhD from the University of Texas at Dallas, and completed postdoctoral fellowships in nuclear medicine at the University of Massachusetts Medical Center and in radiological sciences/biomedical physics at UCLA Medical Center. His research interests have involved potential applications of physics to the biological and medical sciences, particularly with cerebrovascular diseases and stroke. He has published his work in journals such as *American Scientist, Physics Today, Neurosurgery,* and *Stroke.* In addition, he has written several books including *The Physics of Cerebrovascular Diseases*: *Biophysical Mechanisms of Development, Diagnosis and Therapy,* and *Schaum's Outline of Biology.* He currently teaches general and advanced physics courses.

Candice McCloskey Campbell, PhD, received her doctorate in organic chemistry from Georgia Tech in 1985. She has been teaching at the undergraduate level since 1987. She currently teaches at Georgia Perimeter College in Dunwoody, Georgia. Her professional work has been in synthetic organic chemistry and mechanistic organic chemistry. She has been active with the Two-Year College Chemistry Consortium to enhance the chemistry curriculum at the two-year college level.

Shaun Murphree, PhD, is Professor and Chair of Chemistry at Allegheny College in Meadville, Pennsylvania. He received a BA in chemistry from Colgate University (Hamilton, New York) and a PhD in organic chemistry from Emory University (Atlanta, Georgia), and he conducted postdoctoral study at Wesleyan University (Middletown, Connecticut). His current research interests include microwave-assisted organic synthesis (MAOS), synthetic methodology, and heterocyclic synthesis. In addition to the present work, he has coauthored a monograph on microwave chemistry, several chapters and reviews on heterocyclic synthesis, and numerous articles in both the synthetic chemistry and chemistry education literature.

Amy B. Wachholtz, PhD, MDiv, MS, is an Assistant Professor of Psychology at the University of Colorado Denver. Dr. Wachholtz graduated with a Master of Divinity degree from Boston University where she specialized in Bioethics. She then continued her education to earn her PhD in Clinical Psychology from Bowling Green State University where she had a dual specialization in Behavioral Medicine and Psychology of Religion. She completed her internship through fellowship training at Duke University where she focused on medical psychology and pain management. She also recently completed a postdoctoral Master's degree in Psychopharmacology. Her research and clinical interests focus on 1) bio-psycho-social-spiritual model of chronic pain disorders and 2) the complexities of treating of co-morbid pain and opioid addiction in both acute pain and chronic pain situations. She enjoys teaching students from a wide variety of disciplines both in the classroom and on the clinical floors of University of Colorado Medical Center.

Jennifer M. Warner, PhD, is the Director of the University Honors Program and a member of the faculty in the Department of Biological Sciences at the University of North Carolina at Charlotte. She received her BS in biology from the University of North Carolina at Chapel Hill, her MS in biology with a focus in microbiology from the University of North Carolina at Charlotte, and her PhD in curriculum and teaching from the University of North Carolina at Greensboro. Her current research interests revolve around variables that influence student success and retention in the sciences. She currently teaches a variety of courses including principles of biology, human biology, the nature of science, and pathogenic bacteriology.

Kathy A. Zahler, MS, is a widely published author and textbook writer. She has authored or coauthored numerous McGraw-Hill Education preparation guides for tests, including the GRE®, the Miller Analogies Test, the Test of Essential Academic Skills (TEAS®), and the Test Assessing Secondary Completion™ (TASC™).

How to Use This Book

Welcome to McGraw-Hill Education's *3 MCAT Practice Tests*. You've made the decision to pursue a medical career, you've studied hard, you've taken and passed the most difficult science courses, and now you must succeed on this very tough exam. We're here to help you.

The three full-length MCAT sample tests in this book have been created by a team of teachers and test-prep experts. Together, they have helped thousands of students score high on all kinds of exams. Here, they have pooled their knowledge, experience, and test-taking expertise to make this the most effective practice program available.

These practice tests simulate the real exam in structure, format, and degree of difficulty. Of course, these practice tests can provide only an approximation of how well you will do on the actual MCAT. However, if you approach them as you would the real test, they should give you a very good idea of how well you are prepared.

In this book you will find:

➤ **A general introduction to the MCAT,** including basic facts about the structure and format of the test and the kinds of questions you will encounter.

➤ **Important test-taking strategies** that can help you raise your score.

➤ **Explanations for every question.** After you take each test, read carefully through these explanations, paying special attention to those you answered incorrectly or had to guess on. If necessary, go back and reread the subject review sections in the corresponding chapters.

ONLINE RESOURCES

This book also provides you with access to a wealth of online review content. Covering all four major sections of the MCAT, these online resources provide concise summaries of the most important concepts found on the exam, extensive illustrations that clarify the most challenging topics, and tools to help approach specific question types in the most effective way. This extensive review material is divided into three sections:

➤ **Biological and Biochemical Foundations of Living Systems.** This section looks at Part 1 of the MCAT, which assesses your knowledge of foundational concepts in biology and biochemistry and your understanding of how biological processes function, both separately and together, in living systems, including the human body.

➤ **Chemical and Physical Foundations of Biological Systems.** Covering Part 2 of the MCAT, this section assesses your knowledge of foundational concepts in general chemistry, organic chemistry, and physics and your understanding of how chemical and physical processes function, both separately and together, in living systems, including the human body.

➤ **Behavioral and Social Sciences & Critical Analysis.** This review section provides in-depth coverage of all the topics tested in Parts 3 and 4 of the exam: Psychological, Social, and Biological Foundations of Behavior and Critical Analysis and Reasoning Skills. Part 3 of the exam tests your knowledge of basic concepts in psychology and sociology that are important for understanding how behavioral and sociocultural factors affect health outcomes and the provision of health care. Part 4 of the exam tests your ability to analyze, evaluate, and apply information from reading passages in a wide range of social sciences, general sciences, and humanities areas.

These review materials include dozens of extra practice questions.

Visit MHPracticePlus.com/MCAT to access the online review materials. You will be able to download textbook-quality PDFs to study on your computer or laptop.

Introducing the MCAT

Read This Section to Learn About

➤ MCAT Basics
➤ The Computerized Test Format
➤ Where and When to Take the MCAT
➤ How to Register for the MCAT
➤ Taking the MCAT More Than Once
➤ Your MCAT Scores
➤ How Medical Schools Use MCAT Scores
➤ Reporting Scores to Medical Schools
➤ For Further Information
➤ The Format of the Test
➤ What Is Tested in the Science Sections
➤ What Is Tested in Critical Analysis and Reasoning Skills
➤ General Test-Taking Strategies

MCAT BASICS

The Medical College Admission Test (MCAT) is a standardized exam that is used to assess applicants to medical schools. The test is sponsored by the Association of American Medical Colleges (AAMC) in cooperation with its member schools. It is required as part of the admissions process by most U.S. medical schools. The test is administered by Prometric, a private firm that is a leading provider of technology-based testing and assessment services.

The questions on the MCAT are basically designed to measure your problem-solving and critical-thinking skills. Two test sections assess your mastery of fundamental concepts in biology, biochemistry, general chemistry, organic chemistry, and physics. A third section tests your understanding of concepts in psychology, sociology, and biology that are important to understanding how behavioral and sociocultural factors affect health outcomes and the provision of healthcare. For most questions in these sections, choosing the correct answer requires more than just a rote response; you must calculate a solution, interpret and evaluate given data, or apply a particular scientific principle to a given situation. You will need to demonstrate that you can reason scientifically and employ the principles of research methodology and statistics. There is also a fourth section that tests your ability to analyze, evaluate, and apply information from reading passages on topics in ethics, philosophy, cross-cultural studies, and population health.

According to the AAMC, the skills tested on the MCAT are those identified by medical professionals and educators as essential for success in medical school and in a career as a physician. The importance of the biological, biochemical, and physical sciences is self-evident. Psychological and sociological concepts are included, according to the AAMC, because "knowledge of the behavioral and social determinants of health and wellness [is] becoming more important in medical education," and "tomorrow's doctors need to know [these concepts] in order to serve a more diverse population and to understand the impact of behavior on health and wellness."

THE COMPUTERIZED TEST FORMAT

You will take the MCAT on a computer. You will view the questions on the computer screen and indicate your answers by clicking on on-screen answer ovals. As you work through the on-screen questions, you will be able to highlight relevant portions of the reading passages for easy reference. You will also be able to strike out answer choices that you know are incorrect. This will help you use the process of elimination to pick the correct answer. You will also be allowed to make notes on scratch paper (although all of your notes will be collected at the end of the test). Within each test section, you will be able to go back, review questions that you have already answered, and change your answer if you decide to do so. However, once you have finished a test section, you cannot go back to it and make any changes.

Don't be concerned if you are not a whiz with computers; the skills required are minimal, and in any case, on test day you will have the opportunity to access a computer tutorial that will show you exactly what you need to do.

WHERE AND WHEN TO TAKE THE MCAT

The MCAT is offered at approximately 275 sites in the United States (including the U.S. territories of Puerto Rico and the Virgin Islands) and at 12 sites in Canada. All of these sites are testing labs operated by Prometric. The test is also offered at numerous locations outside North America, including sites in Europe, Great Britain, the Middle East, Africa, Asia, and Australia.

There are 22 test dates every year. Two of the dates are in January, and the rest are in the period from April through early September. Most test dates are weekdays, but a few are Saturdays. On some dates, the test is given only in the morning; on others, it is given only in the afternoon. On a few dates, the test is given in both morning and afternoon sessions.

It is a good idea to take the MCAT in the spring or summer of the year before the fall in which you plan to enroll in medical school. That way, you have enough time to submit your scores to meet the schools' application deadlines.

For up-to-date lists of testing sites and also for upcoming test dates, make sure to check the official MCAT website at www.aamc.org/mcat.

HOW TO REGISTER FOR THE MCAT

You can register for the MCAT online at www.aamc.org/mcat. Online registration for each test date begins six months prior to that date. Registration is available until two weeks before the test date. It's a good idea to register early, because seating at the testing centers may be limited and you want to make sure you get a seat at the center of your choice. When you register, you are charged a fee, which you can pay by credit card. If you wish to change your test date, you can do so online.

TAKING THE MCAT MORE THAN ONCE

If your MCAT score is lower than expected, you may want to take the test again. You can take the MCAT up to three times in the same year. However, the AAMC recommends retesting only if you have a good reason to think that you will do better the next time. For example, you might do better if, when you first took the test, you were ill, or you made mistakes in keying in your answers, or your academic background in one or more of the test subjects was inadequate.

If you are considering retesting, you should also find out how your chosen medical schools evaluate multiple scores. Some schools give equal weight to all MCAT scores; others average scores together, and still others look only at the highest scores. Check with admissions officers before making a decision.

YOUR MCAT SCORES

When you take the MCAT, your work on each of the four test sections first receives a "raw score." The raw score is calculated based on the number of questions you answer correctly. No points are deducted for questions answered incorrectly. Each raw score is then converted into a scaled score. Using scaled scores helps make test-takers' scores comparable from one version of the MCAT to another. For each of the four sections, scaled scores range from 118 (lowest) to 132 (highest). Scaled scores for the entire test range from 472 (lowest) to 528 (highest).

Your score report will be mailed to you approximately 30 days after you take the MCAT. You will also be able to view your scores on the online MCAT Testing History (THx) System as soon as they become available. (For details on the THx system, see the MCAT website.) MCAT score reports also include percentile rankings that show how well you did in comparison to others who took the same test.

HOW MEDICAL SCHOOLS USE MCAT SCORES

Medical college admission committees emphasize that MCAT scores are only one of several criteria that they consider when evaluating applicants. When making their decisions, they also consider students' college and university grades, recommendations, interviews, and involvement and participation in extracurricular or health care–related activities that, in the opinion of the admission committee, illustrate maturity, motivation, dedication, and other positive personality traits that are of value to a physician. If the committee is unfamiliar with the college you attend, they may pay more attention than usual to your MCAT scores.

There is no hard-and-fast rule about what schools consider to be an acceptable MCAT score. The AAMC recommends that admissions officers should not limit acceptance to students who score in the upper third of the range. Instead, they should focus on applicants who score "at the top of the curve," that is, those whose scores lie at the top of the curve on the graph of the percentage of applicants who achieved each score point total. Statistically speaking, those students are likely to graduate successfully from medical school and to pass later qualifying exams on their first try. The AAMC says that this focus is "consistent with wholistic review practices" and "is designed to draw attention to applicants who might otherwise be overlooked." The "top of the curve" scaled score for each MCAT test section is 125; for the entire exam it is 500.

Note that many medical schools do not accept MCAT scores that are more than three years old.

REPORTING SCORES TO MEDICAL SCHOOLS

Your MCAT scores are automatically reported to the American Medical College Application Service (AMCAS), the nonprofit application processing service used by nearly all U.S. medical schools. When you use this service, you complete and submit a single application, rather than separate applications to each of your chosen schools. Your scores are submitted to your designated schools along with your application. There is a fee for using AMCAS. If you wish to submit your scores to other application services or to programs that do not participate in AMCAS, you can do so through the online MCAT Testing History (THx) System.

FOR FURTHER INFORMATION

For further information about the MCAT, visit the official MCAT website at

www.aamc.org/mcat

For questions about registering for the test, reporting and interpreting scores, and similar issues, you may also contact:

Association of American Medical Colleges
Medical College Admission Test
655 K Street, NW, Suite 100
Washington, D.C. 20001-2399

THE FORMAT OF THE TEST

The MCAT consists of four separately timed sections as outlined in the following chart.

MCAT: Format of the Test		
Section	**Number of Questions**	**Time Allowed (minutes)**
1. Biological and Biochemical Foundations of Living Systems *Break: 10 minutes*	59	95
2. Chemical and Physical Foundations of Biological Systems *Break: 10 minutes*	59	95
3. Psychological, Social, and Biological Foundations of Behavior *Break: 10 minutes*	59	95
4. Critical Analysis and Reasoning Skills	53	90
Totals	230	375 (= 6 hours, 15 minutes)

WHAT IS TESTED IN THE SCIENCE SECTIONS

The natural sciences sections of the MCAT (Sections 1 and 2) test your mastery of the concepts and principles of biology, biochemistry, general chemistry, organic chemistry, and physics as they apply to living systems, including the human body.

The behavioral and social sciences section of the MCAT (Section 3) tests your understanding of the behavioral and sociocultural factors that play a role in health care. These three sections have three main organizing principles:

1. **Foundational concepts:** what the AAMC calls the "big ideas" in the sciences that underlie the subjects taught in medical school
2. **Content categories:** the topics that support the foundational concepts
3. **Scientific inquiry and reasoning skills:** the skills needed to solve scientific problems

Foundational Concepts and Content Categories

According to the AAMS, the foundational concepts and categories for sections 1, 2, and 3 of the MCAT are as follows:

1. BIOLOGICAL AND BIOCHEMICAL FOUNDATIONS OF LIVING SYSTEMS

Foundational Concept 1: *Biomolecules have unique properties that determine how they contribute to the structure and function of cells and how they participate in the processes necessary to maintain life.*

Content categories:

➤ Structure and function of proteins and their constituent amino acids

➤ Transmission of genetic information from the gene to the protein

➤ Transmission of heritable information from generation to generation and the processes that increase genetic diversity

➤ Principles of bioenergetics and fuel molecule metabolism

Foundational Concept 2: *Highly organized assemblies of molecules, cells, and organs interact to carry out the functions of living organisms.*

Content categories:

➤ Assemblies of molecules, cells, and groups of cells within single cellular and multicellular organisms

➤ Structure, growth, physiology, and genetics of prokaryotes and viruses

➤ Processes of cell division, differentiation, and specialization

Foundational Concept 3: *Complex systems of tissues and organs sense the internal and external environments of multicellular organisms and, through integrated functioning, maintain a stable internal environment within an ever-changing external environment.*

Content categories:

➤ Structure and functions of the nervous and endocrine systems and ways in which these systems coordinate the organ systems

➤ Structure and integrative functions of the main organ systems

2. CHEMICAL AND PHYSICAL FOUNDATIONS OF BIOLOGICAL SYSTEMS

Foundational Concept 4: *Complex living organisms transport materials, sense their environment, process signals, and respond to changes using processes that can be understood in terms of physical principles.*

Content categories:

- Translational motion, forces, work, energy, and equilibrium in living systems
- Importance of fluids for the circulation of blood, gas movement, and gas exchange
- Electrochemistry and electrical circuits and their elements
- How light and sound interact with matter
- Atoms, nuclear decay, electronic structure, and atomic chemical behavior

Foundational Concept 5: *The principles that govern chemical interactions and reactions form the basis for a broader understanding of the molecular dynamics of living systems.*

Content categories:

- Unique nature of water and its solutions
- Nature of molecules and intermolecular interactions
- Separation and purification methods
- Structure, function, and reactivity of biologically relevant molecules
- Principles of chemical thermodynamics and kinetics

3. PSYCHOLOGICAL, SOCIAL, AND BIOLOGICAL FOUNDATIONS OF BEHAVIOR

Foundational Concept 6: *Biological, psychological, and sociocultural factors influence the ways that individuals perceive, think about, and react to the world.*

Content categories:

- Sensing the environment
- Making sense of the environment
- Responding to the world

Foundational Concept 7: *Biological, psychological, and sociocultural factors influence behavior and behavior change.*

Content categories:

- Individual influences on behavior
- Social processes that influence human behavior
- Attitude and behavior change

Foundational Concept 8: *Psychological, sociocultural, and biological factors influence the way we think about ourselves and others, as well as how we interact with others.*

Content categories:

➤ Self-identity

➤ Social thinking

➤ Social interactions

Foundational Concept 9: *Cultural and social differences influence well-being.*

Content categories:

➤ Understanding social structure

➤ Demographic characteristics and processes

Foundational Concept 10: *Social stratification and access to resources influence well-being.*

Content category:

➤ Social inequality

Scientific Inquiry and Reasoning Skills

The scientific inquiry and reasoning skills that are tested on Sections 1, 2, and 3 of the MCAT are as follows:

➤ **Skill 1:** Knowledge of Scientific Concepts and Principles

➤ **Skill 2:** Scientific Reasoning and Evidence-Based Problem Solving

➤ **Skill 3:** Reasoning About the Design and Execution of Research

➤ **Skill 4:** Data-Based and Statistical Reasoning

To demonstrate mastery of **Skill 1: Knowledge of Scientific Concepts and Principles**, you need to be able to recall and apply basic scientific concepts and principles to solve problems in science. In many cases, you will need to analyze and interpret information presented in diagrams, charts, graphs, and formulas.

To demonstrate mastery of **Skill 2: Scientific Reasoning and Evidence-Based Problem Solving**, you need to be able to understand and use scientific theories, to propose hypotheses, and to analyze scientific models or research studies in order to identify assumptions, make predictions, and draw conclusions.

To demonstrate mastery of **Skill 3: Reasoning About the Design and Execution of Research**, you need to be able to identify appropriate research designs for investigating specified research questions, to critique and evaluate those designs, to predict results, and to recognize ethical issues involved in research.

To demonstrate mastery of **Skill 4: Data-Based and Statistical Reasoning**, you need to be able to interpret data or to describe or evaluate the results of a research study using statistical concepts.

WHAT IS TESTED IN CRITICAL ANALYSIS AND REASONING SKILLS

The Critical Analysis and Reasoning Skills section of the MCAT (Section 4) tests your ability to comprehend information in a reading passage, to analyze and evaluate arguments and supporting evidence, and to apply concepts and ideas to new situations. The passages in this section cover a wide range of topics in both the social sciences and the humanities. You may encounter readings in philosophy, ethics, cultural studies, and similar topics. All the information you need to answer questions will be provided in the passage; no outside knowledge of the topics is required.

According to the AAMC, the questions in the Critical Analysis and Reasoning Skills section test the following four specific skills:

➤ **Comprehension:** the ability to understand new information or to view facts or ideas in a new light.

➤ **Evaluation:** the ability to analyze ideas or arguments presented in a passage and to make judgments about their reasonableness, their credibility, and the soundness of supporting evidence.

➤ **Application:** the ability to apply information in a passage to new conditions or situations and to predict possible outcomes.

➤ **Incorporation of Information:** the ability to consider how new information affects the ideas presented in a passage, for example, whether it strengthens or weakens an argument or a hypothesis.

GENERAL TEST-TAKING STRATEGIES

The following sections present some general test-taking strategies that apply to the multiple-choice questions on the MCAT. These strategies can help you to gain valuable points when you take the actual test.

Take Advantage of the Multiple-Choice Format

All of the questions on the MCAT are in the multiple-choice format, which you have undoubtedly seen many times before. That means that for every question, the correct answer is right in front of you. All you have to do is pick it out from among three incorrect choices, called "distracters." Consequently, you can use the process of elimination to rule out incorrect answer choices. The more answers you rule out, the easier it is to make the right choice.

Answer Every Question

Recall that on the MCAT, there is no penalty for choosing a wrong answer. Therefore, if you do not know the answer to a question, you have nothing to lose by guessing. So make sure that you answer every question. If time is running out and you still have not answered some questions, make sure to enter an answer for the questions that you have not attempted. With luck, you may be able to pick up a few extra points, even if your guesses are totally random.

Make Educated Guesses

What differentiates great test takers from merely good ones is the ability to guess in such a way as to maximize the chance of guessing correctly. The way to do this is to use the process of elimination. Before you guess, try to eliminate one or more of the answer choices. That way, you can make an educated guess, and you have a better chance of picking the correct answer. Odds of one out of two or one out of three are better than one out of four!

Go with Your Gut

In those cases where you're not 100 percent sure of the answer you are choosing, it is often best to go with your gut feeling and stick with your first answer. If you decide to change that answer and pick another one, you may well pick the wrong answer because you have over thought the problem. More often than not, if you know something about the subject, your first answer is likely to be the correct one.

Take Advantage of Helpful Computer Functions

On the MCAT, you have access to certain computer functions that can make your work easier. As you work through the on-screen questions, you are able to highlight relevant portions of the reading passages. This helps you save time when you need to find facts or details to support your answer choices. You are also able to cross out answer choices that you know are incorrect. This helps you use the process of elimination to pick the correct answer.

Use the Scratch Paper Provided

The MCAT is an all-computerized test, so there is no test booklet for you to write in. However, you are given scratch paper, so use it to your advantage. Jot down notes, make calculations, and write out an outline for each of your essays. Be aware, however, that you cannot remove the scratch paper from the test site. All papers are collected from you before you leave the room.

Because you cannot write on the actual MCAT, don't get into the habit of writing notes to yourself on the test pages of this book. Use separate scratch paper instead. Consider it an opportunity to learn to use scratch paper effectively.

Keep Track of the Time

Make sure that you're on track to answer all of the questions within the time allowed. With so many questions to answer in a short time period, you're not going to have a lot of time to spare. Keep an eye on your watch or on the computerized timer provided.

Do not spend too much time on any one question. If you find yourself stuck for more than a minute or two on a question, then you should make your best guess and move on. If you have time left over at the end of the section, you can return to the question and review your answer. However, if time runs out, don't give the question another thought. You need to save your focus for the rest of the test.

Don't Panic If Time Runs Out

If you pace yourself and keep track of your progress, you should not run out of time. If you do, however, run out of time, don't panic. Because there is no guessing penalty and you have nothing to lose by doing so, enter answers to all the remaining questions. If you are able to make educated guesses, you will probably be able to improve your score. However, even random guesses may help you pick up a few points. In order to know how to handle this situation if it happens to you on the test, make sure you observe the time limits when you take the practice tests. Guessing well is a skill that comes with practice, so incorporate it into your preparation program.

If Time Permits, Review Questions You Were Unsure Of

Within each test section, the computer allows you to return to questions you have already answered and change your answer if you decide to do so. (However, once you have completed an entire section, you cannot go back to it and make changes.) If time permits, you may want to take advantage of this function to review questions you were unsure of or to check for careless mistakes.

About the Practice Tests

The Practice Tests in this volume are designed to help you determine your readiness to take the actual MCAT. Each test has four separately timed sections as shown in the chart.

Section	Number of Questions	Time Allowed (minutes)
1. Biological and Biochemical Foundations of Living Systems	59	95
Break: 10 minutes		
2. Chemical and Physical Foundations of Biological Systems	59	95
Break: 10 minutes		
3. Psychological, Social, and Biological Foundations of Behavior	59	95
Break: 10 minutes		
4. Critical Analysis and Reasoning Skills	53	90
Totals	230	375 (= 6 hours, 15 minutes)

The questions are designed to match the real exam as closely as possible in format and degree of difficulty. If you approach these tests as you would the real exam, your results will give you a good idea of how well you would score if you took the real MCAT today.

Each test is followed by complete explanations for every question. Study the explanations carefully, particularly for questions that you missed or that you found difficult.

Following each set of Answers and Explanations is an Evaluation Chart. Use it to measure your test-taking readiness and to pinpoint content areas that you may need to review again before taking the real exam.

How to Use the Practice Tests

The following pages present three full-length practice MCATs. The questions have been designed to match real MCAT questions as closely as possible in terms of format and degree of difficulty. If you are at the beginning of your MCAT preparation, you can use these tests as launching points to determine your strengths and weaknesses, and to identify how far your current score is from your score goal. You can use these tests to assess your mastery of the test content, to sharpen your test-taking skills, and to build your confidence for test day.

For best results, follow these four steps:

1. **Take each Practice Test under test conditions.** Find a quiet place where you will not be disturbed. Take the test as if it were the actual MCAT. Work through the test from beginning to end in one sitting. Mark your answers directly on the test pages. Observe the time limit given at the start of each section. If you have not finished a section when time runs out, mark the last question you answered and then note how much longer it takes you to complete the section. This information will tell you if you need to speed up your pace, and if so, by how much.

2. **Answer every question.** On the real MCAT, there is no penalty for wrong answers, so it makes sense to answer every question, even if you have to guess. If you don't know an answer, see if you can eliminate one or more of the answer choices. The more choices you can eliminate, the better your chance of guessing correctly!

3. **Check your answers in the Answers and Explanations section at the end of each test.** Pay particular attention to the explanations for questions you missed.

4. **Fill out the Evaluation Charts.** A chart is located after the Answers and Explanations section for each test. Mark the numbers of the questions you missed, and the chart will show you which sections of the companion volumes of the **MCAT Test Preparation Series** you still need to review.

MCAT
Practice Test 1

Biological and Biochemical Foundations of Living Systems

59 Questions   Time Limit: 95 Minutes

Questions 1–6 are based on the following passage.

Passage I

Leukemia is a term that describes a wide variety of blood cell cancers. Most leukemia cases involve elevated leukocyte counts. In acute cases of leukemia, immature leukocytes proliferate quickly, which leads to many abnormal immature cells in the bone marrow. This inhibits the ability of the bone marrow to produce healthy new leukocytes. This form of the cancer progresses rapidly, and the cells metastasize easily as they move into the bloodstream from the bone marrow. It can be fatal within weeks or months if not treated promptly. In contrast, chronic cases of leukemia typically involve the proliferation of abnormal mature leukocytes. This form of the disease progresses more slowly, and treatment need not always be immediate.

Once classified as acute or chronic, leukemia can be further subdivided into lymphocytic or myelogenous. This distinction depends on which type of leukocyte is abnormal in the patient. In lymphocytic leukemia, the lymphoid cells, such as the lymphocytes, are abnormal. In the myelogenous form, the myeloid cells, such as basophils, neutrophils, and eosinophils, are affected.

Chemotherapy drugs are often used in the management of leukemia cases. There are numerous categories of these drugs, and they have varied mechanisms of action. In treatment, several drugs are used in combination because some of the drugs are cell-cycle specific while others are not. Alkylating agents are capable of disrupting the function of DNA. Tubulin-binding agents are designed to interfere with microtubule formation. Other drugs are designed to interfere with DNA polymerase, DNA repair mechanisms, or protein synthesis, or to act as purine analogs. Many of these drugs cannot enter into the brain when injected or ingested, so if the cancer has spread to this area, special methods must be used to introduce the drugs to the brain.

1. What would be the BEST explanation as to why people with chronic forms of leukemia can live longer untreated than those with acute cases of leukemia?
   A. Chronic cases involve types of leukocytes that have less important functions in the body.
   B. Chronic cases of leukemia involve abnormal cell division of mature cells, so there are still some immature cells that can proliferate into normal mature cells.
   C. The immune system is less likely to recognize and destroy abnormal immature leukocytes than it would be to recognize and destroy abnormal mature leukocytes.
   D. all of the above

2. What is the most logical explanation for why certain drugs may NOT be able to reach the brain if they have been ingested or injected?
   A. These drugs have a chemical nature that does not allow them to cross the blood-brain barrier.
   B. These drugs are so toxic that they are broken down before they reach the brain.
   C. Most of these drugs target only cancerous cells that normally would not be in the brain.
   D. The drugs that have been ingested have likely been denatured by the acids in the stomach.

3. A variety of risk factors exist for leukemia. Some of these factors include exposure to radiation, certain viral infections, and inherited tendencies. What do all of these factors have in common?
   A. All involve problems with protein translation in the cells.
   B. All can cause an increase in the production of cellular growth factors that enhance cell proliferation.
   C. All cause changes to the DNA that can lead to the production of altered proteins that can influence the development of cancer.
   D. All cause problems with transcription in the cells.

4. Many leukemia patients require antibiotic treatments frequently. Why would this be the case?
   A. Some antibiotics are known to be toxic to certain types of cancer cells and may help to damage the cancerous cells.
   B. The antibiotics might help to increase the function of the patient's immune system.
   C. The antibiotics can help prevent bacterial infections in the patient whose leukocyte function is compromised by the cancer.
   D. The antibiotics can help prevent viral infections in the patient.

5. Of the types of drugs mentioned in the passage, which category is most likely to be cell-cycle specific?
    A. tubulin-binding agents
    B. protein synthesis inhibitors
    C. purine analogs
    D. alkylating agents

6. It is not uncommon for leukemia patients to receive stem cell transplants. Why might this be a productive treatment option?
    A. The stem cells are capable of differentiating into new blood cells, which include the leukocytes, erythrocytes, and platelets.
    B. The stem cells can damage and replace the cancerous leukocytes.
    C. The stem cells can act as immune system modulators, enhancing the function of the entire system.
    D. The stem cells can temporarily replace the function of the cancerous cells and slow down the progression of the disease.

Questions 7–12 are based on the following passage.

Passage II

The kidneys are responsible for filtering certain components of blood and producing urine from them. In an adult, the kidneys are typically capable of processing about 1 to 1.5 liters of water per hour depending on the individual and conditions within the body. In a condition known as water intoxication, a person ingests more water (usually 3 or more liters in a single sitting) in a shorter period of time than the kidneys can process. In a child, the amount of water required to induce water intoxication is much less.

As the excess water moves from the digestive system, it accumulates in the plasma and extracellular fluids. Electrolytes such as sodium are drawn out of the cells in an attempt to equilibrate the concentrations inside and outside of the cells. As more and more water enters the extracellular fluids, the plasma sodium concentration drops, leading to a condition called *hyponatremia*, defined as a plasma sodium concentration less than 130 mmol/liter. Due to the effects of osmosis, water begins entering the cells. The cells will begin to swell and may eventually burst, if the condition is not reversed in a timely manner.

The situation becomes increasingly problematic as the cells and tissues of the central nervous system take in more water. Pressure builds in the brain that causes symptoms that resemble alcohol intoxication. Lightheadedness, nausea, vomiting, and headaches are typical as well. Damage can also occur in the lungs and heart. If not treated promptly, seizures, coma, and death can occur within several hours.

7. During water intoxication, the concentrations of the intracellular and extracellular fluids are not at equilibrium. In this situation, the extracellular fluid would be _____ to the cells.
   A. hypertonic
   B. isotonic
   C. hypotonic
   D. hyperosmotic

8. Imbalances in sodium ion concentrations would MOST likely cause problems with:
   A. neuron function
   B. aerobic cellular respiration
   C. cell division
   D. muscle contraction

9. Of the options listed, what would be the best treatment for someone suffering from water intoxication?
   A. administering a saline solution that is more concentrated than the cells
   B. administering an isotonic solution
   C. administering a solution low in solute concentration
   D. performing dialysis to remove excess water from the plasma

10. Due to the excess water consumed that causes water intoxication, which of the following responses to this excess water would NOT be expected in the body?
    A. an increase in blood volume and pressure
    B. an increase in the secretion of antidiuretic hormone
    C. an increase in urine volume
    D. an increase in glomerular filtration rate

11. The regulation of water and sodium levels in the nephrons is adjusted in two regions of the kidneys where water and sodium can be reabsorbed from the nephron and returned to circulation. Those regions are the:
    A. proximal convoluted tubule and distal convoluted tubule
    B. the loop of Henle and the distal convoluted tubule
    C. the distal convoluted tubule and the collecting duct
    D. the proximal convoluted tubule and the loop of Henle

12. Death that occurs due to water intoxication involves swelling and damage to certain parts of the central nervous system. Damage to which of these structures in the central nervous system would be MOST likely to have fatal consequences?
    A. the cerebrum
    B. the spinal cord
    C. the cerebellum
    D. the medulla oblongata

Questions 13–18 are based on the following passage.

Passage III

Sperm count in human males is influenced by a variety of factors. One of the most important variables affecting sperm count is the number of Sertoli cells located in seminiferous tubules of the testes. The Sertoli cells' primary function is to nurture cells through the process of spermatogenesis by providing them with nutrients and an environment conducive to spermatogenesis. Each Sertoli cell has a set number of spermatozoa that it can support. Sertoli cells have an additional role in forming the blood-testis barrier that provides immune privilege for the seminiferous tubules. This forms a physical barricade that keeps the developing sperm from coming into contact with cells of the immune system.

While it is not clear as to all the factors involved in determining Sertoli cell number, it is apparent that their development is most critical during the first nine months of life and prior to puberty. Events that affect the development of Sertoli cells in young males can influence fertility later in life. There may also be genetic factors involved in determining the number of Sertoli cells formed in a particular male.

The following data were collected from two groups of men. The men in group 1 had a normal sperm count while the men in group 2 were seeking infertility treatment due to a low sperm count. Levels of follicle-stimulating hormone (FSH) and luteinizing hormone (LH) from the pituitary were measured as were the testicular hormones inhibin-B and testosterone in an attempt to determine which hormones seem to be linked to reduced sperm count.

Sample Group	LH	FSH	Inhibin-B	Testosterone
1	5.3 IU/L	5.0 IU/L	190 pg/mL	18.0 nmol/L
2	3.1 IU/L	17.6 IU/L	51 pg/mL	17.8 nmol/L

13. In which group would you expect to see a higher number of Sertoli cells?
    A. group 1
    B. group 2
    C. both groups 1 and 2
    D. impossible to tell from these data

14. Based on the data provided from both groups in the table, it is suggested that there is:
    A. a positive feedback relationship between LH and FSH
    B. a negative feedback relationship between inhibin-B and FSH
    C. a positive feedback relationship between testosterone and FSH
    D. no relationship between these hormones

15. An elevated level of which hormone seems to be the best indicator of sperm count?
    A. LH
    B. FSH
    C. inhibin-B
    D. testosterone

16. Why would it be important for the Sertoli cells to establish a blood-testis barrier and immune privilege?
    A. to prevent the immune cells from attacking the sperm cells, which display different antigens from the other cells in the body
    B. to prevent the developing sperm cells from leaving the reproductive system
    C. to prevent blood from flowing into the testes
    D. to keep the developing sperm cells from entering into the epididymis before they are mature

17. The hormones FSH and LH are also involved in oogenesis in women. When LH surges in the ovarian cycle, what event will result?
    A. endometrium proliferation
    B. ovulation
    C. menstruation
    D. corpus luteum degradation

18. Fully differentiated Sertoli cells lose the ability to proliferate to produce more Sertoli cells. This would mean that they cannot perform:
    A. mitosis
    B. meiosis
    C. apoptosis
    D. binary fission

Questions 19–24 are based on the following passage.

Passage IV

Osteomyelitis is a bone infection often caused by the bacterium *Staphylococcus aureus,* which spreads through the blood to the bones. The infection is quite common after surgeries when soft tissues become infected and the infection moves to the adjacent bones. The long bones of children are particularly susceptible as they have excellent circulation to them during the growth period. In adults, the best circulation is to the vertebrae, and these are the bones that are most likely to develop osteomyelitis.

Osteomyelitis is treated with various antibiotics, but some patients have chronic infections that are not eradicated by antibiotic therapy due to a unique feature of *S. aureus. S. aureus* can be internalized by osteoblasts where the bacteria can continue to survive in the intracellular environment. Inside the osteoblasts, bacteria can induce apoptosis, killing their host cell. Surgical debridement is often required to remove the damaged and dead bone tissue created by the infection.

A major research question deals with how an *S. aureus* infection induces apoptosis in the host osteoblasts. In order for apoptosis to initiate in osteoblasts, the enzyme capsase-8 must be activated. This enzyme serves as a protease that cleaves critical proteins in the cell, causing cell death. Capsase-8 is only expressed under certain circumstances. In the case of osteomyelitis, the *S. aureus* bacteria cause the induction of tumor necrosis factor–related apoptosis-inducing ligand (TRAIL) in the osteoblasts. Then TRAIL activates capsase-8, which triggers a series of events leading to apoptosis and death of osteoblasts.

19. Which of the following potential drugs might be helpful in preventing the death of osteoblasts caused by *S. aureus* infection?
    A. one that increases capsase-8 activity
    B. one that increases TRAIL activity
    C. one that is an antagonist to TRAIL
    D. all of the above

20. Osteoblasts are unusual in that they actively engulf *S. aureus*, which survives in the osteoblast and eventually triggers apoptosis. In engulfing the bacteria, the osteoblasts resemble the normal activities of which type of leukocyte?
    A. basophils
    B. lymphocytes
    C. eosinophils
    D. macrophages

21. Osteomyelitis begins when *S. aureus* enters the bloodstream and moves to the bones. Under normal conditions, the nonspecific immune defense that would be activated as bacteria enter the blood would be:
    A. antibody production by plasma cells
    B. cytotoxic T-cell activation
    C. the complement system
    D. interleukin secretion

22. Many strains of *S. aureus* that cause osteomyelitis are termed methicillin-resistant *Staphylococcus aureus* (MRSA). These strains have developed resistance to the antibiotic methicillin as well as to other antibiotics. The mechanism by which this antibiotic resistance occurs is by:

    A. the overuse of antibiotics, which causes patients to become resistant to the antibiotics

    B. the overuse of antibiotics, which selects for bacteria that have mutations that allow them to survive in the presence of the antibiotics

    C. mutations, which occur as the bacteria are exposed to antibiotics that can serve as mutagens

    D. all of the above

23. The strains of *S. aureus* associated with osteomyelitis have a variety of cell adhesion molecules called *adhesins* that help them to attach to and be internalized by osteoblasts. These molecules are likely found in which of the following bacterial structures?

    A. the nucleoid

    B. the ribosomes

    C. the capsule

    D. spores

24. Osteoblasts are normally involved in building new bone matrix. Their activity is stimulated by the hormone _____ made by the _____.

    A. calcitonin; thyroid

    B. parathyroid hormone; parathyroid glands

    C. osteotonin; bone marrow

    D. none of the above

Questions 25–30 are based on the following passage.

Passage V

Endothelin is a vasoactive peptide involved in a variety of processes, including the control of blood flow. Endothelin is capable of binding to two different receptors. There are receptors for endothelin located on smooth muscle (ETA) and receptors for endothelin located on vascular endothelium (ETB). When endothelin binds to ETA, it initiates vasoconstriction by narrowing blood vessels. However, when endothelin binds to ETB, vasodilation occurs due to the widening of blood vessels. The activity of the ETB receptor seems to counterregulate the ETA effects and prevents excessive vasoconstriction.

Drug X is a selective receptor antagonist for endothelin. It is designed to bind preferentially to certain endothelin receptors. Drug Y is another selective receptor antagonist for endothelin. It is also designed to preferentially bind to one of the endothelin receptors. Researchers are hopeful that drugs X and Y will be of value in the treatment of conditions such as pulmonary arterial hypertension (PAH). In PAH, excess endothelin is produced, which causes an increase in blood pressure within the pulmonary arteries. Normal pressure in the pulmonary arteries is expected to be about 14 mm Hg, and pressure at or above 25 mm Hg constitutes PAH. Both drugs have been tested in patients with PAH. There were five patients in each group. At the end of the study, the percent decrease in mean pulmonary artery pressure was measured for each patient and reported in the table.

Patient	Drug X	Drug Y	Placebo
1	+10%	−10%	+5%
2	+3%	−5%	0%
3	−5%	+2%	+13%
4	+2%	0%	−4%
5	0%	−7%	−2%
Average decrease	+2%	−4%	+2.4%

25. Based solely on the data provided, which conclusion should be drawn concerning the effectiveness of drugs X and Y?
    A. Drug X is a more effective treatment for PAH because most patients had a slight or no increase in pulmonary blood pressure while taking the drug.
    B. The placebo is the best treatment for PAH because some patients taking the placebo had a decrease in pulmonary blood pressure.
    C. Drugs X and Y should be used as combined therapy to maximize their effects.
    D. Drug Y is a more effective treatment for PAH because the majority of patients taking the drug had a decrease in pulmonary blood pressure.

26. Which endothelin receptor is drug X selectively binding to?
    A. ETA only
    B. ETB only
    C. both ETA and ETB
    D. neither ETA nor ETB

27. If a patient has PAH, the heart can become overly stressed which can ultimately lead to heart failure. Which area of the heart is MOST likely to initially be affected by an increased blood pressure in the pulmonary arteries?
    A. the right and left atria
    B. the right and left ventricles
    C. the right ventricle
    D. the left ventricle

28. A patient overexpresses the ETB receptor. Explain what should happen to the patient's pressure.
    A. It should remain the same as long as the ETA receptor is also expressed.
    B. It should decrease due to elevated levels of vasodilation.
    C. It should increase since overexpression of ETB will block available ETA receptors.
    D. It should stay stable since other systems in the body will compensate.

29. Suppose a patient suffers from chronic systolic and diastolic hypertension due to an inherited defect in an endothelin receptor. How would the kidneys attempt to alleviate the hypertension?
    A. by decreasing water absorption in the nephrons
    B. by decreasing urine output thus increasing blood volume
    C. by increasing the amount of aldosterone secreted from the adrenal glands
    D. by increasing the amount of antidiuretic hormone secreted from the pituitary gland

30. In addition to regulation of vessel diameter, ETA is known to have other roles in the body. When activated by a specific type of endothelin, ETA can synergize with growth factors to cause rapid cell proliferation. Based on this information, it is MOST likely that ETA can be involved with:
    A. an increase in metabolism
    B. the development of cancer
    C. immune system hypersensitivities
    D. increased stress to the kidneys and liver

Questions 31–36 are based on the following passage.

Passage VI

An endocrinologist has been studying an enzyme that she suspects is the rate-limiting step in the conversion of cholesterol to estrogen. It is reported in the literature that female mice with a mutation in the gene coding for this enzyme reach sexual maturity earlier than mice without the mutation. Controlled experiments are completed using breeding pairs of wild-type mice and the mutant strain of mice. The plasma estrogen concentration is measured in female offspring at 3 weeks of age, prior to sexual maturity, which typically occurs by 6 weeks of age. The results, in estrogen pg/mL of plasma, are seen in the following table.

Trial	Wild Type*	Mutant Strain*
1	2.3	8.5
2	8.1	4.5
3	4.4	16.2
4	7.6	5.5
5	3.2	3.8
6	8.2	12.5
7	5.5	10.7
8	6.3	8.6

*in estrogen pg/mL of plasma

31. What conclusion can be made based on the data?
    A. The presence of the wild-type enzyme increases estrogen concentration.
    B. The presence of the wild-type enzyme increases cholesterol concentration.
    C. The presence of the mutant enzyme increases estrogen concentration.
    D. The presence of the mutant enzyme increases cholesterol concentration.

32. The rate-limiting step in a metabolic pathway:
    A. requires the lowest activation energy
    B. is the fastest step in a metabolic pathway
    C. is always the last reaction in the pathway
    D. is the slowest step in a metabolic pathway

33. Recent studies have shown that cholesterol levels in women can vary significantly depending on where a woman is in her reproductive cycle. Most notable is the fact that total and LDL cholesterol levels typically decline at the points in the cycle where estrogen levels are at their highest. Based on this, we would expect that total and LDL cholesterol levels would be the lowest:
    A. following menopause
    B. during menstruation
    C. during ovulation
    D. prior to puberty

34. In addition to serving as a precursor for steroid biosynthesis, cholesterol has a variety of other roles in the body including:
    A. maintenance of structural integrity and fluidity in plasma membranes
    B. nucleotide biosynthesis
    C. transport of molecules through the plasma membrane
    D. maintaining osmotic balance between cells and their surrounding environment

35. Based on the data presented, it is likely that:
    A. Wild-type mice reach sexual maturity faster than the mutant strain.
    B. The mutant strain mice will not reach sexual maturity.
    C. The mutant strain mice have a lower cholesterol level than wild-type mice.
    D. Wild-type mice will not reach sexual maturity.

36. If plasma cholesterol levels were to be measured, what would you expect to see in female mice that have reached sexual maturity as compared to female mice that are far from reaching sexual maturity?
    A. Cholesterol levels would be increased in wild-type mice that have reached sexual maturity as compared to wild-type mice that have not reached sexual maturity.
    B. Cholesterol levels would be the same in wild-type mice that have reached sexual maturity as compared to wild-type mice that have not reached sexual maturity.
    C. Cholesterol levels would be increased in mutant strain mice that have reached sexual maturity as compared to mutant strain mice that have not reached sexual maturity.
    D. Cholesterol levels would be decreased in mutant strain mice that have reached sexual maturity as compared to mutant strain mice that have not reached sexual maturity.

Questions 37–42 are based on the following passage.

Passage VII

Human immunodeficiency virus (HIV) is known to infect T cells and macrophages possessing the CD4 receptor. In addition to the CD4 receptor, there are a variety of coreceptors that are also needed for certain strains of HIV to infect cells. One of these coreceptors is called CCR5 and is needed for the most common strains of HIV (called R5) to infect their host cells. The more CCR5 receptors a cell has, the greater the rate of infection for the cell. Some individuals have the delta-32 allele of CCR5 that leads to a decreased risk of HIV infection.

Women are at a much higher risk for contracting HIV from a male partner than a male is for contracting HIV from a female partner. Some of the increased risk for women is dependent on sex hormones. It has been hypothesized that women have different risks of contracting HIV at different points in their reproductive cycles. For example, women may be at a greater risk of contracting HIV following ovulation during the last 2 weeks of their cycle as opposed to the first 2 weeks of their cycle prior to ovulation. The difference between risk of infection before and after ovulation relates to sex hormones produced at various points in the reproductive cycle. It seems that the estrogen that is produced prior to ovulation provides a somewhat protective, although certainly not absolute, role against HIV infection. For women who do become infected with HIV, studies have shown that women in the first 3 to 5 years after HIV infection carry lower HIV viral loads than men, perhaps due to the influence of estrogen. This suggests a major role for sex hormones in the infection and progression of HIV.

37. According to the hypothesis presented concerning estrogen's role in HIV infection, which of these individuals would be at LEAST risk for HIV infection?
    A. a female producing elevated levels of testosterone
    B. a female with an ovarian tumor that causes increased secretion of estrogen
    C. a female who has had her ovaries removed
    D. a male with a reduced testosterone level

38. Women are at a higher risk of contracting HIV following ovulation. Based on the normal events of the female reproductive cycle, which hormone might account for the increased risk of HIV infection in women following ovulation?
    A. increased levels of progesterone
    B. increased levels of follicle-stimulating hormone
    C. increased levels of estrogen
    D. increased levels of luteinizing hormone

39. As a result of chronic infection with HIV, the CCR5 gene is generally up-regulated over time. This would MOST likely account for:
    A. an increased number of host cells becoming infected as the result of prolonged infection
    B. the elimination of HIV from the body in some individuals
    C. increased protection in women as the result of estrogen
    D. resistance of cells carrying the CCR5 receptor to infection

40. Some populations with the delta-32 CCR5 mutation seem to have close to 100% protection against HIV, while other populations with the delta-32 CCR5 mutation seem to have only partial protection. What could account for this difference?
    A. There is an environmental influence on expression of the delta-32 CCR5 phenotype.
    B. The delta-32 CCR5 allele exhibits incomplete dominance. Homozygotes have complete protection while heterozygotes have only partial protection.
    C. The expression of the delta-32 CCR5 allele can be masked by epistasis.
    D. Those that have only partial protection against HIV infection have been exposed to larger doses of HIV.

41. HIV belongs to a unique category of viruses termed retroviruses. Which of the following enzymes would be unique to retroviruses?
    A. DNA polymerase
    B. RNA polymerase
    C. reverse transcriptase
    D. helicase

42. Drugs such as AZT and ddI are nucleoside analogs used in HIV-infected patients. Both are chemically modified versions of the nucleotides that make up DNA and RNA. These modified nucleosides interfere with normal replication and transcription. The MOST important goal of these drugs would be:

    A. to prevent the replication of host cell DNA so that the host cell cannot function
    B. to prevent the transcription of host cell RNA so that no proteins can be expressed
    C. to prevent the viral nucleic acid from entering the host cells
    D. to prevent replication of the viral genome

Questions 43–48 are based on the following passage.

Passage VIII

In the past, there has been a great deal of controversy over the existence of viable but nonculturable (VBNC) states in bacteria. While normal culturing methods cannot detect these VBNC cells, there are a variety of molecular assays that can be used to indicate metabolic activity in the cells. Additionally, these cells can be resuscitated from VBNC states to a culturable state under appropriate conditions. The VBNC state has been observed in numerous species of bacteria and most recently in yeasts.

Escherichia coli is one of many species of bacteria that are able to enter and resuscitate from VBNC states. Certain strains of *E. coli* cause a variety of infections in humans. Urinary tract infections (UTIs) in women are frequently caused by *E. coli* that exist as harmless residents in the intestinal tract. These infections can be treated using antibiotics to kill the *E. coli.* However, about 30 percent of women treated for UTIs end up with a recurrence. For those who support the VBNC theory, it has been hypothesized that recurrent UTIs are caused by VBNC *E. coli* that resuscitate to initiate a new infection. These VBNC cells may not be killed using antibiotic therapies normally used to treat UTIs. Only culturable cells cause the symptoms of a UTI.

The following graph shows the number of *E. coli* bacteria present in a patient following antibiotic therapy for a UTI. Day 1 indicates the number of bacteria present at diagnosis. A urine sample was collected each day and cultured for the presence of *E. coli* as measured in colony-forming units per milliliter of urine (cfu/ml). An assay was also used to determine the number of metabolically active cells that were potentially alive but not culturable (VBNC). The data are as follows:

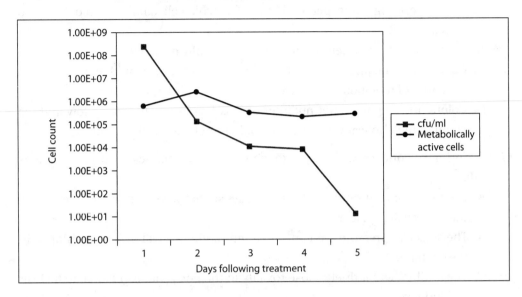

43. What can you conclude from the graph?
    A. Antibiotic therapy is highly effective at eliminating all *E. coli*.
    B. While the current infection has been effectively treated, this patient may be at risk for a recurrent UTI.
    C. The antibiotic therapy used for this patient was not sufficient to eliminate the infection.
    D. Antibiotic therapy has increased the total number of *E. coli* cells in this patient.

44. Which piece of information would be the BEST support for the existence of the VBNC state?
    A. the presence of DNA in the alleged VBNC cells
    B. the presence of an intact plasma membrane in the alleged VBNC cells
    C. the presence of specific proteins in the alleged VBNC cells
    D. the detection of transcription in the alleged VBNC cells

45. Why would women be more likely to contract a UTI caused by *E. coli* as compared to men?
    A. It is likely that the intestinal tracts of women contain a higher number of the *E. coli* bacteria as compared to men.
    B. The urethra of a female is closer to the intestinal tract than in a male, making it easier for the *E. coli* bacteria from the intestinal tract to gain access to the urinary tract.
    C. The *E. coli* bacteria in women are more likely to be resistant to antibiotic treatments.
    D. The immune system is less efficient in women, making infection more likely to occur.

46. If the antibiotic treatment used in the graph was continued for a period of 30 days, the MOST likely prediction would be that the:
    A. Colony-forming units per milliliter of *E. coli* cell counts would begin to increase.
    B. Metabolically active cell counts would eventually decrease.
    C. Colony-forming units per milliliter of *E. coli* cell counts would remain low and the count of metabolically active cells would gradually decrease.
    D. Colony-forming units per milliliter of *E. coli* cells would remain low and the count of metabolically active cells would remain about the same.

47. The primary concern with the extended use of antibiotics to treat infections is that:
    A. People become immune to the antibiotics so that when they really need them, the drugs will be useless.
    B. The selective pressures of continued antibiotic use will induce resistance in the bacteria.
    C. The antibiotics routinely cause toxicity in the body that can damage the liver and kidneys.
    D. The antibiotics encourage the overgrowth of resident bacteria in the body.

48. One theory concerning VBNC cells is that they are simply on their way to dying. A piece of evidence that would refute that theory would be:
    A. if some of the VBNC cells did die
    B. if the VBNC cells resuscitated
    C. if apoptosis was observed in the cells
    D. if no metabolic activity was observed

Questions 49–59 are not associated with a passage.

49. Which of the following explanations could account for the fact that dominant alleles that cause fatal disorders are less common than recessive alleles that cause fatal disorders?
    A. Every person carrying a single fatal dominant allele dies, whereas most individuals who carry a single recessive lethal allele live and reproduce.
    B. Recessive fatal alleles must cause sterility.
    C. Dominant alleles that cause fatal disorders are more serious than recessive lethal disorders.
    D. Dominant alleles are generally less common than recessive alleles.

50. A certain type of cell makes antibodies that are secreted from the cell. It is possible to track the path of these as they leave the cell by labeling them with radioactive isotopes. Which of the following might be the path of antibodies from where they are made to the cell membrane?

    A. Golgi complex to lysosomes to cell membrane
    B. rough endoplasmic reticulum to Golgi complex to cell membrane
    C. nucleus to Golgi complex to cell membrane
    D. smooth endoplasmic reticulum to lysosomes to cell membrane

51. A scientist suspects that the food in an ecosystem may have been contaminated with radioactive phosphates over a period of months. Which of the following substances could be examined for radioactive phosphate to test the hypothesis?

    A. the carbohydrates produced by plants in the area
    B. the DNA of the organisms in the area
    C. the lipids produced by organisms living in the area
    D. all of the above

52. Neurons contain a high concentration of potassium ions relative to the fluids surrounding them. How could a neuron acquire even more potassium?

    A. active transport
    B. osmosis
    C. endocytosis
    D. diffusion

53. At the end of the electron transport chain in aerobic cellular respiration, the final acceptor of the electrons is _____, which will then produce a molecule of _____.

    A. CO_2; O_2
    B. NAD^+; NADH
    C. O_2; H_2O
    D. ADP; ATP

54. A geneticist allows a cell to replicate in the presence of radioactive nucleotides. Which of the following would occur?

    A. The DNA in one of the daughter cells would be radioactive but not in the other daughter cell.
    B. The mRNA made by the daughter cells would be radioactive.
    C. The DNA in each of the daughter cells would be radioactive.
    D. The DNA would not be radioactive in either of the daughter cells.

55. How does DNA differ from RNA?
    A. DNA nucleotides use deoxyribose sugar; RNA uses ribose sugar.
    B. DNA uses the bases A, U, C, and G; RNA uses the bases A, T, C, and G.
    C. DNA is produced in transcription; RNA is produced in translation.
    D. RNA is a double-stranded molecule; DNA is a single-stranded molecule.

56. A human cell undergoes mitosis. Each of the resulting cells have _____ chromosomes.
    A. 8
    B. 23
    C. 46
    D. 92

57. When a nonsteroid (peptide) hormone binds to a receptor on the cell surface:
    A. the hormone moves into the nucleus where it influences gene expression
    B. the hormone-receptor complex moves into the cytoplasm
    C. a second messenger will form within the cell
    D. the cell becomes inactive

58. The attachment site for RNA polymerase on the DNA template is called the:
    A. promoter
    B. regulator
    C. operon
    D. repressor

59. Consider a bacterial cell that performs anaerobic respiration. If that bacterial cell had access to 6 molecules of glucose, how many molecules of ATP would it be able to produce?
    A. 2
    B. 6
    C. 12
    D. 36

STOP. This is the end of Section 1.

Chemical and Physical Foundations of Biological Systems

59 Questions   **Time Limit: 95 Minutes**

Questions 1–5 are based on the following passage.

Passage I

Many alkenes can be hydrated simply by treatment with a strong acid in the presence of water. The limitation of this method is that a carbocation is generated along the mechanistic pathway, opening the door to rearrangements, as shown in the sulfuric acid–catalyzed hydration of 3,3-dimethylbut-1-ene here:

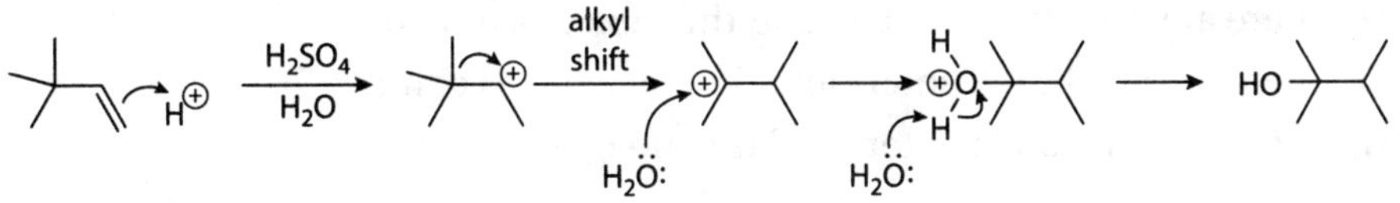

One workaround for this problem is the oxymercuration-demercuration sequence, as shown here:

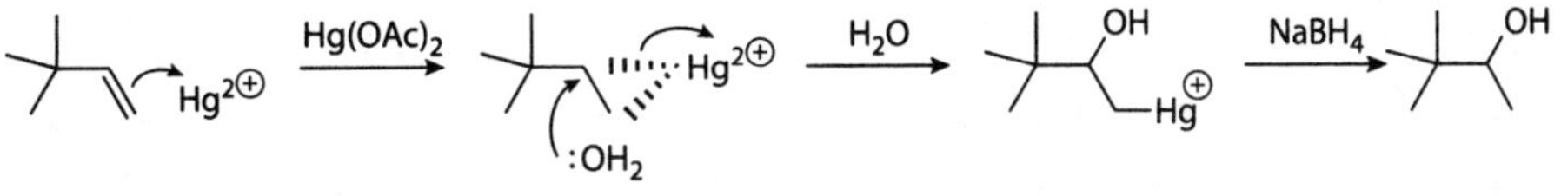

Consider the hydration of 3,6-dimethylcyclohex-1-ene under two separate conditions, for which four different alcohol products are proposed:

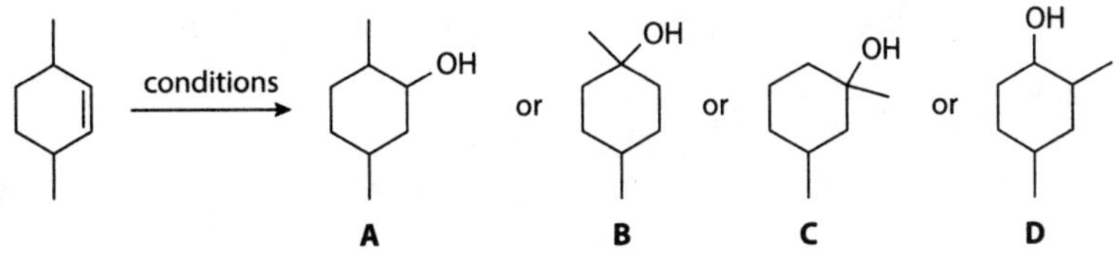

1. The most reasonable major hydration product of 3,6-dimethylcyclohex-1-ene using water and sulfuric acid is:
   A. Product A
   B. Product B
   C. Product C
   D. Product D

2. The most reasonable major hydration product of 3,6-dimethylcyclohex-1-ene using oxymercuration-demercuration is:
   A. Product A
   B. Product B
   C. Product C
   D. Product D

3. The structure giving six unique ^{13}C-NMR signals is most consistent with:
   A. Product A
   B. Product B
   C. Product C
   D. Product D

4. Which of the following statements is MOST true for *trans*-3,6-dimethylcyclohex-1-ene?
   A. There are two chiral centers and the molecule is chiral.
   B. There are two chiral centers and the molecule is achiral.
   C. There are no chiral centers and the molecule is chiral.
   D. There are no chiral centers and the molecule is achiral.

5. The by-product of demercuration is:
   A. Hg^0
   B. Hg^+
   C. Hg^{2+}
   D. Hg^{3+}

Questions 6–8 are not associated with a passage.

6. A peregrine falcon of 9 N is a bird known for its ability to reach extremely high speeds as it pursues prey. A bird in flight is subject to four forces: weight, drag, lift, and thrust. Which free body diagram accurately illustrates the direction of the forces acting on the bird assuming the bird is moving at constant velocity?

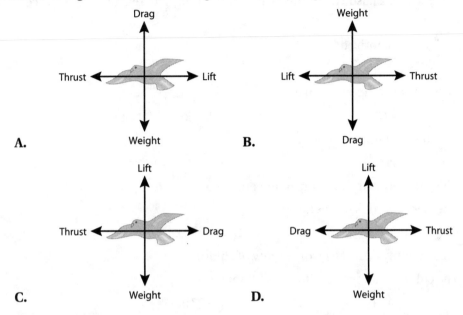

7. Blood is pumped from the heart at a rate of 5 L/min into the aorta of typical radius 1.2 cm. The velocity of blood as it enters the aorta is MOST nearly:

   A. $9 \dfrac{\text{cm}}{\text{s}}$

   B. $12 \dfrac{\text{cm}}{\text{s}}$

   C. $18 \dfrac{\text{cm}}{\text{s}}$

   D. $32 \dfrac{\text{cm}}{\text{s}}$

8. In response to a heart attack, the normal heart rhythm is restored by a cardiac defibrillator, which transmits approximately 15 amperes of current through the chest during a time interval of 7 milliseconds. The amount of charge that flows during that time is:

   A. 0.1 C
   B. 0.6 C
   C. 1.0 C
   D. 1.2 C

Questions 9–14 are based on the following passage.

Passage II

The reaction between sodium metal and chlorine gas is spontaneous and releases energy. The energy that is released is the enthalpy of formation of solid sodium chloride, which is also called the heat of formation. The reaction takes place in five elementary steps:

1. Sodium is vaporized.

$$Na\ (s) \rightarrow Na\ (g) \qquad\qquad \Delta H^o_{rxn} = 92\ kJ$$

2. Chlorine decomposes into atoms.

$$\frac{1}{2}\ Cl_2\ (g) \rightarrow Cl\ (g) \qquad\qquad \Delta H^o_{rxn} = 121\ kJ$$

3. Gaseous sodium atoms ionize.

$$Na\ (g) \rightarrow Na^+\ (g) + e^- \qquad\qquad \Delta H^o_{rxn} = 496\ kJ$$

This quantity is the first ionization energy of sodium vapor.

4. The electron adds to a chlorine atom.

$$Cl\ (g) + e^- \rightarrow Cl^-\ (g) \qquad\qquad \Delta H^o_{rxn} = -349\ kJ$$

This quantity is the electron affinity of chlorine.

5. The chloride ion reacts with the sodium ion.

$$Cl^-\ (g) + Na^+\ (g) \rightarrow NaCl\ (s) \qquad \Delta H^o_{rxn} = -771\ kJ$$

Addition of the five elementary equations gives the sum equation for the formation of solid sodium chloride. Most of the energy that is given off is due to the formation of solid sodium chloride from the gaseous ions. In solid sodium chloride, each positive ion is surrounded by 6 negative ions, and each negative ion is surrounded by 6 positive ions in a cubic lattice array. The lattice energy of an ionic compound is a measure of the attractive forces between the ions. The higher the lattice energy, the stronger the attractions and the higher melting the solid. Lattice energies depend on the charge and on the size of the ions in the array. If the size is constant, increasing charge increases the lattice energy. If the charge is constant, increasing size lowers the lattice energy.

Some lattice energies are given in the table.

Compound	Lattice Energy in kJ/mole
LiCl	834
KCl	701
Na$_2$O	2481
MgO	3795
Na$_2$S	2192

9. When 1 mole of sodium metal reacts with 1 mole of chlorine gas to form solid sodium chloride, what is the heat of formation?
   A. $-771\,kJ$
   B. $+771\,kJ$
   C. $-411\,kJ$
   D. $+411\,kJ$

10. What is the electron configuration of chloride?
    A. $1s^22s^22p^63s^23p^5$
    B. $1s^22s^22p^63s^23p^6$
    C. $1s^22s^22p^63s^23p^64s^1$
    D. $1s^22s^22p^63s^23p^63d^1$

11. Why is the lattice energy of Na_2S so much greater than that of NaCl?
    A. Two sodium ions are needed for every sulfide.
    B. Sulfide has a greater charge than chloride and is about the same size.
    C. Sulfide is much smaller than chloride.
    D. Chloride has a negative one charge, whereas sulfide has a negative two charge.

12. Which of the following represents the lattice energy of sodium chloride?
    A. $+771\,kJ$
    B. $-771\,kJ$
    C. $+411\,kJ$
    D. $-411\,kJ$

13. Which Lewis dot structure BEST represents the sodium ion?
    A. Na
    B. Na$^\bullet$
    C. Na$^+$
    D. Na$^-$

14. The reaction of chlorine gas and sodium metal also produces light. How is the light produced?
    A. The electrons absorb heat energy and release it as light.
    B. Light is emitted when the electrons become gaseous.
    C. Light is emitted when the metal atom becomes gaseous.
    D. Light is emitted when the chlorine becomes atomic.

Questions 15–19 are based on the following passage.

Passage III

Image formation in the human eyeball occurs when parallel light rays refract through the eye lens and converge on the retina. Hyperopia, or farsightedness, is a common vision problem that occurs as a result of these light rays entering the eyeball but converging behind the cornea. This results in the ability to see distant objects clearly with vision becoming blurry for close objects. Hyperopia, as is the case with many vision problems, can generally be corrected with eyeglass lenses, specifically a converging lens, as shown in the figure. A converging lens positioned in front of a hyperopic eye acts to focus the light rays sooner so that they converge on the retina rather than behind the retina.

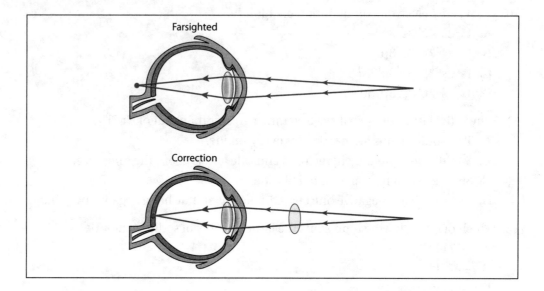

Correction of hyperopia is accomplished with a converging lens tailored to characteristics unique to the person. The following table lists four different scenarios of a converging lens, with each scenario detailing the distance of an identical object placed in front of the same converging lens as well as the focal length of the lens.

Characteristics of a Converging Eyeglass Lens		
Converging Lens Scenario	Object Distance (p) (cm)	Focal Length (f) (cm)
1	3f	f
2	2f	f
3	f	f
4	$\dfrac{f}{2}$	f

15. Which converging lens scenario will NOT produce an image?
   A. Lens Scenario 1
   B. Lens Scenario 2
   C. Lens Scenario 3
   D. Lens Scenario 4

16. Which converging lens scenario will produce an image that is virtual and upright?
    A. Lens Scenario 1
    B. Lens Scenario 2
    C. Lens Scenario 3
    D. Lens Scenario 4

17. The image distance for Lens Scenario 2 is:
    A. 3f
    B. between 2f and 3f
    C. 2f
    D. f

18. The magnification of the image for Lens Scenario 1 indicates that, with respect to the object, the image:
    A. is reduced by 2.
    B. remains the same.
    C. is enlarged by 2.
    D. is enlarged by 3.

19. The focal length is related to the object distance and the image distance according to:

    A. $\dfrac{(\text{object distance})\,(\text{image distance})}{\text{image distance} + \text{object distance}}$

    B. $\dfrac{(\text{object distance})\,(\text{image distance})}{\text{image distance} - \text{object distance}}$

    C. $\dfrac{\text{image distance} + \text{object distance}}{(\text{object distance})\,(\text{image distance})}$

    D. $\dfrac{\text{image distance} - \text{object distance}}{(\text{object distance})\,(\text{image distance})}$

Questions 20–22 are not associated with a passage.

20. Which of the following Fischer projections MOST accurately describes the boxed molecule?

A.
```
    Me
Br ─┼─ H
Br ─┼─ H
    Me
```

B.
```
    Me
Br ─┼─ H
H ─┼─ Br
    Me
```

C.
```
    Me
H ─┼─ Br
Br ─┼─ H
    Me
```

D.
```
    Me
H ─┼─ Br
H ─┼─ Br
    Me
```

21. For the following reaction, the most reasonable starting material is:

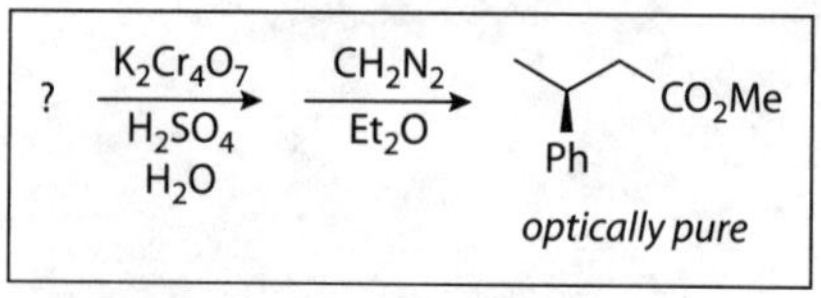

$$? \xrightarrow[\substack{H_2SO_4 \\ H_2O}]{K_2Cr_4O_7} \xrightarrow[Et_2O]{CH_2N_2} \underset{\substack{Ph \\ \text{optically pure}}}{\text{CO}_2\text{Me}}$$

A. 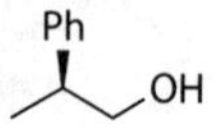
Ph
OH

B. 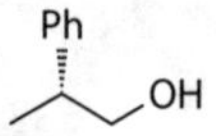
Ph
OH

C. 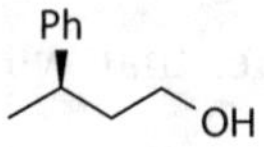
Ph
OH

D. 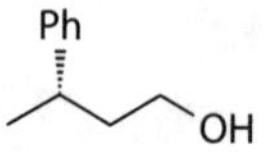
Ph
OH

22. For the following reaction, the most likely product is an:

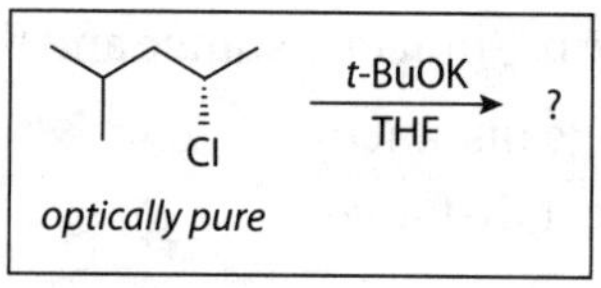

$$\xrightarrow[\text{THF}]{t\text{-BuOK}} ?$$
Cl
optically pure

A. ether with optical activity
B. ether without optical activity
C. alkene with optical activity
D. alkene without optical activity

Questions 23–27 are based on the following passage.

Passage IV

An important class of oxidation-reduction reactions is called single displacement. In single displacement reactions, one element takes the place of another in a compound. The reactivity series for metals is a summary of the results of many single displacement experiments. A metal that is above another is more reactive and will take the place of the lower, less reactive metal in a compound.

For instance, a student places a sample of zinc metal into a solution of nickel (II) nitrate. The zinc reacts to displace the nickel ions as follows:

$$\text{Zn } (s) + \text{Ni(NO}_3)_2 \ (aq) \rightarrow \text{Ni } (s) + \text{Zn(NO}_3)_2 \ (aq)$$

The reactivity series also predicts the reactivity of a metal with water. Only a few metals—the Group I metals and calcium, strontium, and barium from Group II— react with water at room temperature. This reaction is similar to a single displacement because the metal displaces the hydrogen in water. It is often called a hydrogen displacement reaction.

Dilute acid, usually hydrochloric acid, can be used to compare the reactivity of metals that do not react with water.

Experiment

A student reacts samples of copper, cobalt, and iron metal with dilute hydrochloric acid with the following results:

Metal	Reaction with HCl
Cu	No reaction
Co	Slow reaction with formation of small bubbles
Fe	Rapid reaction with formation of large bubbles

Activity Series
K Na Ca Mg Al Mn Zn Cr Fe Ni Sn Pb Cu Ag Au
Better Reducing Agent   **Better Oxidizing Agent**

A general rule for the main group metals is that the reactivity of metals within a group increases going down the column, and the reactivity decreases going from left to right across a row. For transition metals, the reactivity does not change in a regular manner across a row but does decrease going down a column.

23. Which of the following BEST represents the reaction of calcium with water?

   A. $Ca\ (s) + H_2O\ (l) \rightarrow CaOH\ (s) + H\ (g)$

   B. $Ca\ (s) + H_2O\ (l) \rightarrow Ca(OH)_2\ (s) + H_2\ (g)$

   C. $Ca\ (s) + 2H_2O\ (l) \rightarrow Ca(OH)_2\ (s) + H_2\ (g)$

   D. $Ca^{+2}\ (aq) + 2H_2O\ (l) \rightarrow Ca(OH)_2\ (aq) + H_2\ (g)$

24. Which of the following is the first metal in the activity series that does NOT react with water?

   A. Mg

   B. Al

   C. Mn

   D. Zn

25. Where would cobalt be expected to fall in the activity series?

   A. between lead and copper

   B. to the left of iron

   C. between iron and copper

   D. to the right of copper

26. Which of the following statements is NOT true?
    A. Nickel will displace silver from silver (I) nitrate.
    B. Chromium reacts with dilute hydrochloric acid.
    C. Calcium will displace aluminum from aluminum nitrate.
    D. Tin will displace nickel from nickel (II) nitrate.

27. What is the electron configuration of chromium?
    A. $[Ar]4s^2 3d^4$
    B. $[Ar]3d^5 4s^1$
    C. $[Ne]3d^5 4s^1$
    D. $[Ar]4s^0 3d^6$

Questions 28–30 are not associated with a passage.

28. Which of the following metals is diamagnetic?
    A. calcium
    B. aluminum
    C. titanium
    D. copper

29. Iodine-131, a radioisotope typically employed in the diagnosis of thyroid disorders, has a mass number, A, of 131 and an atomic number, Z, of 53. The number of neutrons, N, of iodine-131 is:
    A. 131
    B. 78
    C. 53
    D. 25

30. Ten milliliters of blood is drawn for routine testing. Assuming the density of human blood is $1.06 \, g/cm^3$, the weight of the blood sample is:
    A. 0.1 N.
    B. 1.0 N.
    C. 10.0 N.
    D. 20.0 N.

Questions 31–35 are based on the following passage.

Passage V

The S_N2 reaction is applicable to a wide variety of substrates, and it is impacted by many parameters. First, a good leaving group is required for S_N2 to take place. Second, nucleophilic displacement is dependent upon a strong nucleophile; however, most potential nucleophiles exhibit both basic and nucleophilic character. As nucleophiles become more basic, the competing pathway of bimolecular elimination (E2) begins to predominate.

boron 5 **B** 10.811	carbon 6 **C** 12.011	nitrogen 7 **N** 14.007	oxygen 8 **O** 15.999	fluorine 9 **F** 18.998
aluminium 13 **Al** 26.982	silicon 14 **Si** 28.086	phosphorus 15 **P** 30.974	sulfur 16 **S** 32.065	chlorine 17 **Cl** 35.453
			selenium 34 **Se** 78.96	bromine 35 **Br** 79.904
				iodine 53 **I** 126.90

Two more parameters also exert influence on reactivity: the electrophilic center (i.e., primary, secondary, or tertiary) and the solvent (i.e., nonpolar, polar protic, or polar aprotic). A student mixes equimolar quantities of 2-chloropropane, 2-iodopropane, sodium methoxide (NaOMe), and sodium methyl thiolate (NaSMe) in a solvent of methanol, and observes both S_N2 and E2 reactivity.

31. In comparing methoxide (MeO$^-$) and methyl thiolate (MeS$^-$), methoxide is:
    A. more nucleophilic and more basic
    B. more nucleophilic and less basic
    C. less nucleophilic and more basic
    D. less nucleophilic and less basic

32. In comparing chloride (Cl$^-$) and iodide (I$^-$), chloride is:
    A. the better leaving group and the better nucleophile
    B. the better leaving group and the poorer nucleophile
    C. the poorer leaving group and the better nucleophile
    D. the poorer leaving group and the poorer nucleophile

33. The fastest S_N2 reaction would occur between:
    A. methoxide and 2-iodopropane
    B. methoxide and 2-chloropropane
    C. methyl thiolate and 2-iodopropane
    D. methyl thiolate and 2-chloropropane

34. If temperature is increased,
    A. the rate of E2 increases; the rate of S_N2 decreases
    B. the rate of S_N2 increases; the rate of E2 decreases
    C. the rate of both reactions increases
    D. the rate of both reactions decreases

35. Which of the following solvents would provide for the fastest S_N2 reaction?
    A. methanol
    B. dimethyl sulfoxide
    C. tetrahydrofuran
    D. diethyl ether

Questions 36–42 are based on the following passage.

Passage VI

Cervical traction devices employ forces transmitted through a system of pulleys to correct deformities of the neck and spine by maintaining their proper alignment. The physics involved in these devices are based on Newton's second law of motion and Atwood's machine.

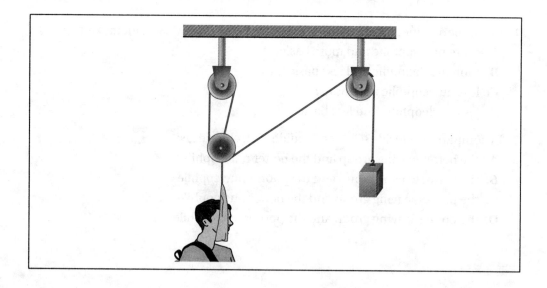

Newton's second law of motion states that a net force, F_{net}, acting in a given direction on an object of mass, m, will result in an acceleration, a, of the object in that same direction, i.e.:

$$\sum F = ma$$

or

$$\sum F_x = ma_x \quad \text{and} \quad \sum F_y = ma_y$$

Atwood's machine, illustrated in the following figure, uses a block-and-pulley system to determine the acceleration of the system as well as other variables such as the falling distance of either mass and the tension in the string connecting the masses.

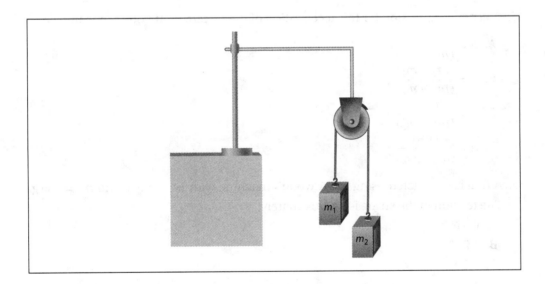

In a typical experimental setup, the Atwood machine is assembled with a massless string around a pulley. Connected on either end of the string are two masses, m_1 and m_2, where $m_1 \neq m_2$. The pulley is considered to be massless as well as frictionless. When the connected masses are released, both masses will accelerate at the same rate with the larger mass accelerating downward and the smaller mass accelerating upward.

Students were asked to conduct experiments using Atwood's machine with a constant total mass of 300 g. They were given hanging weights in increments of 10 g and could place any number of weights on either side of Atwood's machine as long as the total mass equaled 300 g.

36. For a typical Atwood's machine setup, the free-body diagram of the side with m_1 is:

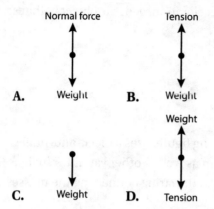

37. A general expression for the acceleration of the system in Atwood's machine is:

A. $a = \dfrac{(m_2 - m_1)}{(m_1 + m_2)}g$

B. $a = \dfrac{(m_2 + m_1)}{(m_1 + m_2)}g$

C. $a = \dfrac{(m_2 \cdot m_1)}{(m_1 + m_2)}g$

D. $a = \dfrac{(m_2)}{(m_1 + m_2)}g$

38. A trial is conducted using the Atwood's machine with $m_1 = 140\,g$ and $m_2 = 160\,g$. The tension in the string is approximately:

A. 0.8 N

B. 1.2 N

C. 1.5 N

D. 1.9 N

39. Students applied masses to the Atwood's machine setup such that $m_1 = 80\,g$ and $m_2 = 220\,g$. The acceleration of the system is:

A. $1.7\,\dfrac{m}{s^2}$

B. $2.4\,\dfrac{m}{s^2}$

C. $3.3\,\dfrac{m}{s^2}$

D. $4.6\,\dfrac{m}{s^2}$

40. In an experimental trial in which the students used masses $m_1 = 110\,g$ and $m_2 = 190\,g$, the students determined the tension in the string to be:

A. 1.4 N

B. 1.9 N

C. 2.8 N

D. 3.3 N

41. An assumption of the calculation for the acceleration of the system of masses in Atwood's machine is that the pulley is frictionless. If one uses a pulley with friction, the expression for the acceleration of the system now becomes:

   A. $a = \dfrac{m_2 g - m_1 g - f}{(m_1 + m_2)}$

   B. $a = \dfrac{m_1 g - m_2 g - f}{(m_1 + m_2)}$

   C. $a = \dfrac{-f}{(m_1 + m_2)}$

   D. $a = \dfrac{(m_1 + m_2)}{m_2 g - m_1 g - f}$

42. In an experiment using a pulley with friction, the students collect data and create a graph of acceleration versus mass difference. From the graph, the students can determine the frictional force from the:

   A. x-variable
   B. y-variable
   C. slope
   D. y-intercept

Questions 43–47 are based on the following passage.

Passage VII

The Jones oxidation is a classical methodology for the oxidation of secondary alcohols to ketones. The conditions involve the combination of potassium dichromate ($K_2Cr_2O_7$), a shelf-stable crystalline solid, and aqueous sulfuric acid (H_2SO_4). This is simply a way to produce chromic acid (H_2CrO_4) in situ:

$$KO-\overset{\overset{O}{\|}}{\underset{\underset{O}{\|}}{Cr}}-O-\overset{\overset{O}{\|}}{\underset{\underset{O}{\|}}{Cr}}-OK \quad \xrightarrow[\text{H}_2\text{O}]{\text{H}_2\text{SO}_4} \quad 2\,HO-\overset{\overset{O}{\|}}{\underset{\underset{O}{\|}}{Cr}}-OH$$

Under the reaction conditions, chromic acid produces equilibrium concentrations of chromium trioxide (CrO_3), which is the key oxidizing agent in the Jones oxidation:

$$HO-\overset{\overset{O}{\|}}{\underset{\underset{O}{\|}}{Cr}}-OH \quad \underset{}{\overset{H^+}{\rightleftharpoons}} \quad O{=}\overset{\overset{O}{\|}}{Cr}{\diagdown}_O \;\;+\;\; H_2O$$

Chromium trioxide reacts with alcohols to provide chromate esters, which proceeds as follows:

With primary alcohols, however, the reaction does not stop at the aldehyde stage. In the presence of acid and water, the initially formed carbonyl compounds are in equilibrium with their hydrates:

The hydrates can form chromate esters with one of the hydroxyl groups, just as the alcohol substrates do. When $R' = H$, this proton is easily lost to provide the carboxylic acid. Therefore, under Jones conditions, secondary alcohols yield ketones, but primary alcohols give carboxylic acids:

If aldehydes are desired from primary alcohols, the oxidation can be carried out with pyridinium chlorochromate (PCC), a shelf-stable crystalline solid that also provides chromium trioxide:

pyridinium chlorochromate
(PCC)

43. Ketones are NOT oxidized to carboxylic acids under Jones conditions because:
   A. They do not form hydrates with water.
   B. Their hydrates cannot form chromate esters.
   C. The chromate esters of their hydrates cannot decompose by proton loss.
   D. The chromate ester decomposition is reversible.

44. Pyridinium chlorochromate (PCC) is selective for the production of aldehydes from primary alcohols because:
   A. It can be weighed out very accurately.
   B. It does not introduce water into the reaction.
   C. The pyridine prevents overoxidation.
   D. The environment is less acidic.

45. Consider the Jones oxidation of heptane-1,6-diol:

The MOST likely product of this reaction would be a(n):
A. hydroxy ketone
B. hydroxy acid
C. oxo aldehyde
D. oxo acid

46. Consider the PCC oxidation of heptane-1,6-diol:

The MOST likely product of this reaction would be a(n):
A. hydroxy ketone
B. hydroxy acid
C. oxo aldehyde
D. oxo acid

47. A tertiary alcohol is treated with the Jones reagent, and the reaction mixture is worked up and purified. The MOST likely compound isolated is a(n):
A. alcohol
B. ketone
C. aldehyde
D. carboxylic acid

Questions 48–52 are based on the following passage.

Passage VIII

α-D-glucose and β-D-glucose are interconverted through a process known as mutarotation, which proceeds via a ring-opened intermediate, as shown:

In solution, α-D-glucose and β-D-glucose exist in a 9:16 ratio at equilibrium, but this is not what would be predicted from sterics alone. The discrepancy is largely due to the anomeric effect, which involves the interaction of the lone pairs on the ring oxygen with the C-1 hydroxy group.

48. The best term for describing the difference between α-D-glucose and β-D-glucose is:
    A. enantiomers
    B. diastereomers
    C. regioisomers
    D. conformers

49. Aside from the multiple alcohols, the functional group found in both α-D-glucose and β-D-glucose is a(n):
    A. hemiacetal
    B. acetal
    C. aminal
    D. orthoester

50. Aside from the multiple alcohols, the functional group found in the ring-opened intermediate is a(n):
    A. ketone
    B. aldehyde
    C. acid
    D. ester

51. α-D-glucose and β-D-glucose are BEST described as:
    A. hexoses and furanoses
    B. pentoses and furanoses
    C. hexoses and pyranoses
    D. pentoses and pyranoses

52. The BEST rationale for the impact of the anomeric effect on the equilibrium of α-D-glucose and β-D-glucose is:
    A. It stabilizes α-D-glucose and destabilizes β-D-glucose.
    B. It destabilizes α-D-glucose and stabilizes β-D-glucose.
    C. It stabilizes both α-D-glucose and β-D-glucose.
    D. It destabilizes both α-D-glucose and β-D-glucose.

Questions 53–57 are based on the following passage.

Passage IX

In the general chemistry laboratory, it is convenient to carry out most reactions in solution, usually aqueous solution. When solid ionic compounds are mixed together at room temperature, no reaction takes place. But if aqueous solutions of the solids are mixed, a reaction can take place. Common types of reactions in aqueous solution include acid-base reactions, precipitation reactions, and oxidation-reduction reactions.

Compounds have different solubilities in water, as shown in the following table:

Solubilities of Some Substances		
Compound	**Temp (°C)**	**Solubility (g/100 mL water)**
NaCl (s)	0	35.70
NaCl (s)	100	39.10
$PbCl_2$ (s)	20	0.99
$PbCl_2$ (s)	100	3.34
AgCl (s)	10	0.000089
AgCl (s)	100	0.0021
CH_3CH_2OH (l)	20	∞
$CH_3CH_2OCH_2CH_3$ (l)	15	8.43

Ions in water solution are called electrolytes, and a solution of electrolytes will conduct electricity. The ability to conduct electricity is called conductivity, and it is directly related to the concentration of ions in solution. Ionic compounds that are very soluble in water are strong electrolytes. Ionic compounds that are sparingly soluble in water are weak electrolytes. Covalent compounds can be strong, weak, or even nonelectrolytes. It depends on whether the substance can form ions in solution, and if so, the concentration of the ions.

A general rule for predicting whether a reaction will take place when two electrolytic solutions are mixed is that a reaction will take place if one or both possible products are either insoluble, weak, or nonelectrolyte.

Experiment

A student determines if each of a series of compounds was soluble or insoluble in water. The results are as follows.

Compound	Soluble in Water
NaCl	yes
$NaNO_3$	yes
$AgNO_3$	yes
$BaSO_4$	no
$Ba(NO_3)_2$	yes
Na_2SO_4	yes
NaOH	yes
$Ca(OH)_2$	no
Na_3PO_4	yes
$Ca_3(PO_4)_2$	no

53. What is the expected insoluble product when a solution of silver nitrate reacts with a solution of sodium chloride at room temperature?
    A. sodium nitrate
    B. silver nitrate
    C. silver chloride
    D. sodium chloride

54. A student prepares a saturated solution of sodium chloride at 100.0 °C. The student makes 250.0 mL of solution and then cools it to 0.0 °C. How many grams of NaCl will precipitate out when the solution is cooled to 0.0 °C?
    A. 89.3 g
    B. 97.8 g
    C. 8.6 g
    D. 3.4 g

55. What would happen to the conductivity of a mixture of two solutions that produces two insoluble products?
    A. It would remain the same.
    B. It would lessen somewhat.
    C. It would decrease greatly.
    D. It would increase greatly.

56. Which of the following statements can BEST be inferred from the experimental results?
    A. Sodium salts are always soluble.
    B. Group II salts are always soluble.
    C. Phosphates are usually insoluble.
    D. Sulfates are usually soluble.

57. Based on the experimental data, which of the following statements is true?
    A. Silver compounds are always insoluble.
    B. Phosphates are always insoluble.
    C. Sulfates are never soluble.
    D. You can improve the solubility of silver chloride with the addition of ammonia.

Questions 58 and 59 are not associated with a passage.

58. Which of the following shows a pair of substances that differ from the other three?
    A. NH_4^+ and NH_3
    B. H_2SO_4 and SO_4^{2-}
    C. $H_2PO_4^-$ and HPO_4^{2-}
    D. HCl and Cl^-

59. Which of the following represents the proper Lewis structure for fluoride?

A. $:\!\ddot{F}\!\cdot$

B. $:\!\ddot{F}\!:$

C. $:\!\ddot{F}\!:^{+}$

D. $:\!\ddot{F}\!:^{-}$

STOP. This is the end of Section 2.

Psychological, Social, and Biological Foundations of Behavior

59 Questions   **Time Limit: 95 Minutes**

Questions 1–4 are not associated with any passage.

1. Alfred is looking through a telescope with one eye closed watching sailboats enter a harbor. He is able to tell that a 20-foot boat has entered before a 30-foot catamaran. Which of the following cues is Alfred NOT able to use to judge relative distance?
   A. relative size
   B. interposition
   C. retinal disparity
   D. texture

2. With which theoretical paradigm is the German political philosopher Karl Marx MOST associated?
   A. conflict theory
   B. functionalism
   C. symbolic interactionism
   D. avoidance theory

3. According to the bystander effect, which is MOST likely to be true in an emergency?
   A. the greater the number of people present, the slower the response because of increased diffusion of responsibility
   B. the greater the number of people present, the slower the response because of decreased diffusion of responsibility
   C. the greater the number of people present, the faster the response because of increased diffusion of responsibility
   D. the greater the number of people present, the faster the response because of decreased diffusion of responsibility

43

4. Studies examining altruism have shown that which of the following is true?

    A. True altruism is common and found even between highly disparate individuals.

    B. Altruism is more frequent in larger communities due to diffusion of responsibility.

    C. Altruism is more likely to occur between individuals who are likely to reciprocate assistance in the future.

    D. Altruism is more likely to occur when participation is anonymous.

Questions 5–9 are based on the following passage.

Passage I

Described by the psychologist B. F. Skinner, operant conditioning posits that learning can be understood by the interaction between reinforcers and stimuli. Studies from both comparative and human psychology have supported Skinner's initial findings and expanded upon them.

    The following figure shows a hypothetical example of various operant conditioning trials. During these trials, when a rat pressed a bar (as indicated by the hash mark on the graph), the behavior was reinforced by the presentation of a food pellet. The reinforcement schedule differs in each cell of the figure. Time is displayed on the *x*-axis and cumulative responses (bar presses) is displayed on the *y*-axis.

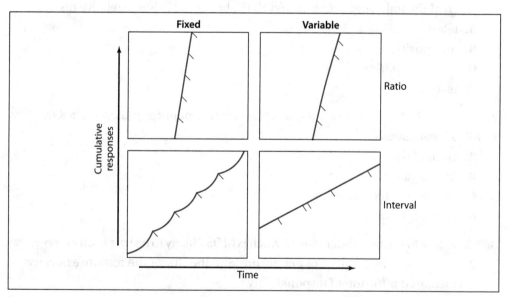

Operant conditioning with each cell representing a different reinforcement schedule.

5. Based on the figure and the concept of operant conditioning, which type of response leads to an increased cumulative response and is MOST likely to result in a more persistent conditioned response?

    A. fixed-ratio

    B. variable-ratio

    C. fixed-interval

    D. variable-interval

45

SECTION 3:
Psychological,
Social, and
Biological
Foundations
of Behavior

6. What would MOST likely happen if, after the bar press, reinforcement was delayed (e.g., a time lag occurred before presentation of the food pellet)?
    A. Conditioning would occur faster, and the slope in each cell of the graph would be steeper.
    B. Conditioning would occur faster but only for the variable reinforcement conditions.
    C. Conditioning would occur more slowly, and the slope in each cell of the graph would be flatter.
    D. Conditioning would occur more slowly but only for the variable reinforcement conditions.

7. Imagine that you are watching a rat complete one of the tasks in the figure above. The rat is pressing the bar at a very high rate and takes a short break from pressing the bar each time the food pellet is delivered. What type of reinforcement schedule are you MOST likely watching?
    A. variable-interval
    B. variable-ratio
    C. fixed-interval
    D. fixed-ratio

8. Based on the ratio-reinforcing graphs, for both fixed and variable conditions, which of the following would you expect?
    A. a predictable response rate for both and a lower resistance to extinction in the variable condition
    B. longer breaks between bar presses for the fixed condition and a higher resistance to extinction
    C. a predictable response rate for both and a greater resistance to extinction in the variable condition
    D. longer breaks between bar presses for the variable condition and a lower resistance to extinction

9. Which of the following is true about conditioning?
    A. In operant conditioning the stimulus behavior always precedes the reinforcement or punishment.
    B. Operant conditioning can be used on animals while classical conditioning cannot be used.
    C. Classical conditioning can explain all learning conditions, but operant conditioning is often used for simplicity.
    D. In classical conditioning the reinforcement must never be paired with an unconditioned stimulus.

Questions 10–14 are based on the following passage.

Passage II

In psychology, research examining moral development has typically focused on age-related differences. One such approach is Lawrence Kohlberg's theory that individuals progress through three levels of morality: preconventional, conventional, and postconventional. Kohlberg identified these levels based on participants' reactions to stories that present moral dilemmas. For example, participants were asked to respond to a story in which a poor man named Heinz steals a drug for his wife who would die without the drug.

The following figure depicts the moral reasoning levels that Kohlberg found within each age group on his scale. In each graph, the proportion of responders tested who showed the indicated level of moral reasoning is shown on the *y*-axis and the age of the responders is shown on the *x*-axis.

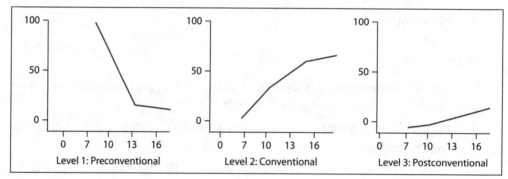

Representations of performance on Kohlberg's task with proportion of responders on the *y*-axis and age on the *x*-axis.

10. If the data pattern steadied out at 17 years old, which level would be demonstrated by the greatest proportion of responders?
    A. conventional
    B. postconventional
    C. preconventional
    D. both postconventional and preconventional equally

11. Based on the data shown, when does conventional morality develop?
    A. before age seven
    B. at age seven
    C. between the ages of 7 and 16
    D. after age 16

47

SECTION 3:
Psychological,
Social, and
Biological
Foundations
of Behavior

12. Which of the following is true about Kohlberg's theory of moral development?
    A. All adults eventually reach the postconventional stage.
    B. Moral judgments can be understood in context based on stages of moral development.
    C. The majority of children are born with the ability to tell right from wrong based on constructed moral principles.
    D. Morality is predefined with specific answers that align with societal laws.

13. According to Kohlberg's theory, which of the following is a characteristic of stage 3 morality?
    A. basing decisions only to avoid punishment or reward
    B. basing decisions on society's rules and the avoidance of punishment
    C. basing decisions on social approval of peers rather than on laws
    D. basing decisions on personally constructed moral principles rather than on societal teachings

14. James is a manager at a store. He sees a coworker temporarily abandon the checkout desk in order to help an elderly customer to her car. This act is a violation of company policy. James reports the coworker to corporate management for discipline. James is MOST likely in which stage of moral development?
    A. postconventional
    B. conventional
    C. preconventional
    D. adaptive

Questions 15–19 are based on the following passage.

Passage III

Researchers studying vision use various methods to investigate human perceptual experience. Research on spectral sensitivity of the rod receptors (scattered throughout the retina) and cone visual receptors (mainly concentrated in the fovea area of the retina) highlights the relationship between perception and physiology.

Signal detection methods have been used to measure the differences in how perception adjusts to low-light environments. Participant responses can be plotted based on sensitivity versus length of time in the dark. The dark adaptation curve can be plotted showing how rods and cones differ in their sensitivity to light over time.

The following graph shows a plot of three calculated dark adaptation curves.

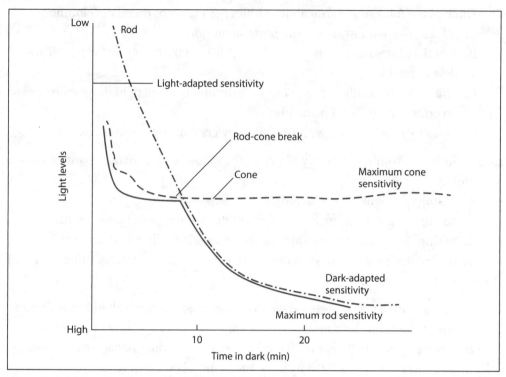

Three dark adaptation curves. Both dashed lines indicate receptor-specific curves, while the solid line is a plot of human light sensitivity with both receptor types included.

15. The dark adaptation curve can be plotted by asking participants to fixate on a specific point and then using signal detection methods with a test light. What is the MOST likely way that researchers would be able to isolate the responses of each receptor type, based on the physiology of the eye?

   A. by using colored versus white lights to differentially activate the rods and cones
   B. by changing the location of the test light from the focal point to the periphery
   C. by asking participants to cover one eye while performing the comparison tasks
   D. by alternating the brightness using flashing lights in order to preferentially activate one receptor type rather than the other

16. Signal detection methods are used to plot the dark adaptation curve. Based on these methods, what would be the threshold used for correctly detecting the presence of the test light?

   A. A participant is considered to have detected the light if he or she can identify the comparison light presence 50% of the time.
   B. A participant is considered to have detected the light if he or she can identify the comparison light presence 25% of the time.
   C. A participant is considered to have detected the light if he or she can identify the comparison light presence 75% of the time.
   D. Any time a participant identifies a light to be present, the light is considered to have been perceived.

49

SECTION 3:
Psychological,
Social, and
Biological
Foundations
of Behavior

17. Based on the dark adaptation curves, which of the following statements is true?
    A. Rods are more sensitive than cones after 5 minutes in the dark.
    B. Cones are more sensitive than rods after 15 minutes in the dark.
    C. Rods are more sensitive than cones at the rod-cone break.
    D. Rods are more sensitive than cones after 20 minutes in the dark.

18. Which of the following statements is true?
    A. Rods are responsible for color vision, which explains color sensitivity under low-light conditions.
    B. Cones are responsible for color vision, which explains greater color sensitivity under low-light conditions.
    C. Rods do not respond preferentially to wavelengths in the light spectrum, which explains why colors are not detectable in low-light conditions.
    D. Both rods and cones respond to specific colors in the light spectrum; loss of color vision in dark conditions is the result of fewer photons of light.

19. Based on the research described above and the physiology of the eye, what is the MOST likely explanation for increased rod sensitivity after the rod-cone break?
    A. Cones are poorer at light adaptation because large groups of them are connected to one interneuron.
    B. Cones are better at light adaptation because they respond to specific wavelengths of light.
    C. Rods are poorer at light adaptation because they are less prone to pigment bleaching.
    D. Rods are better at light adaptation because large groups of them are connected to one interneuron.

Questions 20–24 are based on the following passage.

Passage IV

Research has examined how the presence of others affects how humans behave in different social contexts. This research has examined performance for different types of tasks and has also evaluated how group size affects performance.

The following hypothetical data represents the amount of time an individual devotes to solving a long series of mathematical word problems before selecting an answer (regardless of accuracy of that answer). In this example, effort is measured by the amount of time spent working to solve a multistep word problem either using algebra or calculus. The time spent by the individual was measured for each type of task when performed alone and when performed in a group. In the graph, the number of minutes spent by the individual is shown on the y-axis and the math category is shown on the x-axis.

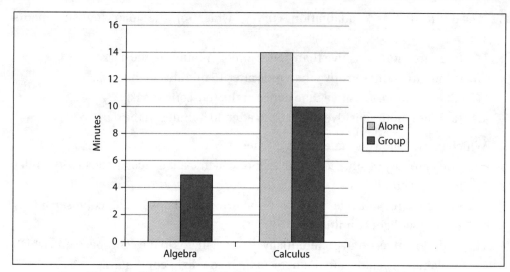

Number of minutes an individual spends to solve math problems.

20. Based on the graph, which of the following statements is true?
    A. The individual spent a longer amount of time solving calculus problems in a group compared to solving calculus problems alone.
    B. The individual spent about the same amount of time solving calculus problems in a group relative to solving them alone.
    C. The individual spent a longer amount of time solving algebra problems alone relative to solving them in a group.
    D. The individual spent a longer amount of time solving algebra problems in a group compared to solving them alone.

21. Based on research examining group performance, which of the following terms BEST explains why the individual spent less effort on solving calculus word problems when working as part of a group?
    A. social facilitation
    B. social loafing
    C. deindividuation
    D. bystander effect

22. Based on research examining group performance, which of the following terms BEST explains why the individual spent more effort on solving algebra word problems when working as part of a group?
    A. social facilitation
    B. social loafing
    C. deindividuation
    D. bystander effect

51

SECTION 3:
Psychological,
Social, and
Biological
Foundations
of Behavior

23. What would you expect to be the MOST likely result if the complexity of the calculus problems increased (e.g., doubled in length and number of steps)?
    A. The individual would step up and expend more effort on solving the problems because he or she would feel more personally responsible.
    B. The individual would reduce the amount of effort spent on solving the problems because he or she would assume that others would step up to complete the task.
    C. The group would likely subdivide the problems into smaller tasks resulting in more individual effort overall.
    D. The amount of effort would remain unchanged.

24. Based on research examining social loafing, which of the following is true?
    A. The effort expended is the result of the participant's perception of diffusion of responsibility.
    B. The effort expended is influenced by the physical limitations that result from group work.
    C. Effort coordination explains all differences in performance for group activities.
    D. The effort expended is the result of expectations from others about an individual's work in a group.

Questions 25–29 are based on the following passage.

Passage V

Understanding the various causes of psychological disorders is a central focus of research in psychology. Further, clinical psychologists must consider factors that influence the incidence rate and characteristics of clinical populations that they treat.

The following graphs depict data from a study by L. R. Snowden and F. K. Cheung, who examined demographic differences in the incidence rate of schizophrenia. The first figure shows the percentage rates for schizophrenia diagnosis among individuals admitted for psychiatric care who classified themselves as "African American," "White," "Hispanic American," or "Asian American and other."

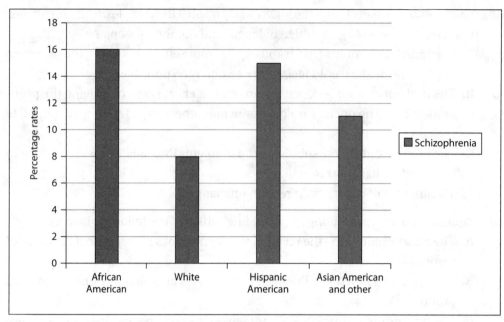

Rates of schizophrenia diagnosis for individuals admitted for psychiatric care by ethnicity. *Source*: Reproduced with permission from L. R. Snowden & F. K. Cheung. "Use of inpatient mental health services by members of ethnic minority groups." *American Psychologist*, 1990:45(3), 347.

The following graph shows the percentage rates for mood disorder diagnosis among individuals admitted for psychiatric care, by the same ethnicity classifications.

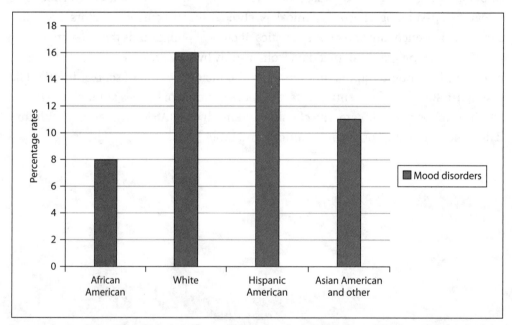

Rates of mood disorder diagnosis for individuals admitted for psychiatric care by ethnicity. *Source*: Reproduced with permission from L. R. Snowden & F. K. Cheung. "Use of inpatient mental health services by members of ethnic minority groups." *American Psychologist*, 1990:45(3), 347.

53

SECTION 3:
Psychological,
Social, and
Biological
Foundations
of Behavior

25. Based on this research, members of which ethnicity are MORE likely to be diagnosed with schizophrenia, and members of which ethnicity are MORE likely to be diagnosed with mood disorders, respectively?
    A. White; Asian American and other
    B. African American; Hispanic American
    C. African American; White
    D. Hispanic American; Hispanic American

26. Based on the data, which possible conclusion can be ruled out completely?
    A. Ethnicity has no impact on the likelihood that an individual will experience a particular mental disorder.
    B. Ethnicity is fully responsible for the likelihood an individual will experience a particular mental disorder.
    C. Clinicians see no ethnicity differences in admittance rates for some disorders.
    D. Clinicians often classify disorders based on existing biases.

27. What would be the BEST logical follow-up study to further examine the differences in diagnosis of mental disorders by ethnicity?
    A. Measure the social and economic status and stress of each person diagnosed with schizophrenia and mood disorder.
    B. Send the patients to a different facility to retest the diagnosis.
    C. Compare the differences in diagnostic criteria and determine the amount of overlap between the diagnostic criteria for mood disorders and schizophrenia.
    D. Investigate why mood disorders are underrepresented in the admission samples by conducting additional surveys.

28. Based on psychological research investigating the causes of schizophrenia, which of the following is NOT true?
    A. Schizophrenia has a genetic component that can be inherited from biological parents, but genetic factors alone cannot account for the development of the disorder.
    B. The production and activity of specific chemical substances in the brain have been found to be associated with schizophrenia.
    C. Environmental factors contribute to the development of schizophrenia.
    D. A person has a 100% chance of developing schizophrenia if both of his or her parents have schizophrenia.

29. The vulnerability-stress (a.k.a. diathesis-stress) model of schizophrenia is BEST exemplified by which of the following?

   A. The more stress to which a person who is genetically predisposed to schizophrenia is exposed, the greater the likelihood that person will experience a psychotic break.

   B. Everyone becomes equally vulnerable to schizophrenia under high stress regardless of their genetic predisposition.

   C. Only negative life stressors increase the likelihood of a psychotic break in genetically predisposed individuals, while positive life stressors do not increase vulnerability.

   D. An individual is more vulnerable to schizophrenia if his or her biological family experiences stress because schizophrenia is so strongly based on genetics.

Questions 30–34 are based on the following passage.

Passage VI

Psychologists have examined how love develops over time. Their research has typically attempted to divide love into different facets whose interrelationships change over time. One such model of love developed by Robert Sternberg is shown in the following diagram and graph.

Sternberg's model has three components: commitment, intimacy, and passion, which in combination result in multiple types of love.

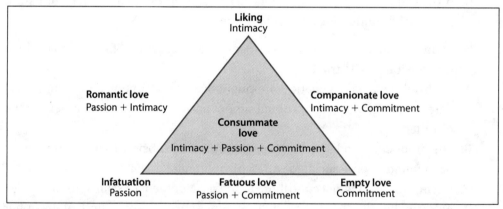

Sternberg's model of love.

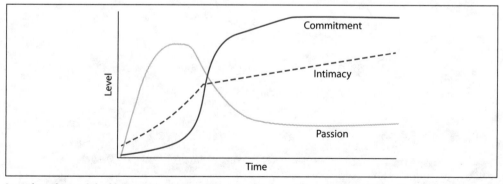

Sternberg's model of love with changes that occur over time. *Source*: From R. J. Sternberg. *The Triangle of Love: Intimacy, Passion, Commitment*. Basic Books, 1988.

55

SECTION 3:
Psychological,
Social, and
Biological
Foundations
of Behavior

30. Based on the graph, which of the following is true?
    A. Intimacy decreases over time.
    B. Passion increases rapidly early and then increases slowly over time.
    C. Commitment initially increases slowly; then it rapidly increases.
    D. Intimacy decreases as passion increases.

31. According to Sternberg's view of love, which of the following is true?
    A. Passion is unnecessary and is abandoned over time.
    B. Intimacy increases but is inherently the same as compassion.
    C. Commitment is crucial and is positively correlated to relationship stability.
    D. Passion is the most important facet for long-term love.

32. Which facet of love is characterized by intense emotion and includes tender sexual feelings?
    A. romantic love
    B. companionate love
    C. commitment
    D. intimacy

33. Which of the following statements about the types of love is MOST likely true?
    A. Fatuous love and liking can coexist in this model.
    B. Passion reaches a zenith early and then declines because you cannot like someone and be passionate about that person at the same time.
    C. In order to succeed over the long term, a relationship must maintain consummate love.
    D. Companionate love increases over time in long-term relationships.

34. Danna has been dating Mark off and on for the past two years. She enjoys the time she spends with him, but she considers him rather shallow. She still dates other people but has strong sexual feelings toward Mark. Danna is most likely experiencing which type of love?
    A. commitment
    B. companionate love
    C. intimacy
    D. infatuation

Questions 35–39 are based on the following passage.

Passage VII

Student performance on tests has been investigated by sociologists as an indicator of how social structures influence learning. The following graph represents student performance by state on a standardized mathematics test called the Trends in International Mathematics and Science Study (TIMSS). The average TIMSS scores and standard error were calculated and are displayed in the graph below. Average scores for each state are displayed individually, and the nationwide U.S. average is also shown as a separate data point. Benchmark (target) scores are also represented in the graph.

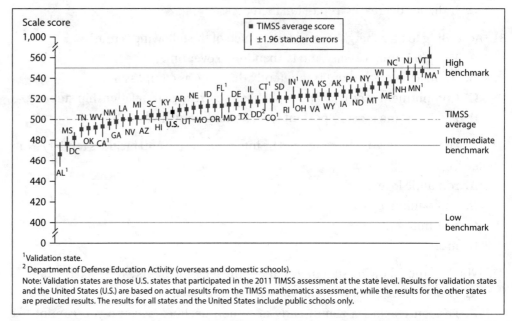

Average TIMSS score by state. *Source*: From U.S. Department of Education, Educational Services, National Center for Education Services, National Assessment of Educational Progress (NAEP), International Association for the Evaluation of Educational Achievement (IEA), Trends in International Mathematics and Science Study (TIMSS), 2011.

35. Which of the following statements is true about the data shown in the graph?
    A. The majority of state average scores were below the national average.
    B. The majority of state average scores were above the national average.
    C. The majority of state average scores were above the high benchmark.
    D. Half of the state average scores were above the national average and half were below.

36. Using the data in the graph, a sociologist is investigating how low-scoring states are attempting to improve their performance by incorporating historically low-performing groups into local programs and services. This approach is MOST closely related to which theoretical concept?
    A. human theory
    B. functionalism
    C. symbolic interactionism
    D. conflict theory

57

SECTION 3:
Psychological,
Social, and
Biological
Foundations
of Behavior

37. Which of the following BEST indicates one way a functionalist would interpret the data in the graph?
    A. The data show that the states are equally able to reinforce the status quo in regard to their own state population.
    B. The data show the historical inequities between various state populations.
    C. The data show that education is effective in reinforcing the relative socioeconomic status (SES) status quo between various state populations.
    D. The data show that performance indicators are not relevant.

38. In terms of the overall economy, teaching in the state school system is considered to be part of which level of production?
    A. primary
    B. secondary
    C. tertiary
    D. functional

39. Jim is a sociologist who works at a public policy center in a state where TIMSS scores are well above the national average. His group is concerned with maintaining the state's lead in educational ranking in order to fend off competition from other states for high-skilled jobs. His policy center creates several initiatives to ensure that the state's schools keep their high rank and reputation for quality. Jim is MOST likely from which theoretical background?
    A. conflict theory
    B. functionalism
    C. symbolic interactionism
    D. social adaptation theory

Questions 40–44 are based on the following passage.

Passage VIII

Studies collecting data on age distribution within populations have a long history in sociological research. The accompanying figure depicts the age distribution for males and females in Japan. The three graph "pyramids" show historical data for 1960 and 2010 and projections for 2060 based on current low birth rates. Each graph is separated into young, adult, and elderly populations.

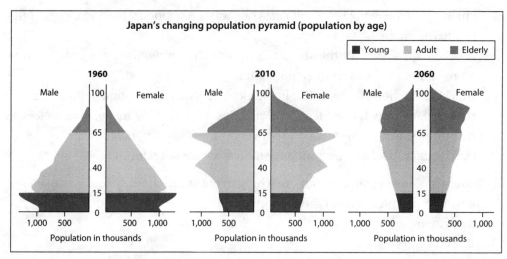

Japanese population characteristics by age over time. *Source*: (for 1960 and 2010) Ministry of Internal Affairs and Communications, Population Census of Japan; (for 2060 projection) National Institute of Population and Social Security Research, Population Projections for Japan (January 2012), based on medium-variant fertility and mortality assumptions.

40. Which conclusion can be drawn from the data in the figure?
   A. The share of the elderly population in Japan will decrease over time relative to the rest of the population.
   B. The share of the young population in Japan will remain largely unchanged over time relative to the rest of the population.
   C. The share of the young population in Japan will increase over time relative to the rest of the population.
   D. The share of the elderly population in Japan will increase over time relative to the rest of the population.

41. What might be a likely result of introducing a new "transitional youth" category to data projections for the years following 2010?
   A. There would be more transitional youth in the population in 2060 than in 2010.
   B. There would be fewer transitional youth in the population in 2060 than in 2010.
   C. There would be no change in the number of transitional youth in the population in 2060 compared to 2010.
   D. There would be a decrease in the share of the elderly population in 2060 because of the addition of a new category.

42. If immigration were increased over time to compensate for the low birth rate, which of the following would MOST likely occur?
   A. Social and cultural characteristics would become more diverse across the population.
   B. Social and cultural characteristics would become more uniform across the population.
   C. Immigration would have a negligible impact because cultural groups tend not to change over time.
   D. The age distribution structure within the population would remain unchanged.

59

SECTION 3:
Psychological,
Social, and
Biological
Foundations
of Behavior

43. If current age distribution trends continue in Japan, which of the following is likely in regard to the role of the elderly in society?
    A. The elderly are likely to have less influence on public policy as their share of the population declines.
    B. The elderly are likely to have more influence on public policy as their share of the population increases.
    C. The influence of the elderly on public policy is likely to be about the same in the future as it is today.
    D. The elderly are likely to have issues adapting to new societal norms and pressures.

44. If immigration were increased over time to compensate for the low birth rate, and if the immigrants became socially and culturally integrated into the native population, which of the following would be true?
    A. The racial composition of the native population would necessarily change.
    B. The ethnicity of the overall population would change.
    C. The racial composition of the immigrant population would necessarily change.
    D. The ethnicity of the overall population would remain basically the same.

Questions 45–49 are based on the following passage.

Passage IX

There are multiple reasons for racial and ethnic mental health treatment disparities in the United States. These differences have implications for mental health care. The following bar graph illustrates some of these disparities.

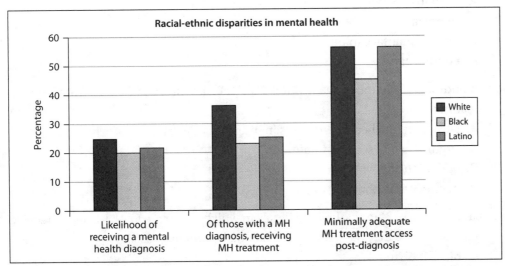

Racial and ethnic disparities in mental health. *Source*: Data from: A. A. Ault-Brutus. "Changes in racial-ethnic disparities in use and adequacy of mental health care in the United States, 1990–2003," *Psychiatric Services*, 2012:63(3), 531–540.

45. Which of the following is true based on the bar graph?
    A. Black individuals are as likely as white individuals to have access to minimally adequate mental health treatment post diagnosis.
    B. Latino individuals are as likely as white individuals to have access to minimally adequate mental health treatment post diagnosis.
    C. White individuals are as likely as Latino individuals to be diagnosed with a mental illness.
    D. White individuals are as likely as black individuals to be diagnosed with a mental illness.

46. George, an African American, was raised in surroundings of the lowest socio-economic status (SES). By working very hard in school, he earned an associate's degree in accounting. He began to take cocaine to keep up with his studies, and just before graduation began using heroin as well. He now experiences withdrawal without the drug and spends most of his time in efforts to obtain the drug. His student loans are coming due, but he has not been able to find a job because of his addiction. Based on the graph, what is the best explanation for why George is likely to continue to have an addiction problem and to remain in the lower SES?
    A. culture of poverty theory
    B. social reinforcement theory
    C. social mobility
    D. human capital

47. Lack of what form of capital is the likely primary barrier preventing George from seeking treatment and achieving social mobility?
    A. human capital
    B. financial capital
    C. environmental capital
    D. cultural capital

48. In addition to finances, what other barriers may prevent George from seeking treatment?
    A. lack of mental health providers in his geographic area
    B. stigma against seeking treatment
    C. both of the above
    D. neither of the above

49. Based on the bar graph, the individuals in which group are LEAST likely to receive treatment once they have received a mental health diagnosis?
    A. black individuals
    B. Latino individuals
    C. white individuals
    D. both Latino and black individuals

61

SECTION 3:
Psychological,
Social, and
Biological
Foundations
of Behavior

Questions 50–54 are based on the following passage.

Passage X

High levels of sustained stress have been studied by a number of researchers. Psychological stress can create escalations in the HPA axis that shift the body out of homeostasis.

An important theory describing the psychophysiological effects of stress was developed by the Austrian-Canadian endocrinologist Hans Selye. This theory posits a general adaptation syndrome (GAS) characterized by three stages: alarm reaction, resistance, and exhaustion.

Selye's model is shown in the following figure. The three phases are shown in order from left to right with stress plotted on the *y*-axis from low to high.

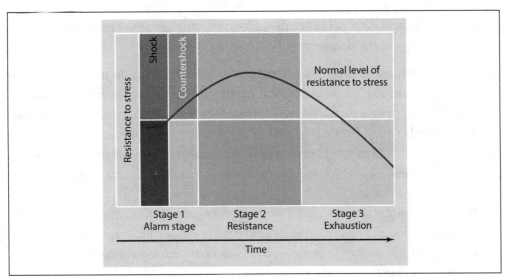

Selye's general adaptation syndrome. *Source*: Adapted with permission from J. W. Santrock. *Adolescence*, 15th ed., McGraw-Hill Education, 2014.

50. Based on Selye's general adaptation syndrome and your knowledge of stress physiology, which of the following is experienced during the alarm reaction stage?
    A. Bodily resources are mobilized and metabolism speeds up.
    B. Adaptability increases until it is depleted completely.
    C. Psychological resources become more moderate and sustained.
    D. People are irritable, impatient, and angry.

51. A person who is going through a divorce constantly complains about feeling tired, avoids family members who disapprove of the divorce, spends time with supportive friends, and engages in meditation in an effort to control feelings of irritation and anger. Which phase of GAS is the person MOST likely in, and how long might this condition last?

    A. Shock; the reaction will only last for a few days.

    B. Countershock; the reaction can persist for hours, days, or years.

    C. Exhaustion; the reaction will last for only a few days.

    D. Resistance; the reaction can persist for hours, days, or years.

52. Which of the following statements is true based on GAS theory?

    A. Resistance reactions are not adaptive and should be avoided.

    B. Resistance reactions are activities to reduce the impact of stress and avoid exhaustion.

    C. Physiological exhaustion is a necessary stage for any stress response.

    D. Physiological exhaustion results in increased stress.

53. An interpretation of the GAS theory posits that stressful life events occurring in combination can damage physical health. Extrapolating from the graph and integrating your knowledge of stress physiology, how would multiple simultaneous stressful events affect an individual?

    A. Multiple stressors would allow a person to repeatedly restart the process in the alarm stage, which would help that person improve resistance to stress and avoid exhaustion.

    B. Multiple simultaneous stressors may overwhelm an individual's stress resistance activities and push him or her into the exhaustion stage more quickly.

    C. It would not matter because individuals rarely encounter multiple stressors simultaneously.

    D. Stressful life events are difficult to classify or study, so we cannot begin to guess how multiple stressors would affect people.

54. Jeremy was driving on a dark road at night when a deer suddenly ran out of the brush and narrowly missed his car. Jeremy realized that there were likely more deer along the road. With his heart pounding, he turned off the road and continued to a lighted expressway with high fences. According to Selye's general adaptation syndrome theory, Jeremy was likely experiencing which of the following?

    A. a resistance reaction

    B. an alarm reaction

    C. physiological exhaustion

    D. autonomic rebound

63

SECTION 3:
Psychological,
Social, and
Biological
Foundations
of Behavior

Questions 55–59 are based on the following passage.

Passage XI

Researchers have long studied human memory. In a classic series of studies, the German psychologist Hermann Ebbinghaus investigated the storage and recall of information in memory. Based on his findings, he developed the so-called forgetting curve, a way of illustrating the rate at which people forget the information they have learned. The forgetting curve has been studied in a variety of different environments and for a variety of different stimuli.

On day 1 of a memory research study, participants were asked to learn a list of items. Researchers then tracked the proportion of the list that the participants remembered as time passed. On day 2, some participants were asked to relearn the list. Again, the proportion remembered was tracked over time. On day 3, some participants were asked to relearn the list a second time, and the proportion they remembered was tracked over time. On day 4, some participants were asked to relearn the list a third time, and the proportion they remembered was tracked over time.

The data from this study produced the following set of forgetting curves. Each line represents the memory of the learned or relearned list. The proportion of the list remembered is shown on the *y*-axis (memory), and the time interval for forgetting is shown on the *x*-axis (time remembered in days).

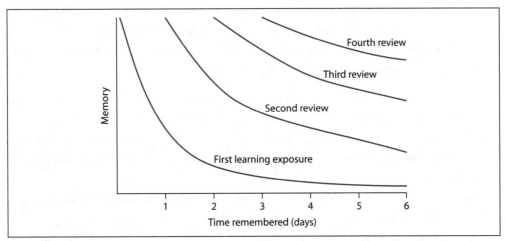

Forgetting curves. Each curve represents the memory of a learned or relearned list.

55. Based on the graph, which of the following statements BEST characterizes forgetting?
    A. Most forgetting occurs gradually over a long period of time.
    B. Most forgetting occurs after only a few days.
    C. Most forgetting occurs soon after information is learned.
    D. Most forgetting occurs at a constant rate over time.

56. The relearning periods shown in the graph indicate what about each relearning episode?
    A. Relearning has no impact on the proportion of a list remembered over time.
    B. Relearning reduces the proportion of a list remembered over time.
    C. Relearning improves memory only following the first relearning episode.
    D. Relearning increases the proportion of a list remembered over time.

57. Which of the following statements is FALSE based on the data shown in the graph?
    A. The greatest difference in retention levels occurs between learning time one and time two.
    B. Relearning is positively correlated with retention of information, but information loss still occurs over time.
    C. Relearning must occur at least four times for optimal retention.
    D. Relearning impacts the rate of forgetting only after several relearning episodes.

58. Suppose that one summer you take a training course on the maintenance and service of a certain piece of complex machinery. At the end of the course, you take a qualifying test. If you retake the test every summer for the next few years, based on the graph, how would you expect to perform on the test?
    A. Test performance would decline sharply at first but decline less and less in later years.
    B. Test performance would decline gradually over the years and then stabilize.
    C. Test performance would decline sharply at first and continue to decline rapidly until eventually you were unable to remember anything at all.
    D. Test performance would decline only slightly from year to year until eventually you were unable to remember anything at all.

59. Suppose that you have been asked to remember a series of passwords for online sites. You are not permitted to write them down but can study a list of the passwords once a week for several months. Each week you are asked to enter the passwords with no errors prior to studying the list. Based on the graph, how would you expect to perform each week?
    A. There would be a sharp decline in your memory each week regardless of the number of times you studied the list.
    B. There would be a gradual decline in your memory each week until the number of remembered passwords stabilized.
    C. There would be a gradual decline in your memory each week regardless of the number of times you studied the list.
    D. There would be a significant decline in your memory in the first week, but the decline would become less abrupt each week after you studied the list.

STOP. This is the end of Section 3.

Critical Analysis and Reasoning Skills

53 Questions   **Time Limit: 90 Minutes**

Directions: This section includes eight reading passages. Each passage is followed by a group of questions. Read each passage, and then select the one best answer to each question based on what you have read.

Questions 1–6 are based on the following passage.

Passage I

According to Professor John MacKinnon, certain places are more likely than others to house new or rediscovered species. First, scientists should look in areas that are geologically stable. Areas with regular earthquakes or volcanic eruptions are less likely to contain species that go back thousands of years because, obviously, the frequent upheavals are not conducive to steady growth or a comfortable way of life. Second, scientists are most likely to find undiscovered or rediscovered species in remote, isolated areas. Cultivated areas are inhospitable to many animals. Often, cultivation eliminates the trees or shrubs that house and protect animal life. A stable climate is a third thing to look for. Stability of climate ensures that the animals that live in the region have had no reason to leave for warmer or wetter environments.

Although most of the recent discoveries and rediscoveries of animal species have taken place in tropical, humid regions, some have occurred in rarely explored mountain habitats. A fourth key thing scientists should look for, according to MacKinnon, is an area with a variety of unusual species that are specific to that area. Of course, this requirement refers back to requirement number two, isolation. An area that is very isolated or difficult to access will naturally have species that cannot be found anywhere else.

In 1994 American biologist Peter Zahler took his second trip to the isolated valleys of the Diamer region in northern Pakistan. He was searching for the woolly flying squirrel, a dog-sized squirrel last seen in 1924. As he describes it, he had narrowed down his search to two animals, using the criteria *mammal, not too small, relatively unknown*, and *in need of conservation intervention*. Because he did not wish to spend time in the steamy environment of the Congo basin, he eliminated the aquatic genet from his list and decided to concentrate on the woolly flying squirrel, which lived in the high Himalayas where there were fewer bugs and no tropical diseases. Working with a guide, Zahler moved from valley to valley. He quizzed the local residents about the squirrel. Many recalled hearing tales about the strange animal, but all insisted it was extinct.

Zahler continued to set traps, listen to squirrel legends, and ask questions. He dodged avalanches, skirted valleys patrolled by armed warlords, and crossed mountains on narrow goat paths. Policemen told him that the squirrels indeed existed in caves above the valley, and that they excreted a substance, *salajit*, that was used as an aphrodisiac. One day, two large, machine gun–toting men entered his camp. After some small talk, one asked whether he would be willing to pay for a live squirrel. The pair claimed to be *salajit* collectors. Zahler agreed to pay top dollar, never envisioning that 2 hours later, he would be presented with a woolly flying squirrel in a bag. Following that surprise, Zahler located evidence of live squirrels throughout the region. The squirrel certainly obeyed all of MacKinnon's regulations. Despite frequent avalanches, the Himalayas are a geologically stable area with a harsh but stable climate and a number of rare species. Not only were the squirrels' caves remote and isolated, it was often necessary to rappel down or climb up sheer cliffs to reach them.

Each rediscovery gives scientists a vital second chance to protect and preserve our rarest, most fragile species. With scientists and students from Pakistan, Zahler began work on a program to protect the squirrel's habitat. Only the advent of war in Afghanistan forced him to abandon the area, and he remains connected to scientists in Pakistan who are continuing the effort.

1. According to the passage, all of these are true EXCEPT:
   A. Woolly flying squirrels excrete an unusual substance.
   B. The Himalayas contain a variety of unique species.
   C. Animals in a drought may leave for a wetter habitat.
   D. The woolly flying squirrel vanished for 70 years.

2. The discussion of the aquatic genet shows primarily that:
   A. Some mammals are unlikely ever to be rediscovered.
   B. Large mammals are more easily tracked and rediscovered.
   C. Endangered mammals are found in many different biomes.
   D. Tropical diseases affect a variety of endangered species.

3. Which of MacKinnon's requirements does the home of the woolly flying squirrel meet?
   I. isolation
   II. geographic stability
   III. climatic stability
   A. I only
   B. II only
   C. I and III only
   D. I, II, and III

4. The author suggests that Zahler decided to search for the woolly flying squirrel because it:

   A. lived in an area that was easily accessible ✗

   B. was neither too small nor too tropical

   C. had been spotted recently by *salajit* collectors

   D. was a legendary creature of great renown

5. According to the passage, which of these locations would be likely to house a new species?

   I. the jungles of Borneo

   II. the mountains of western Iran

   III. the edges of the eastern Sahara

   A. I only

   B. II only

   C. I and II only

   D. II and III only

6. According to the author, rediscovery gives scientists a second chance to protect and preserve rare species. Which of the following information, if true, would most WEAKEN this argument?

   A. Ornithologists hoping for a second sighting of the long-lost ivory-billed woodpecker have triggered a stampede of cameras and news media to the fragile forests where it was recently spotted.

   B. The Audubon Society has set aside part of a forest on Oahu as a potential breeding ground for an endangered warbler once common on several of the Hawaiian islands.

   C. The northern hairy-nosed wombat lives only in one known area, a protected section of Epping Forest National Park in central Queensland, Australia.

   D. Rodent control programs on the Galapagos Islands have managed to stem a threat to endangered petrels, and now 90 percent of their nests result in a successful hatching out of eggs.

Questions 7–12 are based on the following passage.

Passage II

Beaten down, the world against them, exhausted—such was the self-assessment of the Beat Generation, as defined by Jack Kerouac in a 1948 conversation that became part of a 1952 *New York Times* article. At that time, the Beats were in their infancy. In the early '40s, Kerouac attended Columbia University on a football scholarship, but a leg injury ended his football career and forced him to drop out of school. His brief sojourn with the Merchant Marine and the Navy ended badly, and Kerouac limped back to New York to rejoin friends at Columbia, where he met student Allen Ginsberg and the older William S. Burroughs. Most of Kerouac's friends had come of age during World War II, just as Ernest Hemingway and his friends had done during World War I. Just as Hemingway's generation was "Lost," the new generation was "Beat." They found it impossible to find a place in the new, postwar economy. They lived in toxic, brutal poverty and moved constantly, and many of them struggled to find publishers for their oddly constructed, turbulent writings.

Kerouac would be the first of his friends to find a publisher, for his first novel, the rather pedestrian *The Town and the City* published in 1950. The following year, he traveled cross-country with his friend Neal Cassady, a trip that would inspire his most famous work, *On the Road.* Perhaps as much as any Beat work, this frenetic work illustrated the Beat dislike of conformity and desire for movement and new experiences.

Kerouac would continue to write prolifically in the 7 years it took to get *On the Road* published. Meanwhile, Burroughs published *Junkie*, an autobiographical tome on addiction, and Ginsberg published his seminal work, the stream-of-consciousness poem "Howl." "I saw the best minds of my generation destroyed by madness . . . " cried the poet, summing up again the powerlessness of the Beat Generation. Ginsberg used street vernacular and rhythms inspired by the jazz scene of the '50s.

The Beat scene was peripatetic, moving from New York to San Francisco (where "Howl" was published) and later to the left bank in Paris, where Hemingway's Lost scene had emigrated many years earlier. Ginsberg left San Francisco for Paris when his poem "Howl" became the subject of an obscenity trial for its use of colloquial speech and its openness about drugs and homosexuality. He traveled from Paris to Tangier, where Burroughs was living, and helped Burroughs assemble the manuscript of his most famous and infamous work, *Naked Lunch.* Burroughs's book would be published in Paris in 1959 and then in the United States in 1962; again, it would be the center of a long obscenity trial. Both "Howl" and *Naked Lunch* emerged from their trials unscathed; the obscenity charges were determined to be unfounded, and the trials loosened some of the definitions that had bound American literature. In addition, of course, the publicity put the Beats on the front pages of newspapers nationwide.

The Beats were of their time, and they transcended their time. The highway system that crisscrossed the United States in the 1950s gave them the power to move. Suburbia and the man in the gray flannel suit gave them something to despise. The cold war gave them angst and disillusionment. Jazz and the drug culture gave them a way out. Without the Beats to pave the way, sixties culture would have looked quite different, and the gay liberation movement of the 1970s might never have come to pass.

7. The author compares the Beat Generation to the Lost Generation in terms of their:
   A. poverty
   B. openness
   C. prolific output
   D. alienation

8. In the context of the passage, the word *culture* is used primarily to mean:
   A. nation
   B. sophistication
   C. way of life
   D. ethnicity

9. The discussion of Burroughs's obscenity trial best illustrates the author's point that:
    A. The Beat scene was peripatetic.
    B. The Beats affected definitions of literature.
    C. The Beats were inspired by jazz and angst.
    D. The Beats transcended their time.

10. Which of the following assertions does the author support with an example?
    I. Kerouac continued to write prior to the publication of *On the Road*.
    II. The drug culture affected the lives and writings of some Beats.
    III. Sixties culture was influenced by the work of the Beats.
    A. I only
    B. II only
    C. I and III only
    D. II and III only

11. Gregory Corso, another important figure in the Beat crowd, once wrote a poem in the shape of a mushroom cloud entitled "Bomb." If the author included this information in the passage, it would probably be used to:
    A. contrast with Ginsberg's description of "the best minds of my generation"
    B. represent an example of colloquial speech in Beat poetry and prose
    C. support the notion that the cold war colored the Beats' work with angst
    D. illustrate the Beats' dislike for conformity and the postwar economy

12. Suppose the Beat writers were omitted from a major anthology of American literature. This would challenge the author's assertion that:
    A. The Beats affected the gay liberation movement.
    B. The Beats' writing was turbulent and difficult.
    C. The Beats often struggled to find publishers.
    D. The Beats transcended their time.

Questions 13–18 are based on the following passage.

Passage III

Aluminum is the most abundant metallic element in the Earth's crust, but it is never found naturally as an element. Instead, it always appears naturally in its oxidized form as a hydroxide we call bauxite.

Bauxite occurs in three main forms. The forms vary in the number of molecules of water it takes for hydration and in the crystalline structure of the molecule. Gibbsite is a trihydrate form [$Al(OH)_3$]. Bohmite and diaspore are monohydrates [$AlO(OH)$]. Of the three, the main form that is mined is gibbsite. Bauxite may be hard or soft, and it comes in a variety of colors that range from white to red.

Bauxite is formed due to the weathering of alumina-bearing rocks. It often appears as an extensive blanket of ore and is usually mined using surface-mining techniques. By far the largest consumers of aluminum are the United States, Japan, and Germany, but except for a little in Texas and Arkansas, bauxite is nearly nonexistent there. The major producers of bauxite are Australia, which produces around 40 percent of the world's supply, and Guinea, in West Africa. The United States gets much of its supply from Brazil and Jamaica.

The extraction of aluminum from bauxite requires three stages. First, the ore is mined. Then it is refined to recover alumina. Finally, the alumina is smelted to produce aluminum.

The mining is done via the open-cut method. Bulldozers remove the topsoil, and excavators or other types of power machinery are used to remove the underlying layer of bauxite. The bauxite may be washed to remove clay and other detritus.

Refining is done via the Bayer refining process, named after its inventor, Karl Bayer. Ground bauxite is fed into a digester, where it is mixed with a caustic soda. The aluminum oxide reacts with the soda to form a solution of sodium aluminate and a precipitate of sodium aluminum silicate. The solution is separated from the silicate through washing and pumping, and the alumina is precipitated from the solution, where it appears as crystals of alumina hydrate. The crystals are washed again to remove any remaining solution. Then they are heated to remove water, leaving the gritty alumina.

Smelting is done via the Hall-Heroult smelting process. An electric current is passed through a molten solution of alumina and cryolite, which is in a cell lined at the bottom and top with carbon. This forces the oxygen to combine with the carbon at the top of the cell, making carbon dioxide, while the molten metallic aluminum collects at the bottom of the cell, where it is siphoned off, cleaned up, and cast into bars, sheets, or whatever form is needed.

As with all mining of metals, bauxite mining presents certain hazards. Along with the usual mining issues of degraded soil and polluted runoff, chief among them is the omnipresent bauxite dust, which clogs machinery and lungs, sometimes for miles around the mining site. Jamaica and Brazil have seen widespread protests recently against the major bauxite mining companies, which continue to insist that no link between bauxite dust and pervasive lung problems has been proved.

13. In the context of the passage, the word *refined* means:
    A. superior
    B. polished
    C. processed
    D. restricted

14. The discussion of protests shows primarily that:
    A. Bauxite mining takes place in the Third World.
    B. Workers are starting to fight back against the dangers of mining.
    C. Mining companies have misled people for decades.
    D. The government of Brazil works with the mining companies.

15. The passage suggests that the author would MOST likely believe that:
    A. Bauxite mining poses health problems.
    B. The United States should use less aluminum.
    C. Australian bauxite is the best quality.
    D. Karl Bayer was something of a genius.

16. All of these are produced by the Bayer process EXCEPT:
    A. sodium aluminum silicate
    B. sodium aluminate
    C. aluminum manganese
    D. alumina hydrate

17. According to the passage, the most commonly mined form of bauxite contains:
    A. carbon dioxide
    B. iron by-products
    C. caustic soda
    D. three molecules of water

18. The process by which aluminum is extracted from bauxite is most similar to:
    A. the building of steel bridges
    B. the making of copper tubing
    C. the manufacturing of glass
    D. the mixing of cement

Questions 19–25 are based on the following passage.

Passage IV

"I acknowledge Shakespeare to be the world's greatest dramatic poet, but regret that no parent could place the uncorrected book in the hands of his daughter, and therefore I have prepared the Family Shakespeare."

Thus did Thomas Bowdler, a self-appointed editor trained as a physician, explain his creation of a children's edition of Shakespeare that omitted some characters completely, toned down language he considered objectionable, and euphemized such shocking situations as Ophelia's suicide—an accident in Bowdler's version.

Bowdler was hardly the first to tone down the Bard. Poet laureate Nahum Tate rewrote *King Lear*, banishing the Fool entirely and giving the play a happy ending. His version was staged regularly from the 1680s through the 18th century.

Thomas Bowdler was, from all the evidence, a less likely editor. He was born in 1754 near Bath, England, to a wealthy family. He studied medicine but never really practiced, preferring to exercise philanthropy and to play chess, at which he was a master. In his retirement, he decided to try his hand at editorial work. Shakespeare's dramas were his first project. He added nothing to the texts, but by cutting and paraphrasing strove to remove anything that "could give just offense to the religious and virtuous mind."

The result was a 10-volume expurgated version that was criticized widely, although hardly universally. The famed British poet Algernon Swinburne remarked that "no man ever did better service to Shakespeare than the man who made it possible to put him into the hands of intelligent and imaginative children."

There is some indication that Bowdler's sister Harriet did the actual editing of Shakespeare's text. She was a poet and editor in her own right, and clearly more qualified than her brother to lay hands on the Bard of Avon. She may have published the expurgated edition anonymously before allowing her brother to take over the rights. If this is so, it is unsurprising that Harriet would not have wanted her name on the book. If the original Shakespeare were truly objectionable, then it would have been doubly so for a well-bred, unmarried Englishwoman of the day.

Bowdler went on to create children's versions of the Old Testament and of Edward Gibbons's *History of the Decline and Fall of the Roman Empire*, although neither achieved either the success or ridicule of his Shakespeare. Today, of course, we know Bowdler not for his good works, but instead for the eponym derived from his good name. To *bowdlerize* is to censor or amend a written work, often with a connotation of prudishness. The process for which Bowdler is known is one that continues to the present day, as texts deemed too difficult for today's high schoolers are "dumbed-down," library editions of *The Adventures of Huckleberry Finn* have the "n-word" blacked out, and middle-school productions of popular Broadway plays have all expletives deleted. We would be hard-pressed to say that we live in a prudish era, but some of the same impulses that drove Thomas and Harriet Bowdler still exist today.

19. The main argument of the final paragraph is that:
    A. Bowdler did a disservice to the readers of his works.
    B. Bowdler's edited texts have long since vanished into history.
    C. We continue to bowdlerize texts to the present day.
    D. Today we look at Bowdler as a negative influence on writing.

20. The passage implies that Bowdler's sister was a more likely editor than he because:
    A. She would have been truly offended by Shakespeare's plots.
    B. Unlike her brother, she was a published writer and editor.
    C. Bowdler was known for his misuse of the English language.
    D. Women of the time were more likely to read Shakespeare.

21. The passage suggests that Bowdler was influenced by:
    A. prudery
    B. erudition
    C. a poet laureate
    D. a dream

22. The mention of Nahum Tate shows primarily that:
    A. Few dared to change Shakespeare's works during his lifetime.
    B. Actors and directors often changed Shakespeare's words to suit their talents.
    C. Different versions of *King Lear* were used depending on the audience.
    D. The Bowdlers were not the first to alter Shakespeare's texts.

23. Based on the information in this passage, which of these would NOT be bowdlerization?
    I. translating a Japanese folktale into English
    II. eliminating references to witches from a fairy tale
    III. burning copies of *The Satanic Verses*
    A. I only
    B. II only
    C. I and III only
    D. II and III only

24. The author's claim that Bowdler's Shakespeare was not unanimously criticized is supported by:
    A. a quotation from Algernon Swinburne
    B. reference to later children's works by Bowdler
    C. the definition of the eponym formed from his name
    D. the example of Ophelia's revised "suicide"

25. Given the information in the passage, if a bowdlerized version of Shakespeare were available to parents today, which of the following outcomes would MOST likely occur?
    A. Some would ridicule it, and others would buy it.
    B. No one would take it or its author seriously.
    C. Most students would find it too difficult to read.
    D. It would be a dismal failure and be taken off the market.

Questions 26–33 are based on the following passage.

Passage V

The Nobel Peace Prize has often engendered controversy. The Red Cross, yes, but Henry Kissinger? Mother Teresa, perhaps, but Yasser Arafat? Surprisingly, a loud and ongoing controversy surrounds a choice that at first look seems most benign—that of the Guatemalan freedom fighter, Rigoberta Menchú Tum.

Rigoberta Menchú was born in 1959 to a poor Mayan family in Guatemala. At the time of her birth, General Ydígoras Fuentes had just seized power, following the assassination of Colonel Castillo Armas. The year she turned one, there was a failed coup by a military group, many of whom fled to the countryside and would return to lead the rebellion that would wax and wane for the next 36 years.

Guatemala was divided into factions for that entire period, as military governments controlled the nation and guerilla groups controlled the countryside. At the same time, right-wing vigilantes led a campaign of torture and assassination, eliminating students and peasants they deemed to be allied with the guerillas.

In the countryside where Rigoberta lived, the battles were largely over control of farmland. Rigoberta's father was taken into custody and tortured when the army believed he had assisted in the assassination of a plantation owner. Following a rout of the guerillas by the army, the guerillas regrouped and began to take their fight to the capital, beginning a long series of assassinations of government figures.

Rigoberta, her father, and some of her siblings joined the Committee of the Peasant Union (CUC). In rapid succession, Rigoberta lost her brother, father, and mother to the army's own assassination squads. Rigoberta, though only in her early 20s, became a key figure in the resistance, traveling from village to village to educate the Mayan peasants in overcoming oppression, and leading demonstrations in Guatemala City.

Soon Rigoberta was herself a target. She fled to Mexico and continued her life as an organizer, concentrating her focus on peasants' rights. She participated in the founding of the United Representation of the Guatemalan Opposition (RUOG). This period was the most violent of the entire Guatemalan civil war. Under the new president, General Efrain Ríos Montt, massacres of civilians became an everyday occurrence.

Rigoberta traveled to Paris, where she sat down and dictated her life story to anthropologist Elisabeth Burgos Debray. This story, titled *I, Rigoberta Menchú, an Indian Woman in Guatemala*, would galvanize world attention to the plight of Guatemala. Shortly thereafter, Ríos Montt was overthrown in a coup, and the slow work of democratizing Guatemala began. In 1992, Rigoberta would win the Nobel Peace Prize for her life and work.

The controversy is all about the book. It began when anthropologist David Stoll began independent research on the same era about which Rigoberta dictated and discovered discrepancies in her recall of events. Massacres she described were not remembered by the locals; one of her brothers died by shooting rather than by fire, dates were incorrect, and so on. Stoll's discoveries were enough to roil up conservative historians and columnists, who declared Rigoberta's book the grossest propaganda and her career, therefore, unworthy of the Nobel Prize. Not surprisingly, this brought forth charges of racism, sexism, and cultural ignorance from the other side.

The Nobel Committee maintained a stiff upper lip throughout the political back-and-forth and still insists that Rigoberta's prize had to do with her documented good works and not with her personal recorded history. Rigoberta's book is still widely taught, and her place in the history of Central American peasant revolutions seems assured.

26. Which choice(s) by the Nobel Committee does the author seem to indicate was undeserved?
    I. Rigoberta Menchú
    II. Henry Kissinger
    III. The Red Cross
    A. I only
    B. II only
    C. I and III only
    D. II and III only

27. In the context of the passage, the word *custody* means:
    A. fortification
    B. safekeeping
    C. incarceration
    D. supervision

28. Which of the following statements is/are NOT presented as evidence that Rigoberta may have falsified her autobiography?
    I. Massacres she described were not remembered by the locals.
    II. One of her brothers died by shooting rather than by fire.
    III. Rigoberta dictated her life story to anthropologist Debray.
    A. I only
    B. I and II only
    C. III only
    D. II and III only

29. According to the passage, why did Rigoberta leave Guatemala?
    A. She wanted to alert the world to the problems of the peasants.
    B. She was under fire from the army's assassination squads.
    C. She was invited to Paris to dictate her personal memoirs.
    D. She no longer cared to stay after her family was murdered.

30. The author's claim that Rigoberta's book is still widely taught could BEST be supported by the inclusion of:
    A. two students' comments on the ongoing controversy
    B. data on the sales for her book from publication until the present day
    C. a record of bookstores that continue to carry her autobiography
    D. a list of universities that include her book in their required reading lists

31. Which new information, if true, would BEST support conservatives' claims that Rigoberta was a fraud?
    A. the discovery that Rigoberta was really born in early 1960
    B. findings that show Rigoberta educated thousands of Mayan peasants
    C. the discovery that neither Rigoberta nor her parents were part of CUC
    D. findings that show Ríos Montt was overthrown by a peasant army

32. If David Stoll is to be believed, Rigoberta's autobiography seems to be an example of:
    A. "truthiness," the quality of preferring facts one wishes were true to those that are true
    B. "epic," a narrative unified by a legendary hero who reflects the aspirations of a nation or race
    C. "folktale," a story of cumulative authorship from the oral tradition
    D. "manifesto," a credo or position paper in which the leader of a political movement sets forth tenets and beliefs

33. The author of the passage would probably support:
    A. an inquiry that led to the removal of Rigoberta's Nobel Prize
    B. the removal of Rigoberta's autobiography from college curricula
    C. keeping Rigoberta's name in the history books as a freedom fighter
    D. granting the Nobel Prize exclusively to groups, not individuals

Questions 34–40 are based on the following passage.

Passage VI

If our knowledge of the world occurs through the weaving of narratives, as postmodernists would have us believe, then we must judge the truth of each narrative by comparing it with what we value and what we already accept as true. Any metanarrative, or overarching "big story," must be rejected because it attempts to explain away too many individual narratives.

The traditional metanarrative of American history, for example, might posit that the country was forged and tamed by white men who arrived by ship from a continent (Europe) that did not allow them the freedoms they desired. Viewing all of American history through that metanarrative, postmodernists would argue, does not allow us to consider the contributions of other groups to the country we live in today. So constructing a metanarrative can often be exclusionary.

Of course, constructing a series of smaller narratives is just as exclusionary because it frames experience in a limited way. It is easy to see this occurring if you look at any university course list today. How is it possible for American History 4111, "Imperialism and Amerindians, 1600–1840" to coexist alongside American History 4546, "American Military History and Policy"? Does English 340X, "Survey of Women's Literature," subsume or incorporate elements of English 342X, "American Indian Women Writers"? Perhaps we should pity the undergraduate student today. Lacking any overarching metanarrative to provide perspective, how can the poor student wade through the often contradictory mininarratives being thrown his or her way?

There is no question that the old way was wrongheaded and elitist. Survey courses that emphasized the white male perspective were removed from the curriculum in the 1970s, '80s, and '90s, and for good reason. But replacing them with a smorgasbord of mininarratives risks eliminating any sense of a big picture. Can students connect the dots to define a coherent reality, or must their reality be a series of frames with no links among them?

Revising the canon was about ridding our perspective of those racist, sexist, or classist notions that insisted on a single Truth with a capital T. Of course there is no overriding Truth that applies to everyone. For everyone who believes that Thomas Jefferson was a brilliant reformer, there is someone who thinks he was a two-faced slaveholder. Yet, where does it leave us if everyone we know is approaching history, science, literature, or what have you from a slightly different angle? It's bad enough when partisan politics divides us into red states and blue states. How much worse is it to imagine ourselves clad in thousands upon thousands of shades of purple?

The clearest sign that we are not ready to abandon our metanarratives comes in the current and ongoing clash between those who accept evolutionary theory and those who accept the Bible as the written word of God. The latter grant the Earth 6000 years of life, the former give it several million more, and never the twain shall meet. Each of these viewpoints is a metanarrative, a big story that governs people's understanding of the world. Like many metanarratives, each of these completely negates the other.

So on the one hand, metanarratives don't work well because they are too exclusionary. And on the other hand, mininarratives don't work well because they are too narrow. It will be fascinating to watch the canon evolve over the next few decades and to see whether this dichotomy can ever be resolved.

34. The main argument of the passage is that:
    A. Metanarratives provide the best way to view the world.
    B. Metanarratives are usually more restrictive than mininarratives.
    C. Mininarratives are racist, sexist, and classist.
    D. Neither metanarratives nor mininarratives offer a flawless perspective.

35. The passage suggests that the author would MOST likely believe that:
    A. Colleges should offer more courses in American history.
    B. Revising the canon in the late 20th century was a bad idea.
    C. Students today need a more global perspective than their coursework provides.
    D. Divisiveness in politics is preferable to conformity or unilateralism.

36. Which of the following assertions does the author support with an example?
    I. Constructing mininarratives frames experience in a limited way.
    II. We are not ready to abandon our metanarratives.
    III. Constructing a metanarrative may be exclusionary.
    A. I only
    B. III only
    C. I and II only
    D. I, II, and III

37. The ideas in this passage would be MOST useful to:
    A. authors of novels in the postmodern tradition
    B. committees responsible for establishing college curricula
    C. students of ancient Roman or Greek philosophy
    D. journalists, detectives, and other seekers of truth

38. The author states that metanarratives have been replaced on campuses by a "smorgasbord" of mininarratives. The word *smorgasbord* is used to indicate:
    A. freshness
    B. choice
    C. flavor
    D. foreignness

39. Based on the information in the passage, which of these might be considered a metanarrative?
    I. Marxism
    II. rationalism
    III. libertarianism
    A. I only
    B. II only
    C. II and III only
    D. I, II, and III

40. A comparison of a mininarrative to a metanarrative would be MOST similar to a comparison of:
    A. a cropped photograph to a wide-angle photograph
    B. a globe to a world map
    C. a ranch-style house to a palace
    D. a single domestic turkey to a flock of wild turkeys

Questions 41–46 are based on the following passage.

Passage VII

What began as an online personal diary of sorts about a decade ago has become a multimillion-dollar-a-year business that is reshaping the nature of the media, publishing, and marketing. It has the power to catapult unknowns into celebrities, affect political careers, and even influence language. They were known first as "web logs," which evolved into "weblogs" and finally "blogs." In 2004, Merriam-Webster declared *blog* its Word of the Year.

It is estimated that more than 50 million people are blogging, and every second two new blogs are created. Most bloggers use the tool for its original purpose: periodically posting their thoughts on subjects of their choosing for others to read and comment on. But what sounds on the surface to be merely a public display of ideas is in effect changing the nature of media. Print newspapers and magazines have a staff of writers, researchers, and editors who find what they deem to be appropriate (often defined as "nonoffense") material, shape it, and present it to an audience of passive consumers. When those passive consumers use simple websites to disseminate facts and ideas of their choosing, they evolve from passive consumers to active participants, effectively blurring the line between the media and its audience.

Many bloggers choose to focus on news stories that receive little attention from traditional media outlets. They research, report, and comment on information that the public might otherwise not have easy access to. Traditional media companies have stockholders to answer to, and sometimes edit content to eliminate or reduce possible controversial material. Blogs, in comparison, thrive on controversy. Indeed, that is where they most often make their mark. Talking Points Memo, which debuted in 2000, is a left-wing political site whose staff has grown to include eight employees, including five research interns. In December 2002, the blog focused on Senator Trent Lott's comments at a political function that many deemed bigoted, a story that was virtually ignored by print, radio, and television media sources. In less than two weeks, the public outcry grew, and Lott resigned from his post as Senate majority leader.

In addition to their influence, popular bloggers are able to turn their sleuthing and private rants into dollars. Marketers looking for new and more effective ways to reach consumers are increasingly spending money on online advertising. By 2005, it was estimated that $100 million dollars' worth of blogs ads were sold. One blogger in Kentucky uses his site, fark.com, to spread his brand of humor and is earning millions of dollars in ad revenue this year, thanks to the support of theme parks, shampoos, and nutrition bars. But this is predicted to be just the tip of the blogs profitability iceberg. Overall web advertising is expected to grow by 50 percent to $23.6 billion in 2010; much of that will make its way on to blogs.

41. The central thesis of the passage is that:
    A. Blogging was once a solitary activity, but popular blogs now have readerships in the millions.
    B. Advertisers are spending more money on blogs and less on traditional print and broadcasting outlets.
    C. Blogs are not only becoming profitable, but they are also influencing the media and the business of publishing and advertising.
    D. Some bloggers have become millionaires as their popular websites are replete with advertising.

42. The passage implies that bloggers who want to receive, or increase current levels of, advertising revenue must:
    A. strive to be more controversial
    B. build their readership
    C. include more content concerning celebrities and politicians
    D. appeal directly to marketers

43. Suppose evidence was presented to show that traditional media sources were becoming successful in their attempts to compete for blogs' advertising revenue. This new information would MOST challenge the implication that:
    A. Advertisers are spending money on blogs because they present a more effective way to reach consumers.
    B. People choose to read blogs because they don't have to appeal to stockholders.
    C. Popular blogs are better at disseminating information than traditional media sources.
    D. Active participants blur the line between the media and its audience.

44. Which of the following assertions does the author support with an example?
    I. Blogs influence language.
    II. Blogs are used by politicians to shape public discourse.
    III. Blogs disseminate information that traditional media sources neglect.
    A. I only
    B. II only
    C. I and III only
    D. I, II, and III

45. According to the passage, what is one way in which blogs are changing the nature of media?
    A. They are siphoning advertising revenue from traditional news sources.
    B. They are able to affect political careers.
    C. They allow consumers to become active participants in the dissemination of ideas.
    D. They are a public display of ideas.

46. The passage suggests that Talking Points Memo's coverage of a senator's inappropriate comments was:
    A. helpful in attracting advertisers, and therefore revenue-producing
    B. designed to increase readership
    C. an ineffective way to end the senator's career
    D. at odds with news coverage provided by traditional media sources

Questions 47–53 are based on the following passage.

Passage VIII

It is perhaps too easy to think of mathematical truths as objective entities existing in the universe, simply waiting to be "discovered" by brilliant minds such as Pythagoras, Newton, and Descartes. Indeed, such a mentality may be cemented in Western minds raised in the Platonic tradition of a world of ideals that exists outside of the material world we reside in.

But new research in the fields of cognitive science and developmental psychology may be challenging this long-held belief in mathematics as a truth outside of human experience, and recasting mathematics as a product of the brain, an entity that is not discovered by man but rather created by him.

Such a radical paradigm shift has predictably met with stiff resistance, but the evidence in favor of a created mathematics rather than a discovered mathematics is compelling. Study after study has shown that all people possess an innate arithmetic. Babies as young as three or four days old can differentiate between groups of two and three items. And by the age of four months or so, an infant can see that one plus one is two and two minus one is one. Researchers discovered this startling fact by means of a simple experiment, following what is known as the violation of expectation model in developmental psychology. An infant was presented with a scenario in which a researcher held a puppet before the baby's eyes. Then a screen was moved in front of the puppet and another researcher placed a second puppet behind it. The screen was removed and if there were two puppets now visible, the infant registered no surprise (as measured by both the direction of the child's gaze and the duration of her stare). But if the screen was removed and only one puppet appeared, the infant registered perplexity at the situation.

This experiment and others like it strongly suggest that all individuals are born with certain mathematical concepts hardwired into their brains. The ability to quickly and accurately count a small number of items, called *subitizing* by psychologists, is also found in animals. Researchers using experiments similar to the violation of expectation setup described previously have found an innate mathematical ability not just in primates, our closest evolutionary cousins, but in raccoons, rats, parrots, and pigeons. These findings are consistent with the belief that mathematical thinking is a function of the structures in the brain and not a product of the outside world.

Anomalous cases involving brain injuries and disorders also support the idea that mathematical thinking arises from the organization of the brain. There is a documented case of a subject with a PhD in chemistry who suffers from acalculia, the inability to perform basic arithmetic functions. Strangely, this patient is unable to perform simple calculations such as five plus three or eight minus two, but has no problem manipulating abstract algebraic operations. This curious fact has led psychologists to conclude that the part of the brain that handles abstract algebraic operations must be different from the part of the brain that works with more concrete arithmetic functions.

47. The author probably mentions the "Platonic tradition" in order to:
    A. explain why some people may be less accepting of certain conclusions
    B. demonstrate the philosophical and historical underpinnings of mathematical studies
    C. highlight another influential Western figure in mathematical thought
    D. argue that followers of non-Western philosophical traditions are more likely to agree with the author's thesis

48. The author supports the passage's main thesis with all of the following types of evidence EXCEPT:
    A. experiments
    B. case studies
    C. testimonials
    D. comparisons

49. The passage implies that:
    A. Structures for arithmetic calculations are hardwired into the brain, but those for algebraic manipulations are not.
    B. Most animals are able to perform simple arithmetic operations.
    C. Infants at the age of three or four days can already perform simple calculations.
    D. Mathematical concepts are arbitrary.

50. In the context of the passage, the word *curious* means:
    A. marvelous
    B. exotic
    C. odd
    D. novel

51. In the discussion of the violation of expectation experiment, the author assumes that:
   A. Certain observable behaviors accurately indicate inner mental states.
   B. The infants in the study did not know what happened to the puppets behind the screen.
   C. Researchers used the same types of puppets in all of the experiments.
   D. Animals and infants performed at similar levels of competency in the experiments.

52. The central thesis of the passage is that:
   A. Western philosophers were mistaken in their belief in mathematics as an objective truth.
   B. Research in cognitive science and developmental psychology indicates that some animals may have the same mathematical abilities as humans do.
   C. A longstanding attitude toward mathematics may need to be reexamined in light of new evidence.
   D. People create their own mathematical systems based on the structures in their brains.

53. Suppose a team of anthropologists discovered an isolated community of individuals who possessed absolutely no mathematical ability whatsoever. This discovery would have what effect on the author's argument?
   A. It would refute it.
   B. It would support it.
   C. It would neither support nor refute it.
   D. It would be necessary to determine the cause of the individuals' lack of mathematical ability in order to say what effect it would have on the argument.

STOP. This is the end of Section 4.

ANSWERS AND EXPLANATIONS

Section 1. Biological and Biochemical Foundations of Living Systems

Passage I

1. **The correct answer is B.** The passage explains that in acute cases of leukemia, immature leukocytes are involved. This implies that these immature cells are abnormal and may not proliferate into normal mature leukocytes. The passage also indicates that in chronic cases of leukemia, mature leukocytes are affected so that it is possible that some unaffected immature cells may proliferate into functional mature cells. If there are some functional leukocytes, the person would be likely to survive longer without treatment.

2. **The correct answer is A.** The blood-brain barrier is a change in the permeability of blood vessels leading to the brain. Depending on the chemical composition, some drugs can cross and some cannot. Of the choices listed, it seems that if the drugs cannot reach the brain, then they have not crossed the blood-brain barrier. While choice D might seem plausible if a drug was ingested, it would not make sense for a drug that was injected.

3. **The correct answer is C.** Of the items listed in the question, the thing they all have in common is that they are mutagens or involve some genetic change. These mutations to the DNA can lead to the production of altered proteins that can be associated with cancer. While some cancers are associated with changes in cellular growth factors, this would not be the case for all cancers. The translation of proteins is directly from the mRNA, which is derived from the DNA in transcription. There would have to be a change in the DNA for the translation of proteins to be affected.

4. **The correct answer is C.** This question is simply asking about the function of antibiotics. Since a person with leukemia has abnormal leukocytes, there can be problems with the functioning of the immune system such that it does not fight infection well. Antibiotics kill bacteria cells, not viruses, and could help prevent bacterial infections in the leukemia patient who has a compromised immune system.

5. **The correct answer is A.** Some of the choices listed here relate to processes that are not unique to the cell cycle, which regulates cell division. Since cancer involves abnormal cell division, there is a problem with cell-cycle regulation. For example, protein synthesis is not a cell-cycle specific process. Purine analogs can be incorporated during DNA and RNA synthesis, which is also not cell-cycle specific. Alkylating agents interfere with DNA functioning, which is also not specific to

the cell cycle. However, tubulin-binding agents interfere with microtubules, which are used to form spindle fibers during the mitotic phase of the cell cycle. If the spindle fibers are disrupted, chromosome alignment cannot happen properly and cell division will be halted.

6. **The correct answer is A.** Stem cells that originate in the bone marrow serve as the precursor to all blood cells. These include the erythrocytes, leukocytes, and platelets. If a person has leukemia and abnormal leukocytes, a stem cell transplant would allow for the differentiation of new and hopefully normal leukocytes. Stem cells do not have the ability to directly attack other cells, replace the function of abnormal cells, or act as immune system modulators.

Passage II

7. **The correct answer is C.** Solutions that are hypotonic contain less solute and more water than what they are being compared to. In this case, the excess water in the extracellular fluid makes it hypotonic to the cells. This causes water to move into the cells by osmosis. Isotonic solutions have equal solute concentrations both inside and outside the cell. Hypertonic solutions have more solute and less water relative to what they are being compared to. In this case, the intracellular fluid would be hypertonic.

8. **The correct answer is A.** Sodium has a variety of roles in the body. Of the choices listed, sodium is highly involved with the function of neurons. The sodium/potassium pumps maintain an unequal balance of ions across the membrane of neurons during resting potential. During action potential, sodium channels open in order to initiate an impulse. If the sodium ion concentration is out of balance, the neuron function could be compromised.

9. **The correct answer is A.** In this case, administering a solution that is hypertonic to the cells would help. A hypertonic extracellular solution would draw water out of the swollen cells to counteract the effects of water intoxication. An isotonic solution would not help. A solution low in solute concentration would be high in water relative to the cells making the solution hypotonic, which would cause more water to enter the cells. A saline solution would be high in solutes and hypertonic to the cells.

10. **The correct answer is B.** With an extreme increase in water consumption, the plasma and blood volume increases, increasing blood pressure. The kidneys try to deal with this by increasing their filtration rate and increasing urine production to try to eliminate some of the excess water and reduce blood volume and pressure. What should not happen in this situation is to increase the retention of water in the body. Antidiuretic hormone (ADH) normally increases water reabsorption in the nephron. You would expect the secretion of ADH to drop in this circumstance so that more water can be excreted by the kidneys.

11. **The correct answer is B.** In the proximal convoluted tubule, the primary events are the reabsorption of nutrients and water. There are two regions in the nephron

where large amounts of sodium and water are reabsorbed. In the loop of Henle, the countercurrent multiplier system is used, which leads to the reabsorption of salts (sodium and chloride) and water. In the distal convoluted tubule, the hormone aldosterone influences the reabsorption of salts and water followed by osmosis.

12. **The correct answer is D.** This question relies on an understanding of the functions of brain structures. The cerebrum is involved in sensory processing, motor coordination, and association. The spinal cord relays messages to and from the brain and can process some reflex actions. The cerebellum deals with sensory-motor coordination, balance, and complex muscle movement patterns. The medulla oblongata is located in the brain stem; it has reflex centers for vital functions such as ventilation. Damage to the medulla oblongata could potentially be fatal.

13. **The correct answer is A.** The passage explains that Sertoli cells influence spermatogenesis. Therefore, the more Sertoli cells, theoretically, the more sperm should be produced. The two groups of men in this study varied in their sperm count. We are told that group 1 subjects had a normal sperm count while group 2 participants were seeking infertility treatments due to a low sperm count. Based on this information, the men with the higher sperm count should have a higher number of Sertoli cells. This would be group 1.

14. **The correct answer is B.** There are many relationships that could be deduced from these data. Keep in mind that the question says to consider the data from both groups, so we are looking for trends that are similar in groups 1 and 2. Choice A suggests a positive feedback relationship between FSH and LH. This would mean that as one of these hormones increases, so does the other. While this might be possible based on the group 1 data, it is not seen in the group 2 data. Choice C suggests a positive feedback relationship between testosterone and FSH. While this might be plausible for group 2 subjects, it is not for group 1 subjects. This leaves choice B. There is in fact a negative feedback relationship between inhibin-B and FSH. In groups 1 and 2, when inhibin-B was high, FSH was low. This suggests negative feedback. Since there is a relationship between some of these hormones, choice D can be eliminated.

15. **The correct answer is C.** The passage explains that group 1 men have normal sperm counts while group 2 men have low sperm counts. In looking at the data, the testosterone levels between groups 1 and 2 are not significantly different, which indicates that this hormone is not a good indicator of sperm count. The LH data for both groups tend to be fairly low and not drastically different between the groups. For FSH, the level is higher in the group 2 men who have a lower sperm count. Inhibin-B is the only feasible option as it is high in the men with normal sperm counts and low in the men with low sperm counts.

16. **The correct answer is A.** The blood-testis barrier is described in the passage as a barricade to establish immune privilege for the testes. To answer this question,

you need to think about how the sperm cells in the testes would compare to other cells in the body. Sperm cells are haploid, and all are genetically different from each other and from other cells in the body. Because they are genetically different, they should express unique surface antigens. If the cells of the immune system were to contact the sperm, they would be perceived as foreign and could be subject to immune system attack, which would destroy the sperm. For this reason, the blood-testis barrier is required to keep the sperm away from the immune cells. The remaining choices do not make good sense. Sperm cells will eventually leave the reproductive system during ejaculation. It also would not make sense to indicate that the blood flow to the testes needs to be cut off. This would prevent oxygen and nutrient flow to the area. Preventing the sperm from moving to the epididymis before they are ready does not provide an explanation for why the sperm cells need to be kept separate from the cells of the immune system.

17. **The correct answer is B.** This question relies on your knowledge of the female reproductive cycle. In women, as FSH levels climb, follicles are stimulated to grow. These follicles produce estrogen, which exerts positive feedback on LH, whose levels begin to climb. When LH levels peak on the 14th day of the cycle, the follicle ruptures, releasing the egg from the ovary and leaving the corpus luteum behind in the ovary. After ovulation, the corpus luteum secretes both estrogen and progesterone to inhibit GnRH. When GnRH is inhibited, FSH and LH will also be inhibited. Choice B correctly indicates that the LH surge causes ovulation.

18. **The correct answer is A.** This question relies on your knowledge of cell division. Mitosis is the process by which differentiated cells produce identical daughter cells.

Passage IV

19. **The correct answer is C.** Death of osteoblasts due to *S. aureus* infection is the result of induction of apoptosis. Apoptosis is triggered by capsase-8, so increasing the activity of capsase-8 would increase the rate of apoptosis and osteoblast death. Further, capsase-8 is activated by TRAIL made by *S. aureus,* so increasing the TRAIL activity would also increase osteoblast death rates. A drug that is antagonistic to TRAIL would decrease capsase-8 activity and decrease the rate of apoptosis in osteoblasts.

20. **The correct answer is D.** The leukocytes that engulf microbes such as bacteria are macrophages. This process is termed **phagocytosis.** Basophils secrete histamine, which is involved in the initiation of the inflammatory response. Lymphocytes are involved in specific immune system defenses. Eosinophils are involved in the defense response to antigens from unique sources such as parasites.

21. **The correct answer is C.** Complement proteins circulate in the blood in an inactive form. When bacteria enter the blood, the complement proteins are activated, which causes a cascade of reactions that ultimately cause lysis and death of the bacteria. Antibody production or cytotoxic T-cell activation could certainly

be stimulated by bacteria in the blood, but the question stipulated that this must be a nonspecific defense and these defenses are specific. Interleukins are cytokines secreted by immune cells, and they would not directly be able to defend against bacteria in the bloodstream.

22. **The correct answer is B.** Bacteria spontaneously mutate in order to produce diversity in the population. Some bacteria have spontaneous mutations, usually on plasmids, that allow them to survive in the presence of certain antibiotics. If the bacterial population is repeatedly exposed to that antibiotic due to overuse, it exerts selective pressure where only the resistant bacteria survive. These resistant bacteria multiply, and in the next generation a higher frequency of resistance is observed. Antibiotic resistance has nothing to do with people becoming resistant to antibiotics—it is all about the bacterial mutations.

23. **The correct answer is C.** This question relies on your knowledge of bacterial cell structures and functions. The nucleoid is the region of the cell where the one circular loop of chromosomal DNA is located. The ribosomes are responsible for protein synthesis. Bacteria can convert themselves to spores when environmental conditions are poor, allowing them to survive for extended periods of time in harsh conditions. The capsule is a sticky layer surrounding the cell that helps in the attachment of the cell to a surface. It is likely that the adhesins are located here.

24. **The correct answer is A.** Knowledge of the endocrine structures and hormones is needed to answer this question. The hormone calcitonin stimulates the storage of calcium in bone matrix. Its target is the osteoblasts that build new bone matrix. The calcitonin hormone is made by the thyroid gland. Parathyroid hormone is antagonistic to calcitonin and stimulates osteoclasts. Osteotonin is not a real hormone.

25. **The correct answer is D.** Based on the data given, drug Y is the only treatment to show a mean decrease in pulmonary artery pressure, which is the goal of this experiment. While some individual patients in the drug X and placebo groups did show a decrease in pulmonary artery pressure, the overall results for these groups included an increase in mean pulmonary artery pressure.

Passage V

26. **The correct answer is B.** The results from the drug X group indicate that the treatment caused an increase in mean pulmonary artery pressure. This helps us to eliminate choice A, which suggests that drug X is binding to ETA. If this were the case, the drug would be bound to ETA so that endothelin could only bind to ETB. When endothelin binds to ETB, vasodilation occurs, implying a decrease in pressure. This was not seen in the drug X group. Choice B suggests that drug X is selectively binding to the ETB receptor. This would mean that endothelin could only bind to ETA, which does in fact cause an increase in pressure. This would be the correct choice.

27. **The correct answer is C.** To answer this question, you must be familiar with the anatomy of the heart. The right side of the heart is the pulmonary circuit while the left side is the systemic circuit. Deoxygenated blood enters the right atrium of the heart via the superior and inferior vena cava. Blood from the right atrium passes through the tricuspid valve to the right ventricle and then leaves the heart through the pulmonary semilunar valve. Blood is carried via the pulmonary arteries to the lungs where gas exchange occurs. After gas exchange occurs, oxygenated blood returns to the heart via pulmonary veins to enter the left atrium. From there blood passes through the bicuspid valve into the left ventricle. Blood leaves the left side of the heart by passing through the aortic valve into the aorta. If there was a pressure increase in the pulmonary arteries, the right ventricle of the heart would be most likely affected as it is the last chamber that blood is located in before it moves toward the lungs in the pulmonary arteries.

28. **The correct answer is B.** Overexpression of the ETB receptor means that endothelin will have more ETB receptors to bind to. The passage indicates that when endothelin binds to the ETB receptor, vasodilation occurs, which decreases blood pressure. This would suggest that the patient's blood pressure would decrease, the explanation provided by choice B.

29. **The correct answer is A.** This question expects you to be able to consider how the kidneys are involved in regulating blood volume and blood pressure. Water that is reabsorbed in the nephrons returns to the bloodstream to increase plasma volume, which in turn increases blood pressure as the volume of blood increases. When the nephrons absorb more water to increase blood volume, the urine volume decreases. The two hormones aldosterone and antidiuretic hormone help increase the amount of water reabsorbed by nephrons, which in turn decreases urine volume. In order to reduce blood pressure, the kidneys can decrease the amount of water reabsorbed by the nephrons. The less water reabsorbed means there will be less blood volume and less blood pressure. This would ultimately increase urine volume. The question asks how the kidneys might try to reduce hypertension. This would mean that we want less water reabsorbed into the blood, which would decrease blood volume and blood pressure. To do this, urine volume would have to increase.

30. **The correct answer is B.** The question suggests that ETA can be activated by certain types of endothelin, which causes ETA to synergize with growth factors to increase cell proliferation rates. Growth factors are one of many mechanisms used to regulate the cell cycle. Of the choices listed, A, C, and D can be eliminated as they have nothing to do with growth factors and cell proliferation. The only reasonable answer is choice B since one of the many characteristics of cancer is increased cell proliferation.

31. **The correct answer is C.** The data report estrogen concentration. From reviewing the data, it can be seen that the mutant strain generally has a higher estrogen concentration than the wild-type strain.

32. **The correct answer is D.** Rate-limiting steps generally require the highest activation energies and are the slowest steps in a metabolic pathway.

33. **The correct answer is C.** Estrogen levels typically peak prior to ovulation, triggering the LH surge that is responsible for ovulation. For this reason, we would see the highest levels of estrogen around the time of ovulation, which should lead to a decrease in total and LDL cholesterol levels at that time.

34. **The correct answer is A.** One primary role of cholesterol is to stabilize the plasma membrane and to regulate fluidity of the membrane.

35. **The correct answer is C.** Because the mutant mice have a higher estrogen level due to the mutation in the rate-limiting step, it is likely that their cholesterol levels will be lower. Since cholesterol is converted to estrogen, if that process is occurring more rapidly than normal, the cholesterol levels may be lower than normal since the cholesterol is being converted to estrogen.

36. **The correct answer is D.** In the mutant mice, cholesterol is converted to estrogen at a faster rate. We would expect sexually mature mice to have a reduced cholesterol level due to estrogen production as compared to a mouse that is not close to sexual maturity.

37. **The correct answer is B.** The passage explains that estrogen seems to provide some sort of protective role against HIV infection. There is no mention of the role of testosterone with this hypothesis, so we should assume that it is not important to this theory. Therefore, choices A and D can be eliminated. Choice C introduces the idea of a female who has had her ovaries removed. Since the ovaries produce estrogen, assume that this female's estrogen levels would be decreased. Based on the information in the passage, this female should have less protection against HIV infection due to the decreased estrogen levels. Choice B introduces a female who oversecretes estrogen. Since the passage tells us that estrogen provides some protection against HIV infection, this female should be the most likely candidate (of the choices listed) to be protected against HIV infection.

38. **The correct answer is A.** This question requires you to know some of the details of the female reproductive cycle including what hormones are involved following ovulation. Prior to ovulation, both follicle-stimulating hormone (FSH) and luteinizing hormone (LH) are secreted from the anterior pituitary and are involved in follicular growth and maturation. The secretion of both FSH and LH is stimulated by gonadotropin-releasing hormone (GnRH) from the hypothalamus. As the follicles grow and mature, they produce estrogen. During the second week of the cycle, increasing estrogen levels cause a spike in LH levels, which causes ovulation. Recall that following ovulation, the remnant of the follicle that stays in the

ovary is called the corpus luteum. The corpus luteum secretes both estrogen and progesterone, which inhibit the further release of FSH and LH. The question is asking about a unique hormone that causes increased risk of HIV following ovulation. Choices B and D can be eliminated because FSH and LH are hormones most active prior to ovulation. Choice C is not appropriate since estrogen is secreted prior to and following ovulation. The only hormone that is unique to postovulation is progesterone, which makes choice A correct.

39. **The correct answer is A.** Since CCR5 is a coreceptor for HIV, up-regulation of the CCR5 allele should provide more receptors for HIV, making it more likely for more cells to become infected as is indicated by choice A. The remaining choices are not reasonable explanations. Since increased expression of CCR5 should make it easier for cells to become infected, choice B would not be plausible. Choice C does not provide an adequate explanation, particularly since the passage indicates that while in the earlier phases of infection, women carry higher lower loads than men. The passage also indicates that the delta-32 allele of CCR5 provides protection against HIV infection, not the normal CCR5 allele, which eliminates choice D.

40. **The correct answer is B.** To answer this question, you need to rely on your knowledge of genetics. The passage states that the delta-32 CCR5 mutation is protective against HIV infection. The question indicated that there are two different phenotypes noted within the delta-32 CCR5 mutation—one that offers near 100 percent protection against HIV infection and one that offers only partial protection. The best explanation for why two phenotypes (complete protection and partial protection) are observed would be that the delta-32 allele exhibits incomplete dominance. An individual that is homozygous for the allele (meaning he or she inherited two copies of the delta-32 allele) would have full protection, while an individual who is heterozygous (meaning he or she has one normal copy of the allele and one copy of the delta-32 allele) would have an intermediate phenotype (being partial protection). This is indicated by choice B. Since the question indicates that the differences in phenotype (protection) are related to the delta-32 mutation, choices A and D can be eliminated as they suppose that something other than the allele is providing protection. Choice C suggests that epistasis is involved in masking the delta-32 allele. While this might sound remotely plausible, choice B is a much more likely explanation.

41. **The correct answer is C.** You need to know what retroviruses are and have a basic understanding of how they operate to answer this question. Retroviruses have the unique ability to transcribe their RNA to DNA (recall that the central dogma indicates DNA to RNA to protein) so that the viral genetic material can integrate into host cell chromosomes to initiate the latent phase of the life cycle. In order to transcribe the RNA to DNA, the enzyme reverse transcriptase is needed, which is indicated by choice C. The other choices relate to enzymes that are not specific

to retroviruses. DNA polymerase is used by cells to copy DNA during the process of semiconservative replication. RNA polymerase is used by cells to perform the conversion of DNA to RNA (transcription). Helicase is the enzyme in cells that is used to unwind the DNA double helix.

42. **The correct answer is D.** The question explains that AZT and ddI interfere with replication and transcription. During a viral infection, the ideal situation would be to interfere with viral processes while leaving host cell processes unaffected. Choice A suggests that host cell DNA replication should be prevented in order to keep the host cell from functioning and mentions nothing about how this would affect the virus. Choice B is similar in that it does not mention how the virus would be affected. Choice C is not appropriate because it discusses preventing infection. If the patient is already confirmed as infected, then this choice wouldn't make sense. If a person is infected with HIV, then the viral genetic material has already entered the host cells. If replication of the viral genome can be prevented as suggested by choice D, then the progression of the infection can be slowed.

Passage VIII

43. **The correct answer is B.** From the graph provided, it seems that culturable bacteria decreased significantly (almost to 0) during the course of antibiotic therapy, which indicates that the antibiotic treatment was successful at eliminating culturable bacteria. However, the number of nonculturable but metabolically active cells stayed approximately equal during the course of the antibiotic therapy, which suggests that those cells did not respond to the treatment. This eliminates choice A as a possible answer since not all *E. coli* were eliminated by antibiotic treatment. The culturable bacteria causing the infection were eliminated by antibiotic treatment, which removes choice C as a possible answer. Choice D suggests that the treatment increased the number of *E. coli*, which is in direct contrast to what is shown on the graph. The best conclusion is that while the culturable bacteria have been eliminated, the nonculturable bacteria have made the patient at risk for developing another UTI should the nonculturable bacteria resuscitate to culturable form. This is indicated by choice B.

44. **The correct answer is D.** To support the VBNC hypothesis, it is necessary to provide evidence that the cells are metabolically active. The presence of DNA, proteins, or an intact cell membrane within the cell does not necessarily provide sufficient evidence to indicate that the cells are metabolically active because these things could be found in dying or dead cells. This eliminates choices A, B, and C. However, if one could show evidence of transcription occurring within the cells, this would provide good support for the fact that they are metabolically active.

45. **The correct answer is B.** In order to answer this question, you need to be familiar with the anatomy of the male and female reproductive and urinary systems. The passage explains that the *E. coli* bacteria that are normal residents of the digestive tract can cause UTIs when they enter the urinary tract. This means that we are

looking for a difference between men and women that would allow the bacteria to move from the intestinal tract to the urinary tract. There would be no reasonable support to suggest that women have a poorer immune response than men or that the bacteria infecting women are more likely to be resistant to antibiotics. This eliminates choices C and D. The number of *E. coli* in the intestinal tract is insignificant because the only concern is whether they enter the urinary tract to cause infection, which eliminates choice A. In the anatomy of the female system, the urethra is much closer to the anus, which makes for a short traveling distance for the bacteria that are able to get to the urethra. In males, the urethra is longer and farther away from the anus, making it harder for the bacteria to get to the urethra. The anatomical difference suggested by choice B is the only reasonable explanation for why women are more likely to contract UTIs.

46. **The correct answer is D.** Based on the data provided in the graph, the best assumption is that the trends seen in the graph would continue over time. It appears that the antibiotic therapy eliminated the culturable bacteria, so it would be safe to assume that the numbers of culturable bacteria would remain very low. This would eliminate choice A, which says that culturable cell count would increase. Since the cell counts for metabolically active cells did not decrease during the initial antibiotic treatment, there is no reason to assume that they would eventually decrease over a longer period, thus eliminating choices B and C. Based on the fact that the number of nonculturable bacteria did not decrease over the time period shown, we can assume that this is unlikely to change over a longer time course. Assuming that the trends seen in the graph continue, choice D is the most appropriate prediction.

47. **The correct answer is B.** This question relies on an understanding of antibiotic resistance. The overuse of antibiotics puts pressure on bacteria that selects for the bacteria that have mutated to become resistant to antibiotics. The overuse of antibiotics eliminates the susceptible bacteria, which leaves only the resistant bacteria to multiple to large numbers. Choice A suggests that people become immune to antibiotics, which is false. Since antibiotics are designed to target bacteria, bacteria are the only things that can become resistant to antibiotics. Since antibiotics normally kill bacteria, choice D would not make sense since it suggests that the use of antibiotics would increase the populations of resident bacteria. Choice C just isn't logical. Since many antibiotics are used on a routine basis, we know that they don't typically cause massive organ damage.

48. **The correct answer is B.** If the VBNC cells were able to resuscitate to fully metabolically active cells, this would indicate that they were not in the process of dying.

No passage   49. **The correct answer is A.** This question relies on a knowledge of dominant and recessive patterns of inheritance. Dominant alleles are expressed, even in the heterozygous individual. In this case, our example is a dominant allele that causes a fatal condition. Since every individual carrying a single allele of this type would likely not survive, we would expect the frequency of the allele to decrease over time. In contrast, disorders that follow recessive patterns of inheritance require two copies of the allele for expression. Those who are heterozygous do not express the disorder and thus would survive.

50. **The correct answer is B.** Antibodies are proteins that are secreted from the cell. Proteins would be produced and labeled by the rough endoplasmic reticulum. From there, they would be sorted by the Golgi complex and finally directed to the cell membrane for secretion.

51. **The correct answer is B.** This question relies on a knowledge of the basic chemical composition of the biologically important molecules. Carbohydrates and lipids are composed of C, O, and H. However, DNA is a nucleic acid and contains phosphate groups.

52. **The correct answer is A.** This question is asking how to move a potassium ion (which is small) from an area that has a low concentration to an area with a relatively higher concentration. In this case we are moving against the concentration gradient. The transport type that could do this is active transport, using energy to move the ions against their concentration gradient.

53. **The correct answer is C.** During the electron transport chain, oxygen serves as the terminal electron acceptor during aerobic respiration. In addition to serving as an electron acceptor, the oxygen also gathers protons from the electron transport chain, producing water in the process.

54. **The correct answer is C.** This question relies on your knowledge of semiconservative DNA replication where a single double helix is separated in order for both strands of the double helix to serve as templates for the production of new strands.

55. **The correct answer is A.** Of the choices presented, the only accurate choice is A. DNA nucleotides utilize the sugar deoxyribose while RNA nucleotides utilize the sugar ribose. Of the remaining choices, B is incorrect because we know that DNA uses T nucleotides while RNA uses U nucleotides. Choice C is incorrect because RNA is produced in transcription and a protein is produced in translation. Finally, choice D is incorrect because DNA is double-stranded and RNA is single-stranded.

56. **The correct answer is C.** In order to answer this question you need to recall the human diploid number of 46. In mitosis, a diploid parent cell produces two diploid daughter cells.

57. **The correct answer is C.** Steroid hormones exert their effects by entering into cells and binding with a receptor in the cytoplasm. The hormone-receptor complex then enters the nucleus where it acts to alter gene expression in the cell. Since the question is asking about nonsteroid, or peptide, hormones, choices A and B can be eliminated. Choice D can also be eliminated as this is not a plausible explanation. Nonsteroid hormones act as first messengers, binding to their receptors on the

cell membrane. The hormone itself does not enter the cell. The binding of the first messenger to the receptor causes a series of reactions in the cell that ultimately activate second messengers, such as cAMP.

58. **The correct answer is** A. RNA polymerase binds to the promoter site on the DNA template, at which time it is free to begin transcription. The regulator gene is a type of control gene that produces a small protein called a repressor. The operon is a group of linked genes composed of the operator and its adjacent structural genes.

59. **The correct answer is** C. During anaerobic respiration, glycolysis and fermentation occur. The process of fermentation does not produce ATP. The only ATP made during anaerobic respiration is from glycolysis. The net gain of ATP in glycolysis per molecule of ATP is 2. If the cell has access to 6 molecules of glucose and each molecule will produce 2 ATP, then a total of 12 ATP will be produced.

Section 2. Chemical and Physical Foundations of Biological Systems

1. **The correct answer is B.** As described in the passage, treatment of olefins with acid results in a carbocationic intermediate, which is prone to shifts and rearrangements. In this case, a hydride shift is very facile, the driving force being the conversion of a secondary cation into a tertiary variety. Subsequent capture of the electrophilic center with water, followed by proton transfer, leads to Product B.

2. **The correct answer is A.** As described in the passage, the use of mercuric ion prevents the formation of a formal carbocation, and therefore suppresses rearrangements. The intermediate mercurinium ion is captured by water at either secondary position to give an organomercury compound, which is demercurated with sodium borohydride to give Product A.

3. **The correct answer is B.** Product B is the only product with symmetry (specifically, an internal mirror plane); therefore, there are two sets of carbon atoms related by symmetry, which give rise to only one signal for each set. The other three products lack this symmetry element and are expected to exhibit peaks for all 8 carbons in the skeleton.

4. **The correct answer is A.** There are two chiral centers and the molecule is chiral. Both the *cis*- and *trans*-isomers have two chiral centers (the tertiary centers are connected to four different groups); however, the *cis*-isomer possesses a mirror plane that destroys the chirality on a molecular level. In other words, the *cis*-isomer is a *meso* compound. The *trans*-isomer lacks this symmetry element and thus is classified as a chiral molecule.

5. **The correct answer is A.** The demercuration step involves the attack of hydride on the carbon bearing the mercury, resulting in a net $2e^-$ reduction from Hg^{2+} to Hg^0, as shown:

6. **The correct answer is C.** As noted in the text of the problem, the flying bird is subject to four forces: weight, drag, lift, and thrust. Since the bird has mass, it is subject to the force due to gravity or weight, which acts straight downward. Thus, choice B can be eliminated. Drag is the air resistance force encountered in flight, a force that acts opposite to the direction of flight motion. Since the bird in the diagram is moving to the left, drag is a force represented by an arrow directed to the left. This is provided by choice C, the correct choice. Lift is an upward-directed force, and thrust is the pushing force acting to propel the bird in the direction of its motion—to the left.

7. **The correct answer is C.** The blood's volumetric flow rate, Q, is related to flow velocity, v, by the following relation:

$$Q = vA$$

where A is the cross-sectional area of the blood vessel. The volumetric flow rate must first be converted to units of $\dfrac{cm^3}{s}$:

$$Q = 5\,\frac{L}{min} \times \frac{1000\,cm^3}{1\,L} \times \frac{1\,min}{60\,s} = 83.3\,\frac{cm^3}{s}$$

The cross-sectional area of the vessel, A, is:

$$A = \pi r^2 = (3.14)(1.2\,cm)^2 = 4.52\,cm^2$$

Thus, the blood flow velocity is:

$$v = \frac{83.3\,\dfrac{cm^3}{s}}{4.52\,cm^2} = 18.4\,\frac{cm}{s}$$

8. **The correct answer is A.** The current, I, is related to the amount of charge, Δq, that flows during a time interval, Δt, by:

$$I = \frac{\Delta q}{\Delta t} \Rightarrow \Delta q = I \cdot \Delta t = (15\,A)(0.007\,s) = 0.105\,C$$

9. **The correct answer is C.** Because the steps of the reaction and the listed heats of reaction are exactly aligned to how the reaction takes place, there is no need to switch any reactions or reverse any signs for the heats of reaction. This allows you to simply add up the heats of reaction: $+92 + 121 + 496 - 349 - 771 = -411\,kJ$.

10. **The correct answer is B.** The chloride ion has 18 electrons now that it has gained an electron. The new configuration will show a stable octet in the 3s and 3p orbitals combined: $1s^22s^22p^63s^23p^6$.

11. **The correct answer is B.** The lattice energy increases with increasing charge. Clearly the negative two charge of sulfur is greater. Also, sulfur is about the same size as chlorine, meaning that for the (almost) same size ions, the sulfur has double the negative charge.

12. **The correct answer is A.** The lattice energy is always a positive value, eliminating choices B and D. The lattice energy is also the formation of the solid lattice structure from the gaseous ions, the fifth elementary step. Finally, looking at the chart you see that LiCl and KCl have their values listed. Using periodic trends and relationships, the lattice energy for NaCl should fall in between those of LiCl and KCl.

13. **The correct answer is C.** The stable sodium element has 11 protons in the nucleus and 11 orbiting electrons. The sodium ion lacks 1 electron needed for stability, giving it an overall positive charge of +1. The correct Lewis structure for the sodium ion is Na^+.

14. **The correct answer is A.** When heat energy is absorbed, the electrons enter a higher energy state. Light is emitted when the electrons fall back to the ground state.

15. **The correct answer is C.** This question can be solved using the lens equation:

Passage III

$$\frac{1}{\text{object distance}} + \frac{1}{\text{image distance}} = \frac{1}{\text{focal length}}$$

The reader can substitute the values for object distance and focal length from each option into the above equation and solve for the image distance which, for Lens Scenario 3, yields:

$$\frac{1}{\text{image distance}} = \frac{1}{\text{focal length}} - \frac{1}{\text{object distance}} = \frac{1}{f} - \frac{1}{f} = 0$$

which implies an undefined image. The solution could also be determined by drawing a ray diagram.

16. **The correct answer is D.** This problem can be solved using the lens equation:

$$\frac{1}{\text{object distance}} + \frac{1}{\text{image distance}} = \frac{1}{\text{focal length}}$$

The reader can substitute the values for object distance and focal length from each option into the above equation and Lens Scenario 4 yields:

$$\frac{1}{\text{image distance}} = \frac{1}{\text{focal length}} - \frac{1}{\text{object distance}}$$

$$= \frac{1}{f} - \frac{1}{f/2} = \frac{1}{f} - \frac{2}{f} = -\frac{1}{f}$$

In other words, image distance = – focal length. A negative image distance implies a virtual image, which is always upright. The solution could also be determined by drawing a ray diagram.

17. **The correct answer is C.** This question can be solved using the lens equation:

$$\frac{1}{\text{object distance}} + \frac{1}{\text{image distance}} = \frac{1}{\text{focal length}}$$

Substituting the values for object distance and focal length from Lens Scenario 2:

$$\frac{1}{\text{image distance}} = \frac{1}{\text{focal length}} - \frac{1}{\text{object distance}}$$

$$= \frac{1}{f} - \frac{1}{2f} = \frac{2}{2f} - \frac{1}{2f} = \frac{1}{2f}$$

In other words, image distance = 2f, given by choice C.

18. **The correct answer is A.** The image magnification, m, can be determined from the equation:

$$m = -\frac{\text{image distance}}{\text{object distance}}$$

One first needs to determine the image distance for Lens Scenario 1 by using the lens equation:

$$\frac{1}{\text{object distance}} + \frac{1}{\text{image distance}} = \frac{1}{\text{focal length}}$$

Substituting the values for object distance and focal length from Lens Scenario 1:

$$\frac{1}{\text{image distance}} = \frac{1}{\text{focal length}} - \frac{1}{\text{object distance}}$$

$$= \frac{1}{f} - \frac{1}{3f} = \frac{3}{3f} - \frac{1}{3f} = \frac{2}{3f}$$

In other words, image distance $= \dfrac{3f}{2}$ cm. Substituting the information provided for Lens Scenario 1 yields:

$$m = -\frac{\text{image distance}}{\text{object distance}} = -\frac{\dfrac{3f}{2}\ \text{cm}}{3f\ \text{cm}} = -\frac{1}{2}$$

The fact that m is negative implies that the image is inverted with respect to the object. The value of $\dfrac{1}{2}$ implies that it is smaller than the object or reduced by 2.

19. **The correct answer is A.** One first starts with the lens equation and then solves for the focal length, f:

$$\frac{1}{\text{focal length}} = \frac{1}{\text{object distance}} + \frac{1}{\text{image distance}}$$

$$= \frac{\text{image distance} + \text{object distance}}{(\text{object distance})(\text{image distance})}$$

Thus, the focal length is:

$$\text{focal length} = \frac{(\text{object distance})\,(\text{image distance})}{\text{image distance} + \text{object distance}}$$

20. **The correct answer is C.** The molecule in the box is already in an eclipsed conformation required for a Fischer projection. Therefore, since the bromines are on opposite sides in the dash-wedge projection, they must also be on opposite sides in the Fischer, and we can exclude choices A and D. The remaining choices (B and C) are enantiomeric—distinguishing between the two is best carried out by imagining a vantage point from above the dash-wedge representation, as shown:

It is then apparent that the upper bromine would point to the right and the lower bromine would be directed to the left of the observer.

21. **The correct answer is D.**

The chemical transformation involves a Jones oxidation of the primary alcohol to form a carboxylic acid, followed by treatment with diazomethane to form the methyl ester, as shown:

The stereochemistry of the chiral center has not changed; its identity to the given product can be shown by a vertical flip:

22. **The correct answer is D.** The product is an alkene without optical activity. The starting material, (S)-2-chloro-4-methylpentane, possesses a good leaving group on a secondary center with adjacent protons. Therefore, all four common pathways (S_N1, S_N2, E1, and E2) are available to it. However, potassium *tert*-butoxide

is a strong hindered base that is unlikely to engage in substitution reactions (i.e., favors elimination). Once the elimination occurs, the chiral center is destroyed; therefore, the product cannot exhibit optical activity.

optically pure   t-BuOK / THF / E2   achiral

Passage IV

23. **The correct answer is C.** Choice A shows the wrong formula for calcium hydroxide, and choice B is not correctly balanced. Choice D shows calcium ion reacting, instead of the appropriate calcium metal. The complete, balanced equation is choice C.

24. **The correct answer is A.** Looking at the series, K and Na will react with water as they are very reactive metals. Only calcium, strontium, and barium from Group 2 *do* react with water. Mg does not and is the first in the series *not* to react with water.

25. **The correct answer is C.** Cobalt is more reactive than the copper and less reactive than iron. This puts the activity of copper between the two. There is no basis from the passage to compare cobalt's activity to that of lead.

26. **The correct answer is D.** Nickel is better at losing electrons than silver. Therefore, silver ions will attract electrons from nickel and become solid silver. Only copper, silver, and gold will be resistant to acid from the series. Chromium will react with acid. Calcium is better at losing electrons than aluminum. Therefore, aluminum ions will attract electrons from calcium and become solid aluminum. Choice D is false because tin has a lesser tendency to lose electrons than nickel.

27. **The correct answer is B.** Chromium has 24 electrons, and it has one of the anomalous electron configurations of $1s^2 2s^2 2p^6 3s^2 3p^6 \underline{3d^5 4s^1}$.

No passage

28. **The correct answer is D.** A diamagnetic element is characterized by the fact that all of its electrons are paired. Of the four choices, the only metal that fits this description is copper.

29. **The correct answer is B.** The number of neutrons is the mass number A minus the atomic number Z. Thus, the number of neutrons of iodine-131 is $N = A - Z = 131 - 53 = 78$.

30. **The correct answer is A.** The weight of an object or a substance can be calculated using the following equation:

$W = mg$

Weight = (mass)(acceleration due to gravity)

To find the mass of the blood sample, one uses the density equation:

$$\rho = \frac{m}{V}$$

where $\rho =$ density, $m =$ mass, and $V =$ volume. Given in the problem are the density of blood ($\rho = 1.06\,\text{g/cm}^3$) and the volume of blood ($V = 10\,\text{mL} = 10\,\text{cm}^3$). Rearranging the above equation for mass and substituting known values yields:

$$m = \rho V = (1.06\,\text{g/cm}^3)\,(10\,\text{cm}^3) = 10.6\,g$$

However, in order to substitute into the equation for weight, mass must be expressed in terms of kilograms, not grams, which results in 0.0106 kg. Thus, $W = (0.0106\,\text{kg})\,(9.8\,\text{m/s}^2) = 0.104\,\text{N}$.

31. **The correct answer is C.** Sulfur is lower on the periodic table, therefore methyl thiolate is both more polarizable (thus, more nucleophilic) and larger (less basic).

32. **The correct answer is D.** Just as sulfur is lower on the periodic table than oxygen, iodine is lower than chlorine; therefore, iodide is more polarizable and more nucleophilic than chloride. The same top-to-bottom trend makes iodide less basic than chloride. Neither is terribly basic; nevertheless, inasmuch as chloride is the stronger base (i.e., weaker conjugate acid), it is the poorer leaving group.

33. **The correct answer is C.** Methyl thiolate is the stronger nucleophile; iodide is the better leaving group. Therefore, the most favorable reaction will be between those two species.

34. **The correct answer is C.** Increasing temperature always increases rate. The rate enhancement for elimination will be greater because of entropy effects, but both processes will be faster.

35. **The correct answer is B.** Methanol is a polar protic solvent, which tends to retard S_N2 by strongly coordinating to the nucleophile. Ether and THF are not protic, but they are only moderately polar. Dimethyl sulfoxide (DMSO) is a very polar aprotic solvent, which coordinates cations very effectively but leaves the anion "naked" and more prone to engage in nucleophilic attack.

36. **The correct answer is B.** Before you can draw a free-body diagram representing the mass, you must first identify the forces acting on the mass. Because the object has mass, it has weight that acts downward. In addition, because the mass is attached to a string, the string exerts a force of tension through the string, directed upward. The free-body diagram that correctly represents these forces in magnitude and direction is the diagram depicted in choice B.

37. **The correct answer is A.** In order to determine the acceleration of the system, one must apply Newton's second law to each of the two masses in Atwood's machine. Since each mass is moving in the y-direction:

m_1: $\quad\quad \sum F_y = ma_y \quad\quad\quad\quad m_2$: $\quad\quad \sum F_y = ma_y$

$\quad\quad\quad T - m_1 g = m_1 a \quad\quad\quad\quad\quad\quad m_2 g - T = m_2 a$

$\quad\quad\quad\quad T = m_1 a + m_1 g \quad\quad\quad\quad\quad\quad T = m_2 g - m_2 a$

Setting the two expressions for the tension, T, equal to one another yields:

$$m_1 a + m_1 g = m_2 g - m_2 a$$

Solving for a yields:

$$a = \frac{(m_2 - m_1)}{(m_1 + m_2)} g$$

38. **The correct answer is C.** The information given in the problem was that Atwood's machine has $m_1 = 140\,\text{g}$ and $m_2 = 160\,\text{g}$. As was shown in the solution to the previous problem, the tension expressed in terms of either of the masses is:

$$T = m_1 a + m_1 g \quad \text{or} \quad T = m_2 g - m_2 a$$

Either expression can be used, but the acceleration of the system needs to be determined. The general expression for the acceleration (which was the basis for the previous problem) is:

$$a = \frac{(m_2 - m_1)}{(m_1 + m_2)} g$$

Substituting given values:

$$a = \frac{(0.16\,\text{kg} - 0.14\,\text{kg})}{(0.14\,\text{kg} + 0.16\,\text{kg})} \left(9.8\,\frac{m}{s^2}\right) = 0.65\,\frac{m}{s^2}$$

Substituting into the equation in terms of m_1:

$$T = m_1 a + m_1 g = (0.14\,\text{kg})\left(0.65\,\frac{m}{s^2}\right) + (0.14\,\text{kg})\left(9.8\,\frac{m}{s^2}\right)$$

$$= 0.091\,\text{N} + 1.372\,\text{N} = 1.46\,\text{N}$$

You could also substitute into the equation in terms of m_2 and obtain the same result for T:

$$T = m_2 g - m_2 a = (0.16\,\text{kg})\left(9.8\,\frac{m}{s^2}\right) - (0.16\,\text{kg})\left(0.65\,\frac{m}{s^2}\right)$$

$$= 1.568\,\text{N} - 0.104\,\text{N} = 1.46\,\text{N}$$

39. **The correct answer is D.** The expression for the acceleration (determined in the second problem of this set) is:

$$a = \frac{(m_2 - m_1)}{(m_1 + m_2)} g$$

where $m_1 = 80$ g and $m_2 = 220$ g. Substituting all given values:

$$a = \frac{(0.22\,\text{kg} - 0.08\,\text{kg})}{(0.08\,\text{kg} + 0.22\,\text{kg})}\left(9.8\,\frac{m}{s^2}\right) = 4.57\,\frac{m}{s^2}$$

40. **The correct answer is A.** To determine an expression for the tension in Atwood's machine, you can begin with the same two equations of motion for the two masses derived from Newton's second law of motion or:

$$m_1: T - m_1 g = m_1 a \quad m_2: m_2 g - T = m_2 a$$

Solving both equations for the acceleration, a, yields:

$$m_1: a = \frac{T - m_1 g}{m_1} \quad m_2: a = \frac{m_2 g - T}{m_2}$$

Setting the expressions equal to each other and solving for T yields:

$$T = g\left(\frac{2 m_1 m_2}{m_1 + m_2}\right)$$

Substituting all given information yields the tension, T:

$$T = \left(9.8\,\frac{m}{s^2}\right)\left(\frac{2 \cdot 0.11\,\text{kg} \cdot 0.19\,\text{kg}}{0.11\,\text{kg} + 0.19\,\text{kg}}\right) = 1.37\,\text{N} \approx 1.4\,\text{N}$$

41. **The correct answer is A.** To find the effect of pulley friction on the system in Atwood's machine, one must first apply Newton's second law to the system:

$$\sum F_{net} = m_2 g - m_1 g - f = (m_1 + m_2)\,a$$

where downward is considered to be positive. Solving for the acceleration yields:

$$a = \frac{m_2 g - m_1 g - f}{(m_1 + m_2)}$$

42. **The correct answer is D.** This question requires basic knowledge of the equation of a line which is:

$$y = mx + b$$

where y is the y variable, x is the x variable, m is the slope, and b is the y intercept. The acceleration of the system using a pulley with friction is:

$$a = \frac{m_2 g - m_1 g - f}{(m_1 + m_2)}$$

which can be rewritten as:

$$a = \frac{(m_2 - m_1)\,g}{(m_1 + m_2)} - \frac{f}{(m_1 + m_2)}$$

$$= \frac{g}{(m_1 + m_2)}(m_2 - m_1) - \frac{f}{(m_1 + m_2)}$$

where a is the y-variable, $\dfrac{g}{(m_1 + m_2)}$ is the slope (m), ($m_2 - m_1$) is the x-variable, and $\dfrac{-f}{(m_1 + m_2)}$ is the y-intercept. Calculating the y-intercept from the graph and substituting for the two masses, one can calculate the frictional force, given by choice D.

Passage VII

43. **The correct answer is C.** The chromate esters of their hydrates cannot decompose by proton loss. Both ketones and aldehydes form carbonyl hydrates, and those hydrates form equilibrium quantities of chromate ester. However, in the case of ketones, the decomposition of the inorganic ester would require the departure of a carbocation, for which there is a considerably higher barrier than for a proton.

44. **The correct answer is B.** Without water, no carbonyl hydrate can be formed, thus trapping the aldehyde at that stage.

45. **The correct answer is D.** The most likely product would be an oxo aldehyde. Jones conditions will oxidize the secondary alcohol to the ketone and the primary alcohol to the carboxylic acid.

46. **The correct answer is C.** The most likely product would be an oxo aldehyde. The PCC will oxidize the secondary alcohol to the ketone and the primary alcohol to the aldehyde.

47. **The correct answer is A.** The most likely compound isolated is an alcohol. For much the same reason that ketones do not overoxidize, tertiary alcohols are resistant to oxidation by chromium (VI) reagents, since it would require the departure of a carbocation in the chromate ester decomposition step.

48. **The correct answer is B.** α-D-glucose and β-D-glucose differ by a single stereocenter. If one or more—but not all—stereocenters are different, the two compounds are diastereomers. In an enantiomer, each and every stereocenter must have changed. Thus, the enantiomer of D-glucose is L-glucose:

49. **The correct answer is A.** The hemiacetal functionality is highlighted in glucose shown. Note that the hemiacetal carbon is in the same oxidation state as a carbonyl group, which is revealed by 2 bonds to oxygen. In an acetal, 2 alkoxy groups are attached to 1 carbon; in a hemiacetal, one is a hydroxy group and the other is an alkoxy group:

50. **The correct answer is B.** Mutarotation involves the cleavage of the hemiacetal to form an intermediate aldehyde, which can reform the hemiacetal with different stereochemistry:

51. **The correct answer is C.** The difference between hexoses and pentoses is in the total number of carbons contained in the sugar—hexoses are C6 compounds and pentoses are C5 compounds. The difference between furanoses and pyranoses is in the size of the ring formed—furanoses form 5-membered rings and pyranoses form 6-membered rings. The nomenclature is derived from the simple cyclic ethers:

52. **The correct answer is A.** With respect to the lone pairs on the ring oxygen, the β-hydroxy group suffers from unfavorable dipole-dipole interactions, whereas the α-isomer minimizes this electrostatic repulsion, resulting in lower energy:

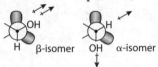

Passage IX

53. **The correct answer is C.** All nitrates and chlorides are soluble. However, chlorides of silver, lead, and mercury are not soluble. The expected product is silver chloride.

54. **The correct answer is C.** At 100 °C, the amount of NaCl dissolved will be 39.12 grams. But because this amount is per 100 mL of water, you need to adjust for using 250 mL of water. Doing so, you get 39.12 grams $\times 2.5 = 97.8$ grams dissolving in 250 mL of water. At 0 °C, the saturated solution will hold 35.7 grams $\times 2.5 = 89.3$ grams. So the difference of 8.6 grams will precipitate out of solution.

55. **The correct answer is C.** In order to conduct electricity, there must be free ions in solution. By creating products that are insoluble, the number of free ions is minimal.

56. **The correct answer is A.** All sodium salts are soluble. Looking over the other choices, there are compounds containing other cations that are sometimes soluble and sometimes not. The experimental data indicate that the only true statement here is choice A.

57. **The correct answer is D.** The first three choices are all false statements. Silver nitrate is an example of a soluble silver compound. Sodium phosphate is an example of a soluble phosphate compound. An example of a soluble sulfate compound is ammonium sulfate. Looking at choice D, you have the following reaction in water: $AgCl(s) \longleftrightarrow Ag^+ (aq) + Cl^- (aq)$. The addition of ammonia to the solution forms a complex ion with silver ion. This reaction proceeds as: $Ag^+ (aq) + 2NH_3 (aq) \rightarrow Ag(NH_3)_2^+ (aq)$. As the ammonia removes the silver ions from solution, the equilibrium is shifted to the right and the silver chloride becomes more soluble.

No passage

58. **The correct answer is B.** Looking at the choices, three of the pairs are conjugate acid-base pairs, which differ by an H^+. However, choice B has the two substances differing by 2 H^+ ions. The conjugate base of sulfuric acid would be HSO_4^-. HSO_4^- would also be the conjugate acid of SO_4^{2-}.

59. **The correct answer is D.** A total of 9 ions are formed when hydroxyapatite dissolves. Because the coefficient of each ion becomes the power of the concentration, you have $[x]^5 \cdot [x]^3 \cdot [x]^1 = [x]^9$.

Section 3. Psychological, Social, and Biological Foundations of Behavior

1. **The correct answer is C.** Alfred cannot use retinal disparity because one of his eyes is closed. Retinal disparity occurs when the brain processes the difference in the images each eye receives and, using each visual perspective, integrates them into a 3-D representation of the environment.

No passage

2. **The correct answer is A.** Conflict theory states that society is fundamentally in conflict when there is an uneven distribution of resources, and that power struggles between groups of people create divisiveness across gender, race, and socioeconomic status.

3. **The correct answer is A.** The bystander effect is characterized by slowness in response due to diffusion of responsibility. The more people who are present, the less an individual is likely to feel responsible to respond to the emergency because of the collective presence of other individuals.

4. **The correct answer is C.** Altruism is more likely to occur between individuals who are likely to reciprocate assistance in the future. Studies of altruistic behavior have shown that helping others occurs more frequently among family members and in smaller communities and where it is most likely to be reciprocated in the future.

5. **The correct answer is B.** During variable-ratio trials the rat is reinforced after a specific number of bar presses. The number of presses varies over time. As a result, the rat presses the bar more vigorously. Further, this type of reinforcement has a higher resistance to extinction because the reinforcement schedule itself varies.

Passage I

6. **The correct answer is C.** Conditioning would occur more slowly, and the slope in each cell would be flatter. The longer the delay between the response and reinforcement, the more slowly conditioning occurs.

7. **The correct answer is D.** Fixed-ratio responses are characterized by a high rate of bar presses, and the short break taken by the rat is indicative of a fixed period of bar presses. Under fixed reinforcement the rat will press the bar quickly because responses are tied to the number of presses and not a time interval.

8. **The correct answer is C.** Ratio reinforcement usually results in predictable response patterns under each of the conditions (fixed and variable), with steady responding in a 1:1 ratio, and multiple rapid bar presses in the variable response ratio condition with long breaks in between. The variable nature of the reinforcement results in greater resistance to extinction in later trials as the rat continues with the behavior even in the absence of reinforcement in hopes of eventually getting a reinforcement.

9. **The correct answer is A.** In operant conditioning the stimulus always precedes the reinforcement or punishment. In the model of operant conditioning, the punishment or reinforcement of a behavior results in the increase or decrease of

that behavior. The behavior is elicited by the stimulus and therefore precedes the conditioning.

Passage II   10. **The correct answer is A.** The largest proportion of responders are in the conventional level because most people never reach the postconventional level. This is consistent with Kohlberg's model and is expected based on the data pattern.

11. **The correct answer is C.** Conventional morality develops between the ages of 7 and 16. It develops as preconventional morality extinguishes. The key period for this change is between 7 and 16 years old.

12. **The correct answer is B.** Moral judgments can be understood in context based on stages of moral development. In Kohlberg's model, the reasons given by the research subjects for answering questions a particular way defined which level of development was being exhibited.

13. **The correct answer is D.** Stage 3 morality is characterized by the basing of decisions on personally constructed moral principles rather than on the likelihood of reward or punishment, or society's rules or laws. According to Kohlberg, someone functioning at this level would be able to reject personal fulfillment and unjust laws in order to make moral decisions.

14. **The correct answer is B.** James is displaying behavior consistent with the conventional stage of moral development. In this stage decisions are based on society's rules and laws with judgments based on relatively absolute criteria (black/white, right/wrong).

Passage III   15. **The correct answer is B.** Changing the location of the comparison light allows researchers to isolate where the light from the test stimuli reaches the retina. When the comparison light is located at the fixation point, the light falls on the fovea, where the cones are located. When the test light is presented away from the fixation point (in the periphery), the rods are activated.

16. **The correct answer is A.** The participant is considered to have detected the light if he or she can identify the comparison light presence 50% of the time. Using signal detection, the presence and absence of the test light is manipulated along with the intensity of the light.

17. **The correct answer is D.** The rods are maximally sensitive after 20 minutes in the dark and are more sensitive overall. Cones are initially more sensitive than rods but become less so after the rod-cone break. At the breakpoint, cones and rods are equally sensitive. Rods only become more sensitive at a lower level of light after the breakpoint.

18. **The correct answer is C.** Rods cannot distinguish between different wavelengths, therefore rod-based light perception is on the black and white gradient and is the primary form of human visual perception after the rod-cone break.

19. **The correct answer is D.** Rods are better at light adaptation because large groups of them are connected to one interneuron. The interneuron amplifies the signal

from each rod receptor decreasing resolution while increasing overall sensitivity to light.

20. **The correct answer is D.** The individual spent a longer amount of time solving algebra problems in a group compared to solving them alone.

21. **The correct answer is B.** The results are consistent with social loafing. This concept is exemplified when an individual reduces his or her effort on a task based on the assumption that other members of the group will "step up" to complete the task. Social loafing is more likely to occur in the context of a more difficult or cognitively-demanding task.

22. **The correct answer is A.** Social facilitation is exemplified when an individual increases his or her effort on a task in a group situation; Social facilitation is more likely to happen when the task is relatively easy or simple to complete.

23. **The correct answer is B.** The individual would reduce the amount of effort spent on solving the problems because he or she would assume others would step up to complete the task. This result is consistent with social loafing, which posits that as group size and task complexity increase, the amount of effort expended by individuals decreases.

24. **The correct answer is A.** The effort expended is the result of the participant's perception of diffusion of responsibility. Social loafing is characterized by the reduction in effort by individuals when they work in groups. This result is consistent even when individuals *think* that they are working alone regardless of whether or not they are *actually* working alone. The individual's perception about the presence of others is more critical to this process than the actuality of the presence of others.

25. **The correct answer is C.** Individuals identifying as "African American" are more likely to be diagnosed with schizophrenia, and individuals who identify as "White" are more likely to be diagnosed with a mood disorder.

26. **The correct answer is C.** Clinicians see no ethnicity differences in admittance rates for some disorders. This conclusion can be ruled out because the observable data collected contradict this statement. However, it is not possible to determine the degree of influence that ethnicity has on the rates of diagnoses or on the incidence rate in these studies since it only assesses those admitted for psychiatric care. It does not measure the rate of diagnosis or population prevalence of psychiatric disorders.

27. **The correct answer is A.** A logical follow-up study would measure the social and economic status and stress of each person diagnosed with schizophrenia and mood disorder. This is the most correct answer because such a study would further investigate the environmental causes for mental disorders. This additional research also fits with the vulnerability-stress view of schizophrenia.

28. **The correct answer is D.** A person has a 100% chance of developing schizophrenia if both of his or her parents have schizophrenia. This answer is incorrect because

even though schizophrenia is heritable, genetic factors alone are not responsible for the development of the disorder and a child inherits 50% of each parent's genotype. This would not guarantee that a child would receive the genetic sequence that is required to be susceptible to this complex, polygenic disorder of schizophrenia.

29. **The correct answer is A.** The more stress to which a person who is genetically predisposed to schizophrenia is exposed, the greater the likelihood that person will experience a psychotic break. The vulnerability-stress view suggests that environmental stressors are correlated to the expression of schizophrenic symptoms. As these stressors increase, the likelihood increases that a person biologically predisposed to schizophrenia will exhibit symptoms. The research is still ongoing with regard to answer C and the vulnerability-stress model does not currently recognize differences in positive and negative stress. Answer D would require the individual to experience stress along with the biological family to fulfill the requirements of the model. If the individual was adopted and has no contact with the biological family, the biological family's stress will not trigger a schizophrenic break.

Passage VI 30. **The correct answer is C.** Commitment initially increases slowly; then it rapidly increases. The model depicts commitment increasing slowly. Then as passion begins to drop, commitment increases rapidly.

31. **The correct answer is C.** Commitment is crucial and is positively correlated to relationship stability. Various studies have shown that commitment is predictive of relationship stability. Commitment is also shown in the model to be at the highest level for the greatest length of time.

32. **The correct answer is A.** Romantic love is characterized by intense emotions and sexual feelings. The passion component develops quickly and early in the relationship and declines rapidly as commitment increases.

33. **The correct answer is D.** Companionate love develops over time and is characterized in Sternberg's model by commitment and intimacy. Choice A is incorrect because if the individual components that make up fatuous love and liking were present, it would be consummate love.

34. **The correct answer is D.** Although Danna has been with Mark for some time, their relationship is best categorized as infatuation due to the lack of commitment and intimacy in the context of strong sexual feelings.

Passage VII 35. **The correct answer is B.** The majority of state average scores were above the national average. Sixteen of the states listed were below the national average and 34 were above. Most state average scores exceeded the national average.

36. **The correct answer is D.** Conflict theory posits that the difference in prestige and resources creates fundamental power struggles between groups of people and that these power struggles create divisiveness across groups. In the example given, the

sociologist is examining differences in groups that are historically underperforming and evaluating how power divisiveness is being minimized.

37. **The correct answer is C.** The data reflect attempts to reinforce the status quo between various state populations. Functionalists view education as structured in such a way that it reinforces the status quo. It keeps societies stable and seeks to avoid disruptions in the system.

38. **The correct answer is C.** Teaching in the state school system is part of the service, or tertiary, sector of the economy. The primary sector includes the extractive industries such as mining and forestry. The secondary sector includes the manufacturing industries.

39. **The correct answer is B.** Jim is attempting to maintain the status quo and is attempting to prevent disruptions in the existing system. His work is consistent with functionalism.

40. **The correct answer is D.** The share of the elderly population in Japan will increase over time relative to the rest of the population. In the graphs, the share of elderly people, shown as the top portion of each population "pyramid," is projected to increase over time relative to the shares of young and adult persons (shown as the bottom and middle portions of each population "pyramid"). Passage VIII

41. **The correct answer is B.** There would be fewer transitional youth in the population in 2060 than in 2010. The transitional youth category is an additional age group between the ages of 15 and 30. It would overlap the existing youth and adult populations and would show the same overall pattern of reduction shown in both those populations over time.

42. **The correct answer is A.** Social and cultural characteristics would become more diverse across the population. This result is consistent with more mobile societies and reflects the changing demographics that would be evident from an addition of individuals from different backgrounds.

43. **The correct answer is B.** The elderly are likely to have more influence on public policy as their share of the population increases.

44. **The correct answer is D.** The ethnicity of the overall population would remain basically the same. Ethnicity is a social construct, and if the immigrants became culturally integrated into the native culture, that would not change the ethnicity of the overall population. Race, on the other hand, is determined by biological and genetic factors. Racial composition may or may not change with an immigrant group, depending on the biological makeup of the original and immigrant groups.

45. **The correct answer is B.** Latino individuals are as likely as white individuals to have access to minimally adequate mental health treatment post diagnosis. While Latino individuals are less likely than whites to be diagnosed with mental illness, they are as likely to receive minimally adequate treatment post diagnosis. Passage IX

46. **The correct answer is B.** Individuals of lower socioeconomic status (SES) who have mental health difficulties have fewer financial resources and less access to mental health care, and are therefore less able to seek treatment. The culture of poverty theory would ignore the reduced access to mental health treatment and attribute George's problems to his poor choices related to drug use. This scenario speaks against social mobility rather than describes it. Human capital does not apply because George has the education to improve his SES.

47. **The correct answer is B.** As a young person with no financial resources, George has less access to mental health care. Additionally, now that he is no longer a student, he likely does not have access to the student counseling center at his school.

48. **The correct answer is C.** Both the stigma related to seeking mental health care and the lack of mental health providers in lower SES areas are likely to affect George's ability to receive treatment.

49. **The correct answer is A.** While black individuals are the least likely to receive a mental health diagnosis, they also have the least access to minimally adequate mental health treatment and are the least likely to receive treatment once diagnosed.

Passage X 50. **The correct answer is A.** Bodily resources are mobilized and metabolism speeds up. During the alarm stage people experience increased physiological arousal. They will become anxious and frightened. The response is similar to the fight-or-flight syndrome.

51. **The correct answer is D.** Resistance; the reaction can persist for hours, days, or years. In GAS, people experiencing resistance generally have a negative emotional and physical reaction (e.g., being tired, irritable, impatient, and angry). However, they are able to intentionally engage in adaptive stress management activities (meditation, seeking social support) to reduce the negative impact of stress. Exhaustion is characterized by extreme physical and mental fatigue. However, it is also characterized by the lack of ability to engage in adaptive stress management activities to resist stress.

52. **The correct answer is B.** Resistance reactions are adaptive and can help reduce the impact of stress. This is consistent with GAS theory. Resistance reactions are those activities that the individual uses to resist the negative impact of stress on the mind and body in order to reduce the likelihood of entering the exhaustion stage.

53. **The correct answer is B.** Multiple simultaneous stressors may overwhelm an individual's stress resistance activities and push him or her into the exhaustion stage more quickly. Individuals are able to resist stress until it overwhelms their adaptive resistance activities, after which the individual falls into exhaustion. Multiple simultaneous moderately stressful events will impact the efficacy of stress resistance activities and push the individual into the exhaustion stage faster than only a single stressor of moderate severity.

54. **The correct answer is A.** Jeremy reacted by adapting and making behavioral changes in response to the stressful situation in an attempt to reduce the stress. This is a characteristic of a resistance reaction.

55. **The correct answer is C.** The forgetting curve is characterized by an initial rapid decrease in the proportion remembered, followed by a slow flattening out over time.

56. **The correct answer is D.** Based on the forgetting curve, each relearning episode increases the amount retained over time. Recall is better for the first few days with each relearning episode.

57. **The correct answer is D.** Relearning impacts the rate of forgetting only after several relearning episodes. In the graph, relearning impacts the rate of forgetting as early as the first relearning episode, although repeated relearning episodes slow the rate of forgetting. Even in the context of multiple relearning episodes, forgetting does still occur over time, but repetition slows this rate of loss.

58. **The correct answer is A.** Test performance would decline sharply at first but decline less and less in later years. There is no relearning in this scenario and the results would be consistent with the slope of the forgetting curve.

59. **The correct answer is D.** There would be a significant decline in your memory in the first week, but the decline would become less abrupt after each time that you studied the list. Each relearning interval will increase the amount retained on subsequent tests.

Section 4. Critical Analysis and Reasoning Skills

Passage I

1. **The correct answer is D.** The woolly flying squirrel did not really vanish; *salajit* collectors knew of its existence. Choices A, B, and C are supported by information in the passage.

2. **The correct answer is C.** Zahler chooses not to track the aquatic genet because he prefers to look for a creature that does not live in a tropical biome. There is no support for the notion that tropical diseases affect these mammals (choice D). The other two choices may or may not be true, but they are not supported by the author's mention of the aquatic genet in the article.

3. **The correct answer is D.** Paragraph 1 gives MacKinnon's requirements for rediscovery or discovery of species. The woolly flying squirrel's home in caves in the Himalayas certainly meets the requirement for isolation (choice A), but as paragraph 4 points out, it also meets the requirements for geographic and climatic stability, making choice D the correct answer.

4. **The correct answer is B.** The discussion of how Zahler chose this animal to study appears in paragraph 3. He wanted a mammal that was not too small, relatively unknown, and in need of conservation intervention. Because he did not wish to deal with heat or diseases, he passed up the aquatic genet for the woolly flying squirrel. That makes choice B the best answer.

5. **The correct answer is A.** To answer this question, you must apply MacKinnon's requirements to your knowledge of geography. MacKinnon suggests that dry climates are not conducive to rediscovery, making the Sahara an unlikely answer (choice D). Western Iran is prone to earthquake activity, making it a less likely choice than the more remote, steamy jungles of Borneo. Choice A is the best answer.

6. **The correct answer is A.** Information that weakens the argument will argue against rediscovery's being a way to protect species. Of the information given, choices B, C, and D suggest ways that species are being protected. Only choice A mentions something that might actually harm a rediscovered species.

Passage II

7. **The correct answer is D.** Both the Beat and the Lost Generations came of age during war and found it hard to cope in the postwar world. Both tended toward exile and alienation, making choice D the best answer.

8. **The correct answer is C.** The word *culture* is used twice—to refer to "the drug culture" and to "sixties culture." Choices A, B, and D make no sense in this context, so the only possible connotation is choice C.

9. **The correct answer is B.** According to the author, "the trials loosened some of the definitions that had bound American literature." The trials, then, did not affect the movement of the Beats (choice A) or their influences (choice C); they affected modern definitions of literature (choice B).

10. **The correct answer is B.** To answer this question correctly, you must ask yourself, "Is there at least one example of I, II, or III anywhere in the passage?" Statement I

says that Kerouac continued to write before his *On the Road* was published, but there are no examples of what he wrote. Statement III says that the Beats influenced sixties culture, but there are no examples of works from that era that showed the Beats' influence. Statement II says that the drug culture affected some Beats. The author gives the example of Burroughs, who wrote *Junkie* about his own addiction, and also mentions "Howl" and its emphasis on drug culture. Because only statement II has supporting examples, the only correct response is (choice B).

11. **The correct answer is C.** It is the subject matter, not the form of Corso's poetry that ties it to the angst of a postwar generation. Including "Bomb" in the passage would help support the point made in choice C.

12. **The correct answer is D.** If the Beats were omitted from an important anthology, it could only indicate that they were not considered important enough to include. That would negate choice D, the notion that they transcended their time. It would not say anything about choice A or C, and the fact that Beat writing was difficult (choice B) would not be enough to eliminate it from an anthology.

Passage III

13. **The correct answer is C.** Refining is one of the three steps in the creation of aluminum. It involves the separation of a solution through distillation and addition of chemicals. Although *refined* is a multiple-meaning word that in context may have any of the four definitions listed, only choice C works in the context of this passage.

14. **The correct answer is B.** Choice A is true, but it has nothing to do with the protests. There is no evidence to support choice D. Choice C may or may not be true; it is implied, but it is not a major point. The mention of protests mainly indicates choice B, that workers are beginning to question the dangers of mining.

15. **The correct answer is A.** There is nothing to support choice B or C, and the author is completely objective when it comes to the discussion of Karl Bayer (choice D). In the final paragraph, the author states, "As with all mining of metals, bauxite mining presents certain hazards," indicating that choice A is the best answer.

16. **The correct answer is C.** Paragraph 6 describes the process of refinement and its by-products. Those that are mentioned in the paragraph include choices A, B, and D. There is no mention of choice C, which is an alloy of aluminum and an element not involved in this refining process.

17. **The correct answer is D.** According to paragraph 2, the most commonly mined form of bauxite is gibbsite, a trihydrate form of bauxite. If it is trihydrate, then it contains three molecules of water (choice D). There is no evidence in the passage to support any of the other choices.

18. **The correct answer is B.** The three-step process that produces aluminum is described as involving mining, refining, and smelting. It is typical of the process that results in most metal products that we use, so it is parallel to copper production (choice B). None of the other three products results from the same three-step process.

19. **The correct answer is C.** The final paragraph mentions Bowdler's works other than Shakespeare and discusses the fact that we derive a verb from his name. The main idea of the paragraph, however, is that Bowdler's form of editing continues to the present day (choice C); several examples of present-day bowdlerization are given.

20. **The correct answer is B.** Bowdler himself was trained as a doctor; the passage makes clear that he was not an editor. His sister, however, was a poet and editor, and therefore was more likely than he to have made the editorial changes that led to the revised Shakespearean texts. There is no evidence in the passage to support choice C or D, and although there is some implication that choice A is true, it does not explain why she would have been a more likely editor than he.

21. **The correct answer is A.** There is no mention of a dream (choice D), the poet laureate is used as an example of prior editing but not as an inspiration for Bowdler himself (choice C), and Bowdler was not a scholar, making choice B an unlikely answer. Instead, his desire was to make Shakespeare accessible to children, and in its unexpurgated state, he felt that was impossible. Choice A is the best answer.

22. **The correct answer is D.** Look for the answer that is supported by the text. Although choices A, B, and C may in fact be true, none of them receives support in the passage. The author's reason for including mention of Nehum Tate is to show that the Bowdlers were not the first to edit Shakespeare.

23. **The correct answer is C.** Remember that the answer will NOT be an example of bowdlerization. First, you must find the definition of bowdlerization in the text: "to censor or amend a written work, often with a connotation of prudishness." Item I is not an example of this; simply translating from one language to another requires neither censorship or amendment. Item III is not an example either; although some may say that book burning is a radical form of censorship, it does not fit the definition here. Only II, which deals with the censorship of a detail in a text, fits the definition. Since I and III do not, choice C is the correct answer.

24. **The correct answer is A.** Although choices B, C, and D appear in the passage, none of them supports the claim that Bowdler's revised Shakespeare was not universally despised. The quote from Swinburne (choice A), however, does—Swinburne praises Bowdler for creating a Shakespeare that can be put in the hands of children.

25. **The correct answer is A.** Because the author makes the point that bowdlerization still occurs today, it is not likely that everyone would revile such a text (choice B) or see that it failed (choice D). More likely would be that it would receive some condemnation but also make some sales (choice A). Although a point is made about "dumbing down" texts for high school students (choice C), the author does not appear to support this, nor is it proof that students would not understand the bowdlerized Shakespeare.

26. **The correct answer is B.** "The Red Cross, yes, but Henry Kissinger?" asks the author. The author finds the controversy over Rigoberta "surprising" and states,

"her place in the history of Central American peasant revolutions seems assured." That indicates that as far as the author is concerned, the committee's choice of Rigoberta is not undeserved (I), but the choice of Kissinger may well be (II). Since the author gives the Red Cross (III) a thumbs-up, only choice B fits the passage.

27. **The correct answer is C.** For vocabulary-in-context questions like this one, always locate the word in question because the distracters are likely to be alternate meanings of that word. Here, the passage states, "Rigoberta's father was taken into custody and tortured when the army believed he had assisted in the assassination of a plantation owner." The only answer that makes sense in this context is choice C.

28. **The correct answer is C.** The question asks you to find the one or more statements that do NOT support the premise that Rigoberta falsified her book. To do that, you must find the statements that do support that premise and eliminate those. Statements that do support the premise will indicate some kind of disconnect between what she said and what was true. Those statements include I and II. Statement III, on the other hand, is simply a statement of fact. It does not support the premise that she falsified the book. The answer is choice C.

29. **The correct answer is B.** This question calls for a cause-and-effect relationship. You must find the cause of Rigoberta's departure. That is not simply something that happened before her departure (choice D), or something that was true but not a direct cause (choice A). The cause appears in the sentence "Soon Rigoberta was herself a target." She left because otherwise she might have been assassinated (choice B).

30. **The correct answer is D.** This question is purely speculative, since the author did not include information to support the statement. If the author had, it would have had to be information that told more about the teaching of Rigoberta's book in schools. Two students' comments (choice A) would not be enough evidence, and choices B and C might show that the book is still sold but not that it is widely taught. Only choice D includes reasonable evidence.

31. **The correct answer is C.** You are asked here to assess the relative relevance of evidence. Falsifying a birth date (choice A) might be evidence of a minor deception, but it would not be enough to support charges of fraud. Falsifying a critical part of her history as it relates to her reputation, as choice C would do, would certainly indicate a desire to deceive.

32. **The correct answer is A.** David Stoll objects to what he considers Rigoberta's misleading the public on matters of fact. That would not mean that her work was an epic (choice B) or a folktale (choice C) because those are specific genres of literature that do not fit his accusations. Nor would he call her work a manifesto (choice D) because he does not accept her as a leader. He might, however, use the trendy word *truthiness* to describe what he feels to be a bending of the truth.

33. **The correct answer is C.** To answer this kind of question, you must compare what you know about the author's point of view with the choices given. The author, unlike some of the people in the passage, seems to have a positive view of Rigoberta, as evinced in the line, "her place in the history of Central American peasant revolutions seems assured." That means that choices A and B would be unlikely views of this author, and there is no evidence to support choice D one way or the other. The best answer is choice C.

Passage VI

34. **The correct answer is D.** The author finds that metanarratives are often racist, sexist, or classist; but that mininarratives are often too restrictive or exclusive to be useful. The best answer is choice D.

35. **The correct answer is C.** You must make this prediction based on what the author has said in the passage. Two examples of courses in American history are given to support the notion that some mininarratives are incompatible, but there is no indication that offering more courses would help (choice A). The author mentions revising the canon (choice B) in paragraphs 4 and 5 but implies that it was a good and necessary idea. Red states and blue states are mentioned in passing, but there is little else to indicate the author's feelings about politics (choice D). The best answer is choice C; the author is concerned that students today find it hard to see a "big picture" due to their immersion in competing mininarratives.

36. **The correct answer is D.** Supposition I is supported by the examples of competing American history courses. Supposition II is supported by the clash between evolutionary theory and strict Bible interpretation. Supposition III is supported by the example of a Eurocentric look at American history (see paragraph 2). Since all three suppositions are supported by examples, choice D is the best answer.

37. **The correct answer is B.** The main idea of the passage has to do with the tension between metanarratives and mininarratives, especially as they affect the way we learn things. This would be most useful for people who develop curricula.

38. **The correct answer is B.** *Smorgasbord* is a Swedish word meaning "a buffet meal featuring a variety of dishes." It is this variety, or choice, to which the author refers. Even if you do not know the word, you should be able to guess this from context.

39. **The correct answer is D.** All three philosophies are all-encompassing ways to look at the world, so all three could be considered metanarratives. Since all three are valid, the answer is choice D.

40. **The correct answer is A.** A mininarrative looks at the world through a limited lens. A metanarrative provides more of a big picture. The best analogy is choice A.

Passage VII

41. **The correct answer is C.** This question asks you to find the main idea. To find the main idea, you must read actively and summarize as you go. There are no titles on MCAT passages to reveal the central thesis, so you must derive it from the text. To determine the correct answer, review the choices. You need to select the one that is not only true according to the passage, but also not so specific

that it excludes one or more of the author's main points. The author indicates that millions of people are blogging but does not mention how many people read popular blogs. Therefore choice A is not supported by the text and can be eliminated. Similarly, the author notes that advertisers are spending more money on blogs than they have in the past but does not reveal that traditional print and broadcasting outlets are receiving less money (choice B). While choice D is true according to the passage, it is not general enough to be the central thesis. Choice C is the correct response, echoing the general statement made at the beginning of the passage, and being broad enough to encompass the author's points made throughout the text.

42. **The correct answer is B.** This question asks you to draw conclusions about a fact presented in the passage. It is a skill most often applied to fiction, but it works in this case for nonfiction as well. The word *implies* tells you that the answer is not directly stated. It is up to you to return to the passage and make inferences based on what is written. The passage states that *popular* bloggers are the ones making money from advertising. There is no general information given about what makes a blog popular; one blogger earns money from humor, while another presents controversial political discourse. There is nothing in the passage to suggest that content about celebrities equates with popularity, eliminating choice C. There is also no reason given to infer that bloggers are, or should be, appealing to marketers (choice D). Although there is one example of a popular blog that is controversial, the other example regarding a humorous website makes choice B the correct answer. Marketers want to advertise on sites that are read by many people, regardless of content.

43. **The correct answer is A.** You must apply new evidence to an assertion in the passage for this question. Specifically, what fact presented by the author would be challenged by evidence that traditional media sources were successfully competing for blogs' advertising revenue? Choices B and D are true statements according to the passage, but they do not relate to the new evidence and should be eliminated. There is nothing in the passage to suggest that blogs are better at disseminating information, so choice C should also be eliminated. A careful rereading of the final paragraph reveals that marketers spend money on blogs and other online advertising because they want "new and more effective ways to reach consumers." Therefore, choice A is correct.

44. **The correct answer is C.** This question involves analyzing an argument. The assertion that blogs influence language (I) is supported by the example of a dictionary giving the distinction of "word of the year" to *blog*. There is no example given of politicians using blogs for any reason (II). Since the assertion that blogs include otherwise neglected news (III) is supported by the story about Trent Lott, both I and III are true, and choice C is correct.

45. **The correct answer is** C. This question tests your ability to locate supporting details or evidence. In questions of this kind, everything you need to know is found directly in the text. The last line of paragraph 2 contains the information: "When those passive consumers use simple websites to disseminate facts and ideas of their choosing, they evolve from passive consumers to active participants, effectively blurring the line between the media and its audience." There is nothing in the passage to suggest that the advertising revenue diverted to blogs is changing the nature of the media (choice A). While the passage does present evidence that blogs can affect political careers (choice B) and they are a public display of ideas (choice D), this evidence is not related to a change in the nature of the media. Choice C is the only correct response.

46. **The correct answer is** D. For questions such as this one, you must draw a conclusion by going beyond the facts of the passage to determine the correct answer. The coverage of Senator Lott is an example of the expansion of what is considered to be newsworthy, not an example of how blogs are attracting advertisers and their money (choice A). There is no suggestion that the coverage was designed to do anything other than report on the news, so choice B is also incorrect. Since Lott resigned from his position as Speaker of the House, the story was not ineffective, eliminating choice C. Choice D is the correct answer because paragraph 3 clearly states that traditional media sources often don't cover what they deem to be controversial news stories, "virtually ignoring" Lott's remarks.

Passage VIII 47. **The correct answer is** A. This evaluation question asks you to analyze an argument. Specifically, you need to figure out why the author mentioned the Platonic tradition. In the first paragraph, the author states that the prevailing view of mathematics is an "easy" one that may be "cemented" in the minds of people. Later, in the third paragraph, the author states that the new view of mathematics has met with "stiff resistance." Thus, the mention of the Platonic tradition helps to explain why there is resistance to the conclusions of the new paradigm, which is what choice A says.

48. **The correct answer is** C. To answer this question, you must assess evidence. Since this is an EXCEPT question, you're looking for the choice that is not present in the passage. The passage does discuss experiments, choice A, in the section about violation of expectation tests. The part about the PhD in chemistry who suffered from acalculia is a case study (choice B). Finally, the author presents a comparison (choice D) when showing how animals and humans have similar abilities. That leaves choice C as the correct answer.

49. **The correct answer is** D. This question asks you to draw conclusions about an assertion that is not directly stated. The second paragraph states that mathematics is created by man, which implies that mathematical concepts are to some degree arbitrary. Choice A is contradicted by the passage in the final paragraph when the

author says that the acalculia patient "has no problem manipulating abstract algebraic operations." Choice B is not supported because the passage only mentions that *some* animals have mathematical abilities. Choice C is incorrect; infants at the age of a few months can perform simple calculations. At younger ages they can only differentiate between two and three items.

50. **The correct answer is C.** This question involves interpreting vocabulary. The word *curious* appears in the final passage. In that paragraph, the author discusses "anomalous" cases and describes the situation as "strange." This makes choice C, "odd," the best choice. There is no indication that the author thinks the fact is superb or excellent ("marvelous," choice A), of foreign origin ("exotic," choice B), or new ("novel," choice D).

51. **The correct answer is A.** In order to answer this question, you must be able to judge credibility. The author cites the violation of expectation experiment as support for the author's claim that mathematics is an innate part of human cognition. In order for these experiments to be credible, the author is assuming that the researchers can accurately determine that the infants are in fact surprised when the number of puppets changes. The only evidence for this is the direction and duration of the stares of the subjects. Accepting these results as evidence indicates the author believes outward signs accurately indicate inner emotional states; otherwise, the evidence would not support the argument.

52. **The correct answer is C.** This question requires you to find the main idea. The passage states that a longstanding view of mathematics as an objective reality is being challenged by new evidence in the fields of cognitive science and developmental psychology. This is what choice C expresses. Choice A is incorrect because the main idea of the passage does not concern Western philosophers. The passage does not claim that animals have the same mathematical abilities as humans do, making choice B wrong. Choice D is not supported by the passage at all.

53. **The correct answer is D.** This question asks you to apply new evidence. This question is very difficult because you must understand both the nature of the author's argument and the effect of new evidence on it. The passage argues that mathematical thinking is a product of the innate structures of the brain and mathematical "truths" are created by people. Finding a group of people that lacks mathematical ability might seem to refute the argument as choice A indicates, but upon closer examination it is not the best answer. The author does allow that certain changes in the brain may destroy the ability to perform mathematical operations. Thus, the community of math-deficient people may have a genetic mutation that prevents them from doing math. If so, it would not harm the author's argument. If, however, the group had no brain abnormalities and possessed no mathematical abilities, it would challenge the author's belief that mathematical thought is hardwired into the brain. Thus, choice D is the best answer.

EVALUATION CHART

Use this evaluation chart to analyze your results on the science sections (Sections 1, 2, and 3) of the Practice Test 1. The chart matches each test question to specific content areas that you can review as part of this book's **online resources**. (See page ix, How to Use This Book.) Check the Answers and Explanations section to see which questions you got correct and which ones you missed. For each question that you missed, find the question number in the left column of the chart below. Look in the right column to find the location of the related review material. If you missed questions in a specific content area, you need to pay particular attention to that area as you study for the MCAT.

Item Number	Content Area
Biological and Biochemical Foundations of Living Systems	
1.	Chapter 9: Structure and Integrative Functions of the Main Organ Systems
2.	Chapter 8: Structure and Function of the Nervous and Endocrine Systems and Ways in Which These Systems Coordinate the Organ Systems
3.	Chapter 2: Transmission of Genetic Information from the Gene to the Protein
4.	Chapter 6: Structure, Growth, Physiology, and Genetics of Prokaryotes and Viruses
5.	Chapter 3: Transmission of Heritable Information from Generation to Generation and Processes That Increase Genetic Diversity
6.	Chapter 9: Structure and Integrative Functions of the Main Organ Systems
7.	Chapter 5: Assemblies of Molecules, Cells, and Groups of Cells Within Multicellular Organisms
8.	Chapter 9: Structure and Integrative Functions of the Main Organ Systems
9.	Chapter 5: Assemblies of Molecules, Cells, and Groups of Cells Within Multicellular Organisms
10.	Chapter 9: Structure and Integrative Functions of the Main Organ Systems
11.	Chapter 9: Structure and Integrative Functions of the Main Organ Systems
12.	Chapter 8: Structure and Function of the Nervous and Endocrine Systems and Ways in Which These Systems Coordinate the Organ Systems
13.	Chapter 9: Structure and Integrative Functions of the Main Organ Systems
14.	Chapter 8: Structure and Function of the Nervous and Endocrine Systems and Ways in Which These Systems Coordinate the Organ Systems
15.	Chapter 9: Structure and Integrative Functions of the Main Organ Systems
16.	Chapter 9: Structure and Integrative Functions of the Main Organ Systems
17.	Chapter 9: Structure and Integrative Functions of the Main Organ Systems
18.	Chapter 7: Processes of Cell Division, Differentiation, and Specialization
19.	Chapter 3: Transmission of Heritable Information from Generation to Generation and Processes That Increase Genetic Diversity
20.	Chapter 3: Transmission of Heritable Information from Generation to Generation and Processes That Increase Genetic Diversity

(Continued)

Item Number	Content Area
21.	Chapter 3: Transmission of Heritable Information from Generation to Generation and Processes That Increase Genetic Diversity
22.	Chapter 3: Transmission of Heritable Information from Generation to Generation and Processes That Increase Genetic Diversity
23.	Chapter 3: Transmission of Heritable Information from Generation to Generation and Processes That Increase Genetic Diversity
24.	Chapter 3: Transmission of Heritable Information from Generation to Generation and Processes That Increase Genetic Diversity
25.	Chapter 7: Processes of Cell Division, Differentiation, and Specialization
26.	Chapter 9: Structure and Integrative Functions of the Main Organ Systems
27.	Chapter 9: Structure and Integrative Functions of the Main Organ Systems
28.	Chapter 6: Structure, Growth, Physiology, and Genetics of Prokaryotes and Viruses
29.	Chapter 6: Structure, Growth, Physiology, and Genetics of Prokaryotes and Viruses
30.	Chapter 8: Structure and Function of the Nervous and Endocrine Systems and Ways in Which These Systems Coordinate the Organ Systems
31.	Chapter 9: Structure and Integrative Functions of the Main Organ Systems
32.	Chapter 9: Structure and Integrative Functions of the Main Organ Systems
33.	Chapter 9: Structure and Integrative Functions of the Main Organ Systems
34.	Chapter 9: Structure and Integrative Functions of the Main Organ Systems
35.	Chapter 9: Structure and Integrative Functions of the Main Organ Systems
36.	Chapter 3: Transmission of Heritable Information from Generation to Generation and Processes That Increase Genetic Diversity
37.	Chapter 8: Structure and Function of the Nervous and Endocrine Systems and Ways in Which These Systems Coordinate the Organ Systems
38.	Chapter 4: Principles of Bioenergetics and Fuel Molecule Metabolism
39.	Chapter 9: Structure and Integrative Functions of the Main Organ Systems
40.	Chapter 5: Assemblies of Molecules, Cells, and Groups of Cells Within Multicellular Organisms
41.	Chapter 9: Structure and Integrative Functions of the Main Organ Systems
42.	Chapter 8: Structure and Function of the Nervous and Endocrine Systems and Ways in Which These Systems Coordinate the Organ Systems
43.	Chapter 9: Structure and Integrative Functions of the Main Organ Systems
44.	Chapter 9: Structure and Integrative Functions of the Main Organ Systems
45.	Chapter 2: Transmission of Genetic Information from the Gene to the Protein
46.	Chapter 3: Transmission of Heritable Information from Generation to Generation and Processes That Increase Genetic Diversity
47.	Chapter 6: Structure, Growth, Physiology, and Genetics of Prokaryotes and Viruses
48.	Chapter 2: Transmission of Genetic Information from the Gene to the Protein
49.	Chapter 6: Structure, Growth, Physiology, and Genetics of Prokaryotes and Viruses
50.	Chapter 4: Principles of Bioenergetics and Fuel Molecule Metabolism
51.	Chapter 9: Structure and Integrative Functions of the Main Organ Systems
52.	Chapter 6: Structure, Growth, Physiology, and Genetics of Prokaryotes and Viruses
53.	Chapter 6: Structure, Growth, Physiology, and Genetics of Prokaryotes and Viruses
54.	Chapter 4: Principles of Bioenergetics and Fuel Molecule Metabolism

Item Number	Content Area
55.	Chapter 3: Transmission of Heritable Information from Generation to Generation and Processes That Increase Genetic Diversity
56.	Chapter 7: Processes of Cell Division, Differentiation, and Specialization
57.	Chapter 2: Transmission of Genetic Information from the Gene to the Protein
58.	Chapter 2: Transmission of Genetic Information from the Gene to the Protein
59.	Chapter 4: Principles of Bioenergetics and Fuel Molecule Metabolism

Chemical and Physical Foundations of Biological Systems
Item Number Content Area

1.	Chapter 6: The Unique Nature of Water and Its Solutions
	Chapter 9: Structure, Function, and Reactivity of Biologically Relevant Molecules
2.	Chapter 6: The Unique Nature of Water and Its Solutions
	Chapter 9: Structure, Function, and Reactivity of Biologically Relevant Molecules
3.	Chapter 4: Separation and Purification Methods
4.	Chapter 9: Structure, Function, and Reactivity of Biologically Relevant Molecules
5.	Chapter 9: Structure, Function, and Reactivity of Biologically Relevant Molecules
6.	Chapter 1: Translational Motion, Forces, Work, Energy, and Equilibrium in Living Systems
7.	Chapter 2: Importance of Fluids for the Circulation of Blood, Gas Movement, and Gas Exchange
8.	Chapter 3: Electrochemistry and Electrical Circuits and Their Elements
9.	Chapter 7: The Nature of Molecules and Intermolecular Interactions
	Chapter 10: Principles of Chemical Thermodynamics and Kinetics
10.	Chapter 5: Atoms, Nuclear Decay, Electronic Structure, and Atomic Chemical Behavior
11.	Chapter 7: The Nature of Molecules and Intermolecular Interactions
	Chapter 10: Principles of Chemical Thermodynamics and Kinetics
12.	Chapter 7: The Nature of Molecules and Intermolecular Interactions
	Chapter 10: Principles of Chemical Thermodynamics and Kinetics
13.	Chapter 5: Atoms, Nuclear Decay, Electronic Structure, and Atomic Chemical Behavior
14.	Chapter 7: The Nature of Molecules and Intermolecular Interactions
15.	Chapter 4: How Light and Sound Interact with Matter
16.	Chapter 4: How Light and Sound Interact with Matter
17.	Chapter 4: How Light and Sound Interact with Matter
18.	Chapter 4: How Light and Sound Interact with Matter
19.	Chapter 4: How Light and Sound Interact with Matter
20.	Chapter 7: The Nature of Molecules and Intermolecular Interactions
21.	Chapter 9: Structure, Function, and Reactivity of Biologically Relevant Molecules
22.	Chapter 4: How Light and Sound Interact with Matter
23.	Chapter 6: The Unique Nature of Water and Its Solutions
	Chapter 7: The Nature of Molecules and Intermolecular Interactions
24.	Chapter 6: The Unique Nature of Water and Its Solutions
	Chapter 7: The Nature of Molecules and Intermolecular Interactions
25.	Chapter 7: The Nature of Molecules and Intermolecular Interactions

(Continued)

Item Number	Content Area
26.	Chapter 7: The Nature of Molecules and Intermolecular Interactions
27.	Chapter 5: Atoms, Nuclear Decay, Electronic Structure, and Atomic Chemical Behavior
28.	Chapter 7: The Nature of Molecules and Intermolecular Interactions
29.	Chapter 5: Atoms, Nuclear Decay, Electronic Structure, and Atomic Chemical Behavior
30.	Chapter 2: Importance of Fluids for the Circulation of Blood, Gas Movement, and Gas Exchange
31.	Chapter 9: Structure, Function, and Reactivity of Biologically Relevant Molecules
32.	Chapter 9: Structure, Function, and Reactivity of Biologically Relevant Molecules
33.	Chapter 9: Structure, Function, and Reactivity of Biologically Relevant Molecules
34.	Chapter 9: Structure, Function, and Reactivity of Biologically Relevant Molecules
35.	Chapter 9: Structure, Function, and Reactivity of Biologically Relevant Molecules
36.	Chapter 1: Translational Motion, Forces, Work, Energy, and Equilibrium in Living Systems
37.	Chapter 1: Translational Motion, Forces, Work, Energy, and Equilibrium in Living Systems
38.	Chapter 1: Translational Motion, Forces, Work, Energy, and Equilibrium in Living Systems
39.	Chapter 1: Translational Motion, Forces, Work, Energy, and Equilibrium in Living Systems
40.	Chapter 1: Translational Motion, Forces, Work, Energy, and Equilibrium in Living Systems
41.	Chapter 1: Translational Motion, Forces, Work, Energy, and Equilibrium in Living Systems
42.	Chapter 1: Translational Motion, Forces, Work, Energy, and Equilibrium in Living Systems
43.	Chapter 9: Structure, Function, and Reactivity of Biologically Relevant Molecules
44.	Chapter 9: Structure, Function, and Reactivity of Biologically Relevant Molecules
45.	Chapter 9: Structure, Function, and Reactivity of Biologically Relevant Molecules
46.	Chapter 9: Structure, Function, and Reactivity of Biologically Relevant Molecules
47.	Chapter 9: Structure, Function, and Reactivity of Biologically Relevant Molecules
48.	Chapter 9: Structure, Function, and Reactivity of Biologically Relevant Molecules
49.	Chapter 9: Structure, Function, and Reactivity of Biologically Relevant Molecules
50.	Chapter 9: Structure, Function, and Reactivity of Biologically Relevant Molecules
51.	Chapter 9: Structure, Function, and Reactivity of Biologically Relevant Molecules

Item Number	Content Area
52.	Chapter 9: Structure, Function, and Reactivity of Biologically Relevant Molecules
53.	Chapter 6: The Unique Nature of Water and Its Solutions
54.	Chapter 6: The Unique Nature of Water and Its Solutions
55.	Chapter 6: The Unique Nature of Water and Its Solutions
56.	Chapter 6: The Unique Nature of Water and Its Solutions
57.	Chapter 6: The Unique Nature of Water and Its Solutions
58.	Chapter 7: The Nature of Molecules and Intermolecular Interactions
59.	Chapter 7: The Nature of Molecules and Intermolecular Interactions

Psychological, Social, and Biological Foundations of Behavior

Item Number	Content Area
1.	Chapter 1: Sensing the Environment
2.	Chapter 10: Understanding Social Structure
3.	Chapter 5: Social Processes That Influence Human Behavior
4.	Chapter 9: Social Interactions
5.	Chapter 6: Attitude and Behavior Change
6.	Chapter 6: Attitude and Behavior Change
7.	Chapter 6: Attitude and Behavior Change
8.	Chapter 6: Attitude and Behavior Change
9.	Chapter 6: Attitude and Behavior Change
10.	Chapter 7: Self-Identity
11.	Chapter 7: Self-Identity
12.	Chapter 7: Self-Identity
13.	Chapter 7: Self-Identity
14.	Chapter 7: Self-Identity
15.	Chapter 1: Sensing the Environment
16.	Chapter 1: Sensing the Environment
17.	Chapter 1: Sensing the Environment
18.	Chapter 1: Sensing the Environment
19.	Chapter 1: Sensing the Environment
20.	Chapter 5: Social Processes That Influence Human Behavior
21.	Chapter 5: Social Processes That Influence Human Behavior
22.	Chapter 5: Social Processes That Influence Human Behavior
23.	Chapter 5: Social Processes That Influence Human Behavior
24.	Chapter 5: Social Processes That Influence Human Behavior
25.	Chapter 4: Individual Influences on Behavior
26.	Chapter 4: Individual Influences on Behavior
27.	Chapter 4: Individual Influences on Behavior
28.	Chapter 4: Individual Influences on Behavior
29.	Chapter 4: Individual Influences on Behavior
30.	Chapter 9: Social Interactions
31.	Chapter 9: Social Interactions
32.	Chapter 9: Social Interactions
33.	Chapter 9: Social Interactions
34.	Chapter 9: Social Interactions
35.	Chapter 10: Understanding Social Structure
36.	Chapter 10: Understanding Social Structure
37.	Chapter 10: Understanding Social Structure
38.	Chapter 10: Understanding Social Structure

(Continued)

Item Number	Content Area
39.	Chapter 10: Understanding Social Structure
40.	Chapter 11: Demographic Characteristics and Processes
41.	Chapter 11: Demographic Characteristics and Processes
42.	Chapter 11: Demographic Characteristics and Processes
43.	Chapter 11: Demographic Characteristics and Processes
44.	Chapter 11: Demographic Characteristics and Processes
45.	Chapter 12: Social Inequality
46.	Chapter 12: Social Inequality
47.	Chapter 12: Social Inequality
48.	Chapter 12: Social Inequality
49.	Chapter 12: Social Inequality
50.	Chapter 3: Responding to the World
51.	Chapter 3: Responding to the World
52.	Chapter 3: Responding to the World
53.	Chapter 3: Responding to the World
54.	Chapter 3: Responding to the World
55.	Chapter 2: Making Sense of the Environment
56.	Chapter 2: Making Sense of the Environment
57.	Chapter 2: Making Sense of the Environment
58.	Chapter 2: Making Sense of the Environment
59.	Chapter 2: Making Sense of the Environment

MCAT

Practice Test 2

Biological and Biochemical Foundations of Living Systems

59 Questions   **Time Limit: 95 Minutes**

Questions 1–6 are based on the following passage.

Passage I

Maintenance of proper pH throughout the body is critical to homeostasis and is carried out through the collective efforts of multiple systems in the body. Failure of the kidneys or respiratory system can have drastic consequences on the body's ability to regulate blood pH. In order to regulate pH in the blood, a buffering system is used, which is shown. This reaction is completely reversible and is driven in either direction depending on the concentration of the reactants. A change to one item in this reaction will in turn affect the concentration of all of the other items. These reactions are catalyzed by the enzyme carbonic anhydrase:

$$CO_2 + H_2O \rightleftharpoons H_2CO_3 \rightleftharpoons H^+ + HCO_3^-$$

carbon dioxide   water   carbonic acid   bicarbonate ion

Generally, there are not many problems with the body's ability to have plenty of HCO_3^- ions in reserve. However, if HCO_3^- ion levels should become too low, the kidneys can generate more. In the distal convoluted tubule and collecting ducts of the nephrons, carbonic anhydrase converts CO_2 into H_2CO_3, which dissociates into H^+ and HCO_3^-. Kidney failure or damage to the carbonic anhydrase enzyme can cause major problems in the ability to regulate blood pH.

When the kidneys fail, their functions must be mimicked or death will occur. Dialysis is used as a means to perform some of the normal functions of the kidneys, which includes the maintenance of acid-base balance. During dialysis, the patient's blood is exposed to dialysis fluid. The dialysis fluid has been prepared such that it will perform a variety of functions that include balancing blood pH, removing wastes from the blood, and removing excess fluids. While dialysis treatment is not nearly as efficient as natural kidney function, it can be used for extended periods of time in many patients with satisfactory results.

1. Based on the buffering equation shown in the passage, if H^+ ion concentration increased, which of the following would occur?
    A. The concentration of carbonic acid would increase.
    B. The concentration of carbon dioxide would decrease.
    C. Bicarbonate ion concentration would increase.
    D. Carbonic anhydrase activity would be reduced.

2. Increased levels of H_2CO_3 in the plasma should cause:
    A. a decrease in ventilation rate
    B. an increase in ventilation rate
    C. an increase in plasma pH
    D. a decrease in the osmotic concentration of urine

3. Suppose plasma levels of carbon dioxide were elevated. On a cellular level, where does this carbon dioxide come from?
    A. It is produced during protein synthesis.
    B. It is a by-product of nucleic acid metabolism.
    C. It is a by-product of glucose metabolism.
    D. It is produced as a direct conversion from oxygen gas in the cells.

4. Many dialysis patients do not produce any urine, so dialysis must be used to manage their fluid levels. In order to remove excess fluids from the blood during dialysis, the patient's blood must be:
    A. isotonic as compared to the dialysis solution
    B. hypertonic as compared to the dialysis solution
    C. hypotonic as compared to the dialysis solution
    D. the same pH as the dialysis solution

5. A class of drugs known as carbonic anhydrase inhibitors is known to increase the excretion of Na^+, K^+, and HCO_3^- ions via urine while allowing for the retention of H^+ ions. This should cause:
    A. an increase in urine volume due to osmotic effects
    B. a decrease in urine volume due to increased water reabsorption at the distal convoluted tubule
    C. a decrease in urine pH due to the excretion of HCO_3^- ions
    D. no changes to the normal properties of urine since Na^+, K^+, and HCO_3^- ions are normally secreted in the urine

133

SECTION 1:
Biological and
Biochemical
Foundations of
Living Systems

6. One of the goals of dialysis is to remove several small, toxic solutes from the blood. In order for the toxins to move from the blood into the dialysis solution, which of the following processes must occur?
   A. active transport
   B. diffusion
   C. osmosis
   D. facilitated diffusion

Questions 7–12 are based on the following passage.

Passage II

Tuberous sclerosis is a genetic disorder characterized by the growth of benign tumors in the brain and on other organs of the body, including the heart, lungs, skin, and kidneys. The prevalence of the condition is about 1 in every 6000 newborns. The symptoms of the disease are variable in their severity, which may take years to fully develop and are often misdiagnosed. One common symptom seen in many tuberous sclerosis patients is kidney problems such as cysts. While the cysts typically cause no major problems, occasionally the cysts may bleed, which causes blood loss and anemia and may lead to kidney failure.

The disease is caused by mutations in two genes, tuberous sclerosis complex 1 and 2 (TSC1 and TSC2), although only one gene needs to be affected to have the disease. The TSC1 gene produces a protein called hamartin, while the TSC2 gene produces the protein tuberin. Both hamartin and tuberin act as tumor suppressors in the body. A typical pedigree for tuberous sclerosis is shown with affected individuals being shaded:

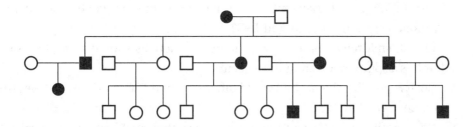

While most cases of tuberous sclerosis are acquired according to the pattern shown in the pedigree, some individuals acquire tuberous sclerosis through a process called gonadal mosaicism. In these cases, the parents do not have apparent mutations in TSC1 or TSC2 in their somatic cells, but they have passed the mutation to their children.

The prognosis for individuals with tuberous sclerosis depends on the severity of their symptoms. Some common symptoms are learning disabilities, seizures, mental retardation, skin abnormalities, and kidney failure. Most individuals with tuberous sclerosis live to a normal life expectancy.

7. Based on the pedigree provided, what is the MOST likely pattern of inheritance for tuberous sclerosis?
   A. sex-linked recessive
   B. sex-linked dominant
   C. autosomal recessive
   D. autosomal dominant

8. If an individual overexpressed both TSC1 and TSC2, you would expect that:
   A. The individual would be likely to develop a severe case of tuberous sclerosis.
   B. The individual should develop a mild case of tuberous sclerosis.
   C. The individual would produce excess hamartin and tuberin to protect against tumor formation.
   D. The individual would produce minimal amounts of hamartin and tuberin, which would allow for some protection against tumor formation.

9. In order for gonadal mosaicism to be the cause of tuberous sclerosis, a mutation must have occurred in the TSC1 or TSC2 gene during:
   A. mitosis in embryonic development
   B. meiosis in embryonic development
   C. mitosis of brain and skin cells during childhood
   D. meiosis in at least one of the parents

10. Would two individuals who had tuberous sclerosis always have children with the disorder?
   A. Yes. If both parents have tuberous sclerosis, all of their gametes will contain mutated versions of TSC1 and TSC2.
   B. Yes. All children of parents with tuberous sclerosis should have the disease unless a spontaneous mutation occurs.
   C. No. It is possible that a child could inherit normal TSC1 and TSC 2 alleles from parents who have the disease.
   D. No. If both parents have tuberous sclerosis, their children will be carriers of the disease but will not display any symptoms of the disease.

11. An individual born with TSC as a result of gonadal mosaicism has parents that do not have the disease. If a pedigree of three or fewer generations were to be constructed for this individual and their family, the pattern of inheritance that would likely be suspected is:
   A. sex-linked recessive
   B. sex-linked dominant
   C. autosomal recessive
   D. autosomal dominant

135

SECTION 1:
Biological and
Biochemical
Foundations of
Living Systems

12. Some tuberous sclerosis patients who develop kidney cysts are often undiagnosed until kidney damage or blood loss and anemia occur. Which of the following problems might a patient with anemia have?
    A. a reduced oxygen-carrying capacity
    B. a high hematocrit count
    C. an elevated erythrocyte count
    D. problems with blood clotting

Questions 13–18 are based on the following passage.

Passage III

The discovery and development of various types of anesthesia have revolutionized modern medicine, allowing many medical procedures to be performed with minimal discomfort to the patient. Local anesthesia is used to induce loss of sensation in a particular area, while general anesthesia is used to induce loss of sensation along with loss of consciousness. Both procaine (also known as novocaine) and lidocaine are drugs used for local anesthesia, and they have similar mechanisms of action. The drugs affect neurons in the local areas to which they are applied by preventing the opening of Na^+ gated channels in the neurons.

Procaine and lidocaine have their own advantages and disadvantages. For example, procaine has the ability to cause vasoconstriction in addition to its analgesic properties. However, lidocaine induces anesthesia faster and for a longer period of time than procaine. In addition to being used as an anesthetic, lidocaine is often used in the treatment of ventricular fibrillation, a condition where the cardiac muscle displays rapid, uncoordinated, and weak rhythms. The drug causes decreased excitability of the ventricles by blocking Na^+ gated channels, while the sinoatrial node in the right atrium is unaffected by the drug.

Procaine has a half-life of up to 0.5 hours in patients. When procaine is metabolized in the body, it is converted to para-aminobenzoic acid (PABA) in the plasma by the enzyme pseudocholinesterase, and PABA is then excreted by the kidneys. Lidocaine is twice as potent as procaine, but lidocaine is also twice as toxic. The half-life of lidocaine in patients is typically between 1.5 and 2 hours. Lidocaine is metabolized in the liver by two enzymes that produce the metabolites monoethylglycinexylidide and glycinexylidide.

13. If lidocaine is provided intravenously to a person with compromised liver function and a person with normal liver function, one hour later you would expect to see:
   A. an increased plasma concentration of lidocaine in the patient with normal liver function as compared to the patient with compromised liver function
   B. a decreased plasma concentration of glycinexylidide in the patient with normal liver function as compared to the patient with compromised liver function
   C. an increased level of monoethylglycinexylidide in the urine of the patient with normal liver function as compared to the patient with compromised liver function
   D. all of the above

14. How would blocking gated Na^+ channels prevent the transmission of messages in nerves?
   A. If gated Na^+ channels are blocked, Na^+ concentrations remain higher inside the neuron than outside of the neuron.
   B. If gated Na^+ channels are blocked, the neuronal membrane cannot depolarize.
   C. Blocking Na^+ channels would prevent the Na^+/K^+ pumps from properly functioning.
   D. Blocking Na^+ channels would prevent neurotransmitters from binding to receptors at the synapse.

15. A neuron under the influence of an anesthetic such as lidocaine would MOST likely:
   A. display decreased neurotransmitter release at the synapse
   B. show increased enzymatic degradation of neurotransmitters in the synapse
   C. show increased reuptake of neurotransmitters in the synapse
   D. display a more negative charge outside the neuron as compared to inside the neuron

16. Which type of neuron would be affected by lidocaine?
   A. motor neurons
   B. interneurons
   C. sensory neurons
   D. glial cells

17. What benefits would come from using an anesthetic such as novocaine, which causes vasoconstriction in addition to analgesic effects, during a surgical procedure?
   A. to keep blood pressure low
   B. to prevent infection
   C. to minimize bleeding during the procedure
   D. to prevent inflammation following the surgery

137

SECTION 1:
Biological and
Biochemical
Foundations of
Living Systems

18. The passage states that when lidocaine is given for ventricular fibrillation the sinoatrial node is unaffected. The sinoatrial node normally functions as:
    A. a valve in the heart
    B. the pacemaker of the heart
    C. the barricade between the right and left side of the heart that keeps oxygenated and deoxygenated blood from mixing
    D. a regulator of blood pressure in the heart

Questions 19–24 are based on the following passage.

Passage IV

Nitric oxide (NO) is a gas that plays important regulatory roles in mammalian processes as diverse as inflammation, blood flow, kidney function, and development. Nitric oxide is created from L-arginine using the enzyme nitric oxide synthase (NOS). In studies using mouse models, NO has been shown to be a critical regulator of early embryo development. Manipulation of NO in the mouse embryo at the two-cell stage of development can prevent further development of the embryo to the blastocyst stage of development.

In order to determine a more specific role for NO in early development, 2-day mouse embryos (composed of two cells) were subjected to treatment by either sodium nitroprusside (SNP) or L-arganine methyl ester (L-NAME). Sodium nitroprusside is a NO donor, while L-NAME is a NOS inhibitor. In addition to a control group, three concentrations of SNP and three concentrations of L-NAME were tested. Each group consisted of 100 embryos. After the appropriate treatment, the number of embryos continuing to the blastocyst stage was counted and reported as follows:

Group	Treatment	Number of Embryos Reaching the Blastocyst Stage
1	Control	84
2	$0.1 \mu M$ SNP	88
3	$1.0 \mu M$ SNP	45
4	$10.0 \mu M$ SNP	0
5	$0.1 \mu M$ L-NAME	52
6	$1.0 \mu M$ L-NAME	35
7	$10.0 \mu M$ L-NAME	9

19. Which of the following would be the MOST appropriate treatment for the control group in this experiment?
    A. treatment with a known amount of SNP associated with a known value of NO needed to continue development
    B. treatment with SNP at a level lower than $0.1 \mu M$
    C. treatment with L-NAME at a dosage higher than $10.0 \mu M$
    D. treatment with neither SNP nor L-NAME

20. Based on the results of these experiments, which of the following conclusions is MOST strongly supported by the data?
    A. Minimal amounts of NO are optimal for development, but increased levels can be harmful.
    B. Increased amounts of NOS lead to the highest rates of embryo survival.
    C. The effects of L-NAME on development are not dose dependent.
    D. Increasing the inhibition of NOS is more detrimental to embryo development than increasing the amount of NO.

21. In order to further investigate the beneficial role of NO on early mouse embryo development, which experimental group should be further investigated?
    A. group 1
    B. group 2
    C. group 4
    D. group 6

22. Considering the fact that mouse development shares many similarities with human development, from which structure would the 2-day-old embryos in this experiment be harvested?
    A. the uterus
    B. the vagina
    C. the oviducts
    D. the ovaries

23. Which of the following BEST characterizes the blastocyst stage of development?
    A. a solid ball composed of many cells that undergo mitosis
    B. a diploid, fertilized egg
    C. a ball of cells containing a fluid-filled cavity
    D. a loosely formed ball of cells that performs meiosis

24. Diabetics typically have lower levels of nitric oxide (NO) than individuals without diabetes. Low levels of NO can be associated with vascular inflammation and vascular damage, leading to reduced blood flow to extremities. Which of the following may help a diabetic patient?
    A. administration of L-NAME
    B. administration of SNP
    C. administration of L-NAME and SNP
    D. administration of SNP and an L-NAME antagonist

Questions 25–30 are based on the following passage.

Passage V

For many years, researchers have been interested in developing edible vaccines that would provide protection against various bacterial and viral diseases. An edible vaccine

139

SECTION 1:
Biological and
Biochemical
Foundations of
Living Systems

is a genetically modified organism (GMO) that is created when genes from the bacteria or virus being vaccinated against are inserted into plant cells. As the plants grow, they produce proteins from the bacteria or virus that the researchers are attempting to vaccinate against. When a person eats the plant, the viral or bacteria proteins serve as antigens, which initiates a primary immune response.

Some of the plants that are of interest in edible vaccine development are bananas, potatoes, tomatoes, corn, rice, tobacco, and soybeans. While early research focused on growing crops that produced edible products such as bananas, the most recent research is focused on extracting material from the leaves and seeds of the plants, dehydrating it, and putting it into capsules that can be swallowed. This allows for a more predictable dosage of the vaccine and eliminates concerns that the crops containing the vaccine would be accidentally eaten by individuals who are not in need of the vaccine. The term *edible vaccine* has now been replaced with the term *plant-derived oral vaccine*.

The development of plant-derived oral vaccines solves many problems associated with injectable vaccines. Because plant-derived oral vaccines are grown in crops, there is no problem with storage or refrigeration that is required of most traditional vaccines. These plant-derived vaccines also require no special training to administer. Additionally, when a vaccine is taken orally, it provides mucosal immunity due to the production of IgA antibodies by the immune system—in addition to systemic immunity. Since 90 percent of diseases enter the body through a mucus membrane, a vaccine that coerces mucosal immunity is of great benefit in the prevention of many diseases.

25. Suppose that an individual has been given a plant-derived oral vaccine against a specific virus. How could you determine whether the vaccine was effective?
    A. Test for the presence of interleukins in the blood of the patient.
    B. Test for the presence of interferons in the blood of the patient.
    C. Test to determine whether the complement system in the blood had been activated.
    D. Test for the presence of antibodies to the viral antigen.

26. In order to engineer a plant-derived oral vaccine, genes from the microbe to be vaccinated against must be placed into the plant genome. Which of the following choices would be the most reasonable way to achieve this goal?
    A. Perform polymerase chain reaction (PCR) to amplify copies of the bacterial or viral genes and then insert the copies into the plant cells by transduction.
    B. Insert the bacterial or viral genes of interest into a plasmid, which can serve as a vector to transfer the gene to the plant cell.
    C. Clone the genes into a bacterial cell and allow it to conjugate with a plant cell.
    D. Use DNA hybridization to allow the genes of interest from the bacterial or viral genome to hybridize with the plant DNA.

27. The goal of any type of vaccination is to induce active immunity without people getting ill from the disease that they are being vaccinated against. In order to have long-term effectiveness, the vaccine must cause the development of which type of cells in the immune system?
    A. cytotoxic T cells
    B. helper T cells
    C. plasma cells
    D. memory cells

28. When a vaccine is given orally, it must pass through the digestive system before being absorbed into the bloodstream, whereas injected vaccines enter the bloodstream directly. What problems might vaccine developers be concerned about with a plant-derived oral vaccine that has to pass through the digestive tract?
    A. There would be concern that the vaccine would not work quickly enough if it had to travel through the digestive tract.
    B. There would be concern that stomach acidity might damage the bacterial or viral proteins that were expressed by the plant cells of the vaccine.
    C. There would be concern that the vaccine might elicit an inflammatory response in the digestive tract.
    D. all of the above

29. Plant-derived oral vaccines produce bacterial or viral proteins that serve as antigens in the body. Which of these events would occur first when a new antigen enters the body?
    A. production of antibodies from plasma cells
    B. presentation of the antigen by a macrophage
    C. secretion of interleukin-2 from helper T cells
    D. attack of the antigen by cytotoxic T cells

30. A traditional vaccine that is administered either intramuscularly or subcutaneously would be expected to cause the formation of which type of antibodies initially following administration?
    A. IgE
    B. IgG
    C. IgM
    D. IgA

Questions 31–36 are based on the following passage.

Passage VI

Interleukins are cytokines or cell-signaling molecules. They come in many varieties and play numerous roles in modulating all aspects of the immune response. Interleukins are produced by many types of cells, and their secretion occurs rapidly, and typically

141

SECTION 1:
Biological and
Biochemical
Foundations of
Living Systems

briefly, as needed. Interleukins travel to target cells where they bind to receptors on the target cell, ultimately causing a cascade of events in the target that alter the behavior of that cell. Different types of microbes stimulate the release of different types of interleukins. The type of interleukins secreted will ultimately influence how the system responds to the infection.

An immunologist suspects that a recently discovered interleukin called interleukin X might be important in protecting against hepatitis C viral (HCV) infection. In order to test this possibility, two strains of mice are used—a knockout strain and a wild-type strain. The strain of knockout mice used in this study has a loss of function mutation in the interleukin X gene. During the experiments to determine whether this new interleukin X might protect against HCV, the mice are exposed to an analog of HCV. Three weeks later, liver biopsies are taken from each of the mice. From the biopsied liver tissues, nucleic acids are extracted and polymerase chain reaction is used to detect the presence of HCV.

In the following data table, you will see data from 10 sets of mice in this experiment. A plus sign (+) indicates that PCR testing detected the presence of HCV and a minus sign (−) indicates that PCR testing did not detect the presence of HCV.

Animal Number	1	2	3	4	5	6	7	8	9	10
Wild-type	−	+	−	−	+	−	−	−	−	−
Knockout	+	+	−	+	+	−	+	−	+	+

31. From the data presented, what can you conclude about the potential for this new interleukin X to protect against HCV infection in mice?
    A. The new interleukin provides no protection against viral infection.
    B. The new interleukin provides complete protection against viral infection.
    C. The new interleukin may provide some level of protection against viral infection.
    D. The new interleukin enhances viral infection.

32. Based on the data shown here, which of the following would provide support for the potential of the new interleukin X to prevent viral infection?
    A. finding that wild-type mice tested negative for HCV in the presence of reduced interleukin X levels
    B. finding that knockout mice tested negative for HCV in the presence of supplemental interleukin X
    C. finding that knockout mice tested negative for HCV in the absence of supplemental interleukin X
    D. finding that wild-type mice tested negative for HCV in the presence of increased interleukin X levels

33. In this experiment, the polymerase chain reaction is used as a means to detect the presence of the hepatitis C virus. How does this technique work?
   A. Targeted primers bind to a specific nucleic acid sequence and amplify that target sequence, if it is present.
   B. It uses primers specific to certain amino acid sequences to determine the presence of specific proteins.
   C. It detects the presence of specific mRNAs to quantify the expression of specific genes.
   D. It detects metabolic activity unique to the target organism it is attempting to detect.

34. Interleukins are just one of many immune modulators. In a typical viral infection, what other immune modulator would you expect to see secreted as part of the innate immune defenses?
   A. interferons
   B. antibodies
   C. growth factors
   D. complement proteins

35. The hepatitis C virus is a single-stranded RNA virus. A potential inhibitor of viral replication would include a substance that is antagonistic to:
   A. DNA polymerase
   B. RNA polymerase
   C. reverse transcriptase
   D. DNA gyrase

36. Suppose that this newly discovered interleukin X is proven to be effective against viral infection. In which of the following cases would we expect an individual to test negative for the hepatitis C virus?
   A. an individual with decreased expression of interleukin X
   B. an individual with decreased expression of the receptor for interleukin X
   C. an individual with increased expression of the receptor for interleukin X
   D. an individual with a mutation in the receptor for interleukin X

Questions 37–42 are based on the following passage.

Passage VII

The process of quorum sensing is observed in a variety of species. It involves a system of communication between organisms that is dependent on population density. Bacteria are notorious for using quorum sensing (QS) via the secretion of secreted signaling molecules, called autoinducers (AI), to coordinate their gene expression once a threshold density of population is reached. Not only can bacteria communicate via QS within their species, but they can also cross-talk through QS between different

143

SECTION 1:
Biological and
Biochemical
Foundations of
Living Systems

species. In order to participate in quorum sensing, bacteria require a way to produce an autoinducer and a way to respond to autoinducers via binding to specific receptors.

One example of how bacteria use quorum sensing to their advantage is to regulate the gene expression of virulence factors. During infection, if a small number of bacteria were to express their virulence factors, this would largely have no impact on the host. Instead, bacteria wait until a quorum is reached in terms of population size, indicating that the population is large enough to express virulence factors. These virulence factors relate to such abilities as escaping the immune response, invasion, and spreading within the host.

We know that we are facing a current healthcare crisis related to the loss of effectiveness of many traditional types of antibiotics based on bacterial resistance. This provides a major impetus for identifying novel ways to target bacterial pathogens that avoid the use of antibiotics. Several chemical compounds and molecules have been identified as facilitators of quorum sensing inhibition. Typically, these factors can serve as signal-targeting enzymes or small-molecule inhibitors of signal synthases and receptors.

37. Autoinducers often act in positive feedback loops. This would mean that the production of an autoinducer would lead to:
    A. the production of more autoinducer
    B. the production of less autoinducer
    C. upregulation of autoinducer receptors
    D. downregulation of autoinducer receptors

38. What sort of advantage would quorum sensing provide to bacterial populations as compared to the organisms within the population acting independently of one another?
    A. Quorum sensing allows bacteria to express genes collectively when the impact of those gene products will be maximized on their host.
    B. Quorum sensing allows individual bacteria to express a higher level of virulence than they could when acting in the absence of quorum sensing.
    C. Quorum sensing reduces the metabolic expenses for the majority of the population while increasing metabolic expenses for just a few members of the population.
    D. Quorum sensing allows members of a population to outcompete other populations for resources within the host.

39. Decreased density of a bacterial population should lead to:
    A. increased expression of autoinducers
    B. decreased expression of autoinducers
    C. increased expression of virulence
    D. increased enzymatic degradation of autoinducers

40. Quorum sensing is used frequently within populations of bacteria such as *Pseudomonas aeruginosa* that form biofilms within their host. Once a quorum is reached, expression of the genes required for biofilm formation occurs. From the bacterial perspective, what direct advantage does the formation of biofilms provide?

   A. It provides a strong attachment to surfaces of the host.

   B. It enhances virulence expression of the organisms involved in the biofilm.

   C. It provides increased resistance to antibiotics.

   D. It enhances the secretions of toxins.

41. N-Acyl homoserine lactones (N-AHLs) are one type of autoinducer produced by certain species of bacteria. Different types of bacteria can produce N-AHLs with unique molecular structures by making minor changes to the core structure of the molecule. Given the structure of the molecule, what would be the MOST likely way they could do this?

   A. by altering the R group side chains

   B. by altering fatty acid chains

   C. by glycosylating the core structure

   D. by methylating the core structure

42. Targets of traditional antibiotics include all of the following EXCEPT:

   A. ribosomes

   B. metabolic processes

   C. the cell wall

   D. the nucleus

Questions 43–48 are based on the following passage.

Passage VIII

Genetically modified (GM) foods contain DNA from more than one source. The goal of creating GM foods is to modify the organisms to express new and useful traits. A few examples involve engineering crops to be resistant to bacterial or viral infections, to be resistant to herbicides, to ripen more slowly, to survive extreme temperature changes, to contain vaccines, or to create crops that are more nutritious.

One GM food that has received media attention over the years is golden rice. This GM product was first introduced in 2000 and was engineered to provide carotene that is a precursor to vitamin A. The carotene in the rice provides the golden color. Vitamin A deficiency is a major problem in underdeveloped parts of the world, killing more than one million people a year, most of whom are children. This vitamin is critical for the development and maintenance of epithelial tissues, for vision, and for growth.

Rice plants normally produce carotene in the inedible parts of the plant. To be able to access and use the carotene, it was necessary to engineer the rice to produce it in the edible grains. In order to achieve this goal, two genes from daffodil plants, *psy* and *lyc*,

145

SECTION 1:
Biological and
Biochemical
Foundations of
Living Systems

and a bacterial gene called *crt1* were added to the rice genome. These genes engineered a pathway that produces lycopene, which is eventually converted to carotene. Each of these genes was placed under the control of a grain-specific promoter so that the products were produced in the rice grains.

While golden rice was produced to provide carotene, which the human body can convert into the essential vitamin A, the rice provided much less carotene than was anticipated. Golden rice 2, a modified version released in 2005, contains a much larger amount of carotene and, as such, is a better source of the vitamin. Field tests were conducted in 2009, and human consumption trials were completed in 2012. However, neither version has been grown in large-scale quantities at this time.

43. Genetically modified organisms (GMOs) can be produced in a variety of ways. In the case of golden rice, genes from the daffodil plant and bacteria were added to the rice genome. Which of the following would be necessary to remove the genes from these other organisms so that they could be added to rice?
    A. reverse transcriptase
    B. a viral vector
    C. restriction enzymes
    D. polymerase chain reaction

44. The engineering of golden rice to have several exogenous genes that can be induced under the control of a single promoter would MOST resemble:
    A. an operon system
    B. hybridized DNA
    C. a vector
    D. Okazaki fragments

45. When preparing GM organisms, it can be easier to get a eukaryotic cell to express bacterial genes than it is to get a bacterial cell to express eukaryotic genes. What might be the MOST reasonable explanation for this?
    A. Bacteria are more simplistic organisms, and it is more difficult to get them to express complex eukaryotic genes.
    B. The ribosomes of bacteria are different from eukaryotic ribosomes, and they have difficulty translating eukaryotic mRNA.
    C. Eukaryotic genes contain introns that must be spliced out prior to translation in order to make a functional protein. Bacteria lack the ability to perform RNA splicing.
    D. Bacterial cells recognize eukaryotic DNA as foreign and use nucleases to destroy it before it can be expressed.

46. An example of an epithelial tissue that might be produced and maintained by vitamin A would be:
    A. epidermal tissue
    B. skeletal muscle
    C. adipose tissue
    D. bone

47. Genetically modified organisms, typically plants, are being developed as a means of administering vaccines. If these transgenic plants are to be successful as vaccines, they will need to:
    A. stimulate inflammation in the recipient
    B. express antigens to stimulate adaptive defenses in the recipient
    C. contain antibodies to the organism being vaccinated against
    D. contain memory cells against the organism being vaccinated against

48. A typical GM organism (GMO) would have _____ genes as compared to its non-GM organism equivalent.
    A. the same number of
    B. one or a few less
    C. one or a few more
    D. a lot more

Questions 49–59 are not associated with a passage.

49. The major constituent of blood plasma is:
    A. protein
    B. NaCl
    C. water
    D. cholesterol

50. The hormone responsible for maintaining control of water balance in the human body is:
    A. antidiuretic hormone
    B. luteinizing hormone
    C. adrenocorticotropic hormone
    D. growth hormone

51. The one principal effect *not* attributed to the hormone insulin is:
    A. glycogen formation and storage
    B. conversion of glycogen into glucose
    C. carbohydrate oxidation
    D. inhibition of gluconeogenesis

147

SECTION 1:
Biological and
Biochemical
Foundations of
Living Systems

52. Venous blood coming from the head area in humans returns to the heart through which major vessel?
    A. superior vena cava
    B. aorta
    C. hepatic portal vein
    D. carotid artery

53. During pulmonary gas exchange, oxygen and carbon dioxide always move:
    A. into the alveoli
    B. into the blood
    C. from high to low concentration
    D. out of the blood

54. Prokaryotic and eukaryotic cells generally have which of the following structures in common?
    A. a membrane-bound nucleus
    B. a cell wall made of cellulose
    C. ribosomes
    D. linear chromosomes made of DNA

55. A person is on medication to increase the pH of the stomach. A side effect is that the increased pH causes the normal stomach enzymes to be unable to function. Which component of this person's diet may NOT be completely digested?
    A. proteins
    B. nucleic acids
    C. fats
    D. carbohydrates

56. An extracellular matrix is characteristic of:
    A. nervous tissue
    B. muscle tissue
    C. connective tissue
    D. epithelial tissue

57. Which of these statements BEST explains why your body prefers to perform aerobic respiration as opposed to anaerobic respiration?
    A. Anaerobic respiration does not allow for NADH to be recycled to NAD^+.
    B. Aerobic respiration requires less of an ATP investment than anaerobic respiration.
    C. Aerobic respiration produces far more ATP than anaerobic respiration.
    D. Aerobic respiration is easier for cells to perform than anaerobic respiration.

58. In Mendel's experiments with the pea plant, the gene for height exists in two allelic forms designated T for tall stature and t for short stature. In the second generation of a cross between a homozygous tall parent (TT) and a homozygous short parent (tt), the phenotypic ratio of dominant to recessive pea plants is:

    A. 1:1

    B. 2:1

    C. 3:1

    D. 4:1

59. When a nonsteroid (peptide) hormone binds to a receptor on the cell surface:

    A. The hormone moves into the nucleus where it influences gene expression.

    B. The hormone-receptor complex moves into the cytoplasm.

    C. A second messenger forms within the cell.

    D. The cell becomes inactive.

STOP. This is the end of Section 1.

Chemical and Physical Foundations of Biological Systems

59 Questions   **Time Limit: 95 Minutes**

Questions 1 and 2 are not associated with a passage.

1. Frogs are vertebrates that rely on their leaping ability for mobility and survival. Assuming frogs demonstrate a parabolic trajectory as they leap, which of the following graphs best describes the horizontal and vertical components of the velocity, v, of the frog as a function of time, t?

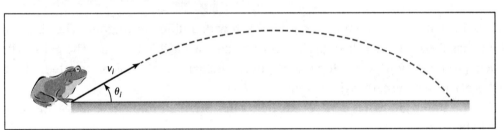

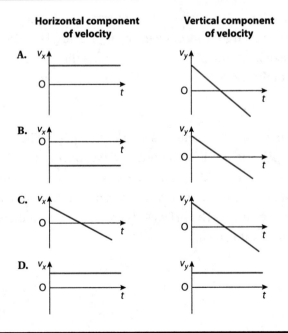

2. To restore cardiac function to a heart attack victim, a cardiac defibrillator is applied to the chest in an attempt to stimulate electrical activity of the heart and initiate the heartbeat. Consider a cardiac defibrillator with a capacitor charged to approximately 6000 V. Assuming the capacitor has a capacitance of 30 μF, the energy released by the capacitor upon discharge of the defibrillator is:

   A. 320 J
   B. 540 J
   C. 750 J
   D. 820 J

Questions 3–7 are based on the following passage.

Passage I

Amino acids are amphiprotic molecules; they contain a carboxylic acid group and a basic amino group. The structure of an α-amino acid can be represented by the structure:

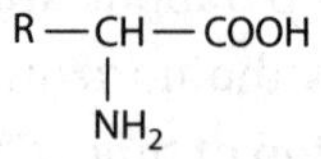

$$R-CH-COOH$$
$$\mid$$
$$NH_2$$

There are 20 common amino acids, each with a different R group. The simplest one has R = H and is called glycine. Glycine has two acidic protons. The carboxylic acid proton is more acidic. It has a pK_a of 2.4. Below this pH, it is protonated. Above this pH, it is in the carboxylate form.

The amino group has a pK_a of 9.8. Below this pH, it is protonated; above this pH it is in the form NH_2.

Every amino acid has a form called the zwitterion, which contains both a positive charge and a negative charge, and net zero charge. The pH at which the zwitterion exists is called the isoelectronic pH, or pI. The pI for a diprotic amino acid is found by taking the average of the pK_a's.

Experiment

A 50.0-mL sample of 0.050 M glycine was acidified to pH 2. Then it was titrated with 0.10 M NaOH. The pH was monitored continuously during the titration using a pH meter. The base was added in 1.0-mL increments until pH 3.0; then it was added in 0.30-mL increments until pH 8.0, when the volume of base added was changed to 1.0-mL increments once more. The pH was recorded after each increment was added, and the titration curve was drawn.

151

SECTION 2:
Chemical and
Physical
Foundations of
Biological Systems

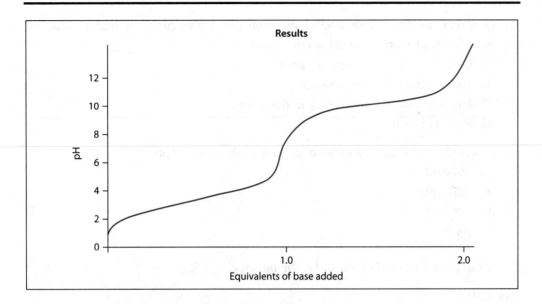

The flattish areas of the titration curve are called buffer zones. Here the pH does not change much upon addition of small amounts of acid or base.

Buffers are necessary in the body because all of our enzymes require a very narrow range of pH for maximum effectiveness.

3. There are two endpoints for this titration. The pH's for those points are:
    A. 2 and 10
    B. 2 and 6
    C. 6 and 10
    D. 6 and 12

4. Which of the following BEST represents the structure of the molecule at pH 2?

    A.
    $$R-CH-COOH$$
    $$|$$
    $$NH_2$$

    B.
    $$R-CH-COOH$$
    $$|$$
    $$NH_3^+$$

    C.
    $$R-CH-COO^-$$
    $$|$$
    $$NH_3^+$$

    D.
    $$R-CH-COO^-$$
    $$|$$
    $$NH_2$$

5. At which of the given pH values does the zwitterion exist?
    A. pH 2
    B. pH 6
    C. pH 10
    D. pH 12

6. Why was the procedure altered between pH 3 and pH 8 by adding 0.30-mL increments instead of 1.0-mL increments?

   A. Less base was needed in this area.

   B. The slope is steeper in this area.

   C. The acid reacts more quickly in this area.

   D. None of the above

7. What volume of NaOH was needed to reach the first endpoint?

   A. 50.0 mL

   B. 25.0 mL

   C. 12.5 mL

   D. 100.0 mL

Questions 8–14 are based on the following passage.

Passage II

A motion sensor, a device that relies on sound to continuously determine the changing location of an object, is used to graphically display its motion in terms of velocity versus time and acceleration versus time graphs.

For example, if the person walks away from the motion sensor, the resulting distance versus time graph will be displayed:

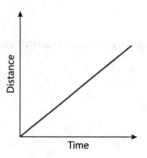

153

SECTION 2:
Chemical and
Physical
Foundations of
Biological Systems

The velocity of the person moving away from the motion sensor at the same rate can be determined by calculating the slope of the graph:

$$\text{velocity} = \text{slope of distance versus time graph} = \frac{\text{rise}}{\text{run}} = \frac{\text{change in distance}}{\text{change in time}}$$

The acceleration of the person can be determined in the same way by calculating the time rate of change of velocity.

A person performs the following series of movements in front of the motion sensor:

➤ *Activity 1:* Starting directly in front of the motion sensor, walk away from the sensor slowly, stand still, and then continue walking away from the sensor slowly.

➤ *Activity 2:* First standing still directly in front of the motion sensor, walk away from the sensor quickly, stand still, and then walk away from the sensor slowly.

➤ *Activity 3:* Standing approximately 3 meters in front of the motion sensor, walk toward the sensor quickly, stand still, and then walk away from the sensor quickly.

➤ *Activity 4:* Standing approximately 3 meters in front of the motion sensor, walk toward the sensor quickly; then move toward the sensor slowly and then stand still.

8. For the person standing directly in front and walking away from the sensor at a steady pace, the velocity versus time graph would be represented by which graph?

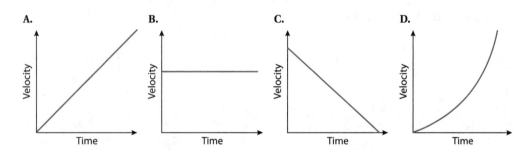

9. For the person standing directly in front of and walking away from the sensor at a steady pace, the acceleration versus time graph would be represented by which graph?

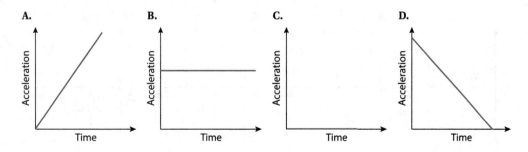

10. If the person were standing approximately 3 meters from the sensor and walked toward the sensor at a steady pace, the distance versus time graph would be represented by which graph?

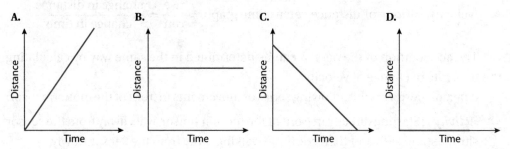

11. For the tasks performed in *Activity 1*, the distance versus time graph would be represented by which graph?

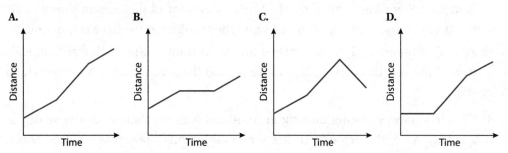

12. For the tasks performed in *Activity 2*, the distance versus time graph would be represented by which graph?

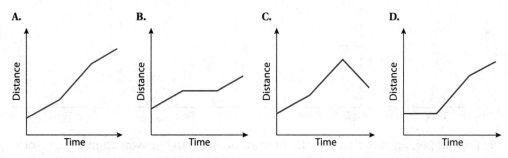

13. For the tasks performed in *Activity 3*, the velocity versus time graph would be represented by which graph?

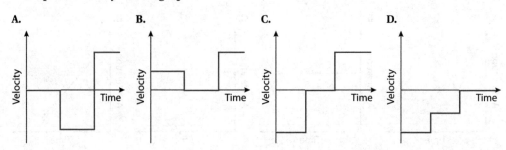

155

SECTION 2:
Chemical and
Physical
Foundations of
Biological Systems

14. For the tasks performed in *Activity 4*, the velocity versus time graph would be represented by which graph?

A. **B.** **C.** **D.**

Questions 15–19 are based on the following passage.

Passage III

The following reaction was carried out according to the narrative experimental shown:

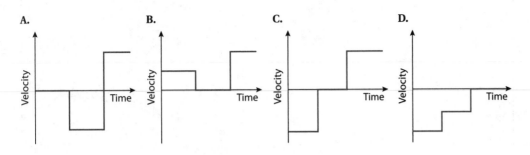

Substance	MW (g/mol)	d (g/mL)
Benzoic acid (**1**)	122.0	–
Thionyl chloride	119.0	1.631
(*S*)-2-methyl-1-butanol (**2**)	88.2	0.819
Dichloromethane	84.9	1.325
(*S*)-2-methylbutyl benzoate (**3**)	192.0	0.992

(*S*)-2-Methylbutyl benzoate (2). Benzoic acid (1.58 g) was dissolved in dichloromethane (20 mL) at room temperature. This solution was treated with thionyl chloride (1.04 mL) and allowed to stir for 45 min, after which (*S*)-2-methyl-1-butanol (1.19 mL) was added. After stirring for 1 hour, the reaction mixture was transferred to a separatory funnel and washed with deionized water (30 mL). The organic phase was collected, dried over sodium sulfate, and concentrated in vacuo to give a crude mixture (1.92 g) that was analyzed by thin-layer chromatography (TLC 1), which showed the product was impure.

The crude mixture was dissolved in dichloromethane (30 mL), returned to the separatory funnel, and subjected to a second aqueous wash. The organic phase was collected, dried over sodium sulfate, and concentrated in vacuo to give a pure product (1.49 g) according to thin-layer chromatography (TLC 2). The pure product was also analyzed by IR spectroscopy.

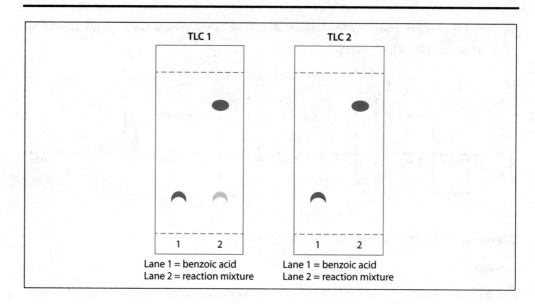

TLC 1

TLC 2

1   2

Lane 1 = benzoic acid
Lane 2 = reaction mixture

1   2

Lane 1 = benzoic acid
Lane 2 = reaction mixture

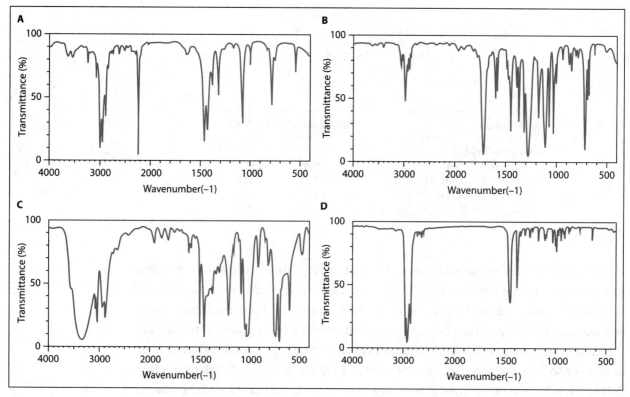

15. When the crude reaction mixture was returned to the separatory funnel for a second aqueous wash, the aqueous phase MOST effective for providing a pure product would be:

   A. deionized water alone
   B. 1 M hydrochloric acid
   C. 1 M sodium hydroxide
   D. saturated sodium chloride

157

SECTION 2:
Chemical and
Physical
Foundations of
Biological Systems

16. The yield of this reaction is:
    A. 60% of theory
    B. 70% of theory
    C. 80% of theory
    D. 90% of theory

17. The IR spectrum MOST likely derived from the product of this reaction is:
    A. Spectrum A
    B. Spectrum B
    C. Spectrum C
    D. Spectrum D

18. If the amount of (S)-2-methyl-1-butanol were increased, how would the rate of the reaction be affected?
    A. The rate would increase.
    B. The rate would decrease.
    C. The rate would be unaffected.
    D. It is impossible to predict the effect on rate.

19. The role of thionyl chloride in this reaction is to:
    A. act as an acid catalyst
    B. act as a base catalyst
    C. convert the acid to a more reactive species
    D. convert the alcohol to a more reactive species

Question 20 is not associated with a passage.

20. Which of the following is the MOST stable conformation of chlorocyclohexane?

    A.

    B.

    C.

    D.

Questions 21–25 are based on the following passage.

Passage IV

Valine can be synthesized via the Strecker synthesis using isobutyraldehyde, as shown here:

In one particular synthesis, step 2 was incomplete, so a mixture of compounds 2 and 3 was encountered at the end. For purification, the reaction mixture was transferred to a separatory funnel and shaken with dichloromethane and 1M NaOH, after which the dichloromethane settled to the bottom.

21. In step 1 of the Strecker synthesis, isobutyraldehyde functions as a(n):
    A. oxidizing agent
    B. reducing agent
    C. nucleophile
    D. electrophile

22. Step 2 of the Strecker synthesis is BEST described as a(n):
    A. oxidation
    B. reduction
    C. hydrolysis
    D. condensation

23. The valine synthesized in the Strecker synthesis is BEST described as:
    A. achiral and optically active
    B. achiral and optically inactive
    C. a racemic mixture and optically active
    D. a racemic mixture and optically inactive

24. In the separatory funnel, compound 2 is MOST likely:
    A. charged and in the top layer
    B. charged and in the bottom layer
    C. neutral and in the top layer
    D. neutral and in the bottom layer

25. The BEST IUPAC name for compound 2 is:
    A. 2-amino-3-methylbutanenitrile
    B. 2-cyano-3-methylpropanamine
    C. 2-(methylethyl)-2-aminoethanenitrile
    D. 1-cyano-1-(methylethyl)methanamine

Questions 26–28 are not associated with a passage.

26. In a direct current circuit, a voltage gradient, ΔV, generates and pushes current, I, through a wire of resistance, R, according to Ohm's law or $\Delta V = IR$. Ohm's law can analogously be applied to blood flow, Q, through a vessel of length, L, by the presence of a pressure gradient, ΔP. In this case, the variables involved in blood flow are related by Poiseuille's law or $Q = \dfrac{\pi r^4}{8\eta L}\Delta P$. Given this, which of the following scenarios would result in the smallest resistance of blood flow?
    A. double the length and double the radius
    B. double the length and halve the radius
    C. halve the length and double the radius
    D. halve the length and halve the radius

159

SECTION 2:
Chemical and
Physical
Foundations of
Biological Systems

27. For an individual who is myopic, or nearsighted, the eyeball is longer than normal, causing visual images to be focused in front of the retina. Myopia can be corrected by:
    A. using a concave lens, which increases the focal length
    B. using a convex lens, which increases the focal length
    C. using a concave lens, which reduces the focal length
    D. using a convex lens, which reduces the focal length

28. Xenon-133, a radionuclide with a half-life of 5.25 days, is often used to assess pulmonary ventilation. If a dose of 28 mCi (millicuries) is administered to a patient in such a study, the radionuclide activity measured after 7 days is:
    A. 1 mCi
    B. 5 mCi
    C. 8 mCi
    D. 11 mCi

Questions 29–33 are based on the following passage.

Passage V

A student performed qualitative tests on a series of unknown chemicals in order to identify them. The unknowns included $NaCl$, $NaHCO_3$, sugar ($C_{12}H_{22}O_{11}$), $MgSO_4$, $Na_2S_2O_3$, cornstarch, and chalk ($CaCO_3$). These are all household chemicals. $MgSO_4$ is Epsom salts, $NaHCO_3$ is baking soda, and $Na_2S_2O_3$ is photographic fixer. The student was asked to identify six unknowns: A, B, C, D, E, and F.

   The qualitative tests were based on the following:
➤ Solubility in water: starch is insoluble, as well as one of the other compounds. The rest are soluble in water.
➤ Chalk produces a gas when treated with acid.
➤ Starch turns blue when treated with iodine.
➤ $MgSO_4$ produces a milky precipitate when treated with aqueous ammonia.
➤ $NaHCO_3$ turns pink when treated with phenolphthalein.
➤ $Na_2S_2O_3$ decolorizes iodine solution.
➤ $NaCl$ conducts electricity in solution.
➤ Sugar does not conduct electricity in solution.

   The student prepared a flowchart that would aid in doing the experiments in a systematic manner and allow efficient identification of the unknowns.

Experiment

The experiments were conducted in the following order. The solubility of each chemical in water was tested first. From those results, the insoluble unknowns were tested next. The unknowns that were soluble in water were tested as aqueous solutions, rather than on the solid samples. First these solutions were treated with ammonia. Those that did not react with ammonia were tested further, with phenolphthalein and then iodine. From these results, the unknowns that had not reacted with any reagent were then tested for conductivity.

Results

Unknown	Solub	Conductivity	Acid	Phenolphthalein	NH_3	I_2
A	Y	Y	N	N	N	N
B	N	Y	Y	N	N	N
C	Y	Y	N	N	Y	N
D	N	N	N	N	N	Y_{BLUE}
E	Y	Y	Y	Y	N	N
F	Y	Y	N	N	N	$Y_{COLORLESS}$

From these results the student was able to identify all six unknowns.

29. Which of the following unknowns, when 1 mole was placed in enough water to make 10.0 liters of solution, showed the least increase in entropy?
    A. $NaHCO_3$
    B. $Na_2S_2O_3$
    C. $CaCO_3$
    D. $MgSO_4$

30. Unknown C was determined to be:
    A. $NaHCO_3$
    B. $Na_2S_2O_3$
    C. $CaCO_3$
    D. $MgSO_4$

31. Unknown A was determined to be:
    A. $CaCO_3$
    B. NaCl
    C. $Na_2S_2O_3$
    D. starch

32. The pK_a of the phenolphthalein used in testing the salts is 9.3. In a separate experiment involving a titration, phenolphthalein is used. For which of the following titrations is phenolphthalein BEST suited?
    A. strong base with a weak acid
    B. weak base with a strong acid
    C. weak base with a weak base
    D. all of the above

161

SECTION 2:
Chemical and
Physical
Foundations of
Biological Systems

33. The milky precipitate formed when $MgSO_4$ reacts with aqueous ammonia solution is $Mg(OH)_2$. Enough magnesium sulfate is used to saturate a solution that, when tested with a pH indicator strip, has a resulting pH of 10. What is the approximate K_{sp} of magnesium hydroxide?
    A. 10^{-12}
    B. 10^{-8}
    C. 10^{-4}
    D. 10^{-3}

Questions 34–38 are based on the following passage.

Passage VI

Plants are able to perform all of the necessary functions and processes to maintain life through photosynthesis—the biochemical conversion of sunlight to the important nutrient, sugar, and the uptake of water through its roots. The uptake of water from the roots, through the stem, and into the tissue of the plant occurs via capillary action—the motion of fluid through extremely small vessels or tubes. Capillary action involves the interaction of the following two types of forces: adhesive forces that allow the water's molecules to adhere or stick to the plant tissues and cohesive forces that provide an attraction between water molecules. Upward movement of the water through the capillary vessels occurs when the adhesive forces are greater than the cohesive forces. The height, h, that the water will ascend up the plant depends upon the surface tension, T, of the water according to the equation:

$$h = \frac{2T}{\rho g r}$$

where ρ is the density of water ($= 1000 \, \text{kg/m}^3$), g is the acceleration due to gravity ($= 9.8 \, \text{m/s}^2$), and r is the radius of the plant stem.

To explore capillary action, the following experiment was conducted to determine the effects of sugar in water transported up the stem of identical carnation flowers. Three beakers were each filled with 0.5 L of water. One beaker (beaker 1) was set aside with no sugar added to the water. Fifteen grams of sugar was added to the water in the second beaker (beaker 2), and 30 grams of sugar was added to the water in the third beaker (beaker 3). Also added to each beaker were 10 drops of red food dye. A carnation was placed in each beaker and observed at 2-hour intervals, marking the height of the dye in the carnation stem. The data are presented in the following table:

Time (hr)	Height of Dye (cm) Beaker 1: No Sugar	Height of Dye (cm) Beaker 2: 15 g Sugar	Height of Dye (cm) Beaker 3: 30 g Sugar
0	0	0	0
2	2.41	0.32	0.15
4	4.17	1.69	0.80
6	5.93	3.06	1.45
8	7.69	4.43	2.10

34. Given that the radius of a carnation stem is 2.5 mm, the surface tension of the water required to reach a height of 8 cm is:
    A. 0.01 N/m
    B. 0.10 N/m
    C. 1.00 N/m
    D. 10.00 N/m

35. The experiment showed that the dye in beaker 1 with no sugar traveled higher up the stem than the dye in beakers 2 and 3, each with increasing amounts of sugar placed in the water. What would be the BEST explanation for the results seen by the experiment?
    A. weight of the water
    B. length of the stem
    C. size of the beaker
    D. type of plant stem

36. For the carnation placed in beaker 3, the hourly rate of ascension of the dye up the carnation stem is approximately:
    A. 0.13
    B. 0.28
    C. 0.69
    D. 0.95

37. For the carnation in beaker 1, the height that the dye will reach after 10 hours would be:
    A. 7.8 cm
    B. 8.4 cm
    C. 9.7 cm
    D. 10.5 cm

38. For the carnation in beaker 2, how long would it take for the dye to reach 10 cm?
    A. 15 hours
    B. 16 hours
    C. 17 hours
    D. 18 hours

Questions 39–43 are based on the following passage.

Passage VII

The treatment of 2-chlorohexane with sodium methoxide or sodium *t*-butoxide at 100 °C leads to a mixture of products, including an S_N2-derived ether and two regio-isomeric alkenes (products of E2 elimination), as shown in the following diagram:

ether   terminal alkene   internal alkene

163

SECTION 2:
Chemical and
Physical
Foundations of
Biological Systems

R	% Ether	% Terminal	% Internal
Me	35	22	44
t-Bu	10	79	11

In both cases, alkene products dominate. However, when t-butoxide is used, the S_N2 product drops from more than a third of the reaction mixture to 10%, and the terminal alkene becomes the major product (versus the internal alkene in the case of methoxide).

39. Which property of t-butoxide (versus methoxide) is the most significant factor in the lower yield of ether?
    A. higher pK_a
    B. increased steric bulk
    C. decreased solvation
    D. higher molar heat capacity

40. For the reaction with methoxide:
    A. The terminal alkene is the kinetic product and the thermodynamic product.
    B. The terminal alkene is the kinetic product; the internal alkene is the thermodynamic product.
    C. The internal alkene is the kinetic product; the terminal alkene is the thermodynamic product.
    D. The internal alkene is the kinetic product and the thermodynamic product.

41. For the reaction with t-butoxide:
    A. The terminal alkene is the kinetic product and the thermodynamic product.
    B. The terminal alkene is the kinetic product; the internal alkene is the thermodynamic product.
    C. The internal alkene is the kinetic product; the terminal alkene is the thermodynamic product.
    D. The internal alkene is the kinetic product and the thermodynamic product.

42. What would be the most reasonable product distribution from the reaction of 2-chlorohexane with isopropoxide at 100 °C?
    A. 40% ether; 40% terminal alkene; 20% internal alkene
    B. 40% ether; 20% terminal alkene; 40% internal alkene
    C. 20% ether; 30% terminal alkene; 50% internal alkene
    D. 20% ether; 50% terminal alkene; 30% internal alkene

43. What would be the most reasonable product distribution from the reaction of 1-chlorohexane with methoxide at 100 °C?
    A. 50% ether; 0% terminal alkene; 50% internal alkene
    B. 50% ether; 50% terminal alkene; 0% internal alkene
    C. 25% ether; 25% terminal alkene; 50% internal alkene
    D. 25% ether; 50% terminal alkene; 25% internal alkene

Questions 44–48 are based on the following passage.

Passage VIII

Visible light is electromagnetic waves that travel at a constant speed of $c = 3.0 \times 10^8 \frac{m}{s}$ and range in wavelength from 400 nm (violet) to 700 nm (red). As light travels from one medium to another, light changes direction or refracts, a phenomenon that is important in image formation. All transparent media, such as air, water, glass, and oil, are characterized by an index of refraction, a value that indicates the amount by which the speed of light through that medium slows down. The index of refraction is defined as:

$$n = \frac{c}{v} = \frac{\text{speed of light in vacuum}}{\text{speed of light in medium}}$$

As light passes from one medium (medium 1) to another medium (medium 2), the angle of refraction of light through medium 2 (as measured with respect to the normal or vertical axis) is related to the angle of incidence of light through medium 1 through Snell's law of refraction:

$$n_1 \sin \theta_1 = n_2 \sin \theta_2$$

This is depicted in the following figure:

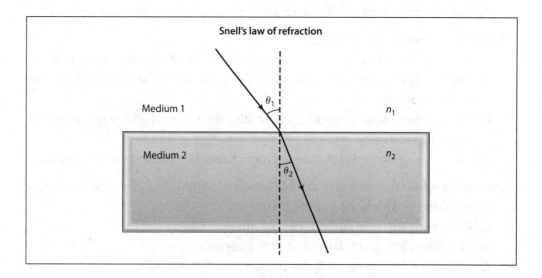

Refraction is important in image formation in the human eye. In the normal vision process, light passes through air ($n_\text{air} = 1.000$) and enters the eyeball through the cornea ($n_\text{cornea} = 1.376$), as shown in the following figure:

165

SECTION 2:
Chemical and
Physical
Foundations of
Biological Systems

Schematic diagram of the human eye

Air
$n = 1.000$

Cornea
$n = 1.376$

Lens
$n = 1.406$

Vitreous
humor
$n = 1.337$

Aqueous
humor
$n = 1.336$

From the cornea, light enters the aqueous humor ($n_{aqueous\ humor} = 1.336$), passes through the lens of the eye ($n_{lens} = 1.406$), and enters a chamber filled with vitreous humor ($n_{vitreous\ humor} = 1.337$), where it then strikes the retina or the screen where the image is formed.

44. Red light of the visible spectrum has a wavelength of 700 nm. The frequency of red light is:
   A. 2.0×10^{14} Hz
   B. 4.0×10^{14} Hz
   C. 2.0×10^{17} Hz
   D. 4.0×10^{17} Hz

45. The speed of light as it travels through the aqueous humor is:
   A. $1.8 \times 10^8 \frac{m}{s}$
   B. $2.0 \times 10^8 \frac{m}{s}$
   C. $2.2 \times 10^8 \frac{m}{s}$
   D. $3.0 \times 10^8 \frac{m}{s}$

46. The speed of light is slowest when it passes through the:
   A. aqueous humor
   B. lens
   C. cornea
   D. vitreous humor

47. If light is incident at 28° through air, the angle it is refracted through the cornea is:
   A. 10°
   B. 14°
   C. 17°
   D. 20°

48. The majority of light refraction occurs in the human eye at the interface between:
   A. air–cornea
   B. cornea–aqueous humor
   C. aqueous humor–lens
   D. lens–vitreous humor

Questions 49–54 are based on the following passage.

Passage IX

The familiar 3% solution of hydrogen peroxide found in the local drugstore decomposes over time to form water and oxygen gas. The equation is:

$$H_2O_2 \ (aq) \rightarrow 2H_2O \ (l) + O_2 \ (g)$$

As the oxygen forms, the mass of the liquid H_2O_2 decreases. The mass difference is equivalent to the mass of oxygen that forms. This reaction occurs very slowly but can be sped up by the addition of a catalyst such as I^-. One experimental method for determining the rate of the catalyzed decomposition of hydrogen peroxide requires measuring the mass difference over time intervals.

The molarity of the hydrogen peroxide solution at each interval can be calculated using a simple stoichiometry approach. The mass of oxygen is converted into moles, which is then multiplied by the ratio 2:1 to determine the moles of hydrogen peroxide that reacted. This value is then subtracted from the initial moles of hydrogen peroxide and then divided by the volume of the liquid sample.

To get the rate of reaction, a short time interval is used; the expression rate $= \Delta [H_2O_2]/\Delta t$ represents the instantaneous rate as t approaches zero.

Data		
Time (sec)	Mass O_2 Formed (g)	M H_2O_2
0	0	0.882
60	2.960	0.697
120	5.056	0.566
180	6.784	0.458
240	8.160	0.372
300	9.344	0.298
360	10.336	0.236
420	11.104	0.188
480	11.680	0.152
540	12.192	0.120
600	12.608	0.094

When the molarity is plotted against the time, a logarithmic curve results that approaches $M = 0$ in an asymptotic fashion. At each point on the curve, the tangent represents the instantaneous rate of reaction. The rate constant for the reaction can be calculated using the rate equation:

$$\ln ([A]_o/[A]_t) = kt$$

167

SECTION 2:
Chemical and
Physical
Foundations of
Biological Systems

49. Which of the following statements is true?
    A. The instantaneous rate is fastest at the beginning of the reaction.
    B. The instantaneous rate is always faster than the average rate of reaction.
    C. The rate at the half-life is equal to one.
    D. All of the above statements are true.

50. The rate over the first 60 seconds of reaction is:
    A. 1.48000 M/sec
    B. 0.34900 M/sec
    C. 0.00308 M/sec
    D. 0.01160 M/sec

51. The rate constant for this reaction is:
    A. [ln .882 – ln .697]/60
    B. [ln (.882 – .697)]/60
    C. [ln .697]/60
    D. [ln .882]/60

52. The half-life of this reaction is approximately:
    A. 150 sec
    B. 190 sec
    C. 300 sec
    D. 450 sec

53. The decomposition of hydrogen peroxide follows first-order kinetics. This means that:
    A. The rate is directly related to the hydrogen peroxide concentration.
    B. The rate is directly related to the oxygen concentration produced.
    C. The rate is logarithmically related to the hydrogen peroxide concentration.
    D. The rate is logarithmically related to the rate constant.

54. The catalyst I^- works to increase the rate of this reaction by:
    A. changing the mechanism of the reaction
    B. lowering the enthalpy of the reaction
    C. raising the enthalpy of the reaction
    D. none of the above

Questions 55–59 are based on the following passage.

Passage X

The two diastereomers of 1-bromo-2,2-dimethyl-4-(dimethylethyl)cyclohexane (compound 1) behave very differently when treated with lithium diisopropylamide (LDA). While both give 3,3-dimethyl-5-(dimethylethyl)cyclohexene (compound 2), the

$(1R, 4R)$-isomer of compound 1 reacts much faster than the $(1S, 4R)$-isomer under the same conditions, as shown in the following diagram:

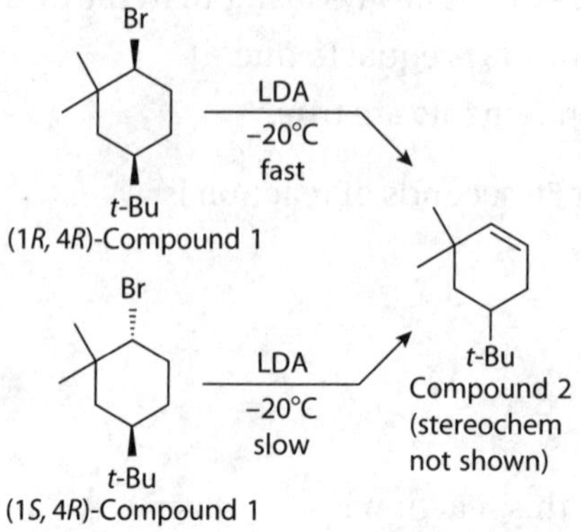

When compound 2 is treated with ozone, followed by dimethylsulfide, compound 3 is formed. Alternatively, when compound 2 is treated with borane, followed by basic hydrogen peroxide, compound 4 is formed, as shown:

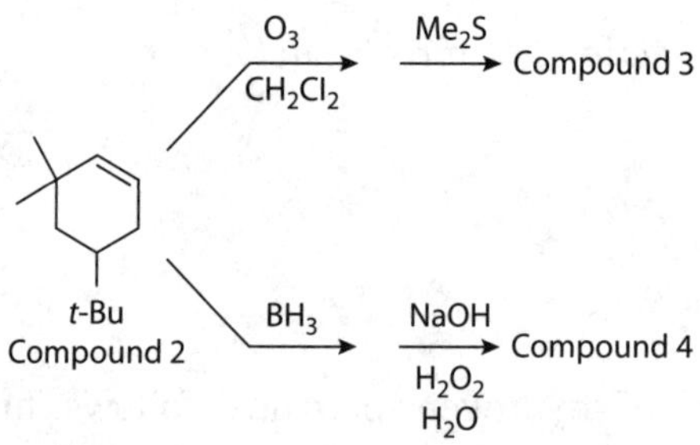

55. The most reasonable mechanism for the first reaction (compound 1 > compound 2) is:
   A. $S_N 1$
   B. $S_N 2$
   C. E1
   D. E2

56. The reason the $(1R, 4R)$-isomer reacts faster than the $(1S, 4R)$-isomer is:
   A. In the $(1R, 4R)$-isomer, steric hindrance from the t-butyl group destabilizes the bromine.
   B. In the $(1S, 4R)$-isomer, steric hindrance from the t-butyl group repels LDA.
   C. The major conformer in the $(1R, 4R)$-isomer aligns dipoles so that it is more polar.
   D. The major conformer in the $(1S, 4R)$-isomer lacks the proper orbital alignment.

57. Compound 2 is MOST accurately described as a:
   A. single enantiomer exhibiting optical activity
   B. single enantiomer exhibiting no optical activity
   C. racemic mixture exhibiting optical activity
   D. racemic mixture exhibiting no optical activity

169

SECTION 2:
Chemical and
Physical
Foundations of
Biological Systems

58. The MOST accurate structure for compound 3 is:

A.

B.

C.

D.

59. The MOST accurate structure for compound 4 is:

A.

B.

C.

D.

STOP. This is the end of Section 2.

Psychological, Social, and Biological Foundations of Behavior

59 Questions   **Time Limit: 95 Minutes**

Questions 1–4 are not associated with any passage.

1. In Dutton and Aron's "swinging bridge" study, which of the following was found to be a critical component of perceived attraction?
   A. Genetic factors influenced whom the participants found attractive.
   B. Childhood proximity and background were strong indicators of attraction.
   C. Lower adrenaline levels in response to more stable bridges were associated with increased attraction.
   D. Higher adrenaline levels in response to more unstable bridges were associated with increased attraction.

2. Kim has been in an automobile accident. He is unable to produce speech but is able to read, understand language, and even sing. Kim most likely has damage to which area of the brain?
   A. Wernicke's area
   B. Broca's area
   C. substansia nigra
   D. fusiform gyrus

3. Janey's family encourages her to continue her education. She works extremely hard and earns her master's degree in education. She is excited about beginning her teaching career and finally earning a paycheck. Her father, who is a school superintendent, arranges for her to have a job in an elementary school in his district. This is an example of which sociological construct?

A. social mobility

B. social stratification

C. nepotism

D. meritocracy

4. Robert is a salesman who sells jewelry door to door. His favorite sales technique involves showing his most expensive piece of overpriced jewelry to his potential customers. When the customer rejects the first piece, he displays a second, less expensive piece. Which of the following terms describes Robert's sales technique?

A. door in the face

B. foot in the door

C. reciprocity

D. ingratiation

Questions 5–9 are based on the following passage.

Passage I

Evolutionary psychology has advanced our understanding of mate selection in humans. A prominent researcher, David Buss, conducted a number of research studies to investigate the evolutionary theory of mate selection in a wide range of cultures.

The following data are a hypothetical adaptation of research looking at mate retention. The data are based on a study by Buss and Shackelford studying mate retention

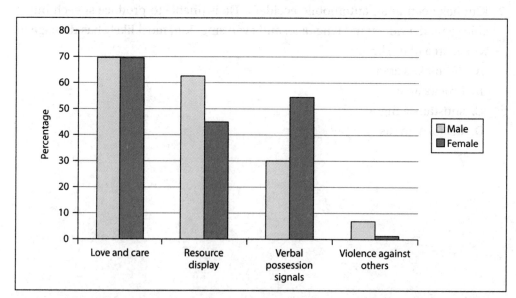

Mate retention tactics by sex. *Source*: Based on research conducted by D. M. Buss & T. K. Shackelford. "Vigilance to violence: Mate retention tactics in married couples." *Journal of Personality and Social Psychology*, 1997:72(2), 346–361. Adapted with permission.

173

SECTION 3:
Psychological,
Social, and
Biological
Foundations
of Behavior

strategies. Participants were asked about tactics that they have engaged in while in a relationship. Love and care are forms of comforting tactics. Resource display includes tactics such as buying presents. Verbal possession includes labels such as "wife" or "boyfriend" or other tactics announcing that a mate is spoken for in social situations. Violence against others represents physical aggression against other people perceived to be making advances toward one's mate. In the graph, the y-axis represents the percent of participants indicating that have used the tactic. The x-axis represents the tactic, with the vertical bars indicating the different sexes.

5. Which of the following statements is true based on the data shown?
    A. Men are more likely to use all four tactics.
    B. Women are more likely than men to engage in violence against others.
    C. Men are more likely than women to use resource display.
    D. Women are more likely than men to use love and care.

6. Which of the following statements represents how evolutionary psychology interprets the results shown?
    A. Men are more likely to use resource display because women value financial status as a characteristic in a mate; high financial status means that a man can support offspring and increase their likelihood of survival.
    B. Men are more likely to use resource display because women like nice gifts from their mate.
    C. Men are more likely to use resource display because it proves that they are powerful, and women are more loyal to powerful men out of fear.
    D. Men are more likely to use resource display because it will attract multiple women; in that case, it is not a problem if a man loses his current mate.

7. Which of the following characterizes how males select mates, according to evolutionary psychology?
    A. Males select mates based mainly on financial status of their potential partner.
    B. Males select mates based mainly on the youth, attractiveness, and good health of their potential partner.
    C. Males select mates based mainly on the education and ambition of their potential partner.
    D. Males select mates based mainly on the industriousness of their potential partner.

8. Which of the following potential follow-up investigations would be most likely to contribute to further understanding of the mate selection process in humans, from an evolutionary psychology perspective?
    A. conducting the study on the same group of participants over time
    B. asking participants to complete a self-assessment and memory test
    C. asking participants to read relationship advice texts and testing them a year later to see if they show different responses
    D. investigating the correlation between behavior and the financial status and perceived attractiveness of the mates

9. If this study included a tactic called nonverbal possession signals (e.g., putting an arm around a spouse), according to evolutionary psychological theory, which gender would likely use this tactic more frequently and why?

   A. *men.* because nonverbal possession signals, like physical violence, are a form of physically protecting your mate from competitors

   B. *men.* because providing engagement and wedding rings to your spouse to wear as a nonverbal possession signal is another way to show competitors your level of resources

   C. *women.* because women often use public displays of affection to show how committed their mates are to them

   D. *women.* because nonverbal possession signals are another means to indicate possession without directly interacting with potential competitors

Questions 10–14 are based on the following passage.

Passage II

Researchers investigating implicit and explicit memory have found that certain disorders may impair explicit memory but not implicit memory. In a historic study, E. K. Warrington and L. Weiskrantz (1970) gave a list of words to amnesics and control participants. All participants then completed four memory tasks. Two were standard measures of explicit memory (recall and recognition tasks), and two were indirect measures of implicit memory in which the participants were asked to complete word fragments by guessing what the completed word or fragment was. Each memory task consisted of participants reading and later being tested on their implicit and explicit memory for a list of words.

The results of this study are shown in the following graph:

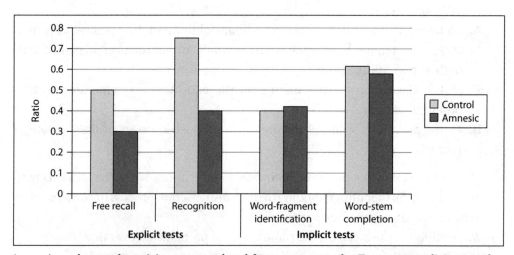

Amnesic and control participants completed four memory tasks. Two were explicit tests (free recall and recognition) and two were implicit tests (word-fragment identification and word-stem completion). *Source*: Adapted with permission from E. K. Warrington & L. Weiskrantz. "Amnesic syndrome: Consolidation or retrieval?" *Nature*. 1970:228(5272), 628–630.

175

SECTION 3:
Psychological,
Social, and
Biological
Foundations
of Behavior

10. What does the graph MOST likely indicate about explicit versus implicit memory for amnesics compared to control participants?
   A. Amnesics perform worse on both explicit memory and implicit memory tasks compared to control participants.
   B. Amnesics perform equally well as control participants on explicit memory and implicit memory tasks.
   C. Amnesics perform better than controls on implicit memory tasks because there is no interference from explicit memories.
   D. Amnesics experience significant impairment for explicit memory tasks but do not experience significant impairment for implicit memory tasks compared to control participants.

11. Prior to Warrington and Weiskrantz's research, psychologists believed that amnesics lacked the ability to encode or store information in long-term memory. However, based on their research, what is the MOST likely explanation for the amnesics' difficulty performing specific memory tasks?
   A. Some amnesic participants are unable to remember new material but can access previously learned information to make judgments about current events.
   B. Some amnesic participants are able to learn new information (encoding) but are unable to explicitly state what they have learned (retrieval).
   C. Amnesic participants do not have any memory impairments when compared to control participants.
   D. Some amnesic participants are unable to learn new information but are able to explicitly recall lists of words.

12. If these results were examined using Endel Tulving's model of memory (episodic, semantic, procedural), which of the following statements is MOST likely to be true?
   A. Amnesic participants are able to encode and access semantic memory but are still impaired in their ability to retrieve the encoded information.
   B. Amnesic participants are able to encode and access episodic memory but are unable to access semantic memory.
   C. Amnesic participants have access only to procedural memories and therefore can only unconsciously follow scripts.
   D. Amnesic participants can encode and access episodic, semantic, and procedural memory with no impairments because these are part of a separate memory system.

13. Based on previous research, what is the brain structure that is MOST likely impaired in the amnesic population?
   A. cerebellum
   B. amygdala
   C. hippocampus
   D. Broca's area

14. Based on previous research, what is the brain structure that is MOST likely associated with the storage of long-term memory?

    A. amygdala

    B. hippocampus

    C. cerebral cortex

    D. Broca's area

Questions 15–19 are based on the following passage.

Passage III

Research investigating different types of memory has found important differences between how those memories are recognized. The results of a hypothetical study are shown in the following graphs. In this study, during a training phase participants were instructed to listen to two separate study lists of musical sections, some familiar and some novel. Later, during a testing phase, participants listened to a mix including all of the initial melodies as well as an equal number of distractors. They were then asked to tell whether they had heard a melody during the training phase and, if so, which of the two study lists the melody was from.

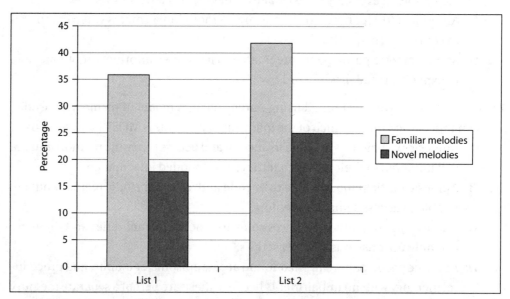

Percent of familiar and novel melodies that were correctly identified as being from a specific study list.

177

SECTION 3:
Psychological,
Social, and
Biological
Foundations
of Behavior

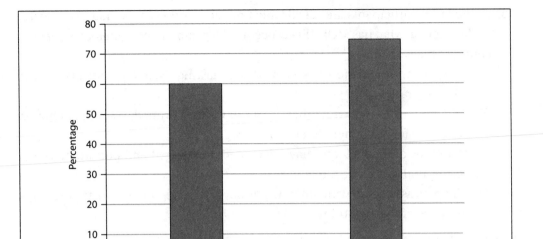

Percent of familiar and novel melodies that were correctly identified as being from one of the two study lists, but not a specific list.

15. Based on the results shown, which of the following is true about the data?
    A. Participants were better able to remember which list a melody was from than whether a melody had been heard during training.
    B. Participants were better able to remember which list novel melodies were from than familiar melodies.
    C. Participants were better able to remember which list familiar melodies were from than novel melodies.
    D. Participants were better able to identify familiar melodies than novel melodies as having been heard during training.

16. Based on memory research, which type of memory is MOST closely associated with list recognition performance?
    A. episodic memory
    B. semantic memory
    C. procedural memory
    D. implicit memory

17. Based on memory research, which type of memory is MOST closely associated with the data depicted for novel melodies in the second graph (percent correctly identified as being from one of the two study lists, but not a specific list)?
    A. episodic memory
    B. semantic memory
    C. procedural memory
    D. implicit memory

18. A year later, participants are asked which melodies on each list had been heard. In the interval, what has MOST likely occurred for remembered melodies over the course of the year?

    A. Long-term potentiation has created long-lasting excitatory circuits for the memory trace.

    B. Synapses associated with other details have been pruned, resulting in higher activation for the remembered melodies.

    C. Memories of the melodies have remained unchanged and performance will correspond to the intact memories.

    D. Synapses associated with other details have been reinforced due to conscious rehearsal of the memories.

19. If familiarity led to confusion about which list a melody was from (i.e., interfered with episodic memory), how would the data in the first graph MOST likely change?

    A. The percentage of melodies correctly ascribed to list 1 would increase, but not the percentage correctly ascribed to list 2.

    B. The percentage of melodies correctly ascribed to list 2 would increase, but not the percentage correctly ascribed to list 1.

    C. The percentage of novel melodies correctly ascribed to both list 1 and list 2 would increase.

    D. The percentage of familiar melodies correctly ascribed to both list 1 and list 2 would decrease.

Questions 20–24 are based on the following passage.

Passage IV

A classic study investigating observational learning was conducted by the psychologist Albert Bandura. In his study he explored whether children would model violent behavior after watching film sequences that featured violence.

In this study, four groups of child participants watched three different film sequences (aggressive-model-rewarded, aggressive-model-punished, and nonaggressive model control). In an additional control group, child participants were not shown a film.

➤ In the aggressive-model-rewarded group, the participants watched a film in which a child was rewarded for violent behavior toward another child.

➤ In the aggressive-model-punished group, the participants watched a film in which a child was punished for violent behavior toward another child.

➤ In the nonaggressive model control group, the participants watched a film in which there was no violent behavior between children.

179

SECTION 3:
Psychological,
Social, and
Biological
Foundations
of Behavior

The results of this study are shown in the following graph. Aggression is shown on the *y*-axis and the experimental and control groups are plotted on the *x*-axis:

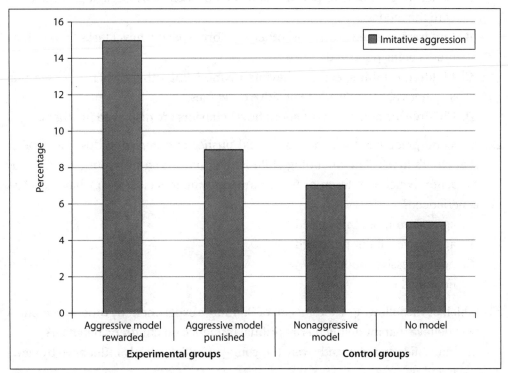

Modeling and aggression. *Source*: Adapted with permission from a study by A. Bandura, D. Ross, & S. Ross. "Vicarious reinforcement and imitative learning," *Journal of Abnormal and Social Psychology.* 1961:67(12), 601–607.

20. Based on the graph, which of the following is true about imitative aggression?
   A. Children who view aggressive behavior and see the behavior rewarded are more likely to engage in imitative aggression.
   B. Children who view aggressive behavior punished are as likely as children who view aggression being rewarded to engage in imitative aggression.
   C. Children who view nonaggressive behavior are as likely as children who view aggressive behavior to engage in imitative aggression.
   D. Children are equally likely to engage in aggressive behavior regardless of whether they see behavioral models or no models at all.

21. According to Albert Bandura, this study highlights specific expectations concerning reinforcement and how reinforcement influences learning in children. In this view, which of the following is MOST probable based on the data from this study?

    A. Children learn how to perform specific novel tasks by engaging in the tasks with the models.

    B. Children passively learn how others perform specific novel tasks by watching others being punished.

    C. Children exhibit specific behaviors by modeling others when they see that another's behavior leads to positive outcomes.

    D. Children are able to report about how behaviors are displayed in others.

22. A second-grade class watches as a child pushes another child down and takes that child's lunch. The offending child is then put into a time-out (isolation) by a teacher. Which condition of Bandura's experiment is closest to what this class experienced?

    A. aggressive-model-rewarded

    B. aggressive-model-punished

    C. nonaggressive model

    D. no model

23. Which of the following is a criticism of Bandura's experiment by other researchers who believe that modeling has a minimal influence on children's behavior?

    A. The children in the study were too young to be definitively influenced by viewing films.

    B. In the study, the children in the control group displayed aggressive behavior similar to that displayed by the experimental groups.

    C. Child actors in the films were not aggressive enough in their depictions to produce violent behavior in child participants.

    D. The children in the study were in too artificial an environment and the tasks completed were not generalizable to real-world conditions.

24. Which of the following would MOST closely match the aggressive-model-rewarded condition of Bandura's study?

    A. Joey watches a friend play a violent video game in which punching small animals results in more points.

    B. Adam watches a feature film in which the lead character hits a pedestrian with his car and is sent to jail.

    C. Sally plays a video game that consists of solving problems using logic.

    D. Cameron watches a feature film showing parents grieving over the loss of a child.

181

SECTION 3:
Psychological,
Social, and
Biological
Foundations
of Behavior

Questions 25–29 are based on the following passage.

Passage V

Education levels and frequent childbirth are linked to poverty levels. Worldwide organizations such as the United Nations Educational, Scientific, and Cultural Organization (UNESCO) and World Health Organization (WHO) track fertility rates, poverty levels, and education across the world as countries experience both economic transitions (e.g., from agrarian to manufacturing) and increased globalization. On the following graphs, each dot represents a country's mean fertility rate plotted against the percentage of girls enrolled in secondary school and the percentage of the population living in poverty.

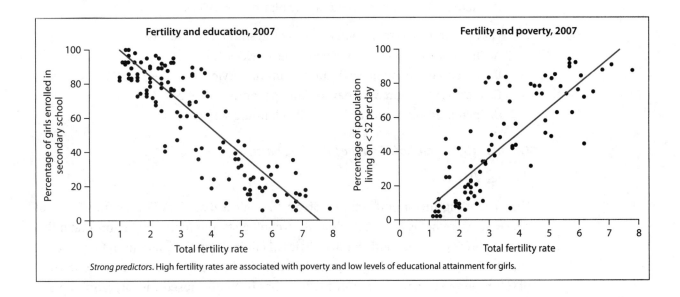

Strong predictors. High fertility rates are associated with poverty and low levels of educational attainment for girls.

25. Based on the graphs, in a country with an average fertility rate of six children per woman, what is the likelihood that a girl will be enrolled in secondary school, and what is the likelihood that she will live in poverty (<$2/day)?
    A. 41% chance of secondary enrollment; 83% likelihood of poverty
    B. 10% chance of secondary enrollment; 68% likelihood of poverty
    C. 5% chance of secondary enrollment; 68% likelihood of poverty
    D. 22% chance of secondary enrollment; 80% likelihood of poverty

26. Which of the following may explain why frequent childbirth alters women's social mobility?
    A. culture of poverty
    B. financial capital per family member
    C. social stratification
    D. increased human capital

27. Based on the graphs, if a man has four children, what is the likelihood that he will be living in poverty and what is the likelihood that he will have a secondary school education?
    A. 50% likelihood of poverty; 57% chance of secondary education
    B. 50% likelihood of poverty; education level unknown
    C. poverty level unknown; 57% likelihood of secondary education
    D. not enough information provided

28. What factor related to cultural capital could shift fertility levels?
    A. increased access to family planning services
    B. increased acceptance of family planning services
    C. increased resources to pay for family planning services
    D. increased education about family planning services

29. What factor related to human capital could shift fertility levels?
    A. increased access to family planning services
    B. increased acceptance of family planning services
    C. increased resources to pay for family planning services
    D. increased education about family planning services

Questions 30–34 are based on the following passage.

Passage VI

Understanding the various causes of psychological disorders is a central focus of research in psychology. Further, clinical psychologists must consider factors that influence the incidence rate and characteristics of clinical populations whom they treat.

The following graph depicts genetic familial relationships and the incidence rate of schizophrenia when one family member has been diagnosed with schizophrenia.

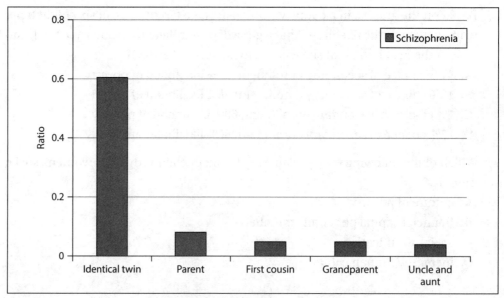

Familial relationship and incidence rate of schizophrenia when one family member is diagnosed with schizophrenia.

183

SECTION 3:
Psychological,
Social, and
Biological
Foundations
of Behavior

This second graph depicts the incidence rate of schizophrenia among children in relationship to each other and to parents when one or more family members have schizophrenia.

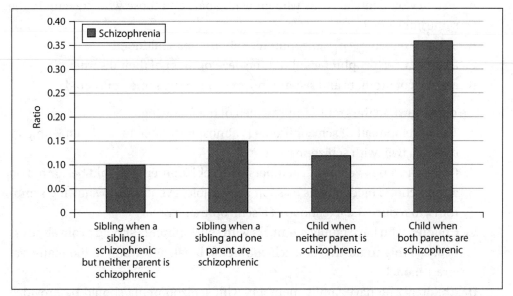

Parental and sibling schizophrenic status and incidence rate of child schizophrenia diagnosis.

30. Based on the graphs, which group is at the highest risk for developing schizophrenia?
   A. children whose parents are both schizophrenic
   B. siblings with one schizophrenic parent
   C. individuals with uncles or aunts who are schizophrenic
   D. individuals with a schizophrenic identical twin

31. These data make the strongest argument for which view of the origin of schizophrenia?
   A. genetic causes
   B. environmental causes
   C. drug use/abuse causes
   D. both genetic and environmental causes

32. Which of the following is NOT associated with schizophrenia in the research literature?
   A. too much GABA or too much activity at the GABA receptors
   B. according to learning theory, family structure and social learning processes
   C. abnormally enlarged ventricles in the brain and reduced blood flow in certain portions of the frontal lobe
   D. sodium channels in specific neuronal pathways that are structured in an abnormal fashion

33. Based on the data in the graphs, which of the following would be the most appropriate follow-up study to investigate both hereditary and environmental factors in schizophrenia?

   A. a survey of identical twins who grew up apart and those who grew up in the same household
   B. a survey of parents of schizophrenics about their childhood
   C. a survey of schizophrenics about the development of their disorder
   D. a survey of brothers and sisters who grew up in the same household

34. The data shown in the graphs imply which of the following?

   A. The development of schizophrenia is almost inevitable for children with parents or a twin with schizophrenia.
   B. Children who have family members with schizophrenia should be started on antipsychotic medications as soon as possible, even prior to showing symptoms, to reduce the likelihood of a schizophrenic break.
   C. Children who have family members with schizophrenia should avoid all stress because this could trigger a schizophrenic break according to the diathesis-stress model.
   D. Children who have family members with schizophrenia should be provided with additional environmental support to reduce the likelihood that they will develop schizophrenia.

Questions 35–39 are based on the following passage.

Passage VII

Research into various states of consciousness has contributed greatly to our understanding about the mechanisms involved in human sleep. This research has provided insight into sleep as a restorative process and has highlighted the negative consequences of sleep deprivation.

The following figure depicts a full 8-hour sleep cycle. In the figure, sleep is divided into several stages based on EEG activity.

185

SECTION 3:
Psychological,
Social, and
Biological
Foundations
of Behavior

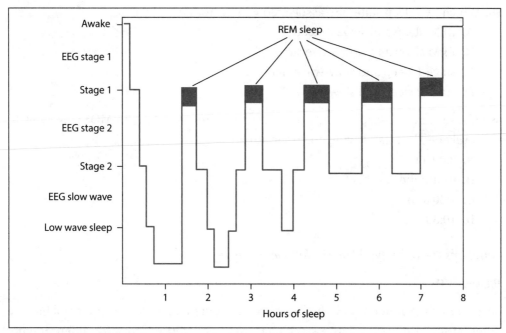

Sleep stages as a function of EEG activity during an 8-hour sleep period.

35. Based on the figure, which of the following statements is true?
    A. The amplitude of the EEG wave becomes smaller as deeper levels of sleep are reached.
    B. The length of REM sleep per sleep cycle generally increases as the night progresses.
    C. The length of time a person is in slow-wave sleep increases as hours of sleep increase.
    D. The frequency of the EEG wave becomes greater as deeper levels of sleep are reached.

36. Most vivid dreaming occurs in which part of the sleep cycle?
    A. REM sleep
    B. stage 2 sleep
    C. slow-wave sleep
    D. equally in all stages of the sleep cycle

37. Based on the figure, about how long is one sleep cycle?
    A. 20 minutes
    B. 4 hours
    C. 8 hours
    D. 90 minutes

38. Which two sleep states are associated with restorative processes?
    A. REM sleep and stage 2 sleep
    B. REM sleep and slow-wave sleep
    C. stage 1 sleep and slow-wave sleep
    D. stage 2 sleep and slow-wave sleep

39. If Jose went to sleep at 10:00 p.m., at what time would he be MOST likely to be awakened by a car driving down the street?
    A. 2:00 a.m.
    B. midnight
    C. 1:30 a.m.
    D. 10:30 p.m.

Questions 40–44 are based on the following passage.

Passage VIII

Research has examined how the presence of others affects how humans behave in different social contexts. This research has examined performance for different types of tasks and has also evaluated how group size affects performance. Studies have examined both internally motivated changes in behavior and losses due to coordination of activity with others (role duplication).

The following data represent a study conducted by B. Latané, K. Williams, and S. Harkins. In their study, they measured sound produced by individuals when asked to cheer or clap. They then manipulated the grouping conditions. Some individuals were alone, others were in actual groups of either two or six. Additional participants were told that they were placed into groups, but actually they were merely blindfolded and equipped with headphones (thus placing them in so-called pseudogroups). The decibels produced by each individual or group of individuals were measured for each condition. The results of this study are depicted in the following figure with group size depicted on the *x*-axis and sound produced in decibels depicted on the *y*-axis.

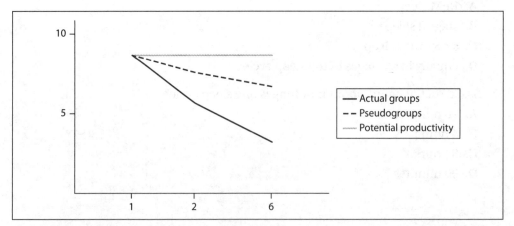

Loss of productivity based on group size and pseudogroup size. *Source*: Adapted with permission from B. Latané, K. Williams, & S. Harkin. "Many hands make light the work: The causes and consequences of social loafing." *Journal of Personality and Social Psychology*, 1979:37(6), 822.

187

SECTION 3:
Psychological,
Social, and
Biological
Foundations
of Behavior

40. Based on the data shown, which of the following statements is true?
    A. Sound level increased the more participants there were in the groups.
    B. Sound level increased more in actual groups than in pseudogroups.
    C. Sound level decreased only when participants thought they were in a group but not when they were in an actual group.
    D. Sound level decreased for participants in actual groups and for participants in pseudogroups.

41. What would you expect to occur if the people in pseudogroups believed that the number of people in their groups was being altered?
    A. The decibel level would increase if the people in pseudogroups believed that there were more people in their groups.
    B. The decibel level would decrease if the people in pseudogroups believed that there were more people in their groups.
    C. The decibel level would decrease if the people in pseudogroups believed that there were fewer people in their groups.
    D. The decibel level would stay the same because there are not actually any more or any fewer people in the supposedly altered pseudogroups.

42. Based on research examining group productivity, what concept BEST explains the difference between the actual groups and the pseudogroups?
    A. loss of coordination
    B. the bystander effect
    C. social loafing
    D. group polarization

43. Based on research examining group productivity, what concept BEST explains the difference between potential productivity and the pseudogroups' productivity?
    A. loss of coordination
    B. the bystander effect
    C. social loafing
    D. group polarization

44. What are the implications for group projects based on these results?
    A. the larger the group size, the more social loafing will occur and the less effort each person will make toward completing a task
    B. the larger the group size, the more effort each person will make toward completing a task
    C. the smaller the group size, the greater the social diffusion of effort
    D. the larger the group size, the less effort any single person will need to contribute to reach a goal

Questions 45–49 are based on the following passage.

Passage IX

Research investigating behavior in social situations has found that social behavior varies depending on the environment. Social behavior can involve either shallow acting or deep acting. Shallow acting requires altering facial expressions and body language so that on the surface, the individual conveys an emotion or opinion to conform to the social situation but does not really experience that emotion/opinion. Deep acting requires alteration of inner beliefs such that the individual believes the emotion or opinion he or she is expressing in order to conform to the situation.

In one study, deep acting and shallow acting in a social situation were examined for customer-service workers. These workers routinely interacted with customers by smiling at them, speaking with them, responding to their queries, and detailing the benefits of various products. Later, stress was assessed for these workers.

Hypothetical results are depicted in the following figure.

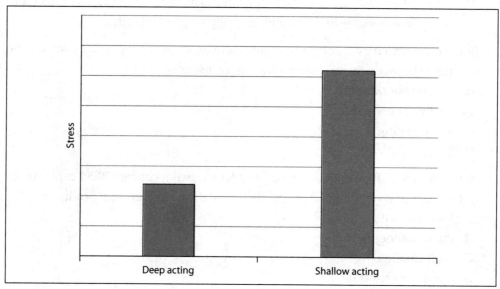

Perceived stress from social interactions involving deep acting and shallow acting.

45. Based on the results of this study, which of the following is true?
   A. Deep acting results in higher stress levels.
   B. Shallow acting results in higher stress levels.
   C. Stress levels are the same for both kinds of social behavior.
   D. Shallow acting is likely to be more common because it is easier.

189

SECTION 3:
Psychological,
Social, and
Biological
Foundations
of Behavior

46. Based on the dramaturgical approach of this study, and the data in the figure, which of the following is true of social interactions?
    A. The more social interactions that require shallow acting, the less perceived stress there will be.
    B. Social interactions should ideally not involve any acting.
    C. Social interactions involving deep acting should result in less stress.
    D. The fewer social interactions that require acting, the greater the stress will be.

47. According to cognitive dissonance theory, why would shallow acting be more stressful than deep acting among customer-service workers?
    A. Making sure that facial expressions and body language are consistent increases autonomic arousal and leads to elevated stress.
    B. Deep acting requires that you change your beliefs; therefore, acting becomes less stressful.
    C. Individuals with social anxiety are more likely to engage in shallow acting.
    D. Deep acting provides more off-stage time compared to on-stage time.

48. Which of the following concepts involves an actor making sure that he or she chooses an "audience" comprised of people who will validate the actor's self-view?
    A. self-verification
    B. backstage self
    C. off-stage behavior
    D. self-referencing

49. According to the dramaturgical approach, when is an individual truly himself or herself?
    A. when the individual is alone (off-stage)
    B. when the individual has minimal interaction with others (on-stage)
    C. when the individual engages in self-talk dialogue (on-stage)
    D. when the individual engages in actions that cannot be seen by others (backstage)

Questions 50–54 are based on the following passage.

Passage X

High levels of stress have been studied by a number of researchers. Research exploring stress and well-being has made some compelling discoveries. A common finding is that people who are under stress are more likely to report being sick than people who are under less stress. A 2002 study by N. Hamrick, S. Cohen, and M. S. Rodriguez examined social connections and incidence of colds or flu. In their study, they asked participants about stressful events and about their social lives. Then they had the participants keep a diary for 3 months.

The accompanying figure shows the results of their study. The vertical bars on the *x*-axis represent participants who have either low or high levels of social contact, and who are under either low or high stress. The *y*-axis shows the percentage of participants who experienced a cold or flu.

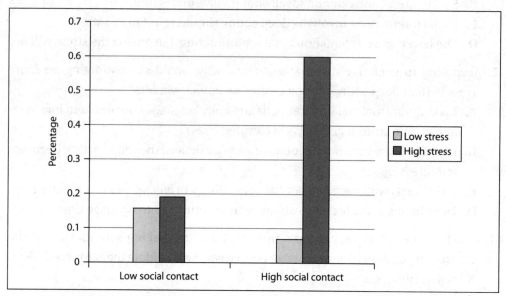

Participants were classified as either high-stress or low-stress and low-social-contact or high-social-contact groups. The percentage of the participants who experienced cold or flu is shown on the *y*-axis. *Source*: Adapted with permission from N. Hamrick, S. Cohen, & M. S. Rodriguez. "Being popular can be healthy or unhealthy: Stress, social network diversity, and incidence of upper respiratory infection." *Health Psychology*, 2002:21(3), 294–298.

50. What does this research indicate about high-social-contact vs. low-social-contact participants?

A. High-social-contact participants under high stress are less likely to become sick than low-social-contact participants.

B. High-social-contact participants under high stress are more likely to become sick than low-social-contact participants.

C. Low-social-contact participants under high stress are less likely to become sick than high-social-contact participants.

D. In general, high-social-contact participants are less likely to become sick than low-social-contact participants.

51. Based on the research depicted in the graph, which of the following is the MOST likely scenario that would contribute to the likelihood of a person becoming sick?

A. giving a small birthday party for a family member

B. getting a negative performance review on a minor job task

C. dropping an expensive electronic device and having it break

D. attending a large "new hire" orientation session for a major promotion in a new company

191

SECTION 3:
Psychological,
Social, and
Biological
Foundations
of Behavior

52. During a highly stressful time period, actions such as meditating or taking breaks to reduce or tolerate the stress are part of which strategy?
    A. accommodation
    B. coping
    C. appraisal
    D. resistance

53. Abby is a member of several on-campus groups. Recently, she has increased her course load and has also taken on extra hours at her part-time job. Based on research, which of the following activities may help Abby reduce her risk of falling ill?
    A. joining a new club
    B. taking a morning run
    C. listening to fast music while studying
    D. consuming more alcoholic drinks on the weekend

54. Which of the following could be considered a physiological reaction to threat in which the autonomic nervous system is active?
    A. resistance
    B. pressure
    C. fight-or-flight response
    D. appraisal

55. Sue was waiting while her friend Betsy was trying on wedding dresses in the dressing room. When Betsy emerged wearing a sleek red dress, Sue was confused as to why Betsy's choice of dress wasn't white. Sue's observation can be described as an example of:
    A. Conflict theory
    B. Symbolic interactionism
    C. Social constructionism
    D. Globalization

56. The stage of sleep that is most beneficial to the body system is:
    A. First stage
    B. Second stage
    C. Third stage
    D. Fourth stage

57. The gland that plays an important role in the body's immune response is:
    A. Thymus gland
    B. Pituitary gland
    C. Pineal gland
    D. Thyroid gland

58. The region of the brain responsible for the understanding of language is referred to as Wernicke's area which is found in which lobe of the brain?
   A. Parietal lobe
   B. Frontal lobe
   C. Occipital lobe
   D. Temporal lobe

59. In the early 1900s, millions of immigrants and their families from European countries passed through the gates of Ellis Island for a life in the United States for reasons including economic hardship, political persecution, and lack of religious freedoms. The life-changing endeavor undertaken by these immigrants is an example of:
   A. financial capital
   B. cultural capital
   C. human capital
   D. social capital

STOP. This is the end of Section 3.

Critical Analysis and Reasoning Skills

53 Questions   **Time Limit: 90 Minutes**

Directions: This section includes eight reading passages. Each passage is followed by a group of questions. Read each passage, and then select the one best answer to each question based on what you have read.

Questions 1–6 are based on the following passage.

Passage I

Sea beans. Ballast waifs. These adorable nicknames do not hint at the destructive nature of invasive plants. Sea beans are those plants whose seeds, buoyed by a pocket of air, float on the tide from one island to another, or even across vast stretches of ocean. Ballast waifs are less natural in origin; they are seeds that arrive on one shore from another in the soil placed in a ship's hold as ballast.

One remarkably lovely and dreadfully damaging ballast waif is *Lythrum salicaria*, the bright purple, spiky flower known commonly as purple loosestrife. Purple loose-strife is not a newcomer to U.S. shores; it arrived from Eurasia, almost certainly via ship, some 200 years ago. It was widely used for medicinal and ornamental purposes throughout the 19th century. Its lovely purple blooms may still be seen in gardens throughout the country, where people love it for its long growing season.

For all its beauty, purple loosestrife is a menace. The same long growing season that makes it so beloved by gardeners makes it a seed-making machine. A mature plant may produce 2 or 3 million seeds a year.

That is not enough for *Lythrum salicaria*, however. It also propagates underground, sending out shoots and stems in all directions. It is also able to cross-pollinate with other species of *Lythrum*.

Scientists took little notice of purple loosestrife until sometime in the 1930s, when a particular strain began colonizing along the St. Lawrence River, an area rife with the sort of wetlands purple loosestrife likes best. Purple loosestrife does not just propagate wildly; it also adapts easily to changes in environment. As it starts up in a new area, it quickly outcompetes native grasses, sedges, and other flowering plants, forming dense stands of purple loosestrife where once heterogeneous wetland meadows existed. This not only eradicates the native plants, but it also removes food sources for migratory birds and other animals.

In recent years, purple loosestrife has had a devastating impact on native cattails and wild rice. It has invaded and destroyed spawning areas for fish. In rural areas, it is beginning to move away from wetlands and adapt to drier areas, encroaching on agricultural lands. In urban areas, it is blocking pipes and drainage canals. It has moved steadily westward and is now found in all states but Florida.

Attempts to control purple loosestrife have been only partially successful. It has proved resistant to many herbicides, and it is impervious to burning, as its rootstock lies beneath the surface and can reproduce from there. It can be mowed down and plowed under, and then replaced with a less invasive plant. This is very labor-intensive in marshy areas that are substantially overgrown, but it may be the only way of eliminating the pest. Plowing it under requires unusually large discs on the plow because it is important to chop up the rootstock. Gardeners who have planted purple loosestrife are encouraged to dig it up and replace it with other, less damaging plants.

The best plan may be to seek a natural enemy of purple loosestrife, a weevil or insect that will destroy the plant. However, finding such an enemy that will target only purple loosestrife while leaving other, preferred plants intact is a daunting task. More important than that, introducing yet another foreign species to American swampland may lead to problems that make our purple loosestrife infestation look mild.

1. According to the passage, all of these are true EXCEPT:
   A. Purple loosestrife propagates through an underground system.
   B. Purple loosestrife has even affected the survival of fish.
   C. Purple loosestrife is best eradicated through controlled burning.
   D. Purple loosestrife is often used in American gardens.

2. The mention of the St. Lawrence River shows primarily that:
   A. Sea beans prefer to travel on freshwater conveyances.
   B. Purple loosestrife does well in marshy areas along rivers.
   C. Most sea beans survive best in northern regions.
   D. Purple loosestrife can be replaced by less damaging plants.

3. Which fact or facts about purple loosestrife add to its power of endurance?
   I. ability to cross-pollinate
   II. easy adaptability
   III. spiky stems and flowers
   A. I only
   B. II only
   C. I and II only
   D. I, II, and III

4. The author suggests that people enjoy growing purple loosestrife because:
   A. It keeps out other weeds.
   B. It makes millions of seeds.
   C. It has a long growing season.
   D. It reduces weevils and insects.

5. According to the passage, where would purple loosestrife easily thrive?
   I. in the subtropical swamps of central Florida
   II. in the wetland meadows of eastern Michigan
   III. along the inland waterways of North Carolina
   A. I only
   B. II only
   C. I and II only
   D. II and III only

6. According to the author, purple loosestrife can be eradicated by being mowed down, plowed under, and replaced with other species. Which of the following information, if true, would most WEAKEN this argument?
   A. *Lythrum salicaria* has been removed from some gardens through the careful use of an Australian slug.
   B. Replanted meadows where purple loosestrife once grew are slowly being taken over by a new, hardier strain of *Lythrum salicaria*.
   C. Cattails are coming back to some New York swampland once devastated by the incursion of *Lythrum salicaria*.
   D. Chopping up the rootstock of *Lythrum salicaria* with a plow adds an unexpected bonus in the form of nitrogen-rich fertilizer.

Questions 7–12 are based on the following passage.

Passage II

Since soldiers first formed armies, there has been martial music. It provided rhythm for drilling and marching, and it raised morale before battle and weakened that of the enemy during battle. From the war drums of Native Americans to the messenger drums of the early Chinese, from the trumpets of the ancient Egyptians to those of the ancient Celts, music has accompanied men into battle.

Fife and drum corps were popular from the Renaissance on, but the military band we think of today did not really exist until the 18th century, when brass instruments and woodwinds were combined in European bands to form a martial sound that could be heard even above the cannons and muskets of the battlefield. That sound was supplemented beginning in 1720 with the novel sound known as Janissary music.

The Janissaries were an elite corps of Turkish soldiers whose music was particularly suited to a military corps. Janissary music used kettledrums, cymbals, triangles, tambourines, and unusual forms of percussion such as the "Jingling Johnny," a tall, decorated pole hung with bells. By 1720, the sound had made its way to Europe by way of a gift from the Turkish sultan to the Polish army of Augustus II. Within a few years, Janissary percussion had been added to military bands in Russia, Austria, and Prussia. So-called "Turkish music" became wildly popular, and it did not take long for the lively military style to find its way into classical composition. This sudden craze presaged the Orientalism that would flavor European art in the next century.

Here in America, when we think of martial music, we think of John Philip Sousa and beloved marches on the order of "The Stars and Stripes Forever." However, 100 years earlier, Joseph Haydn used a Janissary style in his *Military Symphony No. 100 in G Major*, and Ludwig van Beethoven included a "Turkish March" in *The Ruins of Athens*. Wolfgang Amadeus Mozart based his opera *The Abduction from the Seraglio* on Janissary percussion. As the 19th century began, it became popular to add a "Janissary stop" to pianos and harpsichords to provide a percussive accompaniment similar to that produced by the kettledrums of the Janissary corps.

As quickly as it had come, Janissary music passed out of favor, and by the middle of the 19th century, European and American bands had become formal, trained accessories to regiments, consisting typically of flute and piccolo, clarinets, oboe, saxophones, bassoons, horns, cornets, trombones, and percussion. In this country, the importance of martial music may have reached its peak during the Civil War, when every unit and regiment had its own small band. However, even today, according to *Mother Jones*, the Pentagon is the largest employer of musicians anywhere in the world, spending nearly $200 million of taxpayers' money annually on bands from Guam to Washington, D.C.—approximately 10 times what the federal government spends on K–12 music education. No longer do these bands follow men into battle, however; their purpose today is largely ceremonial, and you are more likely to hear them at a state funeral than at the rear of a forced march.

7. The author compares Native American drums to Chinese drums in terms of their:
   A. tone
   B. appearance
   C. purpose
   D. value

8. In paragraph 4, the word *stop* is used to mean:
   A. period
   B. barricade
   C. interruption
   D. knob

9. The discussion of Haydn and Mozart BEST illustrates the author's point that:
   A. Not all martial music is Janissary in flavor.
   B. Janissary music was European in origin.
   C. Martial music influenced classical composers.
   D. Orientalism affected painting as well as music.

10. Which of the following assertions does the author support with an example?
    I. Janissary music used unusual forms of percussion.
    II. You might hear martial music at a state funeral.
    III. John Philip Sousa wrote beloved marches.
    A. I only
    B. II only
    C. I and III only
    D. II and III only

11. In the 18th century, enlisting in the army became known as "following the drum." If the author included this information in the passage, it would probably be used to:
    A. support the notion that martial music was a critical part of military culture
    B. provide an example of idiomatic expressions based on music and art
    C. add details to the segment on the influence of martial music in the Civil War
    D. illustrate the change that followed the introduction of Janissary music

12. The author's mention of the level of funding provided for music education is most likely meant as a:
    A. fascinating comparison
    B. critical comment
    C. humorous aside
    D. predictive claim

Questions 13–18 are based on the following passage.

Passage III

In the history of preemptive wars that end badly, we must consider the Zulu War of 1879. Like many wars of the 19th century, it was declared not by Parliament but rather by people on the scene. Sir Henry Bartle Frere was an emissary of the Queen, sent to Cape Town to find a way to unify the British and Boer colonies with a variety of independent black states to form a Confederation of South Africa. Standing in his way was the Zulu Army, a robust contingent of 40,000 warriors under the leadership of King Cetshwayo.

Frere looked for a way to seize Zululand. He used a series of minor border disputes to prompt an ultimatum to Cetshwayo, demanding that his army disband and be remodeled within 30 days. Cetshwayo refused to reply, which led to a state of war. A month and a half later, a British force invaded Zululand. They moved in three columns toward the royal compound.

On the 22nd of January, the middle column, led by Lord Chelmsford, a favorite of the Queen, split, with Chelmsford leading a large force to support a small reconnoitering party. The 1,750 left at camp soon found themselves surrounded by nearly 20,000 Zulus. Notice was sent to Chelmsford, but he would not be deflected from his plan. The resulting massacre at Isandhlwana reduced the middle column by 1,350 men. Some of the survivors retreated to Rorke's Drift, where they joined a small force of about 100 men who had successfully held off a few thousand warriors.

News of the massacre made its way to England, but Chelmsford, quite the modern military man, had already put a cover-up in place. He managed to convince the Queen and some of the press that Isandhlwana was overcome due to a lack of ammunition, and he put forth Rorke's Drift as a major victory, allowing that minor skirmish to be glorified as the massacre was all but forgotten. He would later blame Isandhlwana on the disobedience of an officer who died there.

Chelmsford's self-supporting propaganda was effective for a while, but as the Zulu War turned even bloodier, albeit more successful for the British, he was eventually recalled and replaced by Field Marshal Wolseley. Wolseley would command the British troops through the final campaigns of the Zulu War, campaigns that culminated in the capture of King Cetshwayo. The British divided up Cetshwayo's kingdom into 13 mini-chiefdoms, granting 11 to Zulus, 1 to a pro-British Basuto chief, and 1 to a white African mercenary. This plan led to many years of civil war, and in 1882, the British restored Cetshwayo to his throne, leaving his son in charge of a nearby territory. In 1883 that son joined with a band of Boer mercenaries and invaded his father's kraal, forcing his father into exile, where he soon died under mysterious circumstances. In league with the Boer who would become the first prime minister of South Africa, Louis Botha, a second son of Cetshwayo's attacked his brother and defeated his army. This son, Dinizulu, would be the last king of the Zulus to have any power. His land is now part of KwaZulu-Natal Province in South Africa.

13. In the context of the passage, the word *campaigns* means:
    A. races between candidates
    B. actions advancing a principle
    C. related military operations
    D. overland hunting expeditions

14. The discussion of Rorke's Drift is used primarily to show:
    A. why the capture of the king was a forgone conclusion
    B. how a minor success deflected attention from a major failure
    C. the many ways that British forces outmaneuvered the Zulus
    D. the use of British nomenclature to rename African landmarks

15. The passage suggests that the author would MOST likely believe that:
    A. Chelmsford was a failure.
    B. Chelmsford was a hero.
    C. Frere was a hero.
    D. Wolseley was a failure.

16. Each of these at some time ruled some or all of Zululand EXCEPT:
    A. a white African mercenary
    B. King Dinizulu
    C. Cetshwayo
    D. Lord Chelmsford

17. Which of these best shows that the British had little understanding of the land they occupied?

    I. Chelmsford initiated a cover-up of events at Isandhlwana.

    II. British forces moved in three columns toward the royal compound.

    III. The British plan for apportionment led to years of civil war.

    A. I only

    B. I and II only

    C. III only

    D. II and III only

18. The author's description of the Zulu War makes it seem MOST similar to:

    A. the peasant uprising known as Kett's Rebellion

    B. the systematic genocide of the Nigeria-Biafra conflict

    C. the amphibious raid by the Allies on Dieppe, Normandy

    D. the removal by force of Saddam Hussein in Iraq

Questions 19–25 are based on the following passage.

Passage IV

The Shawnee people of the Ohio and Cumberland Valleys gave the American elk its other name, *wapiti*. Yet when we think of elk today, we rarely envision them as eastern animals. If we want to see elk in their natural habitat, we travel to Colorado or Montana, where they still roam the mountainous terrain.

Elk were, in fact, once found in the East, from Georgia north to New York and Connecticut. By the time of the Civil War, hunting and habitat destruction had caused their extinction in most eastern states. All of the eastern subspecies are now extinct. Elk County, Pennsylvania, and Elk County, Kansas, were without elk for more than a century.

At the beginning of the 20th century, herds of elk in the Rocky Mountains faced death by starvation as encroaching farms depleted their winter feeding and finally the government decided to intercede. They gathered up elk from Yellowstone National Park and shipped 50 of them to Pennsylvania. The elk were to be protected, with no hunting of them allowed until eight years had passed.

At that early date, 1913, there was little understanding of the kind of acclimatization required when moving large animals from one habitat to another. The elk were released from cattle cars and chased into the wild to fend for themselves. Two years later, 95 more elk were moved from Yellowstone to Pennsylvania.

Elk are large animals with large ranges, and the damage these elk caused to corn-fields was substantial. The elk tended to move toward farming areas because that was where the food was. Farmers and poachers took some elk illegally, but the herds still began to grow. During the 1920s, several hunting seasons went by with harvests of one or two dozen elk, but then the numbers declined dramatically, and the elk were again put under protected status. No real census was taken until 50 years later, in 1971.

At that time, according to the State Wildlife Management Agency, researchers found about 65 animals. Intensive work by the Bureau of Forestry to improve elk habitat, especially through reclamation of old strip mines, brought those numbers up to 135 by the early 1980s. By the year 2000, there were more than 500 elk in Pennsylvania, including many in Elk County.

In 1984 a group of hunters established the Rocky Mountain Elk Foundation, whose mission is to reintroduce elk in the states where they once roamed. The foundation runs into resistance from farmers and antihunting groups and generally requires majority approval from the community before animals are introduced. At present, new herds are established in Arkansas, Kentucky, Michigan, and Wisconsin in addition to Pennsylvania. There is talk of moving herds to Tennessee and to the Adirondack range in New York. It seems fairly clear that improving habitat for elk reintroduction improves conditions for other wildlife—wild turkey, whitetail deer, and black bear, among others.

Unlike the way things were done in the 1910s, today reintroduction is far more closely monitored and controlled. Animals are tested for disease. They are held in a large enclosure until they have acclimated to their surroundings. After a few weeks, they are released, but most have radio collars and/or ear tags that allow researchers to track their movements and habitat use. Research results help foresters know what to plant where in order to keep the herd healthy and help biologists know whether the herd is thriving or is in need of intercession. Land trusts are used to preserve habitat and to keep the elk from moving too close to cropland. The people in charge of elk reintroduction have no desire to live through another annihilation of the eastern *wapiti*.

19. According to this passage, a major early threat to elk populations was:
    A. wolves and cougars
    B. vehicular traffic
    C. disease
    D. hunting

20. Based on information in the passage, about how many elk were moved from Yellowstone to Pennsylvania in the mid-1910s?
    A. 65
    B. 95
    C. 135
    D. 145

21. According to the passage, where might you see elk today?
    A. the Tennessee Valley
    B. Georgia
    C. the Adirondacks
    D. Arkansas

22. Which of the following assertions does the author support with an example or examples?

    I. New herds have been established in several states.

    II. Improving habitat for elk helps other wildlife.

   III. Land trusts are used to preserve elk habitat.

    A. I only

    B. III only

    C. I and II only

    D. I, II, and III

23. According to the passage, what is true of the elk in Pennsylvania today?

    A. They are the same as the elk who lived there 200 years ago.

    B. They are a different subspecies from the old Pennsylvania elk.

    C. They are a different subspecies from the elk found in the Rockies.

    D. They are only distantly related to the elk found in Yellowstone National Park.

24. Which of the following findings BEST supports the author's contention that elk repopulation is carefully monitored?

    A. Farming to raise deer, elk, and reindeer is increasingly popular.

    B. Before 1997, there had not been a wild elk in Kentucky in 150 years.

    C. Rocky Mountain elk were among the original animals at the Hearst Zoo.

    D. Jackson County is testing potential elk herds for chronic wasting disease.

25. Which new information, if true, would most CHALLENGE the claim that elk reintroduction benefits other species as well?

    A. record sightings of wild turkey, pheasant, and grouse on reclaimed land in Pennsylvania

    B. surprising numbers of multiple births in moose from central and western Maine and New Hampshire

    C. a census showing that whitetail deer were migrating northward from Pennsylvania into New York

    D. an increase in temperature of one or two degrees in the headwaters of the Yellowstone River

Questions 26–33 are based on the following passage.

Passage V

In linguistics, *metathesis* refers to the reversal of phonemes in a word. This can come about by accident, as in the common mispronunciation "aks" for *ask* or the common (and correct) pronunciation of *iron* as "i-orn." It may come about on purpose, as in various language games.

    Accidental metathesis may be a process that takes place in the evolution of languages. Over time, for example, the Latin words *miraculum, periculum,* and *parabola* evolved into the Spanish words *milagro, peligro,* and *palabra.* Linguists posit that such changes usually occur when two consonants are of the same type, with similar mouth formations needed to create each one.

The Reverend Archibald Spooner, an Oxford dean, was known for his unintentional transpositions and gave his name to the particular metathesis he represented: *Spoonerisms*. Most famous Spoonerisms once attributed to Spooner are now believed to be apocryphal, but they are nevertheless amusing; for example, his supposed advice to a substandard student: "You have deliberately tasted two worms and will leave Oxford by the next town drain." Spoonerisms are funny when the metathesis involved changes one word into another, and they seem to lend themselves particularly well to off-color jokes.

Everyone is familiar with Pig Latin, in which initial consonant sounds are moved to the end of a word and followed with the syllable "ay." This is not pure metathesis, but it begins with the kind of metathesis known as backslang, in which syllables or letters in a word are reversed to produce a private code. Pig Latin may have begun as a language spoken in prisoner-of-war camps; it was certainly used in such camps during World War II and in Vietnam.

In Pig Latin, the phrase "Over the river and through the woods" becomes "Overay uhthay iverray anday oughthray uhthay oodsway." In other variations of Pig Latin, it might instead be "Overway uhthay iverray andway oughthray uhthay oodsway." There are computer programs that translate from English to Pig Latin and back again, and there is even a version of the Bible written entirely in Pig Latin. For the most part, however, outside of prisoner-of-war camps, Pig Latin is a funny code used by children.

French children and teenagers use a similar code. Called *verlan* (a reversal of *l'envers*, or "reversal"), it is trickier than Pig Latin because it relies much more on phonetics than on spelling. In verlan, the word *café* becomes *féca*, but the word *tomber* ("to fall") becomes *béton*. Verlan becomes even more complex in words that end in silent *e* or which have only one syllable. While just a few words from Pig Latin have entered the vernacular (for example, *amscray* and *ixnay*), many verlan words are common lingo in France.

Historically, for reasons that are not quite clear, butchers have been frequent users of metathesis, creating their own backslang to converse without being understood by patrons. In France, this is called *louchébem* (*boucher*, or "butcher," with the first consonant moved to the end and the letter *l* placed in front). In Australia, it is known as *rechtub klat*. That name, of course, represents the ultimate in metathesis—the reversal of letters instead of merely syllables.

26. In the context of the passage, the word *transposition* refers to a:
    A. reordering of letters or syllables
    B. movement of terms in an equation
    C. rendering into another language
    D. musical performance in a new key

27. Which of the following examples is presented as evidence that butchers are frequent users of metathesis?

    I. Spoonerisms
    II. *louchébem*
    III. Pig Latin
    A. I only
    B. I and II only
    C. II only
    D. II and III only

28. Which example(s) of metathesis does the author call accidental?

    I. verlan and other backslang
    II. *parabola* to *palabra*
    III. the pronunciation of *iron*
    A. I only
    B. II only
    C. I and III only
    D. II and III only

29. The discussion of prisoner-of-war camps shows primarily that:

    A. Pig Latin can be entertaining even in difficult circumstances.
    B. Metathesis developed during the mid-20th century.
    C. Prisoners may revert to childish games to pass the time.
    D. Metathesis is useful and practical as a secret code.

30. The author's claim that most Spoonerisms are apocryphal could BEST be supported by the inclusion of:

    A. a list of transpositions attributed to the Reverend Spooner
    B. examples of modern-day transpositions based on famous Spoonerisms
    C. interviews with Spooner's contemporaries denying their authenticity
    D. Spooner's own letters to relatives, colleagues, and friends

31. Which of these might be an example of accidental metathesis?

    I. saying *interduce* instead of *introduce*
    II. saying *asterix* instead of *asterisk*
    III. saying *cause* instead of *because*
    A. I only
    B. I and II only
    C. II and III only
    D. I, II, and III

32. Based on information in the passage, which of these would be the verlan translation of *critique*?

    A. *euqitirc*
    B. *ticri*
    C. *tiquay*
    D. *quecriti*

33. The passage implies that Pig Latin is NOT pure metathesis because it:
    A. does not transpose phonemes
    B. is not accidental
    C. includes the addition of an extra syllable
    D. does not add to the language

Questions 34–39 are based on the following passage.

Passage VI

Philosophers generally recognize three different conceptions of totality. Atomistic thinkers, such as Descartes and Wittgenstein, believe that the whole is no more than the sum of its parts. A thorough study of these parts, atomists believe, will lead to an understanding of the whole. A contrasting view, held by Schelling, Hegel (although some scholars question whether Hegel's ontology actually conforms to this formalist conception of totality), and members of the structuralist school of philosophy, holds that the whole has an identity of its own, separate from the nature of its component parts. A third view, and perhaps the most challenging to explore, is the dialectical/materialist idea of the whole held by Karl Marx. In this view, the whole is seen not simply as the sum of its parts as atomists believe or as something independent of its parts according to formalist thought. Instead, the whole is conceived of as the constantly changing and evolving interactions between all of its component parts.

In Marx's view, there are no things—static, independent objects or ideas—there are only processes. Everything that makes up the world is constantly in the process of becoming, with both its past and its future encapsulated in the very notion of the object itself. Furthermore, according to the dialectical materialist view, all objects are interdependent and the interactions they have with each other are also parts of their totalities.

Critics of this perspective point out, somewhat justifiably, that such an ontology has a number of difficulties. One of their major objections is that dialectical materialism is impractical to employ in any meaningful way. Consider how thinking of even a simple object such as a chair in this way quickly leads to a surfeit of information, connections, and processes. For a chair is not simply a chair, but the result of the labor of an individual, a process of manufacturing, the needs of a society that requires chairs, and many other factors. And each of these factors has its own past (and future) and myriad other connections as well. The number of relationships increases exponentially, which quickly makes a dialectical worldview utterly overwhelming to even the most agile philosophical mind.

Marxist philosophers attempt to work around this potential pathology by invoking what is called the process of abstraction. Abstraction allows the philosopher to draw certain boundaries around the object, idea, or relationship studied. Typically, these abstractions involve deciding an appropriate time scale to consider, the level of generality necessary for understanding specific interactions, and the vantage point from which to view a particular object of study. Abstraction on these levels allows the philosopher to bring certain relationships and processes into greater focus in order to understand them, while always keeping in mind that such an abstraction necessarily obscures various other connections. Marx famously used this process in his study of capitalism, sometimes viewing the system from the vantage point of the capitalist, other times assuming the perch of the worker, and even at times trying to view the system from the perspective of capital itself. Similarly, sometimes Marx generalized people as simply members of their class in order to gain a better grasp of the relationship between owner and worker. Each new abstraction adds to the understanding of the system, and the process of abstraction must happen again and again in order to bring hidden connections into view.

34. The passage suggests that philosophical conceptions of totality:
    A. have evolved over time from an atomistic view to a dialectical view
    B. have prevented philosophers from grasping the inherent connections involved in all things
    C. are based on three mutually exclusive conceptions of the relationships between part and whole
    D. are limited to three competing and contrasting conceptions

35. The author MOST likely refers to the dialectical materialist view of totality as "most challenging" because:
    A. Few philosophers other than Marx espouse it.
    B. It appears to require unprecedented mental capabilities.
    C. The insights it offers to a philosopher are overwhelming.
    D. It cannot be employed without using the process of abstraction.

36. The author includes the example of the chair in order to:
    A. point out a complication involved with the dialectical perspective
    B. provide an instance of dialectical abstraction
    C. explain how manufactured objects fit into Marx's view of capitalism
    D. demonstrate that dialectical thinking is impossible

37. The author believes that the dialectical materialist conception of totality:
    A. provides insights into the world superior to the ones provided by the atomistic and formalist conceptions
    B. may correctly be found objectionable on certain levels
    C. is impractical when not paired with the concept of abstraction
    D. works best when applied to institutions like capitalism

38. Which of the following would be an example of a dialectical abstraction as detailed in the passage?

A. A philosopher sees a table as the sum of all the processes that went into producing it.

B. A philosopher conceives of capital not as a static thing, but as a constantly evolving interaction.

C. A philosopher studying sexism only looks at developments and changes from the 20th century.

D. A philosopher admits that any insights gained are colored by the particular vantage point he or she takes.

39. The primary purpose of the passage is to:

A. argue for the primacy of a particular philosophical ontology

B. criticize a school of thought as impractical

C. explain how Marx attempted to study capitalism

D. attempt to answer a particular objection to a philosophical practice

Questions 40–47 are based on the following passage.

Passage VII

Biologists use the term "living fossil" to designate a species that maintains many of the features of its ancient ancestors. These species have evidenced very little evolutionary change, indicating not that they are primitive creatures as might be popularly believed, but instead that they are exquisitely suited for their biological and ecological niches and thus have not had any selection pressures to respond to.

The four most celebrated living fossils are the lungfish, the horseshoe crab, the lampshell, and the coelacanth. The horseshoe crab is the relative youngster of the group, belonging to the Jurassic period and having shown little structural changes in its 200-million-year lifespan. The lampshell, a member of the phylum Brachiopoda, is part of an even older lineage, resembling ancestors that lived nearly 400 million years ago.

The oldest members of the living fossil family are the lungfish and the coelacanth, both species that are remarkably similar to their forebears that roamed the Earth almost 425 million years ago. The lungfish, of which there are six surviving species, has the same basic structure and fleshy lobe fins of its progenitor, the sarcopterygian. Of course, the lungfish has long interested biologists not just because of its connections to the distant past but because of the bridge it represents between aquatic species and land dwellers. In fact, the African and South American species of lungfish live part of their lives entirely on land, burrowing into mud and respiring through a tiny breathing hole in their earthy homes. Although the lungfish has remained evolutionarily stable for close to 250 million years, prior to that the species did experience rapid and dynamic evolutionary change. However, by the end of the Permian period, the changes ground to a halt, and the lungfish has persevered happily ever since.

The singular story of the coelacanth stretches all the way from the Silurian period, some 425 million years ago, to the modern day. The coelacanths were well-known from the fossil record and dating technologies placed them in a time when plants were just beginning to encroach on the land. However, biologists thought the species went extinct long before the dinosaurs did. Imagine the surprise when in 1938 a South American trawler captured a strange-looking fish, some five feet in length and a pale blue and silver in color. By an astounding coincidence, the captain of the boat had a relationship with the curator of the East London Museum and had made a habit of sending any interesting finds along to her. Upon seeing this strange specimen, the curator contacted a leading ichthyologist, who, after examining the creature, said he "would not have been more surprised if I had seen a dinosaur walking down the street." But despite all protestations of common sense and amid allegations of forgery and fakery, upon further study, the creature was indubitably a coelacanth. Since that day, explorers have found many more members of the species and have even turned up a second species in the Indian Ocean.

40. The primary purpose of the passage is to:
    A. explain how living fossils can remain unchanged by evolution
    B. describe a dilemma facing evolutionary biologists
    C. detail the interesting story of the coelacanth
    D. provide an overview of a biological category

41. The passage states that describing living fossils as primitive is a misnomer because:
    A. Living fossils are just as advanced as any other species.
    B. The public does not understand how evolution works.
    C. Living fossils continue to evolve.
    D. Living fossils no longer respond to natural selection.

42. Based on the information in the passage, which of the following orderings, from earliest to most recent, is correct?
    A. Jurassic, Permian, Silurian
    B. Permian, Silurian, Jurassic
    C. Silurian, Permian, Jurassic
    D. Silurian, Jurassic, Permian

43. The author probably mentions the lungfish's early evolutionary changes in order to:
    A. clarify the term *living fossil*
    B. show that biologists are divided as to what constitutes a living fossil
    C. indicate that the lungfish might again experience evolutionary change
    D. compare the lungfish to the coelacanth

44. The passage suggests that the author MOST likely believes:
    A. The modern discovery of the coelacanth was somewhat due to luck.
    B. The lungfish is a more interesting living fossil than the coelacanth.
    C. Biologists were wrong to think the coelacanth extinct.
    D. The coelacanth also experiences a period of rapid evolutionary change.

45. In contrast to the other three living fossils, the horseshoe crab:
    A. was alive at the same time the dinosaurs were
    B. has experienced few structural changes
    C. is no longer evolutionarily stable
    D. evolved well after land-dwelling plants did

46. The author MOST likely mentions allegations of forgery and fakery in order to:
    A. underscore how unprecedented the discovery was
    B. indicate that some thought to profit from the discovery
    C. describe the public's reaction to the find
    D. dismiss the concerns of leading biologists of the time

47. Suppose a biologist rejects the classification of coelacanths as living fossils. Which of the following pieces of evidence would be MOST helpful to the biologist's argument?
    A. New dating technologies reveal the coelacanth species is only 300 million years old.
    B. A third species of coelacanth is discovered that differs from the other two known species.
    C. New evidence shows that the coelacanth actually belongs to the same lineage as do rays and skates.
    D. A new species of living fossil is discovered that is even older than the coelacanth.

Questions 48–53 are based on the following passage.

Passage VIII

For years, a great many political scientists have been puzzled by what appears to be the most basic of all political questions: why vote? Of course, it's not that voting is an overly troublesome or burdensome activity; commonsense explanations of voting behavior are often borne out through empirical study. People vote in order to express their preferences for a particular candidate or platform, to demonstrate their civic pride, or to involve themselves in the political process. The puzzle lies instead in the actual act of voting, which in many ways conforms to what social scientists term the "free-rider problem." Any social good that spreads both costs and benefits amongst a number of citizens encourages the citizens to attempt to reap the benefits without incurring the costs. Given the almost infinitesimal chance that any one individual's vote would actually affect the outcome of an election and given that the supporters of the winning candidate all share equally in the benefit of that candidate's election, the costs of voting, no matter how minor they may be, appear to make voting an irrational act. Better to stay home on election day and let the others do the heavy lifting, the thinking goes.

But the fact is people do get up on election day and vote. Various theories have been postulated to explain this seemingly irrational behavior, but there are three factors that political scientists return to again and again: resources, mobilization, and instrumental motivation.

Resources refer to both material possessions such as money and transportation, and immaterial things such as time and political knowledge. Mobilization refers to the pressures the media, political parties, and other groups can exert on an individual in order to make him or her feel compelled to vote. Instrumental motivation is the extent to which a person believes his or her vote will actually affect the outcome of the election.

Of these three critical factors, resources has received the most scholarly attention. According to a classic view of voting behavior, people vote because they have the time and the money to do so. Some political scientists have even calculated what they call a baseline model of political participation. This model attempts to predict political participation based on an individual's level of education, income, and several other occupational variables. Certain individual traits may affect the final decision, but the theory holds that the level of resources is a better predictor of political behavior than any other factor.

Unfortunately, this model, while achieving some success when applied to actual political behavior, suffers from a serious flaw. The model becomes useless when the voting behaviors of citizens from other countries are compared. The differences in voter turnout across educational levels and income are smaller than the differences found in turnout across various countries. Additionally, countries with higher per capita levels of education and income are not necessarily the countries with the highest voter turnout. Indeed, the United States and Switzerland, two countries that are at the top or near to the top of the list in terms of per capita education level and income have some of the lowest voter turnout numbers.

48. According to the passage, the problem that puzzles political scientists is:
    A. what motivates people to vote
    B. why people consider voting an irrational act
    C. what makes people think the benefits of voting outweigh the costs
    D. whether voting is a case of the free-rider dilemma

49. The "thinking" referred to in the last sentence of the first paragraph ("Better to stay home on election day and let the others do the heavy lifting, the thinking goes") would MOST likely be attributed to:
    A. political scientists
    B. free riders
    C. typical voters
    D. political candidates

50. According to the baseline model of political participation, which of the following individuals would be MOST likely to vote?
    A. a lawyer
    B. a Swiss citizen
    C. a U.S. citizen
    D. a homemaker

51. Which of the following does the author indicate is a possible factor in explaining voting behavior?
    I. a large amount of free time
    II. get out the vote drives
    III. a sense of the significance of one's vote
    A. I only
    B. II only
    C. II and III
    D. I, II, and III

52. According to the passage, the baseline model of political participation is:
    A. applicable only to isolated cases of voting behavior
    B. an accurate predictor of voting behavior
    C. more useful in countries with lower voter turnout
    D. more useful in countries with higher voter turnout

53. The passage implies that:
    A. Resources are the key factor in explaining voting behavior.
    B. The effects of mobilization and instrumental motivation on voter turnout have been ignored by scholars.
    C. No theory of voting behavior will successfully explain voter turnout.
    D. Explanations of voting behavior involving mobilization have not received the same attention as other explanations.

STOP. This is the end of Section 4.

ANSWERS AND EXPLANATIONS

Section 1. Biological and Biochemical Foundations of Living Systems

Passage I

1. **The correct answer is A.** Increasing H^+ ion concentration should drive the reaction to the left, which causes the production of carbonic acid (choice A). If the reaction continues, the carbonic acid would be converted to carbon dioxide and water. This would eliminate choice B, which suggests that the carbon dioxide levels would decrease. Since the reaction is driving to the left, bicarbonate ion levels should not increase, so choice C can be eliminated. The passage indicates that carbonic anhydrase catalyzes the reaction in both directions, so its activity should be increased when H^+ ion concentration increases.

2. **The correct answer is B.** Increased levels of H_2CO_3 in the plasma should lead to an increased production of carbon dioxide and water. Increased levels of carbon dioxide are the primary trigger for ventilation. If carbon dioxide levels are high, the ventilation rate should increase. The presence of carbonic acid would decrease pH as opposed to increasing pH (suggested by choice C).

3. **The correct answer is C.** This question is simply asking for how carbon dioxide is produced on the cellular level. You should recall your knowledge of the process of cellular respiration. During aerobic respiration, glucose goes through glycolysis, Krebs cycle, and the electron transport chain. During Krebs cycle, carbon dioxide is released. Therefore, carbon dioxide is formed in the cells as a by-product of glucose metabolism. Protein synthesis and nucleic acid metabolism do not produce carbon dioxide as by-products.

4. **The correct answer is C.** This question is about osmotic effects. We are told that the process of dialysis needs to remove excess fluids (water) from the blood. In order to do this, the dialysis fluid must have more solutes and less water than the blood. This would mean that the dialysis fluid must be hypertonic to the blood. Another way to say this is that the blood must be hypotonic (contain less solutes and more water) than the dialysis fluid (choice C). If the patient's blood was isotonic to the dialysis fluid, there would be no net movement of water. If the blood were hypertonic to the dialysis fluid, water would enter the blood.

5. **The correct answer is A.** Increasing the levels of Na^+, K^+, and HCO_3^- ions excreted in the urine should increase the concentration of the urine. As the urine becomes more concentrated, osmotic effects occur, and extra water will be excreted with the urine in an attempt to dilute the urine. This will increase the urine volume (choice A).

6. **The correct answer is B.** The question indicates that the toxins being referred to are small in size. We can assume that they are at a high concentration in the blood as compared to the concentration of the dialysis fluid. Choice A can be eliminated because active transport moves substances from a lower concentration to a higher concentration. In this case, we want to move the toxins from a higher concentration (the blood) to a lower concentration (the dialysis fluid). This would indicate that diffusion (choice B) would be appropriate. Osmosis deals only with the movement of water, which will not help move the toxins out of the blood.

Passage II

7. **The correct answer is D.** Sex-linked inheritance can be quickly eliminated as males and females seem to be equally affected based on the pedigree. Since autosomal inheritance is obvious, it is necessary to determine if the pattern is characteristic of a dominant or recessive condition. Recessive traits are notorious for "skipping generations" in pedigrees, which means that affected children often come from unaffected parents. To be affected, the individual must be homozygous recessive. The parents do not have the disease, but they are unknowing carriers (heterozygotes), which gives them a 25% chance of having an affected offspring. In dominant autosomal inheritance, the affected individual can be homozygous dominant or heterozygous. This means that in order for a child to have the disease, the child must have inherited at least one mutated allele from his or her parent who also had the disease. The only exception would be if spontaneous mutation occurred. When affected individuals appear in each generation of a pedigree, dominance should be suspected.

8. **The correct answer is C.** TSC1 and TSC2 are the normal alleles. Only mutated versions of these alleles cause tuberous sclerosis, according to the passage. The passage indicates that the gene products of TSC1 and TSC2 are hamartin and tuberin, both of which are tumor suppressors. If an individual were to overexpress TSC1 and TSC2, more of the TSC1 and TSC2 gene products would be produced; so we would suspect that their levels of hamartin and tuberin would be elevated. This should provide extra protection against tumor formation, which is indicated by choice C.

9. **The correct answer is D.** The passage explains that individuals who developed tuberous sclerosis as the result of gonadal mosaicism come from parents who do not have the mutated TSC1 and TSC2 alleles in their somatic cells. Since we already determined that the pattern of inheritance for this condition is autosomal dominant, we know that the affected individual only needs to receive a mutated version of TSC1 or TSC2 from one parent. Since individuals inherit their alleles through the egg and sperm of their parents, it is reasonable to expect that the gonadal mosaicism form of tuberous sclerosis must come from a mutation in the TSC1 or TSC2 gene on one of the parent's gametes. Since gametes are made using the process of meiosis, it would seem that the mutation occurred during this process, leaving choice D as the best answer.

10. **The correct answer is C.** This question relies on the fact that you have already determined that the normal pattern of inheritance for tuberous sclerosis is autosomal dominant. Since affected individuals could be heterozygous for the mutated versions of TSC1 and TSC2, it would be possible that half their gametes carry the normal alleles while the other half would carry the mutated alleles. Assuming both parents with the disease are heterozygous, a Punnett square would indicate that 25% of the offspring would be homozygous recessive and would not have tuberous sclerosis.

11. **The correct answer is C.** We have already established that tuberous sclerosis is an autosomal condition. The passage explains that individuals with the gonadal mosaicism form of tuberous sclerosis come from parents who do not carry the mutated TSC1 and TSC2 alleles in their somatic cells. However, some of their gametes carry the mutation. Since the somatic cells do not have the mutated alleles, these individuals do not appear to have tuberous sclerosis. If a pedigree were to be constructed, it would show two unaffected parents producing a child with the disease. This would resemble autosomal recessive inheritance where "skipping generations" is typical.

12. **The correct answer is A.** This question is asking about anemia, which has many causes. But anemia is always characterized by either a low erythrocyte count or a low hemoglobin count. The question indicated that tuberous sclerosis often occurs as the result of blood loss, which would indicate that the type of anemia occurring would be characterized by low erythrocyte counts and low hemoglobin counts. Since the function of hemoglobin is to transport oxygen, and the hemoglobin and erythrocyte counts are low, it would be expected that oxygen-carrying capacity would be reduced.

13. **The correct answer is C.** The passage explains that lidocaine is metabolized in the liver and produces two metabolites: monoethylglycinexylidide and glycinexylidide. If we are comparing a person with normal liver function to one with compromised liver function, there will be a difference in how long it takes to clear lidocaine from the system. If the liver function is impaired, it is expected that lidocaine will stay in the plasma longer as it waits to be metabolized by the liver. Therefore, the plasma concentration of lidocaine in the liver-compromised patient should be higher after 1 hour than in the patient with normal liver function. The faster lidocaine is metabolized by the liver, the faster the metabolites would be expected to enter the plasma and ultimately be excreted by the kidneys. Choice C is correct because it suggests that one of the metabolites of lidocaine, monoethylglycinexylidide, would be processed by the liver and kidneys more quickly in the normal patient as compared to the liver-impaired patient.

14. **The correct answer is B.** This question requires an understanding of resting potentials and action potentials in the neurons. Recall that resting potentials (polarization) of neuronal membranes are maintained due to an unequal balance of ions that allows for the inside of the neuron to be more negative than the outside

of the neuron. This is primarily due to the action of Na^+/K^+ pumps, which utilize large amounts of ATP to maintain an unequal balance of ions. In the polarized state, Na^+ is found in high concentrations outside the neuron and K^+ is found in high concentrations inside the neuron. The neuron also contains a variety of negatively charged molecules. In order for a message to be sent, the membrane needs to depolarize. This is characterized by the opening of Na^+ gated channels, which allow Na^+ to flood the inside of the neuron, temporarily (and locally) making that area of the neuron more positive inside than outside. This action potential will propagate the length of the neuron, where it will ultimately coerce the release of neurotransmitters into the synapse. Blockage of the Na^+ channels would essentially keep the neuron in resting potential where Na^+ is restricted to outside the neuron. Blocking Na^+ channels prevents the initiation of the action potential or depolarization of the membrane.

15. **The correct answer is A.** Since lidocaine blocks Na^+ gated channels, we have already established that it prevents the initiation of action potentials in the affected neurons. Normally, as action potentials propagate, they eventually cause the release of neurotransmitters into the synapse. Since action potentials are impaired in lidocaine-treated neurons, we should expect that there will be fewer neurotransmitters released into the synapse.

16. **The correct answer is C.** The passage indicates that lidocaine is an analgesic (prevents pain) by blocking Na^+ gates channels in neurons. Since glial cells are not neurons, choice D can immediately be eliminated. In order to prevent pain from being processed, the messages must be prevented from entering the central nervous system where interneurons are located. Therefore, sensory neurons must be blocked. If these are blocked, the interneurons do not receive the pain messages and motor neurons will not act on them.

17. **The correct answer is C.** Vasoconstriction means that vessel diameter narrows, restricting blood flow to the area. The question introduces the idea of using novocaine during surgery. Since the drug causes vasoconstriction, this would actually increase blood pressure, eliminating choice A. The best choice is C. Bleeding is likely to occur during surgery, so vasoconstriction should slow the blood flow, which results in less blood loss.

18. **The correct answer is B.** This question relies on your knowledge of the anatomy of the heart and the conducting system of the heart. The sinoatrial node (SA node) is a group of conducting cells located in the right atrium. Recall that the valves of the heart are atrioventricular (AV) and semilunar valves. The barricade that divides the right and left side of the heart is the septum. The SA node generates electrical signals that control cardiac muscle contractions and serves as the pacemaker for the heart.

Passage IV
19. **The correct answer is D.** It is important to provide controls in experimental designs. Control groups should be treated the same as the treatment groups except for the one variable that is being tested. The control group either receives no treatment or receives a placebo (which is not a form of treatment) to make the subject

believe that he or she is receiving a treatment. Choices A, B, and C all suggest that the control group should be treated with one of the two drugs (SNP or L-NAME), which removes them as viable options. In the experiment described in the passage, the control group should not be provided with either drug (SNP or L-NAME), which is indicated by choice D.

20. **The correct answer is A.** To answer this question, you need to analyze the data provided. Looking at the number of embryos surviving, you should notice that all three groups treated with any dosage of L-NAME had decreased survival as compared to the control group. The passage explains that L-NAME is a NOS inhibitor. If the enzyme needed to convert L-arginine to NO does not work, then NO levels will be decreased. The data suggest that a decreased level of NO provided by the L-NAME treatment is detrimental. Further, the higher the dose of L-NAME, the more inhibition of NOS and the less NO provided, led to a dose dependent decrease in survival that eliminates choice C as an option. The passage also explains that SNP is a NO donor, which increases NO levels. According to the data provided for the SNP groups, a small increase in NO (seen in group 2) seems to increase embryo survival. However, as the SNP dose becomes larger (and the higher the level of NO provided), this will lead to decreased survival. The highest rates of survival were seen in the 0.1 μm SNP group, and survival decreased with increased dosage of SNP. This would eliminate choice B since increasing levels of NOS would increase NO levels similar to SNP treatment. The data show that SNP treatment (which increases NO levels) is most detrimental to embryo survival. Choice D directly contradicts this. The best conclusion is that NO is necessary for development, since the data showed that the NO inhibition leads to decreased survival. However, only a certain amount of NO is needed as high levels also lead to decreased rates of embryo survival.

21. **The correct answer is B.** Group 1 was the control group, so there would be no need to further investigate that group. This eliminates choice A. Groups 4 and 6 showed drastic decreases in embryo survival, eliminating choices C and D. However, group 2 (choice B) showed an increase in embryo survival, which would suggest that further research within that dosage would be appropriate.

22. **The correct answer is C.** The question relies on your knowledge of the anatomy of the female reproductive system and the events of fertilization. As a follicle ruptures in the ovaries, the ovum would be released into the oviducts. Sperm should enter the vagina, moving up the uterus and into the oviducts. Sperm should encounter the ovum in the oviducts where fertilization should occur. This eliminates choices A, B, and D, leaving choice C as the correct choice.

23. **The correct answer is C.** This question also relies on your knowledge of early development. After fertilization, the zygote (a diploid, fertilized egg) begins cleavage, which is rapid mitotic cell division. This results in a solid ball of cells. Eventually, the center of this structure hollows out to form a cavity. This stage of development is the blastocyst stage. Choice A can be eliminated because it suggests that a blastocyst is a solid ball of cells when it really is a hollowed-out structure. Choice B suggests a diploid, fertilized egg, which is actually called a zygote.

Choice D suggests that there is a ball of cells that perform meiosis. Since we know the only cells to perform meiosis are the gametes, choice D can be eliminated. Choice C correctly describes the structure of the blastocyst.

24. **The correct answer is B.** The passage explains that SNP is a NO donor, which increases NO levels. Since decreased levels of NO can cause reduced blood flow to the extremities, increasing levels of NO may improve blood flow for a diabetic patient.

Passage V 25. **The correct answer is D.** This question relies on knowledge of the immune response. Interleukins are cytokines that are secreted during the process of clonal selection in primary immune responses. Since they are not specific toward any one particular antigen, choice A can be eliminated. Interferons are produced as non-specific defenses against viral infections. Virally infected cells secrete interferons that are detected by neighboring cells. Secretion of interferons gives neighboring cells the chance to increase their immune defenses so that they do not become infected by the virus. Since interferons are nonspecific, their presence would not indicate immunity against a specific virus, which eliminates choice B. The components of the complement system circulate in the plasma and are activated by bacteria that may enter the blood. Activation of the complement system ultimately lyses and kills the bacterial cell. Since the question is asking about a virus, choice C can be eliminated because it deals with bacteria. This leaves choice D as the correct response. The detection of antibodies against the viral antigen would indicate that specific defenses were initiated and that plasma cells were activated to secrete antibodies against the viral antigen that was presented by the vaccine.

26. **The correct answer is B.** While polymerase chain reaction (PCR) is used to amplify copies of target DNA, it would not help to get the viral or bacterial genes of interest into plant cells. This eliminates choice A. Choice C suggests that the genes could be cloned into a bacterial cell and transferred to a plant cell by conjugation. Conjugation is unique to certain species of bacteria and occasionally is seen in fungi, but it does not happen in plants. So choice C is eliminated. Choice D suggests that the genes of interest should be hybridized to the DNA of the plant. Since hybridization occurs between complementary base pairs, this would suggest that the DNA sequence of the gene of interest and the plant would have to be the same, which is not the case. This leaves choice B as the best option. Bacterial or viral genes can be spliced into plasmids. The plasmids serve as vectors to deliver the gene of interest to a variety of cell types, including plants.

27. **The correct answer is D.** Once activated, most cells in the immune system do not live long. Activated cytotoxic T cells and plasma cells are inactivated once the antigen that they have been designed to fight has been eliminated. The basis of long-term immune system protection is the development of memory T and memory B cells (choice D). These memory cells are produced upon primary exposure to a specific antigen and have the ability to survive for years within the body. Should the same antigen return, memory cells quickly proliferate into cytotoxic T cells and plasma cells to fight the antigen.

28. **The correct answer is B.** All vaccines take time to work (often weeks before full immunity occurs), so waiting for an oral vaccine to pass through the digestive tract (which takes no more than a few hours) is not of major concern. This eliminates choice A. Choice C suggests that inflammation in the digestive tract might be a problem. Since the inflammatory response is expected as one of the nonspecific immune defenses, it is not of major concern. Since two choices have been eliminated, choice D is no longer an option. This leaves choice B as the correct response. Since the plant has been engineered to express proteins unique to the virus or bacterium being vaccinated against, it is possible that these proteins might be damaged in the stomach. Recall that the function of the stomach is to digest proteins by using the enzyme pepsin.

29. **The correct answer is B.** This question requires an understanding of the specific defenses of the immune system. The ultimate goal of the specific defenses is to allow for the production of antibodies from plasma cells and the production of cytotoxic T cells. However, neither of these things can occur without the activation of a helper T cell. In order to activate the helper T cell, macrophages must phagocytize foreign antigens. The fragments of these antigens will be displayed on the surface of the macrophage. This antigen presenting cell will then activate the helper T cell.

30. **The correct answer is C.** IgM antibodies are produced first in response to exposure to a new antigen. Later, IgG antibodies will be produced.

31. **The correct answer is C.** Based on the data presented, more of the knockout mice tested positive for the virus than the wild-type mice. Since the knockout mice had the new interleukin gene disrupted, they would not produce this new interleukin, which could be the reason that most of the knockout mice tested positive for the virus.

Passage VI

32. **The correct answer is B.** If wild-type mice were provided with supplemental interleukin X and tested negative for HCV, it is possible that this could be attributed to the presence of interleukin X.

33. **The correct answer is A.** The polymerase chain reaction works by using primers specific to a target sequence. In the presence of that sequence, the primers bind and the target sequence is copied. After multiple cycles, many copies of the target gene are present and can be detected. In the absence of that sequence, the primers do not bind and nothing will be amplified.

34. **The correct answer is A.** The question specifically noted that we were looking for something that was part of the innate set of immune defenses. Of the choices provided, interferons are the only option that would be typical in viral infection.

35. **The correct answer is B.** Because this is an RNA virus that must produce additional RNA viruses, the enzyme's RNA polymerase would be the logical target given that it copies RNA. Reverse transcriptase is unique to retroviruses, and DNA polymerase and DNA gyrase would be used for DNA replication.

36. **The correct answer is C.** Of the choices provided, C is the most plausible. Increased expression of receptors for the new interleukin could lead to a higher level of

interleukin activity in the cells. If this interleukin is effective against viral infection, increased activity might lead to better protection.

37. **The correct answer is A.** In positive feedback loops, a stimulus is amplified in the feedback loop. In this case, if the stimulus is the production of an autoinducer, a positive feedback loop would stimulate the production of more autoinducer. This is in contrast to negative feedback loops where the response in the feedback loop is the opposite of the stimulus.

38. **The correct answer is A.** If bacteria can coordinate their efforts to express certain genes, they are more likely to impact their host as compared to if a single cell were to express a gene product on its own. For example, if bacteria were to express a virulence factor, such as a toxin, the impact of that from a single cell would be minimal on the host. However, if the entire population expressed that toxin in a coordinated manner, the impact would be much greater on the host.

39. **The correct answer is B.** As the population of bacteria decreases, and there is less likelihood of a quorum, there is less accumulation of autoinducers within the population. As the population increases, autoinducer expression should increase as well.

40. **The correct answer is A.** The advantage of biofilm formation is that it provides a direct and strong attachment to its host. Biofilms are notoriously difficult to eradicate, and the bacteria within them are provided protection against many variables, sometimes including antibiotics.

41. **The correct answer is A.** This question relies on your knowledge of the structure of organic molecules. The N-AHLs in this question should be recognized as some derivative of an amino acid. Given that information, the most likely way to alter them would be by altering their R group side chains.

42. **The correct answer is D.** Antibiotics must target structures that are unique to prokaryotic cells. Of the choices listed, the nucleus is a structure lacking in prokaryotic cells and therefore could not serve as a target for antibiotics.

43. **The correct answer is C.** Restriction enzymes are known to cut DNA at specific recognition sequences and are valuable tools for excising genes to be transferred from one source to another. Reverse transcriptase is used to copy RNA to DNA. Viral vectors can carry DNA of interest into other cells, but they are not used to remove genes from an organism. Polymerase chain reaction (PCR) is used to produce multiple copies of a target DNA sequence.

44. **The correct answer is A.** A series of several genes under the control of a single promoter is most similar to the inducible operon system in bacteria. Okazaki fragments are produced during semiconservative replication on the lagging strand of DNA. Strands of DNA that are hybridized are complementary to each other. A vector is used to carry DNA from one source into another.

45. **The correct answer is C.** Bacterial ribosomes are in fact different from eukaryotic ribosomes. However, the genetic code is universal so there should be no problem translating the proteins. When eukaryotic DNA is introduced to bacterial cells, it

is contained in a vector such as a plasmid that is a normal component of many bacterial cells. We know that eukaryotic genes contain introns and prokaryotic genes do not. If a eukaryotic gene is placed in a prokaryotic cell, the introns cannot be removed and the mRNA produced will contain introns. When translated, the intended protein will not be produced.

46. **The correct answer is A.** This question is asking which of the types of tissue listed are epithelial. Skeletal muscle is muscular tissue, adipose tissue is connective tissue, and bone is connective tissue. Epidermal tissue is made of stratified squamous epithelial tissue.

47. **The correct answer is B.** Vaccines are designed to work by stimulating the primary immune response of the recipient. This requires the immune system to recognize an antigen and to mount a specific immune response. Ultimately, this leads to the production of memory cells that can survive for long periods of time. When the system is challenged by the actual antigen, different types of memory cells can quickly proliferate into plasma cells and cytotoxic T cells in order to destroy the antigen.

48. **The correct answer is C.** Genetically modified organisms contain one or more additional genes as compared to their non-GM organism equivalents.

49. **The correct answer is C.** Blood is a fluid made up of liquid plasma (55%), the primary component of which is water, and floating cells (45%). The plasma is richly endowed with dissolved proteins, lipids, and carbohydrates.

No passage

50. **The correct answer is A.** This problem can be solved through knowledge of each of the various hormones given in the four options. Antidiuretic hormone maintains control of water balance in the human body by stimulating increased water reabsorption by the kidneys. Luteinizing hormone stimulates secretion of sex hormones by ovaries and testes. Adrenocorticotropic hormone stimulates the adrenal glands. Growth hormone regulates a wide variety of activities involved in growth and metabolism.

51. **The correct answer is B.** The pancreas is the source for two hormones: insulin and glucagon. Among its principal effects, insulin stimulates glycogen formation and storage, stimulates carbohydrate oxidation, and inhibits gluconeogenesis. All of these effects are described in choices A, C, and D. The other hormone, glucagon, stimulates conversion of glycogen into glucose. So choice B is the correct answer.

52. **The correct answer is A.** The superior vena cava is the vein that carries deoxygenated blood from the upper half of the body to the heart into its right atrium. The aorta is the largest and longest of the arteries of the human body that transports oxygenated blood directly from the left ventricle to all other organs and tissues in the body. The hepatic portal vein is the major vein that transports blood from the digestive organs into the liver. The carotid artery is one of two types of arteries (the other being vertebral) that feed blood from the heart and into the head/brain area.

53. **The correct answer is C.** Pulmonary gas exchange is always based on simple diffusion. Diffusion allows for the movement of a substance from an area of high concentration of the substance to an area of low concentration of the substance. Depending on the concentrations, oxygen and carbon dioxide will move in variable directions. Choices A, B, and D indicate that the movement of gases always occurs in a fixed direction, which is incorrect.

54. **The correct answer is C.** Prokaryotic cells lack membrane-bound organelles including a nucleus. Their DNA is circular and does not exist as linear chromosomes. Prokaryotic cells can have a cell wall, but it is typically made of peptidoglycan. The only item on this list that is common between prokaryotic and eukaryotic cells is that they both contain ribosomes needed for protein synthesis within the cell.

55. **The correct answer is A.** This question relies on your knowledge of nutrient breakdown through the digestive system. In the stomach, the primary activity is protein digestion. The enzyme pepsin is activated by the acidity of the stomach. If the stomach pH were to be increased, there may not be enough acid to activate pepsin. This would mean that proteins would not be digested in the stomach. However, the pancreas produces proteinases that can work on protein digestion in the small intestine.

56. **The correct answer is C.** The four major tissue types are listed as choices. Nervous tissue is unique in its communication abilities. Muscular tissue is characterized by bundles of cells with the ability to contract. Epithelial tissue is characterized by sheets or layers of cells that connect to underlying tissues via a sticky basement membrane. Only connective tissues are characterized by cells scattered in a nonliving matrix that often contains fibers such as collagen.

57. **The correct answer is C.** The primary difference between aerobic and anaerobic cellular respiration is the amount of ATP generated. Anaerobic respiration generates 2 ATP per molecule of glucose, while aerobic cellular respiration generates about 36 ATP per glucose molecule.

58. **The correct answer is C.** This problem requires a Punnett square to be performed for each generation. For the first generation, the Punnett square for the genetic cross of TT × tt or:

	T	T
t	Tt	Tt
t	Tt	Tt

In the first generation, the T and t gametes unite to produce individuals with a Tt (heterozygous) genotype. In the second generation, the Punnett square is conducted for the genetic cross of Tt × Tt or:

	T	t
T	TT	Tt
t	Tt	tt

The phenotypic results from this cross are that three of the four pea plants will be tall (TT, Tt, and Tt) and one of the four is short (tt). Thus, the phenotypic ratio of dominant to recessive pea plants is 3:1, given by choice C.

59. **The correct answer is C.** Steroid hormones exert their effects by entering into cells and binding with a receptor in the cytoplasm. The hormone-receptor complex then enters the nucleus where it acts to alter gene expression in the cell. Since the question is asking about nonsteroid, or peptide, hormones, choices A and B can be eliminated. Choice D can also be eliminated as this is not a plausible explanation. Nonsteroid hormones act as first messengers binding to their receptors on the cell membrane. The hormone itself does not enter the cell. The binding of the first messenger to the receptor causes a series of reactions in the cell that ultimately activate second messengers, such as cAMP.

Section 2. Chemical and Physical Foundations of Biological Systems

No passage

1. **The correct answer is A.** As the frog follows the parabolic trajectory, the horizontal component of its velocity, which can be calculated by $v_{i,x} = v_i \cos \theta_i$, is positive and remains constant throughout the entire trajectory. Based on this information, one can readily exclude choices B and C as possible answers. The vertical component of velocity begins with its maximum (positive) value at the origin, calculated by $v_{i,y} = v_i \sin \theta_i$, and then follows according to the equation:

$$v_{f,y} = v_i (\sin \theta) - g \Delta t$$

Thus, at $\Delta t = 0$, the vertical component of velocity of the frog is at its positive maximum value, which decreases until it reaches zero as the frog reaches the maximum altitude or the highest point of its trajectory. As the frog continues past the point of its maximum altitude, the vertical component of velocity begins to increase, but, because the frog is now moving downward, it is negative. The negative values are indicated by the graph moving linearly under the positive x-axis. When the frog lands, the magnitude of the vertical component of velocity is equal to its value at launch but its direction is opposite to that of its launch. The pair of graphs that best represents both components of velocity in projectile motion is choice A.

2. **The correct answer is B.** The energy stored in a capacitor is given by the formula:

$$E = \tfrac{1}{2} CV^2 = \tfrac{1}{2} (30 \times 10^{-6})(6 \times 10^3 \text{ V})^2 = 540 \text{ J}$$

Passage I

3. **The correct answer is D.** The endpoints occur when 1 and 2 equivalents of base have been added. According to the graph, these would be at pH 6 and pH 12.

4. **The correct answer is B.** At pH 2, the amount of H^+ ions in solutions is plentiful. Therefore, both the carboxylic acid and the amino groups are protonated.

5. **The correct answer is B.** Above a pH of 2.4, the carboxylic acid is in the carboxylate form. The amino group is protonated below a pH of 9.8. The zwitterion will exist between pH 2.4 and pH 9.8, making a pH of 6 the correct answer.

6. **The correct answer is B.** A titration is a slow process where titrant is added drop by drop until the endpoint is reached. However, knowing where the steep slope is, one can add more base to begin with and then slow down as the endpoint is approached. Near the endpoint, the slope increases sharply in this area, so smaller increments are needed.

7. **The correct answer is B.** The concentration of the base is twice that of the glycine, so half as much volume is needed to reach the first endpoint. A 50.0-mL sample of 0.050 M glycine will require 25.0 mL of 0.10 M NaOH to reach the first endpoint.

Passage II

8. **The correct answer is B.** Because the person is walking at a steady pace away from the motion sensor, the velocity is constant. For each increment of time, the corresponding slope (rise over run) that is the velocity is equal in value throughout the entire activity. Thus, the graph that best illustrates this activity is choice B.

9. **The correct answer is C.** Because the person is walking at a steady pace away from the motion sensor, the velocity is constant. As noted from the previous problem, the graph on a velocity versus time graph is a horizontal line at a nonzero positive value, determined by magnitude of the person's pace. Acceleration, which can be determined by the time rate of change of velocity over time, is zero, because the velocity is constant. This graph is represented by choice C.

10. **The correct answer is C.** In this activity, the person starts at some distance 3 meters away from the motion sensor, which means the graph would have to start at a positive, nonzero value of distance. This readily eliminates choices A and D as possible answers. Since the person is walking toward the motion sensor, the student is walking toward the origin, represented by choice C.

11. **The correct answer is B.** Activity 1 starts with the person standing directly in front of the motion sensor and then walking away from the sensor slowly. This translates into a positively increasing graph (because the person is walking away from the sensor) with a small slope (because the person is walking slowly). The person then stands still, which means the distance remains the same (horizontal line) over that segment. In the final segment, the person walks away, which reveals a graph similar to the first segment appended to the horizontal graph. This is represented by choice B.

12. **The correct answer is D.** In Activity 2, the person starts by standing still (a horizontal line on a distance versus time graph) in front of the motion sensor. The person then walks away from the sensor quickly, described by a positively increasing graph because the person is walking away from the sensor and with a steep slope because the person is walking quickly. In the final segment, the person continues to walk away, again yielding a positively increasing graph but with a smaller slope because the person is walking as opposed to moving quickly. This is represented by the graph in choice D.

13. **The correct answer is C.** In Activity 3, the person starts from a distance of 3 meters and walks toward the motion sensor quickly. Because the person walks toward the motion sensor, the velocity will be negative and represented by a horizontal line for that segment because the person is walking at a steady pace. Because the person moves quickly, the magnitude of the velocity will be greater than if the person was walking slowly. At this point, choices C and D would both be acceptable choices. The person then stands still, which means the velocity is zero and will be zero throughout the entire segment. The person then walks away from the sensor quickly, which is described by a horizontal line of the same magnitude as the first segment but positive because the person is walking away from the motion sensor. The correct answer is choice C.

14. **The correct answer is D.** In Activity 4, the person starts from a distance of 3 meters and walks toward the motion sensor quickly. Because the person walks toward the motion sensor, the velocity will be negative and represented by a horizontal line for that segment because the person is walking at a steady pace. Because the person moves quickly, the magnitude of the velocity will be greater than if the person was

walking slowly. The person then walks toward the sensor slowly, which is described by a horizontal line of smaller magnitude than the first segment but still negative because the person is walking toward the motion sensor. In the final segment, the person stands still, resulting in a zero velocity (horizontal line along the x-axis). The correct answer is choice D.

Passage III

15. **The correct answer is C.** The aqueous phase most effective for providing a pure product would be 1 M sodium hydroxide. The TLC analysis clearly indicates the presence of benzoic acid in the crude reaction mixture. The challenge becomes how to separate benzoic acid from the desired ester using aqueous extraction alone. By using sodium hydroxide in the aqueous phase, benzoic acid is deprotonated to form benzoate, which is soluble in water, as shown. The desired ester lacks the acidic proton and is therefore unaffected by base.

organic soluble   aqueous soluble

16. **The correct answer is B.** The first task is to determine the limiting reagent, which is the alcohol (as shown):

Substance	MW (g/mol)	d (g/mL)	Amt added	mmol
Benzoic acid (**1**)	122.0	–	1.58 g	13.0
Thionyl chloride	119.0	1.631	1.04 mL	14.3
(S)-2-methyl-1-butanol (**2**)	88.2	0.819	1.19 mL	11.1
Dichloromethane	84.9	1.325	20.00 mL	(solvent)

Therefore, the theoretical yield for the product would be 11.1 mmol × 192 g/mol = 2.13 g. The isolated (purified) yield is 1.49 g (according to the experimental), meaning the actual yield is 1.49 g/2.13 g = 70% of theory.

17. **The correct answer is B.** The defining characteristic of the product in the IR spectrum is the carbonyl stretch, which should appear about 1700 cm^{-1}. Spectrum B is the only one that exhibits this band in the IR. Spectrum A shows a stretch at 2200 cm^{-1}, which indicates a nitrile; Spectrum C shows a stretch at 3300 cm^{-1}, which is consistent with an alcohol; and Spectrum D contains no diagnostic peaks aside from C-H and C-C stretches.

18. **The correct answer is A.** The rate would increase. The second reaction involves the Ad_N reaction between an alcohol and an acyl chloride, as shown here:

Since the subsequent reactions (loss of chloride and proton transfer) are rapid, this is the rate-limiting step. Therefore, the rate law for this reaction would be:

$$\text{rate} = k[\text{BzCl}][\text{ROH}]$$

Increasing the concentration of alcohol (ROH) would then increase the reaction rate.

19. **The correct answer is C.** The reaction between an alcohol and a carboxylic acid is very slow. The formation of an ester can be catalyzed by a strong acid (such as sulfuric acid or p-toluenesulfonic acid). However, in this particular case, the acid is first converted to a much more reactive acyl chloride using thionyl chloride, as shown:

20. **The correct answer is C.** The answer choices are best considered as two sets of two: two boat conformations and two chair conformations. Boat conformations in general are almost always of higher energy owing to the so-called flagpole interactions shown here:

No passage

The distinguishing characteristic between the two chair conformations is that one (choice C) places the chlorine substituent in an equatorial attitude, whereas the other (choice D) forces the substituent to occupy an axial position. An equatorial orientation is almost always energetically preferable.

21. **The correct answer is D.** The first part of the Strecker synthesis involves the nucleophilic addition of ammonia onto the carbonyl carbon of the aldehyde, as shown. The aldehyde therefore functions as an electrophile.

Passage IV

22. **The correct answer is C.** In the second part of the Strecker synthesis, a nitrile group is converted to an acid functionality. The two oxygen atoms in the latter are supplied by water, making this a hydrolysis reaction. Oxidation and reduction can be ruled out by examination of the oxidation state of carbon in the reactant (nitrile) and product (acid). In both compounds, the reactive carbon (in blue) has three bonds to an electronegative element—nitrogen in the nitrile and oxygen in the acid. The oxidation state of the blue carbon is +3 in both cases; therefore, no redox chemistry has occurred.

23. **The correct answer is D.** The valine synthesized in the Strecker synthesis is best described as a racemic mixture and optically inactive. The product of this reaction (valine) clearly has a chiral center; therefore, the two achiral responses are invalid. Since the synthesis launches from an achiral material, and no chiral reagents are introduced along the way, the only reasonable outcome is to have a racemic mixture of enantiomers. Note that the chiral center is set in the first part of the synthesis (attack of cyanide on the iminium intermediate). Since the attack can occur from either face of the iminium with equal probability, we expect to see an exactly 1:1 mixture of enantiomers. Any racemic mixture is optically inactive because for every molecule that rotates light clockwise, there exists an enantiomer, which will rotate light counterclockwise, resulting in no net rotation.

24. **The correct answer is D.** In the presence of sodium hydroxide, the amino acid (3) will become deprotonated and form the aminocarboxylate (i.e., 4), which will be water soluble. The aminonitrile (2), on the other hand, lacks an acidic proton and will remain neutral. Thus, it will be dissolved in the dichloromethane, which the passage indicates is the bottom layer in the separatory funnel.

25. **The correct answer is A.** The best IUPAC name for compound 2 is 2-amino-3-methylbutanenitrile. The nitrile is the higher order functional group, relegating the amine functionality to substituent status. Therefore, the main chain is a butanenitrile (shown in blue). Note that the nitrile carbon is C1 (this is easy to overlook). Attached to the main chain are an amino group at C2 and a methyl group at C3.

No passage   26. **The correct answer is C.** This problem can be solved by substituting the results of each scenario into Poiseuille's law and searching for the largest value. Choice A yields an $8\times$ increase in flow. Choice B results in a $1/32\times$ increase in flow. Choice C yields a $32\times$ increase in flow while choice D results in a $1/8\times$ increase in flow.

27. **The correct answer is A.** By definition of the two types of lenses, a concave lens increases the focal length of an image while a convex lens reduces the focal length of an image. Therefore, choices B and C are incorrect and can be immediately excluded. Since myopia results in image formation in front of the retina, the

appropriate corrective lens would be a concave lens, which increases the focal length of the image, causing the image to focus past this point and on the retina. Choice A is the correct response. Choice D represents the corrective approach for hyperopia or farsightedness.

28. **The correct answer is D.** The problem can be solved using the radioactive decay equation:

$$A = A_o e^{-\left(\frac{0.693}{T_{1/2}}\right)t}$$

where A is the final radionuclide activity measured at some time, t; A_o is the initial radionuclide activity; $T_{1/2}$ is the radionuclide half-life; and t is the radioactive decay time. Adapting the given information to this equation, A is the unknown, $A_o = 28$ mCi, $T_{1/2} = 5.25$ $d = 453{,}600$ s, and $t = 7$ $d = 604{,}800$ s, which yields the following calculation:

$$A = (28 \text{ mCi})(0.397) = 11.1 \text{ mCi}$$

29. **The correct answer is C.** Calcium carbonate (marble/chalk) is insoluble in water   Passage V
    and will produce the least amount of ions to spread out in solution. This is different from the other three, which are soluble and will have ions spread out in solution. Calcium carbonate will be soluble in acid, however, which is why acid rain can erode marble statues.

30. **The correct answer is D.** Unknown C is soluble in water, which eliminates the calcium carbonate. Unknown C also forms a precipitate with NH_3. This will happen when magnesium sulfate reacts with ammonia according to the reaction:

$$2 H_2O\ (l) + 2 NH_3\ (aq) + MgSO_4\ (aq) \rightarrow Mg(OH)_2\ (s) + (NH_4)_2SO_4\ (aq)$$

31. **The correct answer is B.** Unknown A is soluble in water and has negative results for all of the tests except for conductivity, so it must be NaCl.

32. **The correct answer is A.** The endpoint of a titration should best be matched to the pK of the indicator. Because a strong base and weak acid titration will have an endpoint in the basic range, phenolphthalein is best-suited for this titration.

33. **The correct answer is A.** If the pH $= 10$, then the pOH is 4 because pH $+$ pOH $= 14$. Given the pOH $= 4$, the $[OH^-]$ is 1×10^{-4} M. When the K_{sp} expression is written for magnesium hydroxide, we get $K_{sp} = [Mg^{2+}][OH^-]^2$. This then becomes $K_{sp} = [x][x]^2 = [x]^3$. $[1 \times 10^{-4}\text{M}]^3 = 1 \times 10^{-12}$. This is close to the actual value of 1.6×10^{-12}.

34. **The correct answer is C.** You first need to determine a mathematical relationship   Passage VI
    for surface tension, which can be derived from the following equation:

$$h = \frac{2T}{\rho g r}$$

Rearranging the equation for T and substituting all given information yields:

$$T = \frac{\rho g r h}{2} = \frac{\left(1{,}000 \, \frac{kg}{m^3}\right)\left(9.8 \, \frac{m}{s^2}\right)(0.0025 \, m)\,(0.08 \, m)}{2} = 0.98 \, \frac{kg}{s^2} \approx 1.0 \, \frac{N}{m}$$

35. **The correct answer is A.** This problem can be answered by referring to the equation for the height of the dye traveling through capillary action:

$$h = \frac{2T}{\rho g r}$$

Of all of the options presented for consideration, the only one with direct relevance to a variable within the equation is choice A. The weight of the water is reflected by the term ρg, which must be pulled up the stem by the surface tension. The presence of sugar increases the weight of the water to be taken up the stem by capillary action and thus it travels more slowly. At each time interval recorded in the experiment, the dye in beakers 2 and 3 does not travel as high up the stem as the stem placed in beaker 1.

36. **The correct answer is B.** The equation for the line of best fit for the data recorded for beaker 3 is:

$$y = 0.275x - 0.2$$

which is expressed in the form of the equation for a line:

$$y = mx + b$$

where m is the slope of the line. It is the slope that provides the hourly rate of ascension of the dye up the carnation stem. The answer is 0.28.

37. **The correct answer is C.** The equation for the line of best fit for the data recorded for beaker 1 is:

$$y = 0.945x + 0.26$$

or

$$\text{Height of Dye} = 0.945 \times (\text{time}) + 0.26$$

Substituting the value of 10 hours for time yields:

$$\text{Height of Dye} = 0.945 \times 10 \text{ hrs} + 0.26 = 9.71 \text{ cm}$$

38. **The correct answer is D.** The equation for the line of best fit for the data recorded for beaker 2 is:

$$y = 0.58x - 0.42$$

or

$$\text{Height of Dye} = 0.58 \times (\text{time}) - 0.42$$

Substituting the value of 10 cm for the height of dye and solving for time yields:

$$10 \text{ cm} = 0.58 \times (\text{time}) - 0.42$$

$$\text{Time} = 17.9 \text{ hours} \approx 18 \text{ hours}$$

39. **The correct answer is B.** The property of t-butoxide (versus methoxide) that is the most significant factor in the lower yield of ether is increased steric bulk. While t-butoxide does have a higher pK_a, this should also make it more nucleophilic. However, engaging in S_N2 reactivity is sterically more demanding than proton abstraction. Therefore, the bulkier t-butoxide forms less ether.

40. **The correct answer is D.** The thermodynamic product is defined as the one that is thermodynamically more stable. In this case, the internal alkene would be more stable, since it is disubstituted versus the monosubstituted terminal alkene. In an E2 paradigm (which is generally irreversible), one must assume that the major product formed the fastest. In the case of methoxide, this is the internal alkene. Therefore, the internal alkene is both the kinetic and thermodynamic product (actually, the norm).

41. **The correct answer is B.** The terminal alkene is the kinetic product; the internal alkene is the thermodynamic product. The thermodynamics of the products have not changed; thus, the internal alkene is still the thermodynamic product. However, with t-butoxide the terminal alkene forms the fastest; therefore, it is the kinetic product.

42. **The correct answer is D.** The most reasonable product distribution is 20% ether; 50% terminal alkene; 30% internal alkene. Since the steric bulk of isopropoxide is intermediate between methoxide and t-butoxide, it is reasonable to expect the outcome in all cases to be between the bounds of the other two bases. Thus, more ether is formed than with t-butoxide, but less than with methoxide. Furthermore, the terminal alkene is still favored, but less strongly than t-butoxide.

43. **The correct answer is B.** The most reasonable product distribution is 50% ether; 50% terminal alkene; 0% internal alkene. With 1-chlorohexene, it is mechanistically impossible to access the internal alkene. Therefore, the only viable products are the ether (S_N2 product) and the terminal alkene (E2 product).

44. **The correct answer is B.** The wavelength, λ, of light is related to its frequency, f, by the equation:

$$c = f\lambda$$

where c is the speed of light in a vacuum or $3.0 \times 10^8 \frac{m}{s}$. Solving for the frequency yields:

$$f = \frac{c}{\lambda} = \frac{3.0 \times 10^8 \frac{m}{s}}{700 \times 10^{-9} m} = 4.0 \times 10^{14} Hz$$

45. **The correct answer is C.** The speed of light through a medium, v, is related to its index of refraction, n, by:

$$n = \frac{c}{v} = \frac{\text{speed of light in vacuum}}{\text{speed of light in medium}}$$

The index of refraction of the aqueous humor is given in the passage as $n_{\text{aqueous humor}} = 1.336$.

Substituting into the above equation:

$$v = \frac{c}{n} = \frac{3.0 \times 10^8 \frac{m}{s}}{1.336} = 2.2 \times 10^8 \frac{m}{s}$$

46. **The correct answer is B.** The speed of light through the medium is related to its index of refraction by the equation:

$$n = \frac{c}{v} \text{ or } v = \frac{c}{n}$$

So the speed of light is slowest when the index of refraction is the greatest. Of the possible answer choices, the medium with the greatest index of refraction is the lens with $n = 1.406$. Thus, the speed of light is the slowest as it passes through the lens of the human eye.

47. **The correct answer is D.** The angle of refraction is determined by Snell's law of refraction or:

$$n_1 \sin \theta_1 = n_2 \sin \theta_2$$

From information given in the passage:

$$n_1 = n_{air} = 1.000; \theta_1 = \theta_i = 28°; \text{ and } n_2 = n_{cornea} = 1.376$$

Solving for the unknown θ_2:

$$\sin \theta_2 = \frac{n_1 \sin \theta_1}{n_2} = \frac{(1.000)\sin 28°}{1.376} = \frac{0.469}{1.376} = 0.341$$

$$\theta_2 = \sin^{-1}(0.341) = 19.9° \approx 20°$$

48. **The correct answer is A.** When light refraction is at its greatest, the refraction angle is the smallest, which occurs when the ratio of $\frac{n_1}{n_2}$ is the smallest. Of the four possible combinations, the smallest value for the ratio is given by the air–cornea interface.

Passage IX 49. **The correct answer is A.** The only true statement is choice A. At the beginning of the reaction, the concentration of the reactants is greatest. This will give the greatest instantaneous rate. Choice B is not correct because, as the reaction nears its end, the rate at that point will be less than the average rate.

50. **The correct answer is C.** First the change in molarity is needed. Then this is divided by the time interval. The initial rate $= (0.882 - 0.697)/60 = 0.00308$ M/sec.

51. **The correct answer is B.** Using the equation $\ln([A]_o/[A]_t) = kt$, substitution gives:

$$[\ln(.882 - .697)] / 60$$

52. **The correct answer is B.** The half-life is the time it takes for half of the starting material to react. Starting with 0.882 M, the first half-life would be at 0.441 M, which would take between 180 and 240 sec.

53. **The correct answer is A.** Because the decomposition is first order, the rate $= k$ [H_2O_2].

54. **The correct answer is A.** A catalyst lowers the energy of activation of a reaction by changing the mechanism of the reaction.

Passage X 55. **The correct answer is D.** Compound 1 has a good leaving group (bromide), and it is treated with a very strong, hindered base (LDA). Because LDA is so sterically hindered, any kind of substitution (S_N1 or S_N2) is out of the question. Moreover, the generation of a double bond in the product is a tip-off to an elimination reaction. Choosing between an E1 or an E2 reaction, it is important to recognize that E1 reactions generally occur in systems where a base is either weak or nonexistent. Since LDA is a very strong base ($pK_a = 36$), an E2 mechanism is the most reasonable choice.

56. **The correct answer is D.** The major conformer in the (*1S, 4R*)-isomer lacks the proper orbital alignment. In both isomers, the *t*-butyl group (shown in blue) locks the cyclohexane into the chair conformer that gives the *t*-butyl group the equatorial position. Recall that for E2 elimination to proceed quickly, an antiperiplanar relationship must exist between the leaving group (in this case, bromide) and an adjacent proton, which is dictated by the alignment of the σ^* orbital of the C–Br bond with the σ orbital of the C–H bond. The antiperiplanar arrangements are shown below in bold blue. Notice that the (*1R, 4R*)-isomer can achieve the necessary antiperiplanar arrangement, whereas the (*1S, 4R*)-isomer cannot (a C–C bond in the ring is antiperiplanar to the bromine).

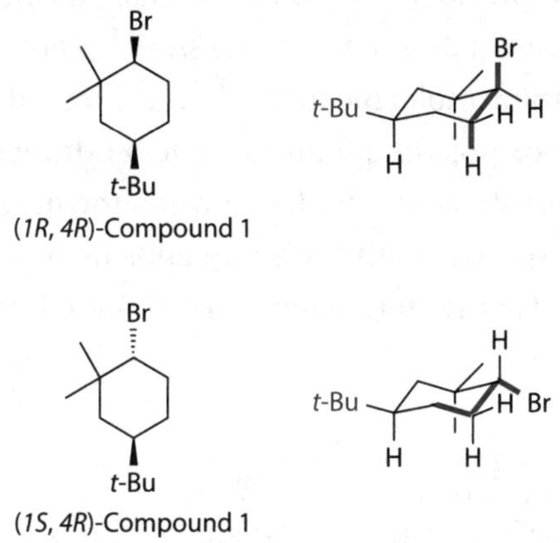

Br
t-Bu
(1R, 4R)-Compound 1
Br
t-Bu
H H
H H
Br
t-Bu
(1S, 4R)-Compound 1
H
t-Bu
H Br
H H

57. **The correct answer is A.** Since the dimethyl group at C2 prevents elimination from the left side, there is only one possible elimination product. Furthermore, since the reaction does not involve the stereochemistry of the *t*-butyl group, the product should be a single enantiomer (the *R*-isomer). Inasmuch as only one enantiomer is present, the product should exhibit optical activity.

Br
LDA
−20°C
fast
t-Bu
(1R, 4R)-Compound 1
t-Bu
(5R)-Compound 2
Br
LDA
−20°C
slow
t-Bu
(1S, 4R)-Compound 1

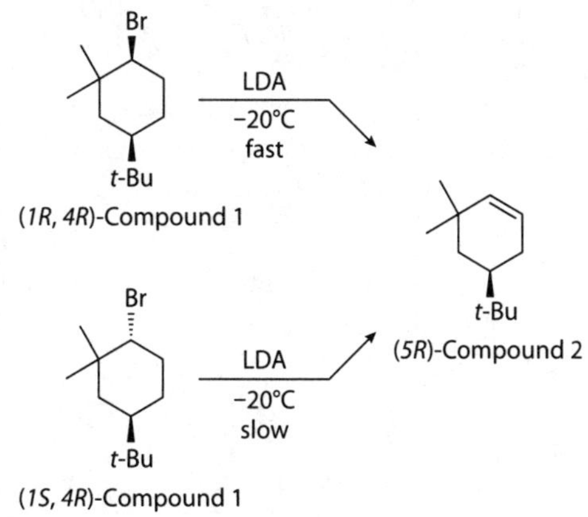

58. **The correct answer is C.** Ozonolysis has the net effect of cleaving the double bond and putting two carbonyl groups in its place. Choices A and B differ from choices C and D by the total carbon count. Note that the starting material (compound 2) has 6 carbons in the ring—these 6 carbons will end up as 6 carbons in the chain of the dialdehyde (compound 3). Choices A and B only have 5 chain carbons; therefore, they can be disqualified. The remaining choices (C and D) differ in the stereochemistry at the *t*-butyl group. Ozonolysis will not affect this stereochemistry, as shown:

59. **The correct answer is C.** Bear in mind that the regiochemistry in hydroboration is driven by sterics alone. In this particular case, there is no clear Markovnikov or anti-Markovnikov product (i.e., both product alcohols are similarly substituted). However, there is a difference in the steric interactions involved in the two approaches of the borane molecule to the double bond. If the boron aligns with the carbon at the 12 o'clock position, there is steric hindrance caused by the dimethyl group, as shown. This interaction is absent when the boron aligns with the carbon at the 2 o'clock position. The hydroxy group ends up at the same position that the boron was added. As for the stereochemistry of the *t*-butyl group, it is unaffected by this chemistry.

Section 3. Psychological, Social, and Biological Foundations of Behavior

1. **The correct answer is D.** The "swinging bridge" study showed that in conditions eliciting a stronger adrenaline reaction, participants rated others as more attractive. This result highlights certain environmental factors that can alter the judgment of attractiveness. This phenomenon is called misattribution of arousal.

2. **The correct answer is B.** Broca's area in the left frontal lobe is responsible for language production in the brain. In this example, the individual understands language (written) but is unable to produce speech. Interestingly, patients can often produce language if they sing, and this is a frequent therapy for individuals with damage to Broca's area.

3. **The correct answer is C.** Though Janey worked hard for her degree and is excited about her career, it is her father who provides a job for her rather than having her interview and receive the position through normal channels. If she received a better job based on her own hard work and better grades, the sociological construct would be meritocracy. A social mobility construct would indicate that she had changed from one socioeconomic status (SES) level to another, but in this instance Janey is maintaining her same SES with a career in the same field as her father. This suggests social reinforcement rather than social mobility. Social stratification indicates that different SES levels exist and does not really apply in this case.

4. **The correct answer is A.** The door-in-the-face technique is characterized by an outrageous request followed by a second, more reasonable request. In this example, the outrageous request is the offer of overpriced jewelry. The reasonable request is the offer of less expensive jewelry.

5. **The correct answer is C.** Men are more likely than women to use resource display. Based on the data shown, men are more likely to engage in resource display as a mate retention strategy.

6. **The correct answer is A.** Evolutionary psychology would explain that men are more likely to use resource display because women value financial status as a characteristic in a mate. Evolutionary psychology posits that women are more likely to pursue mates who can provide resources for potential offspring because that indicates that their future offspring will be more likely to survive and pass on the women's genes.

7. **The correct answer is B.** Males select mates based mainly on the youth, attractiveness, and good health of their potential partner. This answer is consistent with males selecting mates that have characteristics indicating higher potential fertility.

8. **The correct answer is D.** A likely potential follow-up investigation would study the correlation between behavior and the financial status and perceived attractiveness of the mates. This would allow for a comparison of retention strategies used, based on previously identified desirable characteristics in male and female populations.

9. **The correct answer is D.** Women are more likely to use indirect means of communicating to competitors that their spouses are "taken." Nonverbal possession signals allow communication without the threat of violence, which may damage health, childbearing ability, and physical well-being (all of which are key attractors to men, according to evolutionary theory). In this instance, public displays of affection are used as a signal to competitors, not as a way to make a partner commit.

Passage II

10. **The correct answer is D.** Amnesics experience impairment for explicit memory tasks but do not experience impairment for implicit memory tasks compared to control participants. The amnesics score significantly lower on the explicit memory tasks. However, there is no significant difference in performance on the implicit memory tasks.

11. **The correct answer is B.** Amnesic participants were significantly worse at explicit memory tasks compared to control participants. Further, they were able to complete the implicit memory task for a novel (newly learned) list of words. This suggests that they are able to encode new information (i.e., learn) but are unable to explicitly recall or retrieve the previously stored information.

12. **The correct answer is A.** Amnesic patients are able to encode and access semantic memory but are still impaired in their ability to retrieve the encoded information. Amnesic patients are able to perform the implicit memory task, and so are able to encode information. However, they are impaired in their ability to retrieve information unless that information is prompted in the implicit task. Further, it is possible that the patients were able to explicitly recall the experience of learning and form an episodic memory. However, the only answer choice that includes episodic memory can be ruled out because semantic memory is necessary for episodic retrieval in Tulving's model.

13. **The correct answer is C.** The hippocampus has been found to be a critical structure in the storage and retrieval of memories. Patients with damage to the hippocampus have impaired memory formation and retrieval.

14. **The correct answer is C.** Memories are stored in various locations throughout the cerebral cortex through a process called long-term potentiation.

Passage III

15. **The correct answer is C.** Participants were better able to remember which list familiar melodies were from than novel melodies. List recognition was better for familiar melodies than for novel melodies for both studied lists.

16. **The correct answer is A.** Episodic memory is characterized by the ability to identify and consciously re-experience an event that occurred in the past. Procedural, semantic, and implicit memory are characterized as memory of an event without a corresponding knowledge of when it occurred.

17. **The correct answer is B.** Semantic memory is characterized by the ability to recall facts but not remember when an event occurred. In this case, the semantic memory provides the knowledge that the melody is known but is unable to isolate when the melody was heard.

18. **The correct answer is A.** Long-term potentiation has created long-lasting excitatory circuits for the memory trace. Long-term potentiation is the process by which memories are stored and lasting memories are encoded.

19. **The correct answer is D.** The percentage of familiar melodies correctly ascribed to both list 1 and list 2 would decrease. Participants would be unable to ascribe familiar melodies to either list because they would not have a memory of when they heard each melody.

20. **The correct answer is A.** The results show a significant increase in acts of imitative aggression by children who view a film showing aggression being rewarded.

Passage IV

21. **The correct answer is C.** Bandura's research showed that children would imitate aggression when they viewed the aggression rewarded. Learning was not directly tested, and children only needed to view the aggression (reward/punishment) conditions.

22. **The correct answer is B.** The offending child in the example is punished for the child's actions because of the initial aggression. This is consistent with the aggressive-model-punished condition of Bandura's study in which the child is initially aggressive and is later punished for his or her actions.

23. **The correct answer is D.** One major criticism of Bandura's study was that the children were in an artificial environment and displayed aggression toward a toy rather than toward another child (as seen in the film).

24. **The correct answer is A.** Joey watches a friend play a violent video game in which punching small animals results in more points. In this condition, Joey is watching his friend being rewarded for aggressive behavior.

25. **The correct answer is D.** According to the regression lines in the two graphs, in a country with an average fertility rate of six children per woman, a girl has approximately a 22% chance of being enrolled in secondary school and an 80% chance of living on less than $2.00 per day.

Passage V

26. **The correct answer is B.** Each living child alters the financial resources available to each family member, and frequent childbirth may increase health problems for the woman, which may impede her ability to be financially productive. A higher number of children leads to fewer financial resources per child because income does not necessarily rise with the birth of each child. Fewer financial resources means fewer educational opportunities, particularly for female children outside of the United States.

27. **The correct answer is D.** The graphs depict only women's fertility, education, and poverty levels. Men's fertility levels are less well-known. Even in the context of marriage, many of the world's cultures have less strict sexual rules for men, making men's fertility much more difficult to track.

28. **The correct answer is B.** Attitude shifts within a culture toward acceptance of family planning would be a change in cultural capital.

29. **The correct answer is D.** Education increases human capital; therefore, education about family planning services would be an increase in a society's human capital.

30. **The correct answer is D.** The group at the highest risk is individuals with a schizophrenic identical twin. The data show that the highest incidence rate (60%) is for identical twins. Children whose parents are both schizophrenic are the group with the next highest risk at 36%.

31. **The correct answer is D.** The data show a strong genetic link for the incidence rate of schizophrenia. However, in the case of identical twins (100% genetic match), the incidence rate is only 60%. This suggests that additional environmental influences must also be factors in the development of schizophrenia.

32. **The correct answer is A.** The other answer choices have been associated with schizophrenia in the research literature. Too much GABA (which is an inhibitory neurotransmitter) has not been associated with schizophrenia in the research literature, although too little GABA has been proposed as a possible mechanism.

33. **The correct answer is A.** The most appropriate follow-up study would be to survey identical twins who grew up apart and those who grew up in the same household. This is the best answer because it would allow you to study individuals who are exact genetic matches with each other and also allow you to compare same-household (similar environments) twins to different-household (different environments) twins.

34. **The correct answer is D.** Because a child's genetic code cannot be changed but environmental factors also play a role in the development of schizophrenia, a child with schizophrenic family members should receive extra environmental support to reduce the likelihood of developing schizophrenia. Schizophrenia is not inevitable based on genetic factors. Choice C is not a real possibility because avoiding all stress is not possible. Antipsychotic medications have serious negative side effects, and treatment guidelines do not recommend that they be started prophylactically for schizophrenia.

35. **The correct answer is B.** The length of time a person spends in REM sleep per sleep cycle generally increases as the night progresses. Amplitude becomes larger and frequency slows down as deeper levels of sleep are reached. Further, the length of time a person spends in slow-wave sleep decreases as the hours of sleep increase.

36. **The correct answer is A.** Most vivid dreaming occurs during REM sleep. Dreaming can also occur during other stages, but it is typically not as vivid.

37. **The correct answer is D.** Each sleep cycle is approximately 90 minutes in length. The cycle is characterized by the stages.

38. **The correct answer is B.** REM sleep and slow-wave sleep are considered to be associated with restorative processes. REM sleep has been found to decrease as one ages and loss of REM sleep has been found to be associated with cognitive dysfunction (particularly memory). The release of growth hormone during slow-wave sleep has physiological benefits.

39. **The correct answer is D.** At 10:30 p.m., Jose had just begun to enter stage 2 sleep, which is a much lighter sleep state than the sleep states represented by the other answers. During stage 2 sleep, Jose is much more likely to be awakened by small noises that would not affect him during slow-wave sleep (choices B and C) or at the onset of REM sleep (2 a.m.). While the end of REM sleep can result in easier arousal from sleep, the onset of REM sleep is associated with more difficult sleep arousal.

40. **The correct answer is D.** Sound level decreased for participants in actual groups and for participants in pseudogroups. The data show that as the number of people in actual groups increased and the number of (supposed) people in pseudogroups increased, the sound level decreased. Passage VIII

41. **The correct answer is B.** The decibel level would decrease if the people in pseudogroups believed that there were more people in their groups.

42. **The correct answer is A.** Loss of coordination is characterized by a decrease in productivity due to role/work overlap. The actual groups and the pseudogroups are both affected by social loafing. This is because the actual groups and pseudogroups both believe that there are others working with them. However, only the actual group is affected by loss of coordination. This difference is explained by the lack of a feedback loop, which would indicate the work overlap in the pseudogroups (who are only told there are others working with them) compared to the actual groups (who receive feedback from other group members present).

43. **The correct answer is C.** The difference between the potential productivity and the pseudogroups' productivity can best be explained by social loafing because the difference is the result of *believed* group size. The pseudogroup participants are not aware of any actual participation by any other person. So loss of coordination does not have any impact on pseudogroup results.

44. **The correct answer is A.** The greater the number of people working together to complete a task, the more likely it is that social loafing will occur due to a diffusion of responsibility, resulting in decreased effort.

45. **The correct answer is B.** This statement is consistent with the results in the figure and shows that increases in shallow acting are likely to result in increases in stress. Passage IX

46. **The correct answer is C.** In the dramaturgical approach, an individual is always playing some type of role in all social interactions. Based on the research shown, deep acting will result in less stress.

47. **The correct answer is B.** Cognitive dissonance theory suggests that if you change your beliefs, acting becomes less stressful. The theory states that in low-reward situations, it is less stressful for you to alter your beliefs to match existing situations. In this example, customer-service workers engaged in shallow acting (e.g., changing facial expressions, smiling at customers) and deep acting (e.g., detailing the benefits of a product, etc.) in order to interact with customers. Because there is little direct reward for showing enthusiasm and engaging customers, more stress will result with shallow acting in which inner beliefs are not changed. Conversely, for deep acting, cognitive dissonance would result in a shift in inner beliefs to

match deep acting behavior, resulting in less stress compared to that experienced during shallow acting.

48. **The correct answer is A.** Self-verification involves making sure that a person chooses the "audience" that verifies his or her self-view and thus reinforces that person's self-identity.

49. **The correct answer is A.** According to the dramaturgical approach, individuals are truly themselves only when they are alone (offstage). Onstage behavior is characterized by acting, and backstage behavior is still influenced by goal-directed behavior for the audience.

Passage X 50. **The correct answer is B.** High-social-contact participants under high stress are more likely to become sick than low-social-contact participants.

51. **The correct answer is D.** Both positive events and negative events increase stress. The more social contacts, the more likely that a person will be exposed to a cold or flu, and the higher the stress, the more likely the individual will become sick.

52. **The correct answer is B.** Taking steps to master, tolerate, or reduce stress is referred to as coping.

53. **The correct answer is B.** Light exercise such as taking a morning run is a positive coping mechanism and will likely reduce stress.

54. **The correct answer is C.** The fight-or-flight response is characterized by the activation of the autonomic nervous system.

No Passage 55. **The correct answer is B.** Symbolic interactionism, proposed by social psychologist George Mead, proposes that an individual's identity is defined by symbols representative of a society. One example of such a symbol is the traditional white dress of a bride. Sue expected Betsy, a future bride, to have chosen a white wedding dress, aligned with the norms and expectations of Sue's social interactions.

56. **The correct answer is C.** The stage of sleep that is the most beneficial to the body system is the third stage of sleep often referred to as slow wave sleep. During this stage of sleep, the greatest release of growth hormone, most effective wound healing and most active immune responses occur.

57. **The correct answer is A.** The thymus gland plays a critical role in the immune system. The pituitary gland is located in the hypothalamus and releases hormones, among them growth hormones. The pineal gland is involved in the release of melatonin and assisting with the circadian rhythms of the body. The thyroid gland controls energy use, protein production, body sensitivity to other hormones.

58. **The correct answer is D.** Wernicke's area, the region of the brain responsible for the understanding of language is found in the left temporal lobe of the brain.

59. **The correct answer is B.** Cultural capital involves the world outlook and beliefs that are passed on from parents to children. The fact that the immigrants saw the conditions that they were in would not translate into a successful life for their children and made a choice to improve the likelihood of success is an example of cultural capital.

Section 4. Critical Analysis and Reasoning Skills

1. **The correct answer is C.** Skim the passage to locate mention of three out of four assertions. The underground system (choice A) appears in paragraph 4, purple loosestrife's effect on fish appears in paragraph 6, and its use in American gardens (choice D) appears in paragraph 2. Paragraph 7 says that it is "impervious to burning," making choice C the best answer.

2. **The correct answer is B.** This question indirectly asks you to locate an author's reasons for including a detail. Returning to the passage will help you see that the mention of the St. Lawrence River refers to a type of wetland where purple loosestrife does well. The only answer supported by the text is choice B.

3. **The correct answer is C.** All three details are facts about purple loosestrife, but only its ability to cross-pollinate (I) and its easy adaptability (II) are facts that "add to its power of endurance." Since both I and II are correct, the answer is choice C.

4. **The correct answer is C.** The answer appears in paragraph 3: "The same long growing season that makes it so beloved by gardeners makes it a seed-making machine." It is the long growing season (choice C) that gardeners like.

5. **The correct answer is D.** You must infer the answer based on what you have learned about purple loosestrife from the passage. Because it thrives in wetlands and along rivers, either II or III is likely. Although I might in theory be possible, the author does point out, "It has moved steadily westward and is now found in all states but Florida." Since that eliminates I as a choice, the answer must be choice D.

6. **The correct answer is B.** Your choice must weaken the argument that purple loosestrife is best eradicated by digging it up, plowing it under, and reseeding. Choice A would suggest another means of eradication but would not weaken the original argument. Choices C and D do not weaken or strengthen the argument, although both may suggest benefits of the eradication plan. Only choice B throws a monkey wrench in the works: If a new strain of purple loosestrife is growing up where it was once eliminated, then this form of eradication does not really work.

7. **The correct answer is C.** Native American and Chinese drums are mentioned in the first paragraph as examples of drums that accompany soldiers into battle.

8. **The correct answer is D.** A Janissary stop is described as being added to organs and harpsichords, which have a series of stops, or knobs, that adjust tones and add special effects. The only answer that fits the context is choice D.

9. **The correct answer is C.** Haydn and Mozart enter the discussion as examples of classical composers who adopted the forms and characteristics of martial music. This does not mean that Janissary music came from Europe (choice B), and since Haydn and Mozart are musicians, not painters, choice D does not apply.

10. **The correct answer is C.** Skim the passage to find whether examples are given to support each assertion. Looking first at assertion I, you can see that the author

mentions the "Jingling Johnny" as an example of unusual percussion. Since I is a yes, you can immediately eliminate answer choices B and D. The only question remaining is whether the answer is choice A or C, so you must look for examples to support assertion III. The first sentence in paragraph 4 mentions "The Stars and Stripes Forever" as an example of Sousa's beloved marches. Since I and III are both yes responses, your answer must be choice C.

11. **The correct answer is A.** This is a "what-if?" question: What if the author included this particular piece of information? The fact that it refers to the 18th century means that it has no relation to the Civil War (choice C), and the use of drums preceded Janissary music (choice D). The best answer is choice A; it would help support the idea that martial music was a key part of the military at that time.

12. **The correct answer is B.** The author compares the Pentagon's expenditure on music to the government's comparatively paltry expenditure on K–12 music education. Although the information is fascinating (choice A), the shock value involved in the comparison makes it most likely to have been included as a critical remark.

Passage III 13. **The correct answer is C.** Since the whole passage is about military adventures, you should be able to select choice C as the most likely answer without reviewing the passage. The proof is in paragraph 5, where the author refers to "the final campaigns of the Zulu War."

14. **The correct answer is B.** Although Rorke's Drift was a British success story (choice C), the author makes clear that it was a minor success at best and tells how Chelmsford used it to cover up a huge British failure at Isandhlwana.

15. **The correct answer is A.** The author does not seem to think much of the tactics of Frere (choice C), and Wolseley (choice D) is mentioned only in terms of his success after taking over for Chelmsford. In the author's narrative, Chelmsford tried to seize Zululand, but his invasion force was massacred and he was eventually recalled to England. Despite his self-serving propaganda, Chelmsford clearly failed to accomplish his purpose. The best answer is choice A.

16. **The correct answer is D.** King Cetshwayo (choice C) ruled Zululand before he fought the British. After the kingdom was subdivided, a white African mercenary (choice A) ruled one part of it. Later, Dinizulu (choice B) wrested the kingdom from his own brother and ruled briefly. Chelmsford (choice D) never ruled at all.

17. **The correct answer is C.** Your choice must specifically point to a British failure to understand the African culture. Chelmsford's cover-up (I) had nothing to do with the Africans. The three-column advance (II) may have been a tactical error, but it cannot be blamed on a failure to understand Africans. The failure of partition (III), however, indicates that the British did not recognize the divisions among tribal leaders and peoples. Since only III is a yes, the answer is choice C.

18. **The correct answer is D.** To answer this question, you must think about the purpose and aim of the Zulu War. It was not a peasant uprising (choice A) or a war to eradicate a people (choice B); it was a war designed to topple a leader so as

to form a union imposed from outside the region. In that way, it most resembles modern-day Iraq (choice D).

19. **The correct answer is D.** Hunting and habitat destruction are the only reasons mentioned for the depopulation of elk prior to the 20th century.

20. **The correct answer is D.** According to the passage, in 1913, 50 elk were moved from Yellowstone to Pennsylvania. Two years later, 95 more were moved. The total shipped in those years comes to 145.

21. **The correct answer is D.** "At present," says the passage, "new herds are established in Arkansas, Kentucky, Michigan, and Wisconsin in addition to Pennsylvania." There is talk of moving herds to Tennessee (choice A) and the Adirondacks (choice C) in the future. Georgia (choice B) is mentioned only as the original southernmost range of eastern elk; it is not a place where they might be seen today.

22. **The correct answer is C.** A list of states accompanies assertion I, and a list of animal species accompanies assertion II. Since both I and II are supported by examples, the answer is choice C.

23. **The correct answer is B.** As the passage states clearly, "All of the eastern subspecies are now extinct." The reintroduced subspecies is the western subspecies, the one found in Yellowstone. It is a different subspecies from the original Pennsylvania elk.

24. **The correct answer is D.** Your answer must directly support the contention that elk repopulation is carefully monitored. Choices A and C have nothing to do with repopulation; they deal with animals in confined conditions. Choice B deals with wild elk but not with monitoring of the population. Choice D shows an example of monitoring that is taking place today.

25. **The correct answer is C.** The claim is that elk reintroduction benefits other species. Your answer must contradict this contention. Choice A shows a clear benefit to other populations, so it does not contradict the claim. Choice B shows a change in a species that does not live where elk live. Choice D does not refer to other species at all. Only choice C indicates a possible problem; the fact that deer are migrating northward may mean that elk are encroaching on their habitats.

26. **The correct answer is A.** Spooner was known for his transpositions, of which "You have deliberately tasted two worms" (wasted two terms) is an example. Although *transposition* has a variety of possible meanings, here it refers specifically to the exchange of letters or word parts.

27. **The correct answer is C.** The final paragraph discusses two forms of metathesis that derive from the butchers' trade. One is *louchébem* (II), and the other is *rechtub klat.* Since only II is correct, the answer is choice C.

28. **The correct answer is D.** Verlan and other backslang (I) are word games and therefore purposeful, not accidental. The examples of accidental metathesis include the change between Latin originals and Spanish derivatives (II) and mispronunciations or skewed pronunciations of English words (III). Since II and III are correct, the answer is choice D.

29. **The correct answer is D.** Although the origin of Pig Latin appears to be unknown, the author refers to its use in the prisoner-of-war camps of World War II and Vietnam. The implication is that it was used to communicate between prisoners in a language their captors could not understand.

30. **The correct answer is C.** If most Spoonerisms are apocryphal, or fictional, that would not be proved by a list of attributed transpositions (choice A), which would simply seem to support their authenticity. Examples of modern-day transpositions (choice B) would do nothing to support or deny the authenticity of Spoonerisms, and Spooner's letters (choice D) would not help because his transpositions, if they existed, were oral, not written. Interviews with people who knew Spooner (choice C) would be the best way to settle the issue one way or the other.

31. **The correct answer is B.** Saying *cause* instead of *because* (III) is an example of *aphaeresis*, the loss of the initial part of a word. The other two examples show transpositions of phonemes that are accidental. Since I and II are correct, the answer is choice B.

32. **The correct answer is B.** Verlan transposes the phonemes in syllables, often changing the spelling to match the revised word construction. Since *critique* is pronounced /krih-teek/, reversing those phonemes would give you a word pronounced /teek-krih/. The most likely spelling for this is shown in choice B.

33. **The correct answer is C.** Compare what you know about Pig Latin to what you know about metathesis. Pig Latin, like other metathesis, does transpose phonemes, so choice A is incorrect. Metathesis may be accidental or purposeful, so choice B is incorrect. There is no indication that the definition of metathesis includes the rule that such words must add to the language, so choice D does not work. Pig Latin involves more than the reversal of phonemes that marks metathesis; it also involves the addition of the "ay" syllable. The best answer is choice C.

Passage VI 34. **The correct answer is C.** This question involves your understanding of supporting details and evidence. The answer is found at the beginning of the passage, where the author details the three conceptions of totality. Here, the author states that the first two views are "contrasting" and that the third view is "not simply . . . the sum of its parts as atomists believe or . . . something independent of its parts." Thus, all three views are incompatible with each other, and choice C is the correct answer. There is no evidence that the views have evolved from each other (choice A). The materialist view is one of the conceptions of totality, and it has helped philosophers grasp connections, so choice B cannot be correct. Be careful of choice D; the passage states that philosophers "recognize" three different views, but that doesn't mean there are only three views.

35. **The correct answer is B.** This question asks you to assess evidence. What supporting evidence does the author give to back the claim that this view is "challenging"?

The answer lies at the end of the third paragraph, where the author states that the high number of connections and relationships make the view "overwhelming" to even the brightest philosophers. This idea is what choice B expresses. It is not clear from the passage how many philosophers espouse this view (choice A), and the author doesn't say whether that makes the viewpoint challenging. Choice C is wrong because the author says the number of things a philosopher must consider is overwhelming, not the insights. The author says that Marxist philosophers use abstraction (choice D) but never states that it is necessary to the dialectical viewpoint.

36. **The correct answer is A.** This question depends on your ability to analyze an argument. The author uses the chair in the third paragraph as part of his discussion on the critics' objections to a dialectical conception of totality. This is precisely what choice A states. The author has not yet discussed abstraction (choice B) or capitalism (choice C). Choice D is too strong; the author doesn't say dialectical thinking is impossible, just difficult.

37. **The correct answer is B.** In order to answer this question you need to distinguish among fact, opinion, and unsupported assertions. Look in the passage for the author's opinion or belief about the dialectical materialist viewpoint. At no point does the author indicate it leads to superior insights (choice A). *Critics* of the view state that it is impractical to use, but the author doesn't state that is what *he* believes (choice C). And there is no indication that the author thinks it's best used for the study of institutions (choice D). That leaves choice B, which is supported when the author writes that criticisms of dialectical materialism are "somewhat justified." This gives an indication of the author's belief about his subject matter.

38. **The correct answer is C.** This question asks you to draw conclusions. Using the information in the passage, you must conclude which answer choice reflects a process of abstraction. The author states that abstraction allows the investigator to "draw boundaries" around an object or idea studied. One possible abstraction involves "time scale." In choice C, the philosopher puts a temporal boundary around the idea studied. Choices A and B are examples of dialectical thinking but not abstractions. Choice D simply indicates a philosopher is aware of his or her biases, but there are no abstractions made.

39. **The correct answer is D.** To answer this question you'll need to look for the main idea. Choice A is not correct because the author does not say that the dialectical viewpoint is better than the other two. Choice B is mentioned as a criticism of the dialectical viewpoint, but it is not the primary focus of the passage. Marx's view of capitalism (choice C) is mentioned merely in passing and is not the main point of the passage. Choice D is correct because the author describes a viewpoint, details an objection to it, and then discusses how that objection may be overcome.

40. **The correct answer is D.** This question requires you to find the main idea. The passage discusses living fossils, a term biologists use to designate a species that has changed little since its inception. It then provides details on four different living fossils. Choice D is the best description of the passage. The passage doesn't primarily explain how these species remain unchanged as choice A states. Nor does it detail a dilemma (choice B) or focus mainly on the coelacanth (choice C).

41. **The correct answer is B.** In order to answer this question, you must choose an accurate paraphrase of the information in the passage. The first paragraph states that living fossils are not primitive. Rather they are so well-adapted to their environment that there is little need for change. Thinking that evolution necessarily represents advancement is indeed a misunderstanding, as choice B indicates. Choice A is not what the passage states as there is no comparison to other species. Choice C may be true, but it doesn't answer the question. Choice D is not stated in the passage.

42. **The correct answer is C.** This question asks you to solve a problem. Here, you need to use information from the passage to put the time periods in the correct order. The discussion of the horseshoe crab indicates that the Jurassic period is the most recent, some 200 million years ago. The Permian period, at which time the lungfish ceased experiencing major evolutionary changes, was about 250 million years ago. And the Silurian period, from which the coelacanth emerged, was more than 400 million years ago. That makes choice C the correct answer.

43. **The correct answer is A.** You need to analyze an argument in order to answer this question. In the context of the passage, in which the majority of the information explains that living fossils have changed very little, why would the author include a part about rapid evolutionary change? The answer is to show that a living fossil does change and evolve; however, the changes are minor or cease at some point. Choice A is the best answer.

44. **The correct answer is A.** This question requires you to draw conclusions. The author does not state choice A explicitly, but does say that the discovery was aided by an "astounding coincidence." The passage indicates that biologists find the lungfish interesting, but that does not necessarily imply the author believes the same as choice B says. Choice C is not a valid conclusion based on the passage. The author indicates that the discovery of the coelacanth was a major surprise, but that doesn't mean that biologists were wrong to believe it was extinct. There is no evidence to support choice D.

45. **The correct answer is D.** This question asks you to compare and contrast information found in the passage. We know from the second paragraph that the horseshoe crab is the most recent living fossil at 200 million years old. The other three all date from around 400 million years ago. The final paragraph says that at that time, land-dwelling plants were just beginning to evolve. Thus, choice D is the best

answer because the land-dwelling plants had been evolving for about 200 million years by the time the horseshoe crab appeared on the scene. Choices A and B indicate aspects the crab shares with some of the other living fossils. There is no evidence of choice C.

46. **The correct answer is A.** This question tests your ability to analyze an argument. The last paragraph continually emphasizes how the discovery of the coelacanth was an amazing event. The author uses words like *singular, astounding*, and *surprising*. This corresponds to choice A. There is no evidence for choice B or D, and the paragraph does not make it clear that it was the public who reacted with the allegations as choice C indicates.

47. **The correct answer is C.** To answer this question, you must apply new evidence. According to the passage, a living fossil is one that has changed very little over the eons. In order to argue that the coelacanth is not a living fossil, a biologist would need to find evidence of significant change. Showing that the coelacanth actually comes from a different line, as choice C does, would do so. The age of the species is not the issue, as choices A and D indicate. And finding different species, as in choice B, would not affect the status of the coelacanth as a living fossil.

48. **The correct answer is C.** This question asks you to choose an accurate paraphrase. **Passage VIII** The first paragraph explains what puzzles political scientists, so look back at it and try to put the information into your own words. The author states that common-sense explanations of what motivates voters are generally correct, so choice A is wrong. The problem lies instead with why people expend the time and energy to vote when they could reap the benefits without voting and when it is unlikely that their votes will have an impact as choice C, the best answer, states.

49. **The correct answer is B.** You must draw a conclusion to answer this question. The thought expressed in the final sentence of the first paragraph is most similar to what a free rider would believe; namely, a free rider wants to enjoy the benefits of something without incurring the costs. So the best answer is choice B.

50. **The correct answer is A.** To answer this question, you must make a generalization. The passage states that those individuals with more resources are more likely to vote. Of the answers, choice A is best. Lawyers have high levels of education and tend to make a fair amount of money. Choice D might be tempting, but it isn't clear what the education level of the homemaker is, making choice A better. Also, the passage states that Switzerland and the United States have low voter turnout numbers, which eliminates choices B and C.

51. **The correct answer is C.** This question requires you to analyze an argument. Looking back at the passage, the author identifies three main explanatory factors: resources, mobilization, and instrumental motivation. Assertion I is incorrect because the passage does not state a person needs "large amounts" of free time; a person simply needs enough time to vote. Assertion II would correspond to a

mobilization factor, while assertion III indicates a level of instrumental motivation. Thus, choice C is the best answer.

52. **The correct answer is** A. This is a fairly straightforward question that asks about supporting details. In the final paragraph, the author states that the baseline model "achieves some success . . . but is useless" when trying to compare voting behavior among citizens of different countries. Of the answers, choice A best states this. Choice B is wrong because it is too general. As the passage states, the model only works in certain cases. There is no evidence to support choice C or D.

53. **The correct answer is** D. A question that asks what the passage implies is asking you to draw conclusions. The correct answer will not be directly stated, so you'll have to look at what inference you can draw from the given information. Choice A cannot be inferred. The passage states that the theory of baseline political participation holds that resources are the key factor, but this theory is shown to be deficient. Choice B is also incorrect. The author states that resources have received the "most scholarly attention," but that doesn't mean the other two factors have been ignored. There is no support for choice C either, since the author only addresses one theory that has been found lacking. That leaves choice D, the correct answer. The author states that resources have received the most attention, so that implies mobilization has received less attention.

EVALUATION CHART

Use this evaluation chart to analyze your results on the science sections (Sections 1, 2, and 3) of the Practice Test 2. The chart matches each test question to specific content areas that you can review as part of this book's **online resources**. (See page ix, How to Use This Book.) Check the Answers and Explanations section to see which questions you got correct and which ones you missed. For each question that you missed, find the question number in the left column of the chart below. Look in the right column to find the location of the related review material. If you missed questions in a specific content area, you need to pay particular attention to that area as you study for the MCAT.

Item Number	Content Area
Biological and Biochemical Foundations of Living Systems	
1.	Chapter 9: Structure and Integrative Functions of the Main Organ Systems
2.	Chapter 9: Structure and Integrative Functions of the Main Organ Systems
3.	Chapter 4: Principles of Bioenergetics and Fuel Molecule Metabolism
4.	Chapter 5: Assemblies of Molecules, Cells, and Groups of Cells Within Multicellular Organisms
5.	Chapter 9: Structure and Integrative Functions of the Main Organ Systems
6.	Chapter 5: Assemblies of Molecules, Cells, and Groups of Cells Within Multicellular Organisms
7.	Chapter 3: Transmission of Heritable Information from Generation to Generation and Processes That Increase Genetic Diversity
8.	Chapter 7: Processes of Cell Division, Differentiation, and Specialization
9.	Chapter 7: Processes of Cell Division, Differentiation, and Specialization
10.	Chapter 3: Transmission of Heritable Information from Generation to Generation and Processes That Increase Genetic Diversity
11.	Chapter 3: Transmission of Heritable Information from Generation to Generation and Processes That Increase Genetic Diversity
12.	Chapter 9: Structure and Integrative Functions of the Main Organ Systems
13.	Chapter 9: Structure and Integrative Functions of the Main Organ Systems
14.	Chapter 8: Structure and Function of the Nervous and Endocrine Systems and Ways in Which These Systems Coordinate the Organ Systems
15.	Chapter 8: Structure and Function of the Nervous and Endocrine Systems and Ways in Which These Systems Coordinate the Organ Systems
16.	Chapter 8: Structure and Function of the Nervous and Endocrine Systems and Ways in Which These Systems Coordinate the Organ Systems
17.	Chapter 9: Structure and Integrative Functions of the Main Organ Systems
18.	Chapter 9: Structure and Integrative Functions of the Main Organ Systems
19.	Chapter 7: Processes of Cell Division, Differentiation, and Specialization
20.	Chapter 7: Processes of Cell Division, Differentiation, and Specialization
21.	Chapter 7: Processes of Cell Division, Differentiation, and Specialization
22.	Chapter 9: Structure and Integrative Functions of the Main Organ Systems
23.	Chapter 7: Processes of Cell Division, Differentiation, and Specialization

(Continued)

Item Number	Content Area
24.	Chapter 9: Structure and Integrative Functions of the Main Organ Systems
25.	Chapter 9: Structure and Integrative Functions of the Main Organ Systems
26.	Chapter 2: Transmission of Genetic Information from the Gene to the Protein
27.	Chapter 9: Structure and Integrative Functions of the Main Organ Systems
28.	Chapter 1: Structure and Function of Proteins and Their Constituent Amino Acids
29.	Chapter 9: Structure and Integrative Functions of the Main Organ Systems
30.	Chapter 9: Structure and Integrative Functions of the Main Organ Systems
31.	Chapter 9: Structure and Integrative Functions of the Main Organ Systems
32.	Chapter 9: Structure and Integrative Functions of the Main Organ Systems
33.	Chapter 2: Transmission of Genetic Information from the Gene to the Protein
34.	Chapter 9: Structure and Integrative Functions of the Main Organ Systems
35.	Chapter 6: Structure, Growth, Physiology, and Genetics of Prokaryotes and Viruses
36.	Chapter 9: Structure and Integrative Functions of the Main Organ Systems
37.	Chapter 8: Structure and Function of the Nervous and Endocrine Systems and Ways in Which These Systems Coordinate the Organ Systems
38.	Chapter 6: Structure, Growth, Physiology, and Genetics of Prokaryotes and Viruses
39.	Chapter 2: Transmission of Genetic Information from the Gene to the Protein
40.	Chapter 6: Structure, Growth, Physiology, and Genetics of Prokaryotes and Viruses
41.	Chapter 1: Structure and Function of Proteins and Their Constituent Amino Acids
42.	Chapter 6: Structure, Growth, Physiology, and Genetics of Prokaryotes and Viruses
43.	Chapter 6: Structure, Growth, Physiology, and Genetics of Prokaryotes and Viruses
44.	Chapter 2: Transmission of Genetic Information from the Gene to the Protein
45.	Chapter 2: Transmission of Genetic Information from the Gene to the Protein
46.	Chapter 9: Structure and Integrative Functions of the Main Organ Systems
47.	Chapter 9: Structure and Integrative Functions of the Main Organ Systems
48.	Chapter 3: Transmission of Heritable Information from Generation to Generation and Processes That Increase Genetic Diversity
49.	Chapter 9: Structure and Integrative Functions of the Main Organ Systems
50.	Chapter 8: Structure and Function of the Nervous and Endocrine Systems and Ways in Which These Systems Coordinate the Organ Systems
51.	Chapter 8: Structure and Function of the Nervous and Endocrine Systems and Ways in Which These Systems Coordinate the Organ Systems
52.	Chapter 9: Structure and Integrative Functions of the Main Organ Systems
53.	Chapter 9: Structure and Integrative Functions of the Main Organ Systems
54.	Chapter 5: Assemblies of Molecules, Cells, and Groups of Cells Within Multicellular Organisms
55.	Chapter 9: Structure and Integrative Functions of the Main Organ Systems
56.	Chapter 5: Assemblies of Molecules, Cells, and Groups of Cells Within Multicellular Organisms
57.	Chapter 4: Principles of Bioenergetics and Fuel Molecule Metabolism
58.	Chapter 3: Transmission of Heritable Information from Generation to Generation and Processes That Increase Genetic Diversity
59.	Chapter 8: Structure and Function of the Nervous and Endocrine Systems and Ways in Which These Systems Coordinate the Organ Systems

Item Number	Content Area
Chemical and Physical Foundations of Biological Systems	
1.	Chapter 1: Translational Motion, Forces, Work, Energy, and Equilibrium in Living Systems
2.	Chapter 3: Electrochemistry and Electrical Circuits and Their Elements
3.	Chapter 9: Structure, Function, and Reactivity of Biologically Relevant Molecules
4.	Chapter 9: Structure, Function, and Reactivity of Biologically Relevant Molecules
5.	Chapter 9: Structure, Function, and Reactivity of Biologically Relevant Molecules
6.	Chapter 9: Structure, Function, and Reactivity of Biologically Relevant Molecules
7.	Chapter 9: Structure, Function, and Reactivity of Biologically Relevant Molecules
8.	Chapter 1: Translational Motion, Forces, Work, Energy, and Equilibrium in Living Systems
9.	Chapter 1: Translational Motion, Forces, Work, Energy, and Equilibrium in Living Systems
10.	Chapter 1: Translational Motion, Forces, Work, Energy, and Equilibrium in Living Systems
11.	Chapter 1: Translational Motion, Forces, Work, Energy, and Equilibrium in Living Systems
12.	Chapter 1: Translational Motion, Forces, Work, Energy, and Equilibrium in Living Systems
13.	Chapter 1: Translational Motion, Forces, Work, Energy, and Equilibrium in Living Systems
14.	Chapter 1: Translational Motion, Forces, Work, Energy, and Equilibrium in Living Systems
15.	Chapter 8: Separation and Purification Methods Chapter 9: Structure, Function, and Reactivity of Biologically Relevant Molecules
16.	Chapter 8: Separation and Purification Methods Chapter 9: Structure, Function, and Reactivity of Biologically Relevant Molecules
17.	Chapter 8: Separation and Purification Methods Chapter 9: Structure, Function, and Reactivity of Biologically Relevant Molecules
18.	Chapter 8: Separation and Purification Methods Chapter 9: Structure, Function, and Reactivity of Biologically Relevant Molecules
19.	Chapter 8: Separation and Purification Methods Chapter 9: Structure, Function, and Reactivity of Biologically Relevant Molecules
20.	Chapter 7: The Nature of Molecules and Intermolecular Interactions
21.	Chapter 8: Separation and Purification Methods Chapter 9: Structure, Function, and Reactivity of Biologically Relevant Molecules
22.	Chapter 8: Separation and Purification Methods Chapter 9: Structure, Function, and Reactivity of Biologically Relevant Molecules

(*Continued*)

Item Number	Content Area
23.	Chapter 8: Separation and Purification Methods
	Chapter 9: Structure, Function, and Reactivity of Biologically Relevant Molecules
24.	Chapter 8: Separation and Purification Methods
	Chapter 9: Structure, Function, and Reactivity of Biologically Relevant Molecules
25.	Chapter 9: Structure, Function, and Reactivity of Biologically Relevant Molecules
26.	Chapter 2: Importance of Fluids for the Circulation of Blood, Gas Movement, and Gas Exchange
27.	Chapter 4: How Light and Sound Interact with Matter
28.	Chapter 5: Atoms, Nuclear Decay, Electronic Structure, and Atomic Chemical Behavior
29.	Chapter 6: The Unique Nature of Water and Its Solutions
	Chapter 10: Principles of Chemical Thermodynamics and Kinetics
30.	Chapter 6: The Unique Nature of Water and Its Solutions
31.	Chapter 6: The Unique Nature of Water and Its Solutions
32.	Chapter 6: The Unique Nature of Water and Its Solutions
33.	Chapter 6: The Unique Nature of Water and Its Solutions
34.	Chapter 2: Importance of Fluids for the Circulation of Blood, Gas Movement, and Gas Exchange
35.	Chapter 2: Importance of Fluids for the Circulation of Blood, Gas Movement, and Gas Exchange
36.	Chapter 2: Importance of Fluids for the Circulation of Blood, Gas Movement, and Gas Exchange
37.	Chapter 2: Importance of Fluids for the Circulation of Blood, Gas Movement, and Gas Exchange
38.	Chapter 2: Importance of Fluids for the Circulation of Blood, Gas Movement, and Gas Exchange
39.	Chapter 9: Structure, Function, and Reactivity of Biologically Relevant Molecules
40.	Chapter 9: Structure, Function, and Reactivity of Biologically Relevant Molecules
41.	Chapter 9: Structure, Function, and Reactivity of Biologically Relevant Molecules
42.	Chapter 9: Structure, Function, and Reactivity of Biologically Relevant Molecules
43.	Chapter 9: Structure, Function, and Reactivity of Biologically Relevant Molecules
44.	Chapter 4: How Light and Sound Interact with Matter
45.	Chapter 4: How Light and Sound Interact with Matter
46.	Chapter 4: How Light and Sound Interact with Matter
47.	Chapter 4: How Light and Sound Interact with Matter
48.	Chapter 4: How Light and Sound Interact with Matter
49.	Chapter 6: The Unique Nature of Water and Its Solutions
50.	Chapter 6: The Unique Nature of Water and Its Solutions
51.	Chapter 6: The Unique Nature of Water and Its Solutions
52.	Chapter 6: The Unique Nature of Water and Its Solutions
53.	Chapter 6: The Unique Nature of Water and Its Solutions
54.	Chapter 6: The Unique Nature of Water and Its Solutions
55.	Chapter 9: Structure, Function, and Reactivity of Biologically Relevant Molecules

Item Number	Content Area
56.	Chapter 9: Structure, Function, and Reactivity of Biologically Relevant Molecules
57.	Chapter 9: Structure, Function, and Reactivity of Biologically Relevant Molecules
58.	Chapter 9: Structure, Function, and Reactivity of Biologically Relevant Molecules
59.	Chapter 9: Structure, Function, and Reactivity of Biologically Relevant Molecules

Psychological, Social, and Biological Foundations of Behavior

1.	Chapter 9: Social Interactions
2.	Chapter 2: Making Sense of the Environment
3.	Chapter 12: Social Inequality
4.	Chapter 4: Individual Influences on Behavior
5.	Chapter 9: Social Interactions
6.	Chapter 9: Social Interactions
7.	Chapter 9: Social Interactions
8.	Chapter 9: Social Interactions
9.	Chapter 9: Social Interactions
10.	Chapter 2: Making Sense of the Environment
11.	Chapter 2: Making Sense of the Environment
12.	Chapter 2: Making Sense of the Environment
13.	Chapter 2: Making Sense of the Environment
14.	Chapter 2: Making Sense of the Environment
15.	Chapter 2: Making Sense of the Environment
16.	Chapter 2: Making Sense of the Environment
17.	Chapter 2: Making Sense of the Environment
18.	Chapter 2: Making Sense of the Environment
19.	Chapter 2: Making Sense of the Environment
20.	Chapter 9: Social Interactions
21.	Chapter 9: Social Interactions
22.	Chapter 9: Social Interactions
23.	Chapter 9: Social Interactions
24.	Chapter 9: Social Interactions
25.	Chapter 12: Social Inequality
26.	Chapter 12: Social Inequality
27.	Chapter 12: Social Inequality
28.	Chapter 12: Social Inequality
29.	Chapter 12: Social Inequality
30.	Chapter 4: Individual Influences on Behavior
31.	Chapter 4: Individual Influences on Behavior
32.	Chapter 4: Individual Influences on Behavior
33.	Chapter 4: Individual Influences on Behavior
34.	Chapter 4: Individual Influences on Behavior
35.	Chapter 4: Individual Influences on Behavior
36.	Chapter 4: Individual Influences on Behavior
37.	Chapter 4: Individual Influences on Behavior
38.	Chapter 4: Individual Influences on Behavior
39.	Chapter 4: Individual Influences on Behavior
40.	Chapter 9: Social Interactions
41.	Chapter 9: Social Interactions

(*Continued*)

Item Number	Content Area
42.	Chapter 9: Social Interactions
43.	Chapter 9: Social Interactions
44.	Chapter 9: Social Interactions
45.	Chapter 9: Social Interactions
46.	Chapter 9: Social Interactions
47.	Chapter 9: Social Interactions
48.	Chapter 9: Social Interactions
49.	Chapter 9: Social Interactions
50.	Chapter 3: Responding to the World
51.	Chapter 3: Responding to the World
51.	Chapter 3: Responding to the World
53.	Chapter 3: Responding to the World
54.	Chapter 3: Responding to the World
55.	Chapter 10: Understanding Social Structure
56.	Chapter 4: Individual Influences on Behavior
57.	Chapter 4: Individual Influences on Behavior
58.	Chapter 2: Making Sense of the Environment
59.	Chapter 12: Social Inequality

MCAT

Practice Test 3

Biological and Biochemical Foundations of Living Systems

59 Questions   **Time Limit: 95 Minutes**

Choose the best answer to each of the following questions. Questions 1–4 are not based on a passage.

1. Which of the following statements BEST explains why your body prefers to perform aerobic respiration as opposed to anaerobic respiration?
   A. Anaerobic respiration does not allow for NADH to be recycled to NAD+.
   B. Aerobic respiration requires less of an adenosine triphosphate (ATP) investment than anaerobic respiration does.
   C. Aerobic respiration produces far more ATP than anaerobic respiration.
   D. Aerobic respiration is easier for cells to perform than anaerobic respiration.

2. If you replaced the thymine in a double helix with radioactive thymine and you allowed DNA replication to occur once, which of the following results would you expect?
   A. The DNA would not be radioactive in either of the double helices.
   B. The mRNA made from the double helices would be radioactive.
   C. The DNA in each of the double helices would be radioactive.
   D. The DNA in one of the double helices would be radioactive but not in the other one.

3. The glucose made by a plant is used to produce all the other molecules that the plant needs, such as proteins, lipids, and nucleic acids. Which statement would be correct about how plants make these other molecules?

    A. Glucose has all the elements needed to make all of the other molecules.

    B. Glucose has all the elements needed to produce lipids, but must obtain other elements to produce proteins and nucleic acids.

    C. Glucose has all the elements needed to produce lipids and proteins, but must obtain other elements to produce nucleic acids.

    D. None of these statements are correct.

4. In Mendel's experiments with the pea plant, the gene for height exists in two allelic forms, designated T for tall stature and t for short stature. In the second generation of a cross between a homozygous tall parent (TT) and a homozygous short parent (tt), the phenotypic ratio of dominant to recessive pea plants is:

    A. 1:1

    B. 2:1

    C. 3:1

    D. 4:1

Questions 5–8 are based on the following passage.

Passage I

Approximately 0.04% of Caucasians are born with cystic fibrosis. This disease is one of the most common recessive genetic diseases and is often fatal. Cystic fibrosis is characterized by the accumulation of abnormally thick mucus throughout the body and the loss of excess amounts of salt via sweat. The thick mucus builds up and causes major problems in the lungs, which often become infected, and can cause digestive abnormalities such as malnutrition and blockages through the intestinal tract. The severity of the disease is variable, and many other potential complications can arise.

    The gene involved in cystic fibrosis is a mutated allele of the cystic fibrosis trans-membrane regulator (CFTR). At least 900 known mutations of this gene can lead to cystic fibrosis. The normal CFTR gene produces the CFTR protein that is a transmembrane chloride channel in cells of the lungs, digestive tract, skin, and reproductive tract. One mutation termed **delta F508** has a single amino acid change in the protein that marks it for destruction before it ever reaches the membrane to complete its function. Without the proper CFTR in the membrane of cells, the chloride and sodium ion balance is altered such that not enough water leaves the cells to produce mucus of the proper consistency. The thick mucus that results accumulates and causes multiple problems, including the trapping of bacteria that can cause infections. Although there is no cure for cystic fibrosis, better management strategies have increased the life span of people with this genetic disease.

257

SECTION 1:
Biological and
Biochemical
Foundations of
Living Systems

5. Many potential treatments are being evaluated for cystic fibrosis. Of the items listed, which would appear to have the BEST chance of preventing the symptoms of the disease in an affected person?
    A. the use of a drug that increases the production of CFTR
    B. the use of a drug that prevents CFTR from being degraded when it reaches the lysosomes
    C. the use of a drug that increases nutrient absorption in the small intestine
    D. the use of a drug that activates a chloride cell channel other than CFTR

6. The CFTR protein is 1480 amino acids in length. How many codons must have been present in the mRNA used to make the protein?
    A. 493
    B. 1480
    C. 1481
    D. 4440

7. If two parents do not have cystic fibrosis but are carriers for the disease, what are their odds of having a child with cystic fibrosis?
    A. 0%
    B. 25%
    C. 50%
    D. 75%

8. Pancreatic insufficiency occurs in some cystic fibrosis patients. This means that there is a lack of digestive enzymes being secreted from the pancreas to the small intestine. Trypsin levels in particular are quite reduced. What items would the individual have a hard time digesting due to a lack of trypsin?
    A. proteins
    B. carbohydrates
    C. sugar
    D. fats

Questions 9–12 are based on the following passage.

Passage II

Within the cells of the body, mitochondria are present in variable numbers. Some cell types have a few of these organelles, and other cell types have hundreds of mitochondria. An interesting feature of mitochondria that distinguishes them from other organelles is that they have their own DNA, termed **mitochondrial DNA (mtDNA)**. The mtDNA is completely distinct from the nuclear chromosomes and is presumed to have evolved separately from the nuclear DNA. Mitochondrial DNA is circular and consists of 37 genes coding for proteins, transfer RNA (tRNA), and ribosomal RNA (rRNA). Each mitochondrion has about five copies of the mtDNA. All of the mitochondria within the body's cells are descendants of the mitochondria present in an egg cell before it was fertilized. Because all mitochondria are derived from those present in an egg cell, they contain the mtDNA from the mother. Sperm contribute no mitochondria or mtDNA to the egg cell during fertilization. This mode of inheritance is often called maternal inheritance.

Although mtDNA composes a small portion of the cell's total DNA, it is subject to mutation, and several diseases are known to be caused by mutations to mtDNA. One of those diseases is Leber's optic atrophy, which causes deterioration of the optic nerve and a progressive loss of central vision. Most people with this condition have inherited both normal mtDNA and mtDNA that carries the mutation. When mutated mitochondria outnumber normal mitochondria, symptoms of the disease occur.

9. The number of mitochondria in a particular cell type probably relates to:
   A. the size of the cell and the amount of space available
   B. the number of proteins the cell needs to produce
   C. the amount of materials in the cell that need to be degraded and removed
   D. the amount of adenosine triphosphate (ATP) the cell needs to produce

10. Men with mtDNA mutations that cause a disease:
   A. will pass them on only to their sons
   B. will pass them on only to their daughters
   C. will pass them on to both sons and daughters about 50% of the time
   D. will never pass them on to their children

11. Endosymbiotic theory explains why mitochondria have their own DNA. This theory essentially states that at one point, free-living prokaryotic cells were engulfed by another cell, eventually becoming mitochondria. The BEST support for this theory is that:
   A. Mitochondria are membrane-bound organelles.
   B. Mitochondrial DNA resembles that of prokaryotic DNA.
   C. Mitochondria have more than one copy of their DNA.
   D. Mitochondria are found in multiple copies in each cell.

12. Mitochondrial DNA within the cells of a given organism is derived from a single source. Which of the following processes should NOT occur within mtDNA?
   A. transcription
   B. translation
   C. crossing over and recombination
   D. spontaneous mutation

259

SECTION 1:
Biological and
Biochemical
Foundations of
Living Systems

Questions 13–16 are based on the following passage.

Passage III

Nitric oxide (NO) is a remarkable gas that acts as a signaling molecule throughout the body. It is produced by vascular endothelium, smooth muscle, and cardiac muscle cells. Because the half-life of NO is only a few seconds, its effects are short lived, but it is nevertheless essential to many of the body's regulation processes. A few of the known roles of NO include control over blood vessel dilation and pressure, involvement in inflammation, neurotransmission, and the regulation of apoptosis (programmed cell death). It is suspected that NO has many other roles in the body that are yet to be completely understood.

NO is produced in cells when a group of enzymes known as nitric oxide synthases (NOS) convert the amino acid L-arginine to L-citrulline. NO is produced as a by-product of the reaction. The activity of NO is modulated by cyclic guanine monophosphate (cGMP). When present, cGMP increases the vasodilating abilities of NO. The expression of phosphodiesterase (PDE) enzymes causes the degradation of cGMP that suppresses the function of NO.

Because NO acts as a smooth muscle vasodilator, a variety of pharmaceuticals that act on NO have been developed. Nitroglycerin, which decreases the amount of oxygen flowing to the myocardium of the heart, is often used to manage the chest pain of angina that is associated with coronary artery disease. Drugs for erectile dysfunction (ED) such as Viagra, Cialis, and Levitra all work by enhancing NO function and increasing vasodilation and blood flow in the penis during sexual stimulation. Even the nutritional supplement industry has tried to manipulate the effects of NO. Bodybuilders and athletes have been using what are termed **NO hemodilators**, alleging that these supplements increase blood flow to muscles, making them look larger and recover faster after injury.

13. You would expect that drugs such as Viagra work by:
    A. inhibiting PDE enzyme activity
    B. decreasing cGMP activity
    C. decreasing NOS activity
    D. acting as an antagonist to L-arginine

14. Cyclic GMP is a modified form of a:
    A. protein
    B. sugar
    C. nucleotide
    D. lipid

15. Some of the advertisements for NO hemodilator supplements imply that the product contains NO. What would be the MOST likely ingredient in these supplements?
    A. The products would have to contain NO to have any of the alleged effects in the body.
    B. Because the half-life of NO is so brief, the product most likely contains L-arginine, which can be converted to L-citrulline and NO in the cells.
    C. The products would most likely contain the PDE enzyme.
    D. The products would contain L-citrulline and NO.

16. One of the contraindications for men taking ED drugs is that they should not be combined with nitroglycerin. What might be an immediate problem observed with men taking nitroglycerin and ED drugs?
    A. Both drugs cause vasodilation by increasing NO levels. This could cause blood pressure to drop to dangerous levels.
    B. The ED drugs might increase the heart rate to dangerous levels.
    C. The drugs might inhibit immune function and inflammatory responses.
    D. The two drugs might interact, having toxic results for the liver and kidneys.

Question 17 is not based on a passage.

17. If a DNA codon, reading from the 5' end, is C-A-T, then the base sequence of the corresponding anticodon, reading from the 5' end, will be:
    A. C-A-U
    B. G-T-A
    C. A-U-G
    D. A-T-G

Questions 18–20 are based on the following data.

The generalized events in DNA replication can be depicted by the following flowchart:

Double helix → Nicking of a strand → Unwinding → Destabilization and relief of pressure → Initiation → Elongation → Closing of nicks

18. Between which two steps would the enzyme *DNA polymerase* be used?
    A. Double helix→Nicking of a strand
    B. Nicking of a strand→Unwinding
    C. Initiation→Elongation
    D. Elongation→Closing of nicks

19. Between which two steps would the enzyme *topoisomerase* be used?
    A. Double helix→Nicking of a strand
    B. Nicking of a strand→Unwinding
    C. Initiation→Elongation
    D. Elongation→Closing of nicks

261

SECTION 1:
Biological and
Biochemical
Foundations of
Living Systems

20. Between which two steps would the enzyme *DNA ligase* be used?
    - **A.** Double helix→Nicking of a strand
    - **B.** Nicking of a strand→Unwinding
    - **C.** Initiation→Elongation
    - **D.** Elongation→Closing of nicks

Questions 21–24 are not based on a passage.

21. The DNA doubles and chromosomes replicate during which phase of the cell cycle?
    - **A.** G1
    - **B.** metaphase
    - **C.** S
    - **D.** G2

22. When two solutions that differ in solute concentration are placed on either side of a semipermeable membrane and osmosis is allowed to occur, which of the following will be observed?
    - **A.** Water will move from an area of low solute concentration to an area of high solute concentration.
    - **B.** The solute will move from an area of high concentration to an area of low concentration.
    - **C.** There will be no net movement of water.
    - **D.** Water will move from an area of high solute concentration to an area of low solute concentration.

23. A scientist discovers an unidentified unicellular organism. To identify it as eukaryotic, she must determine if it has:
    - **A.** ribosomes
    - **B.** a cell membrane
    - **C.** DNA
    - **D.** mitochondria

24. Which of the following would help you identify an unknown cell type as connective?
    - **A.** the ability to contract
    - **B.** the presence of lots of cells arranged in sheets
    - **C.** the presence of a basement membrane
    - **D.** the presence of collagen fibers

Questions 25–28 are based on the following passage.

Passage IV

The origin of eukaryotic organelles has been subject to speculation for many years. In particular, chloroplasts and mitochondria have some unusual features unlike the other organelles of the cell, which suggests they have had a unique history. The evidence collected as a result of the development of molecular research techniques provides an explanation for the origin of these organelles.

The theory of endosymbiosis is used to explain the presence of organelles such as mitochondria and chloroplasts in modern-day eukaryotic cells. The theory suggests that small prokaryotic cells were at one time engulfed by larger prokaryotic cells. Once inside the larger cells, a symbiotic relationship developed. In the case of mitochondria, it has been speculated that the larger cell was likely anaerobic and ingested a smaller aerobic cell. Once inside, the aerobic cell was able to perform aerobic respiration to produce additional adenosine triphosphate (ATP) for the host cell. To explain the evolution of chloroplasts, it has been suggested that cyanobacteria with the ability to photosynthesize were engulfed by a larger anaerobic prokaryotic cell. Support for this theory exists in the fact that both mitochondria and chloroplasts have double membranes, have their own genetic material that is different from typical eukaryotic chromosomal DNA, and have their own ribosomes.

25. According to the endosymbiotic theory presented in this passage, the original anaerobic cell that engulfed the smaller cell was likely performing this process to produce ATP prior to entering a symbiotic relationship.
    A. glycolysis
    B. electron transport
    C. the Krebs cycle
    D. all of these

26. The genetic material of mitochondria and chloroplasts resembles that of modern-day bacteria as opposed to that of typical eukaryotic genetic material. This would mean which of the following?
    A. The DNA in these organelles exists in linear chromosome form.
    B. The DNA in these organelles exists in plasmid form.
    C. The DNA in these organelles exists in a single loop.
    D. The RNA in these organelles is single stranded.

27. Under normal circumstances, items engulfed by a eukaryotic cell might be broken down by which organelle?
    A. the lysosomes
    B. the smooth endoplasmic reticulum
    C. the Golgi apparatus
    D. the rough endoplasmic reticulum

263

SECTION 1:
Biological and
Biochemical
Foundations of
Living Systems

28. Which of the following would lend additional evidence to the endosymbiotic theory?

   A. discovering a difference in the size of the subunits of the ribosomes inside the mitochondria and chloroplasts as compared to the rest of the cell

   B. finding that the inner membrane of the mitochondria and chloroplasts resembled that of modern bacteria

   C. finding plasmid DNA in the mitochondria and chloroplasts

   D. all of the above

Questions 29–32 are based on the following passage.

Passage V

In the early 1900s, it was noticed that cellular materials that passed from the tumors of chickens with cancer to chickens without cancer would eventually cause cancer to develop in the recipient chickens. In this case it appeared that the cancer was somehow "contagious," and it was suspected that viruses were somehow involved in this infectious type of cancer. Later, it was determined that certain viruses have the ability to genetically transform normal cells to a cancerous state by inserting into the chromosomes of their host cells. The virus that caused cancer was named the Rous sarcoma virus (RSV) after its founder. The RSV has only four genes. The *gag* gene codes for the capsid of the virus, the *env* gene codes for the envelope of the virus, the *pol* gene codes for reverse transcriptase, and the *src* gene encodes for a tyrosine kinase.

Within normal cells, there are proto-oncogenes, which are involved in cell division and development. Because most cells are not reproducing all the time, proto-oncogenes tend to be expressed at low levels or not at all. If viral genetic material inserts into a proto-oncogene, it will be converted to an active oncogene, which stimulates excessive cell division, eventually leading to tumor development. Viruses with this ability are termed **oncogenic** viruses. Some viruses activate an oncogene by inserting their genetic material into a cellular proto-oncogene, whereas some oncogenic viruses actually carry oncogenes into their hosts. Whether the virus inserts into a cellular proto-oncogene or carries an oncogene into the cell, the end result is increased cell proliferation and changes in the cell, which can include lack of contact inhibition and immortality.

29. Oncogenic viruses are known to become latent as they enter into the host cell's chromosomes. Many oncogenic viruses are retroviruses. In order for a retrovirus to insert into the host cell's chromosomes, it must FIRST:

   A. convert its RNA to DNA

   B. translate its RNA

   C. initiate transcription

   D. recombine with the host cell's chromosomes

30. Suppose a drug had been made to target the RSV. This drug attempts to prevent the packaging and release of the virus from its host cell. This drug would MOST likely target which of the RSV genes?

    A. *gag* and *env*

    B. *pol* and *src*

    C. *src* only

    D. *pol* only

31. It is known that some viruses carry activated oncogenes into their hosts. What is the BEST explanation for how a virus could acquire an oncogene?

    A. The virus spontaneously mutates.

    B. The virus acquires the oncogene via conjugation with another virus.

    C. The virus is transformed by DNA from another source.

    D. The virus acquired the oncogene from a previous host.

32. Once an oncogene is activated and a cell becomes cancerous, which of the following would be MOST likely to halt the excessive cell division associated with cancer?

    A. microtubule and mitotic disruption in dividing cells

    B. disruption of protein synthesis

    C. introduction of additional growth factors to the cell

    D. disruption of aerobic cellular respiration

Questions 33–36 are based on the following passage.

Passage VI

Evolutionary theory predicts that given selective pressures, populations will evolve in certain ways. Antibiotic resistance that develops in bacteria is an excellent example of evolutionary selection in action. Spontaneous mutations in bacteria will happen in nature. Due to random chance, some of these mutations provide bacteria the ability to survive in the presence of antibiotics that would normally kill them. These mutations can provide advantages to the bacteria such as the ability to degrade the antibiotics with enzymes, the ability to pump the antibiotic out of the cell, the ability to prevent the antibiotic from entering the cell, and the ability to change target molecules in the cell so that the antibiotic is unable to affect its target. Additionally, most antibiotic-resistance genes can easily be passed from a resistant bacterium to a nonresistant bacterium via the process of conjugation. Transduction by viruses can also carry resistance genes from one bacterium to another. It becomes very easy for an entire bacterial population to become resistant to an antibiotic in a very short period.

Antibiotic resistance is a major public health concern because as bacteria develop resistance to certain antibiotics, those antibiotics are no longer capable of eliminating infections caused by resistant bacteria. Further, some bacteria are able to acquire mutations that provide them with resistance to multiple antibiotics. One such example is methicillin-resistant *Staphylococcus aureus* (MRSA). This type of bacteria can be carried asymptomatically by some people and passed to others where it will cause an infection. One of the most common places for MRSA to be spread is through hospitals. The problem with MRSA is that its multiple resistance leaves it susceptible to very few antibiotics. In fact, strains of MRSA are known to show resistance to nearly every antibiotic available.

265

SECTION 1:
Biological and
Biochemical
Foundations of
Living Systems

33. Why would repeated use of antibiotics select for resistant strains of bacteria?
    A. The antibiotics would force the bacteria to mutate at a greater rate.
    B. The antibiotics would kill the susceptible bacteria, leaving only the resistant ones to multiply.
    C. The antibiotics would directly increase the rate of binary fission in resistant organisms.
    D. All of the above would be logical reasons that the repeated use of antibiotics selects for resistant bacteria.

34. Conjugation is one method bacteria use to pass their resistance genes to other bacteria. During conjugation, the genes transferred are typically located on:
    A. the bacterial chromosome
    B. the ribosome
    C. the mRNA
    D. a plasmid

35. A variety of biotechnology techniques have been developed that allow for manipulated gene transfer. Often, antibiotic-resistance genes are purposefully transferred along with the gene of interest. Why would this be important?
    A. to make sure that the transformed cells can survive in the presence of antibiotics
    B. to be able to use antibiotics as a marker to select between transformed and nontransformed cells
    C. the antibiotic-resistance genes happen to be near the gene of interest being transferred
    D. to prevent infection of the transformed cells

36. When humans take antibiotics to treat infections, we rely on the fact that the antibiotics target the bacterial cells while leaving our own cells unharmed. What cell structure in bacteria is structurally different from eukaryotic cells and could potentially be a target of an antibiotic?
    A. the cell membrane
    B. the DNA nucleotides
    C. the ribosomes
    D. the cytoplasm

Questions 37–40 are not based on a passage.

37. Some human males have three sex chromosomes (XXY) and suffer from a genetic disease known as Klinefelter's syndrome. The symptoms include a failure to develop sexually and an impairment of intelligence. Klinefelter's syndrome is an example of a disease related to:

    A. karyotype
    B. point mutation
    C. homeostasis
    D. bacterial origin

38. In humans, the number of tetrads formed during mitosis is:

    A. 23
    B. 46
    C. 0
    D. 4

39. The centromere, or primary constriction of the chromosome, contains rings of proteins that are intimately associated with a spindle fiber. These rings are called:

    A. somites
    B. centrioles
    C. asters
    D. kinetochores

40. The two sets of chromosomes present in the cells of diploid organisms are derived from:

    A. the doubling of a haploid cell
    B. the contribution of one haploid set from each parent
    C. a reduction process within a tetraploid cell
    D. all of the above

Questions 41–44 are based on the following passage.

Passage VII

Guillain-Barré syndrome (GBS) is a rare condition characterized by destruction of the insulating myelin sheath on neurons located in the peripheral nervous system. Many people who develop GBS usually have it happen within days or weeks following recovery from a respiratory or gastrointestinal infection, but the reason GBS develops is uncertain. Others develop GBS following routine surgeries or vaccinations. GBS has been seen in people of all ages, and it affects men and women equally. The symptoms of GBS typically begin as tingling or weakness in the feet that can lead to paralysis that often ascends through the body. Most of the time, GBS is acute and lasts for a relatively brief period until remyelination of the peripheral nerves can occur. However, for some

267

SECTION 1:
Biological and
Biochemical
Foundations of
Living Systems

people, relapses are common and the condition can be chronic. Rarely, GBS can cause permanent paralysis and respiratory failure.

During GBS, the immune system produces antibodies to the surface antigens of peripheral myelin. These antibodies facilitate the destruction of the myelin, which leads to the neurological symptoms. Although GBS does not have a treatment, procedures such as plasmapheresis, also known as plasma exchange, can be used to alleviate the symptoms of GBS. During plasmapheresis, the blood is removed from the body and separated into cells and plasma. The plasma is discarded so that only the blood cells are returned to the body in donated or synthetic plasma. Another treatment option is the intravenous delivery of immunoglobulin. The antibodies present in the immunoglobulin may block the antibodies produced to the surface antigens of peripheral myelin. Typically, the symptoms of GBS subside within months of their onset when treatments such as plasmapheresis or immunoglobulin are used.

41. GBS affects the myelin of the peripheral nervous system. Which neurons in the body should NOT be affected by GBS?
    A. those in the arms and legs
    B. those in the abdominal cavity
    C. those that innervate the heart
    D. those in the spinal cord

42. GBS can eventually lead to muscle paralysis due to demyelination of peripheral nerves. The BEST explanation for this would be that:
    A. The peripheral nerves can no longer conduct action potentials due to a lack of myelin.
    B. The muscle cells no longer respond to acetylcholine at the neuromuscular junction.
    C. The sodium-potassium pumps in the neurons are not functioning properly.
    D. The brain is failing to send the appropriate signals to the peripheral nerves.

43. Based on the information provided in the passage, GBS could BEST be described as:
    A. a dominant genetic disorder
    B. a sex-linked genetic disorder
    C. an autoimmune disorder
    D. an infectious disease

44. Plasmapheresis seems to help many patients with GBS. The MOST reasonable explanation for why plasmapheresis would alleviate the symptoms of GBS would be that:
    A. Replacing the plasma would decrease the number of lymphocytes attacking myelin of the peripheral nerves.
    B. There would be less of an attack on peripheral myelin when the antibodies against myelin are removed with the plasma.
    C. Replacing the plasma makes the immune system more capable of fighting the infections that are characteristic of GBS.
    D. Replacing the plasma would remove any toxins responsible for the symptoms.

Questions 45–48 are not based on a passage.

45. Which of the following drugs might cause muscle spasms (uncontrolled contractions)?
    A. one that elevates calcium levels
    B. one that prevents the use of adenosine triphosphate (ATP)
    C. one that elongates the sarcomere
    D. one that prevents attachment of myosin heads to actin

46. Diabetes insipidus is an inherited endocrine disorder that causes the kidneys to produce extreme amounts of urine per day that can severely dehydrate the individual with this condition. Management of this disorder involves hormone therapy. Which of the following is the missing hormone in a person with this disorder?
    A. antidiuretic hormone
    B. thyroid-stimulating hormone
    C. glucagon
    D. calcitonin

47. During pulmonary gas exchange, oxygen and carbon dioxide always move:
    A. into the alveoli
    B. into the blood
    C. from high to low concentration
    D. out of the blood

48. The hypothalamus is part of the:
    A. cerebrum
    B. brain stem
    C. diencephalon
    D. spinal cord

Questions 49–52 are based on the following passage.

Passage VIII

The thyroid gland is best known for its role in the regulation of metabolism via tri-iodothyronine (T3) and thyroxine (T4). Thyroid-stimulating hormone (TSH) is secreted by the pituitary gland in response to declining levels of T3 and T4. TSH activates the thyroid gland to release T3 and T4, which are stored as thyroglobulin (bound to protein). T3 is about five times more physiologically potent than T4. Thyroglobulin is enzymatically converted to T3, T4, and globulin, and T3 and T4 are released. T4 is converted in the liver to T3 and reverse T3 (RT3). About 80% of T3 comes from T4 conversion and the other 20% comes directly from the thyroid gland. Reverse T3 blocks the action of T3 and T4 by occupying T3 and T4 cell receptor sites.

269

SECTION 1:
Biological and
Biochemical
Foundations of
Living Systems

A symptom of a thyroid hormone abnormality is the swelling of the thyroid that is referred to as a goiter, which can necessitate a portion or even all of the thyroid gland being surgically removed. After the surgery, synthetic hormones are given in an attempt to regulate the metabolism. Because the thyroid also deals with calcium homeostasis, complete removal of the thyroid can cause calcium levels to become extremely low.

The following data was collected from blood drawn to complete a thyroid panel on a patient suffering from a goiter:

	Patient Values	Expected Normal Values
Triiodothyronine (T3)	6.5 pg/mL	2.3–4.2 pg/mL
Thyroxine (T4)	14.2 µg/dL	4.5–12 µg/dL
Thyroid-stimulating hormone (TSH)	0.10 µIU/mL	0.35–2.5 µIU/L

49. Which conclusion is BEST supported by the data?
    A. This individual has hypothyroidism, which is caused by low levels of TSH.
    B. This individual has hypothyroidism, which is caused by abnormally low levels of thyroglobulin.
    C. This individual has hyperthyroidism, which is due to decreased levels of T3.
    D. This individual has hyperthyroidism, which is caused by elevated levels of T3.

50. After complete thyroid removal (which includes removal of the parathyroids), a patient's blood calcium becomes very low. Which of the following responses could potentially help increase calcium levels?
    A. activation of osteoclasts to degrade bone tissue
    B. activation of osteoblasts to build bone tissue
    C. taking synthetic calcitonin
    D. taking synthetic calcitonin in combination with parathyroid hormone

51. Hyperthyroidism can have multiple causes. All of the following endocrine structures could produce hormones that could potentially be involved with hyperthyroidism EXCEPT:
    A. the hypothalamus
    B. the anterior pituitary gland
    C. the thyroid gland
    D. the adrenal glands

52. An individual is producing normal levels of T3 and T4, but they do not seem to be functioning properly. The MOST likely problem is a deficiency of:
    A. calcium
    B. sodium
    C. potassium
    D. iodine

Questions 53–56 are based on the following passage.

Passage IX

The process of induced erythrocythemia, or blood doping, has become common among certain circles of athletes such as cyclists. The purpose of blood doping is to provide an endurance advantage to the athlete. There are several ways to induce erythrocythemia, including the injection of synthetic oxygen carriers, blood transfusions, and the injection of hormones.

Synthetic oxygen carriers are modified proteins that have a relatively high affinity for oxygen. These can provide short-term increases in the oxygen-carrying ability of blood, but they are quickly degraded. Blood transfusions can be used right before an athletic event. The transfused erythrocytes can be homologous in nature, meaning that they are harvested from a donor's blood, or they can be autologous, meaning they are removed from the athlete 5 to 10 weeks before the event and stored. The cells are then reinfused right before an athletic event. Another approach to blood doping involves injections of the hormone erythropoietin (EPO). The EPO used for this purpose is a recombinant molecule. It is available by prescription for certain medical conditions, but it has been widely abused by some athletes.

Testing for blood doping is not always conclusive. For autologous or homologous transfusions, the only indicator of doping is an elevated hematocrit or hemoglobin count, which is not conclusive evidence of doping. If EPO is being used, it can be detected in the urine but only for short periods. Further, the recombinant version of EPO is hard to distinguish from the natural version, and certain other proteins present in the urine may resemble EPO.

53. What sort of benefit would blood doping provide an athlete?
    A. It would increase the number of white blood cells, making the athlete less likely to develop infections.
    B. It would increase the clotting ability of the athlete's blood, making the athlete less likely to lose large volumes of blood in the event of an injury.
    C. It would increase the number of red blood cells that can provide more oxygen to produce more adenosine triphosphate (ATP) during aerobic cellular respiration.
    D. It would decrease the viscosity of the blood, making it easier for the heart to pump.

54. Some athletes prefer the use of autologous transfusions as compared to homologous transfusions. What would be a potential benefit of an autologous transfusion?
    A. It would provide more erythrocytes, since some of the ones from a homologous transfusion will die while the blood is in storage waiting to be infused.
    B. It would require longer-term advantages in athletic performance as compared to a homologous transfusion.
    C. It would make it easier to train more vigorously right after the blood was removed from the athlete.
    D. It would provide less risk of the transmission of diseases or transfusion reactions as compared to a homologous transfusion.

271

SECTION 1:
Biological and
Biochemical
Foundations of
Living Systems

55. Erythropoietin (EPO) can be a lifesaving drug for patients with certain medical conditions. Which of the following conditions could MOST likely be helped by the injection of EPO?
    A. coronary artery disease
    B. hypotension
    C. renal failure
    D. anemia

56. If the autologous doping procedure requires the removal of cells from the athlete and later those cells are reinfused into that same person, how can this provide an advantage?
    A. The athlete has become used to functioning with fewer red blood cells after the removal, so the reinfusion provides an extra boost before a performance.
    B. The erythrocytes removed from the individual have been naturally replaced after the procedure, so the number of erythrocytes in circulation after the reinfusion is greatly increased.
    C. The reinfusion increases the ability for the cells to tolerate anaerobic respiration and lactic acid production for longer periods.
    D. The autologous procedure really does not provide any measurable benefits to the athlete.

Questions 57–59 are not based on a passage.

57. The hormone that is NOT released by the anterior pituitary gland is:
    A. growth hormone
    B. antidiuretic hormone
    C. thyroid-stimulating hormone
    D. follicle-stimulating hormone

58. Curare is an arrow poison that binds to ACh (acetylcholine) receptors and prevents this neurotransmitter from exerting its usual physiological action. The likely effect of curare is:
    A. diminished heart rate
    B. an increase in nerve conduction
    C. paralysis
    D. rapid breathing

59. Oxygen tensions in the alveoli (AL), the pulmonary artery (PA), and the pulmonary vein (PV) are all different. Given the dynamics of gas exchange in the lungs, the appropriate values of partial pressures for each of these three sites are:
    A. AL: 40 mm Hg; PA: 160 mm Hg; PV: 100 mm Hg
    B. AL: 40 mm Hg; PA: 100 mm Hg; PV: 160 mm Hg
    C. AL: 100 mm Hg; PA: 40 mm Hg; PV: 160 mm Hg
    D. AL: 160 mm Hg, PA: 40 mm Hg; PV: 100 mm Hg

Chemical and Physical Foundations of Living Systems

59 Questions   **Time Limit: 95 Minutes**

Questions 1–5 are based on the following passage.

Passage I

In October 2012, Felix Baumgartner attempted a world-record sky-diving jump from just over 128,000 ft (39,014 m) above the Earth's surface. He was fitted with a customized, pressurized spacesuit that brought his total weight to 260 lbs (1156 N). The spacesuit was designed to collect and transmit important monitoring, communications, and tracking information throughout the jump. Baumgartner then ascended to the jumping altitude housed within a pressurized capsule of weight 2900 lbs (12900 N) attached to a 30×10^6 cubic feet (8.5×10^8 L) helium-filled weather balloon. The weather balloon with the attached capsule ascended at a rate of 1000 ft/min (5.1 m/s), reaching the jumping altitude in approximately two hours.

Once the capsule reached the jumping altitude, the door to the capsule was opened and Baumgartner stepped out and fell forward, beginning his free-fall descent. He continued falling until he reached a maximum speed of 834 mph (373 m/s), which exceeded the speed of sound. This speed was Baumgartner's terminal velocity—the velocity attained in which he was no longer being accelerated downward due to gravity. Once he reached this speed, Baumgartner deployed his parachute and glided safely to Earth's surface.

1. The terminal velocity of a skydiver can be determined in large part by the orientation of the skydiver in free fall. Which orientation would be MOST likely to result in the largest terminal velocity for the skydiver?

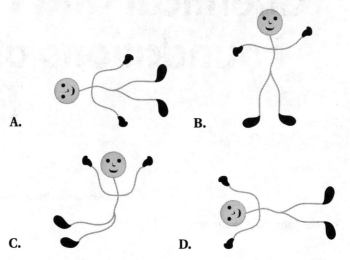

A.   B.

C.   D.

2. Assuming the density of helium is 0.1785 g/cm^3, the weight of the helium used to inflate the balloon was:
   A. $1.5 \times 10^8 \text{ N}$
   B. $1.5 \times 10^7 \text{ N}$
   C. $1.5 \times 10^6 \text{ N}$
   D. $1.5 \times 10^5 \text{ N}$

3. The distance traversed by Mr. Baumgartner before he reached maximum velocity was approximately:
   A. 4800 m
   B. 5480 m
   C. 6350 m
   D. 7100 m

4. The drag force, $F\text{drag}$, can be expressed in terms of the terminal velocity, v_t, as $F\text{drag} = Cv_t^2$, where C is a drag constant. The value of the drag constant for Mr. Baumgartner is:
   A. 0.008 kg/m
   B. 0.680 kg/m
   C. 1.320 kg/m
   D. 5.640 kg/m

275

SECTION 2:
Chemical and
Physical
Foundations of
Living Systems

5. Once the skydiver has reached terminal velocity, the free body diagram that BEST describes the forces acting on a skydiver at terminal velocity is:

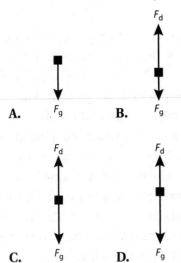

A. F_g B. F_g

C. F_g D. F_g

Questions 6 and 7 are not based on a passage.

6. When hydrogen is heated, the atoms that are formed enter an excited state and energy is released in the form of light. The electrons can move between the various principal energy levels as shown in the following diagram:

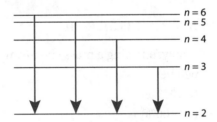

As a result of the electron transitions to the ground state, four bands of light called the Balmer series are produced. Which of the four possible transitions to $n = 2$ in the visible spectrum of hydrogen has the longest wavelength?

A. 3 to 2
B. 4 to 2
C. 5 to 2
D. 6 to 2

7. Thirty milliliters of a solution drawn into a 5-g syringe has a total mass of 80 g. The density of the solution in the syringe is:

A. $1.8\,g/cm^3$
B. $2.5\,g/cm^3$
C. $4.2\,g/cm^3$
D. $5.7\,g/cm^3$

Questions 8–12 are based on the following passage.

Passage II

Bromine, discovered in the early 1800s, has an atomic number of 35 and is located in group 17. Besides being able to exist as a diatomic liquid, bromine can frequently be found in salts and is useful in preparing organic molecules with a range of functions. Some of these uses include pesticides, water purification, prescription drugs, photochemicals, and flame retardants. In some sodas, one can find brominated vegetable oil added as an emulsifying agent. In addition to its strong odor, bromine is a dark, brown-orange liquid at room temperature. Bromine has two stable isotopes, Br-79 and Br-81, and a relative atomic abundance, which causes the atomic mass of bromine to be 79.904. Bromine-80 is one of the many unstable isotopes of bromine. It readily undergoes beta decay to form Kr-80. Bromine can also undergo other modes of decay to form Kr-80. When analyzing organic compounds that have bromine in them, the mass spectrometric analysis of the compound frequently shows a peak of equal intensity at $m/z = 79$ and $m/z = 81$, or M^+ and M^{+2} peaks of equal height as well.

8. From the masses of the isotopes and the atomic mass of bromine, you can conclude that the relative abundances of the isotopes are approximately:
   A. 35.0% Br-79 and 75.0% Br-81
   B. 50.7% Br-79 and 49.3% Br-81
   C. 100% Br-80
   D. 33.3% Br-79, 33.3% Br-80, and 33.3% Br-81

9. When a sample of Br_2 is analyzed using a mass spectrometer, the most prominent features of the analysis will be:
   A. one peak at $m/z = 80$ (100%)
   B. one peak at $m/z = 160$ (100%)
   C. two peaks at $m/z = 79$ (50%) and $m/z = 81$ (50%)
   D. three peaks at $m/z = 158$ (25%), $m/z = 160$ (50%), and $m/z = 162$ (25%)

10. Br_2 is expected to be:
    A. diamagnetic
    B. paramagnetic
    C. polar
    D. denser than diatomic iodine

11. The effective nuclear charge experienced by the valence electrons of bromine will increase the most as you:
    A. move from top to bottom in group 17
    B. move from bottom to top in group 17
    C. move from left to right in period 4
    D. move from right to left in period 4

277

SECTION 2:
Chemical and
Physical
Foundations of
Living Systems

12. If Br-80 were to emit a positron, $_{+1}^{0}e$, instead of a beta particle, it would still be possible to form Kr-80 via other modes of decay. This would need to include:
    A. one mode of beta decay
    B. two modes of beta decay
    C. one mode of alpha decay
    D. two modes of positron decay

Questions 13–15 are not based on a passage.

13. In a direct current circuit, a voltage gradient, ΔV, generates and pushes current, I, through a wire of resistance, R, according to Ohm's law, or $\Delta V = IR$. Ohm's law can analogously be applied to blood flow, Q, through a vessel of length, L, by the presence of a pressure gradient, ΔP. In this case, the variables involved in blood flow are related by Poiseuille's law, or $Q = \frac{\pi r^4}{8\eta L}\Delta P$. Given this, which of the following scenarios would result in the greatest resistance of blood flow?
    A. double the length and double the radius
    B. double the length and halve the radius
    C. halve the length and double the radius
    D. halve the length and halve the radius

14. For an individual who is myopic, or nearsighted, the eyeball is longer than normal, causing visual images to be focused in front of the retina. Myopia can be corrected by:
    A. using a concave lens, which increases the focal length
    B. using a convex lens, which increases the focal length
    C. using a concave lens, which reduces the focal length
    D. using a convex lens, which reduces the focal length

15. The hydrogen atom consists of a single electron of charge $q_e = -1.6 \times 10^{-19}$ C and a single proton of charge $q_p = +1.6 \times 10^{-19}$ C separated by a distance, $r_{ep} = 5.3 \times 10^{-11}$ m. The electrostatic force that exists between the proton and the electron is:
    A. 3.1×10^{-8} N
    B. 4.5×10^{-8} N
    C. 6.8×10^{-8} N
    D. 8.2×10^{-8} N

Questions 16–20 are based on the following passage.

Passage III

Electromagnetic radiation is often described in physics textbooks as a transverse wave that travels in a vacuum at a speed of $c = 3 \times 10^8$ m/s. Formed by coupled oscillating electric and magnetic fields, electromagnetic radiation comprises all of the types of waves represented within the electromagnetic spectrum, varying in frequency, f, and wavelength, λ, according to the equation, $c = f\lambda$. In addition to its wavelike properties, electromagnetic radiation behaves as waves do. However, classic experiments in quantum physics have also discovered that light behaves as a particle. The particle of light, known as a photon, has energy $E = hf$ where h is Planck's constant ($h = 6.63 \times 10^{-34}$ J·s) and f is frequency. This apparent contradiction is accepted as the "wave-particle duality of light." Two classical experiments that substantiated the "wave-particle duality of light" were Fraunhofer single-slit diffraction and the Compton scattering (see figure).

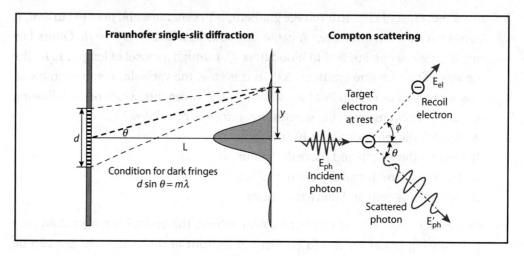

In Fraunhofer single-slit diffraction, monochromatic light is incident parallel to a diffraction grating with a single slit of width d. The light rays will bend around the opening of the slit and project onto a flat screen located a distance, L, from the diffraction grating as a pattern of bright and dark fringes. The pattern of dark fringes (minima) are described by $d \sin \theta = m\lambda$, $m = 1, 2, 3, \ldots$ as the integer value of the particular fringe.

In Compton scattering, a photon of initial energy E_{ph} and wavelength λ_i is incident upon an electron of mass m_e, initially at rest. Upon collision, the photon is deflected with a scattered energy E'_{ph} at an angle θ with respect to the incident axis as well as an increased wavelength, λ_f, given by $\lambda_f = \lambda_i + \left(\frac{h}{m_e c}\right)(1 - \cos\theta)$ where h is Planck's constant, c is the speed of light, and m_e is the rest mass of the electron (9.1×10^{-31} kg). The Compton-scattered electron scatters with an energy E_{el} at an angle φ.

16. According to the nature and description of the two experiments in the passage, you can conclude that:

   A. Single-slit diffraction supports the wave nature of light, whereas Compton scattering supports the particle nature of light.

   B. Single-slit diffraction supports the particle nature of light, whereas Compton scattering supports the wave nature of light.

   C. Both single-slit diffraction and Compton scattering support the wave nature of light.

   D. Both single-slit diffraction and Compton scattering support the particle nature of light.

279

SECTION 2:
Chemical and
Physical
Foundations of
Living Systems

17. If the electromagnetic radiation in the single-slit diffraction experiment were to behave as a particle, the interference pattern would probably look like which of the following?

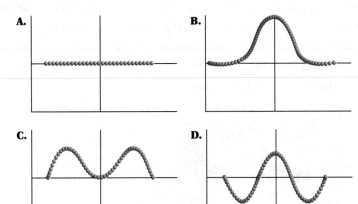

18. The Compton-scattered photon, compared to the incident photon, possesses:
    A. higher energy, higher frequency, and smaller wavelength
    B. higher energy, lower frequency, and smaller wavelength
    C. lower energy, higher frequency, and longer wavelength
    D. lower energy, lower frequency, and longer wavelength

19. In the Compton scattering experiment, the energy of the Compton-scattered electron, E_{el}, can be expressed in terms of the energies of the incident, E_{ph}, and Compton-scattered, E'_{ph}, photons by:

    A. $E_{el} = \dfrac{\left[E_{ph} - E'_{ph} \cos(\theta)\right]}{\cos(\phi)}$

    B. $E_{el} = \dfrac{\left[E_{ph} - E'_{ph} \cos(\theta)\right]}{\sin(\phi)}$

    C. $E_{el} = \dfrac{\left[E_{ph} - E'_{ph} \sin(\theta)\right]}{\cos(\phi)}$

    D. $E_{el} = \dfrac{\left[E_{ph} - E'_{ph} \sin(\theta)\right]}{\sin(\phi)}$

20. An expression for the momentum of a Compton-scattered photon in terms of Planck's constant, h, is:
    A. h/λ
    B. $h\nu$
    C. λh
    D. λ/h

Questions 21–26 are based on the following passage.

Passage IV

A group of students were assigned the task of assembling a slingshot constructed from rubber bands secured with clamps at the edge of a tabletop that is a known distance, Δy, from the floor and then predicting the horizontal range distance, Δx, that a launched projectile (marble) will land from the base of the table. A schematic of the rubber band slingshot is shown in the following illustration:

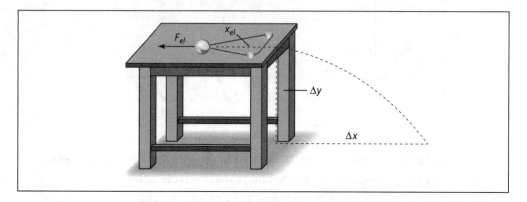

Before the slingshot was constructed, a series of measurements were performed on the rubber band to determine the stretching distance, x_{el}, as a function of an elastic force, F_{el}, applied to the rubber band. The data is shown here:

F_{el} (N)	2	3	4	5
x_{el} (cm)	14	21	26	30

The students used the data to theoretically determine the landing distance of a marble. To compare the effectiveness of their theoretical calculations, the students then launched a marble by stretching the rubber band slingshot to four different values of x_{el}, and recorded the corresponding landing distances, Δx. The data is shown in the following table:

Stretch Distance, x_{el}	2.00 cm	4.00 cm	6.00 cm	8.00 cm
Predicted Value, Δx_{pr}	3.94 m	5.63 m	7.18 m	8.45 m
Observed Value, Δx_{ob}	2.64 m	4.55 m	6.01 m	8.04 m

21. The spring constant for the rubber band used as a slingshot is:
    A. 18.8 N/m
    B. 1.88 N/m
    C. 0.188 N/m
    D. 0.0188 N/m

281

SECTION 2:
Chemical and
Physical
Foundations of
Living Systems

22. The velocity that the marble leaves the table upon release of the stretched rubber band is:

   A. kmx_{el}

   B. $\dfrac{k}{m}x_{el}$

   C. $\sqrt{km}x_{el}$

   D. $\sqrt{\dfrac{k}{m}}x_{el}$

23. The percent error between the values collected for a stretch distance of 2.0 cm is:

   A. 12%

   B. 26%

   C. 33%

   D. 42%

24. The horizontal landing distance, Δx, can be expressed according to:

   A. $\left[\sqrt{\dfrac{k}{m}}x_{el}\right]\left[\sqrt{\dfrac{g}{2\Delta y}}\right]$

   B. $\left[\sqrt{\dfrac{m}{k}}x_{el}\right]\left[\sqrt{\dfrac{2\Delta y}{g}}\right]$

   C. $\left[\sqrt{\dfrac{k}{m}}x_{el}\right]\left[\sqrt{\dfrac{\Delta y}{2g}}\right]$

   D. $\left[\sqrt{\dfrac{k}{m}}x_{el}\right]\left[\sqrt{\dfrac{2\Delta y}{g}}\right]$

25. If the students pull the slingshot back to 10 cm, the horizontal landing distance, Δx, they might expect to see is:

   A. 9.7 m

   B. 10.4 m

   C. 11.9 m

   D. 13.1 m

26. If the marble were doubled in mass, the effect on the horizontal landing distance would be:

   A. decrease by $\sqrt{2}$

   B. increase by $\sqrt{2}$

   C. decrease by 2

   D. no change

Question 27 is not associated with a passage.

27. Which of the following is the MOST stable conformation of chlorocyclohexane?

A.

B.

C.

D.

Questions 28–32 are based on the following passage.

Passage V

A standard imaging procedure in the investigation and evaluation of patients with cardiovascular disease is nuclear stress testing. Nuclear stress testing is often used to determine the extent of coronary artery blockage and assess the damage of heart muscle that arises as a result of a heart attack. In a typical nuclear stress test, the patient first walks on a treadmill to elevate the heart rate. Several minutes into the exercising period, a radiotracer, or a drug tagged with a radioactive element known to target the heart, is injected into the patient's vein and allowed to circulate. As the radiotracer circulates through the blood flow within the heart, the radioactive element decays, emitting gamma radiation that is collected by a gamma ray detector. If a part of the heart's muscle is damaged and not receiving blood flow, the amount of gamma rays detected from this area is less than normal regions of heart muscle. The collected gamma rays are used to produce images of the functional capacity of the heart, allowing the physician to identify any regions of the heart that are functioning below normal capacity.

A common radioactive element used in this testing procedure is thallium-201 (Tl-201). With a half-life of 73 hours, Tl-201 decays to mercury-201 (Hg-201) by electron capture according to:

$$^{201}_{81}\text{Tl} + ^{0}_{-1}e \rightarrow ^{201}_{80}\text{Hg} + ^{0}_{0}\nu$$

The radioactive emissions from Tl-201 are primarily x-rays in the energy range 69 to 83 keV, with gamma rays of energy 135 keV and 167 keV emitted less frequently.

28. In the radioactive decay process of Tl-201, which of the following is true?
   A. A is constant; N increases; Z increases
   B. A is constant; N increases; Z decreases
   C. A increases; N increases; Z is constant
   D. A increases; N is constant; Z is constant

283

SECTION 2:
Chemical and
Physical
Foundations of
Living Systems

29. The wavelength of the 167 keV gamma ray emitted from Tl-201 is (NOTE: $h = 4.15 \times 10^{-15}$ eV · sec; 1 angstrom (Å) $= 1 \times 10^{-10}$ m):
    A. 0.074 Å
    B. 0.183 Å
    C. 0.259 Å
    D. 0.362 Å

30. When compared to x-rays (68–83 keV), gamma rays (167 keV) have:
    A. lower frequency and shorter wavelength, but the same speed
    B. higher frequency and shorter wavelength, but the same speed
    C. lower frequency, longer wavelength, and greater speed
    D. higher frequency, shorter wavelength, and slower speed

31. In a typical nuclear stress test procedure, the percentage of the initial Tl-201 dose that would be present after 24 hours is:
    A. 40%
    B. 55%
    C. 67%
    D. 80%

32. The amount of time required for Tl-201 to decay to 10% of its original dosage is:
    A. 2 days
    B. 5 days
    C. 10 days
    D. 14 days

Questions 33–37 are based on the following passage.

Passage VI

Fritz Haber (1868–1934) was a German chemist who designed a method for making ammonia from nitrogen and hydrogen. This was to Germany's advantage during World War I. The Haber process is an industrial method for making ammonia, NH_3. This process takes N_2 and H_2 gases and combines them at high temperatures (425°C) and high pressures (200 atm) to force the triple-bonded nitrogen gas to react according to the reversible reaction:

$$N_2 + 3H_2 \leftrightarrow 2NH_3 + heat$$

The higher the pressure, the better the rate of reaction will be. A catalyst is also used in the reaction. Once made, ammonia can be used as a fertilizer, household cleaner, precursor to munitions, and smelling salts.

33. The K_{eq} for the reverse reaction is written as:
    A. $[NH_3]^2/[N_2][H_2]^3$
    B. $[N_2][H_2]^3/[NH_3]^2$
    C. $[NH_3]^2/[N_2] + [H_2]^3$
    D. $[N_2][H_2]/[NH_3]$

34. Which of the following scenarios shifts the reaction to the left?
    A. not cooling the ammonia once it is formed
    B. reacting the nitrogen and hydrogen at a higher pressure
    C. adding more nitrogen gas and hydrogen gas to the reaction
    D. using a catalyst

35. Addition of a catalyst will change:
    A. the heat of reaction
    B. the potential energy of the reactants
    C. the potential energy of the activated complex
    D. the point of equilibrium

36. The most probable point in the reaction that serves as the rate-determining step is:
    A. the cooling of the ammonia from a gas to a liquid
    B. the breaking of the bond between the hydrogen atoms
    C. nitrogen and hydrogen atoms reacting to form ammonia
    D. the breaking of the bond between the nitrogen atoms

37. The value of K_{eq} for this reaction can change with temperature. Given the temperatures of 300°C, 400°C, 500°C, and 600°C, which of the following is MOST likely the K_{eq} value when the reaction takes place at 600°C?
    A. 4.3×10^{-3}
    B. 1.6×10^{-4}
    C. 1.5×10^{-5}
    D. 2.3×10^{-6}

Questions 38 and 39 are not based on a passage.

38. Which of the following BEST demonstrates the Lewis definition of an acid–base reaction?
    A. $HCl + NaOH \rightarrow NaCl + H_2O$
    B. $HCl + NH_3 \rightarrow NH_4^+ + Cl^-$
    C. $BF_3 + NH_3 \rightarrow F_3BNH_3$
    D. $CaO + SiO_2 \rightarrow CaSiO_3$

39. Which of the following are the BEST conditions for carrying out the following transformation shown?

    A. sodium methoxide in methanol
    B. methyl iodide in methanol
    C. *p*-toluenesulfonic acid in methanol
    D. sodium iodide in methanol

285

SECTION 2:
Chemical and
Physical
Foundations of
Living Systems

Questions 40–43 are based on the following passage.

Passage VII

When Compound A (shown) is treated with ozone followed by dimethylsulfide, two new products (B and C) are formed, both of which contain carbonyl groups. On the other hand, treatment of Compound A with pyridinium chlorochromate (PCC) results in a single new product (D).

40. What is the best International Union of Pure and Applied Chemistry (IUPAC) name for Compound A?
   A. (2R,3Z)-4-methylhex-3-en-2-ol
   B. (2R,3E)-4-methylhex-3-en-2-ol
   C. (2S,3Z)-4-methylhex-3-en-2-ol
   D. (2S,3E)-4-methylhex-3-en-2-ol

41. The identities of ozonolysis products B and C are BEST described as:
   A. propanal and 2-hydroxypropanal
   B. propanal and 4-hydroxybutanone
   C. 2-butanone and 2-hydroxypropanal
   D. 2-butanone and 4-hydroxybutanone

42. In comparing the physical properties of starting material A and oxidation product D:
   A. The starting material (A) has a lower boiling point and the lower R_f value.
   B. The starting material (A) has a lower boiling point and the higher R_f value.
   C. The starting material (A) has a higher boiling point and the lower R_f value.
   D. The starting material (A) has a higher boiling point and the higher R_f value.

43. The most reasonable pK_a for the starting material (A) is:
   A. −7
   B. 7
   C. 17
   D. 27

Questions 44–48 are not based on a passage.

44. The final result of adenosine triphosphate (ATP) production after anaerobic respiration is:
    A. the same as the amount of ATP made in aerobic respiration
    B. equal to the amount of ATP made in glycolysis
    C. low relative to the amount of ATP made in aerobic respiration
    D. high relative to the amount of ATP made in aerobic respiration

45. The drug 2,4-dinitrophenol (DNP) destroys the H^+ gradient that forms in the electron transport chain. The MOST likely consequence would be:
    A. The cells are forced to perform fermentation.
    B. Adenosine triphosphate (ATP) production increases.
    C. Glycolysis stops.
    D. Oxygen consumption increases.

46. Which set of conditions shown here will NOT favor an S_N2 reaction?
    A. a strong nucleotide
    B. a leaving group on a primary carbon atom
    C. a lower temperature
    D. a solvent of a higher polarity

47. The approximate pK_a value of an organic compound is 50. This organic compound is MOST likely:
    A. an alcohol
    B. a carboxylic acid
    C. a terminal alkyne
    D. an alkane

48. The carbon dioxide exhaled by animals is produced in:
    A. glycolysis
    B. lactate fermentation
    C. Krebs cycle
    D. electron transport chain

Questions 49–52 are based on the following passage.

Passage VIII

Reductive amination of Compound A with dimethylamine in the presence of sodium cyanoborohydride at pH 5.5 results in the formation of *N,N*,2,2-tetramethylpropan-1-amine.

287

SECTION 2:
Chemical and
Physical
Foundations of
Living Systems

On the other hand, Compound A reacts with methylmagnesium bromide to give another product (Compound B), which contains a hydroxyl group.

49. Which of the following is the most reasonable structure for Compound B?

A.

B.

C.

D.

50. Sodium cyanoborohydride is used instead of lithium aluminum hydride (LAH) for the reductive amination because:
    A. Sodium cyanoborohydride is a stronger source of hydride than LAH.
    B. Sodium cyanoborohydride is a milder source of hydride than LAH.
    C. Sodium cyanoborohydride is more sterically hindered than LAH.
    D. Sodium cyanoborohydride is less sterically hindered than LAH.

51. The BEST synthesis of methylmagnesium bromide (MeMgBr) is through:
    A. the treatment of methane with magnesium metal and sodium bromide
    B. the treatment of methane with magnesium bromide
    C. the treatment of bromomethane with magnesium metal
    D. the treatment of methylmagnesium with bromine

52. The functional group present in Compound A is BEST described as a(n):
    A. ketone
    B. ester
    C. alcohol
    D. aldehyde

Questions 53–57 are based on the following passage.

Passage IX

Human tooth enamel is composed of the mineral hydroxyapatite, which has the formula $Ca_5(PO_4)_3OH$. It is insoluble in water, but due to its basicity, it is soluble in acid solution.

Plaque forms on teeth due to a combination of carbohydrates and proteins, called mucin, which produces a film that builds up if not removed by thorough cleaning of the teeth and gums. Plaque traps food particles, which can be fermented by bacteria and produce lactic acid. Saliva does contain buffering agents that can neutralize acid in the mouth, but saliva cannot penetrate solid plaque. Lactic acid levels can drop to as low as pH 4.5 inside the plaque. As the plaque becomes more acidic, hydroxyapatite is converted to calcium hydrogen phosphate, which dissolves in water. The equation is as follows:

$$Ca_5(PO_4)_3OH(s) + 4H_3O^+(aq) \rightarrow 3CaHPO_4(aq) + 2Ca^{+2}(aq) + 5H_2O \qquad (2.1)$$

When the hydroxyapatite reacts, cavities can form. The addition of fluoride to municipal water supplies and to toothpaste has lowered the incidence of cavities in children in the United States. Many children also have fluoride treatments as part of their routine dental care.

Fluoride has the ability to replace the hydroxide ion in hydroxyapatite, forming a compound called fluoroapatite. Fluoroapatite not only has a smaller K_{sp} value than hydroxyapatite, it is less basic as well. Thus it is far less soluble in acid solution. The reaction of fluoride with hydroxyapatite is as follows:

$$Ca_5(PO_4)_3OH\ (s) + F^-\ (aq) \rightleftharpoons Ca_5(PO_4)_3F\ (s) + OH^-\ (aq)$$

The K_{sp} of hydroxyapatite is 7×10^{-37}. The K_{sp} of fluoroapatite is 1×10^{-60}.

53. The dissolution of hydroxyapatite in water is BEST represented by:
  A. $Ca_5(PO_4)_3OH\ (s) \rightleftharpoons 5\ Ca\ (aq) + 3\ PO_4\ (aq) + OH\ (aq)$

  B. $Ca_5(PO_4)_3OH\ (s) \rightleftharpoons Ca_5\ (aq) + (PO_4)_3\ (aq) + OH\ (aq)$

  C. $Ca_5(PO_4)_3OH\ (s) \rightleftharpoons Ca_5\ (PO_4)_3^{+1}\ (aq) + OH^-\ (aq)$

  D. $Ca_5(PO_4)_3OH\ (s) \rightleftharpoons 5\ Ca^{+2}\ (aq) + 3\ PO_4^{-3}\ (aq) + OH^-\ (aq)$

54. Why does the equilibrium of the reaction of hydroxyapatite with fluoride lie to the right?
  A. Fluoride is a weaker base than hydroxide.
  B. Hydroxide can be removed because it is formed by buffers in saliva.
  C. Fluoroapatite is less soluble than the reactant.
  D. The product solidifies onto the surface of the tooth.

55. A larger K_{sp} value means that:
  A. Reactants predominate.
  B. Products predominate.
  C. There is a lower concentration of ions.
  D. The solid is less soluble.

289

SECTION 2:
Chemical and
Physical
Foundations of
Living Systems

56. What is the effect on the solubility of hydroxyapatite if calcium ions are added to a saturated solution?
    A. The equilibrium will shift to the right.
    B. The equilibrium will shift to the left.
    C. There will be no effect.
    D. More hydroxyapatite will ionize.

57. The solubility of hydroxyapatite, x, can be found from:
    A. $K_{sp} = x^3$
    B. $K_{sp} = x^5$
    C. $K_{sp} = x^7$
    D. $K_{sp} = x^9$

Questions 58 and 59 are not associated with a passage.

58. Which of the following represents the proper Lewis structure for fluoride?

    A. $:\overset{\cdot\cdot}{\underset{\cdot\cdot}{F}}\cdot$

    B. $:\overset{\cdot\cdot}{\underset{\cdot\cdot}{F}}:$

    C. $:\overset{\cdot\cdot}{\underset{\cdot\cdot}{F}}:^+$

    D. $:\overset{\cdot\cdot}{\underset{\cdot\cdot}{F}}:^-$

59. The reaction of chalk, $CaCO_3$, produces a gas when treated with acid. This gas is:
    A. oxygen, O_2
    B. carbonic acid, H_2CO_3
    C. carbon dioxide, CO_2
    D. hydrochloric acid, HCl

Psychological, Social, and Biological Foundations of Behavior

59 Questions   **Time Limit: 95 Minutes**

Choose the best answer to each of the following questions. Question 1 is not based on a passage.

1. The theory of hearing that BEST explains perception of low-pitched sounds is called _____. The theory of hearing that BEST explains perception of very high-pitched sounds is called _____.
   A. place theory, frequency theory
   B. frequency theory, place theory
   C. auditory gate theory, place theory
   D. place theory, auditory gate theory

Questions 2–5 are based on the following passage.

Passage I

Researchers studying signal detection have documented various magnitude differences necessary to detect the presence of stimuli (absolute threshold) and to detect changes in the perceptual experience of the stimuli (just noticeable difference). These differences are dependent on the type of sensory experience being measured and can be characterized by proportional differences in magnitude rather than absolute amounts.

A recent study examined the just noticeable difference necessary to perceive tempo changes. In this experiment, signal detection methods were used to examine the amount of change necessary to detect a difference between an initial/target tempo and a comparison stimulus. Two test conditions were evaluated. The initial/target tempo speed was either *slow* (43 beats per minute [bpm]) or *fast* (75 bpm). Comparison tempos were presented that were either sped up or slowed down relative to the initial/target tempo. Participants were asked to identify whether the comparison tempos were the same tempo or a different tempo from the initial/target tempo. The accompanying graph depicts the tempo changes necessary for detection for both the *slow* and *fast* initial/target tempos.

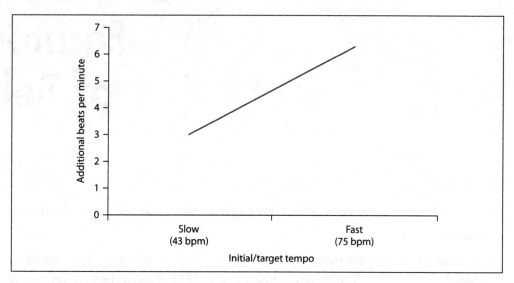

Detecting tempo change (beats per minute). *Source*: Adapted with permission from Thomas, K. (2007). "Just noticeable difference and tempo change." *Journal of Scientific Psychology*, 2, 14–20.

2. If a third initial/target tempo of 60 beats per minute was tested, which of the following would you expect to be TRUE based on the results of this study?
   A. It would take a change in magnitude greater than the *fast* tempo for participants to detect a change.
   B. It would take a change in magnitude smaller than the *slow* tempo for participants to detect a change.
   C. It would take a change in magnitude greater than the *slow* tempo but less than the *fast* tempo for participants to detect a change.
   D. The magnitude of the change necessary for participants to detect a change more than 50 percent of the time would be exactly the same, regardless of the target tempo.

3. Suppose this study used a forced-choice signal detection method. Which type of signal detection response would be MOST likely as the speed of the comparison tempo increased, regardless of the initial/target tempo?
   A. a miss
   B. a false alarm
   C. a correct rejection
   D. a hit

293

SECTION 3:
Psychological,
Social, and
Biological
Foundations
of Behavior

4. Which of the following statements BEST describes Weber's law?
   A. The just noticeable difference (JND) necessary to detect a change in the magnitude of a comparison stimulus (i.e., the tempo) is a constant proportion of the initial/target stimulus.
   B. The JND necessary to detect a change in the magnitude of a comparison stimulus (i.e., the tempo) is a fixed amount, independent of the initial/target stimulus.
   C. The JND necessary to detect a change in the magnitude of a comparison stimulus (i.e., the tempo) is always the same as the absolute threshold to detect the stimulus.
   D. The JND necessary to detect a change in the magnitude of a comparison stimulus (i.e., the tempo) is exactly half of the magnitude necessary to perceive that the stimulus is present.

5. Which of the following conclusions is supported by this study?
   A. The faster the tempo of the initial/target stimulus, the greater the difference required between the initial and comparison tempos for participants to perceive a difference.
   B. The faster the tempo of the initial/target stimulus, the greater the proportion of change needed for participants to perceive a difference.
   C. The slower the tempo of the initial/target stimulus, the greater the difference required between the initial and comparison tempos for participants to perceive a difference.
   D. The slower the tempo of the initial/target stimulus, the greater the proportion of change needed for participants to perceive a difference.

Question 6 is not based on a passage.

6. A researcher inserts electrodes into the brain of a monkey. When the monkey is shown lines aligned at different orientations, the cells respond preferentially to lines of certain particular orientations. It is MOST likely that the researcher has inserted the electrodes into which region of the brain?
   A. occipital lobe
   B. temporal lobe
   C. frontal lobe
   D. parietal lobe

Questions 7–10 are based on the following passage.

Passage II

Jean Piaget, a prominent figure in developmental psychology, believed that the development of all cognitive abilities occurred during the first two years of life. Piaget devised various procedures for examining development in young children. These activities focused on how children (and people) think and how they interact with the world around them. Piaget asserted that biological changes interacted with childhood experiences, resulting in unique developmental stages characterized by schemas, or mental structures. The following table lists the four stages of development identified by Piaget and their function.

Piaget's Stages of Development.

Stage	Age	Purpose
Sensory Motor	Birth–2 years	Coordination of sensations with voluntary motor movement
Preoperational	2–7 years	Increased use of mental images and symbols
Concrete Operational	7–11 years	Increased problem-solving abilities; mastery of conservation; cognition and mental operations are mostly limited to tangible objects and actual events
Formal Operational	11–Adult	Begins to understand and mentally manipulate abstract constructs (e.g., ethics, free will, love)

7. Two children, Tommy and Janet, watch a researcher pour water from a short, wide glass into a tall, narrow glass. When asked, Tommy confidently states that there is now more water in the tall, narrow glass than there was in the short, wide glass. Janet asserts that the amount of water has not changed. Based on Piaget's stages of development, which answer BEST represents this example?

   A. Tommy and Janet are exhibiting egocentrism because they are unable to share each other's viewpoints.

   B. Tommy is not aware of the continued existence of the water once it is poured from one glass to the other, whereas Janet has developed object permanence.

   C. Janet has developed reversibility and understands that the water can be poured back into the original container, whereas Tommy has not yet developed reversibility.

   D. Janet has developed conservation and is aware that the amount of water inside a container is the same even if the dimensions change, whereas Tommy has not yet developed conservation.

295

SECTION 3:
Psychological,
Social, and
Biological
Foundations
of Behavior

8. Amanda's mother hides Amanda's toy rattle beneath a blanket. Amanda does not search for the rattle and appears to be unaware of its existence. Based on Piaget's model, what stage is Amanda in and what concept has she NOT yet mastered?
   A. sensory motor, object permanence
   B. sensory motor, conservation
   C. preoperational, object permanence
   D. preoperational, conservation

9. Based on Piaget's model, what concept is characterized by the ability to absorb new ideas and what concept is characterized by the process of modifying previously developed mental processes?
   A. Accommodation is characterized by the ability to absorb new ideas; assimilation is characterized by the process of modifying previously developed mental processes.
   B. Assimilation is characterized by the ability to absorb new ideas; accommodation is characterized by the process of modifying previously developed mental processes.
   C. Coordination is characterized by the ability to absorb new ideas; consolidation is characterized by the process of modifying previously developed mental processes.
   D. Consolidation is characterized by the ability to absorb new ideas; coordination is characterized by the process of modifying previously developed mental processes.

10. On a rainy day, Juan is asked why it is raining. He replies that it is raining so that he can "play with his toy boat." What developmental stage is Juan likely in, and what concept has he yet to master?
    A. formal operational, decentering
    B. sensory motor, transitivity
    C. preoperational, egocentrism
    D. concrete operational, classification

Question 11 is not based on a passage.

11. Which field of psychology examines positive stresses as well as positive emotions in general?
    A. psychodynamic approach
    B. human-focused psychology
    C. positive psychology
    D. motivation and emotion approach

Questions 12–15 are based on the following passage.

Passage III

The study of emotional experience is often characterized by the attempt to answer the question, "Which comes first, the experience or the label?" Some researchers suggest that the physiological arousal occurs, then the individual contextualizes the experience based on his or her environment, resulting in emotion such as "fear" or "happiness." Other researchers suggest that humans can subconsciously identify the difference in arousal caused by various emotional states or that the arousal and classification occur in parallel.

Recent research has examined the relationship between culture and emotion. One such study examined the differences between how American and Japanese participants contextualize emotion. The researchers examined athletes' use of emotion-related words in interviews. Compared to American athletes, Japanese athletes were found to be more likely to identify emotions with others than with themselves. Based on these findings, the researchers conducted a second experiment in which they asked Japanese and American participants to describe typical emotions experienced by Olympic medalists. The researchers counted the number of emotion-related words and assigned them to either self-focused or self+other–focused groups for comparison.

The results of the second study are shown in the following graph.

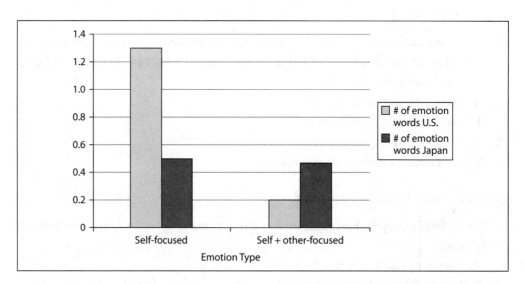

Number of emotion words used by American and Japanese participants. Responses assigned to self-focused and self + other-focused groups. *Source*: Adapted with permission from Uchida, Yukiko, et al. "Emotions as within or between people? Cultural variation in lay theories of emotion expression and inference." *Personality and Social Psychology Bulletin 35*(11), (2009): 1427–1439.

297

SECTION 3:
Psychological,
Social, and
Biological
Foundations
of Behavior

12. Which statement BEST describes how the Schachter–Singer theory of emotion could be used to interpret the results of this study?
    A. The experiences triggered physiological arousal, which caused specific emotions. Because the physiological arousal conditions were similar, the responses between the cultural groups were similar as well.
    B. The experiences triggered autonomic arousal, which the participants then appraised. Each group interpreted their emotional experiences based on cultural differences as a result of the appraisal process.
    C. The experiences activated the thalamus, which simultaneously created both physiological arousal and the emotion. Any differences observed were due to different types of arousal in participants from different cultures.
    D. Experiences between cultures occur in different ways and use different brain regions. The observed cultural differences represent different theories of emotion.

13. Which of the following BEST describes the results of the second study described in the passage?
    A. Japanese athletes described more self+other–focused emotions than self-focused emotions.
    B. Japanese athletes described fewer self-focused emotions than American athletes.
    C. American athletes described more self+other–focused emotions than Japanese athletes.
    D. American athletes described more self+other–focused emotions than self-focused emotions.

14. Which theory of emotion posits that a stimulus creates autonomic arousal, which causes an individual to subconsciously identify an emotional state?
    A. James–Lange theory
    B. Cannon–Bard theory
    C. Schachter–Singer theory
    D. James–Singer theory

15. What additional experiment could be included in future research to further investigate emotion and cultural differences between populations?
    A. asking participants to complete a memory recall task prior to indicating the emotions that they believed the athletes exhibited
    B. conducting the experiment on additional groups from different cultures and comparing the results between them
    C. conducting the experiment on the same group of participants over time but changing the narrative scripts
    D. asking participants to wear heart rate monitors and measuring their arousal while reading narrative scripts

Questions 16 and 17 are not based on a passage.

16. Jane is able to remember and consciously reexperience her 15th birthday party when her parents gave her a Beatles album. She also remembers the Beatles' classic look because her parents described it to her in detail. Which type of memory BEST characterizes the first example, and which type of memory BEST explains the second?
    - **A.** episodic memory, procedural memory
    - **B.** episodic memory, semantic memory
    - **C.** semantic memory, procedural memory
    - **D.** procedural memory, explicit memory

17. At what stage of learning does retroactive interference affect memory?
    - **A.** review
    - **B.** short-term memory
    - **C.** forgetting
    - **D.** encoding

Questions 18–22 are based on the following passage.

Passage IV

Researchers studying vision use various methods to investigate human perceptual experience. In certain instances the perceptual experience mirrors physiology. Research on spectral sensitivity of the rod and cone visual receptors highlights this relationship. The following figure depicts the normalized absorbance of various wavelengths of light by each photoreceptor type. There are three types of cones that each respond preferentially to specific wavelengths in the electromagnetic spectrum. Rods also preferentially respond to specific wavelengths, overlapping the cone receptors' response frequencies.

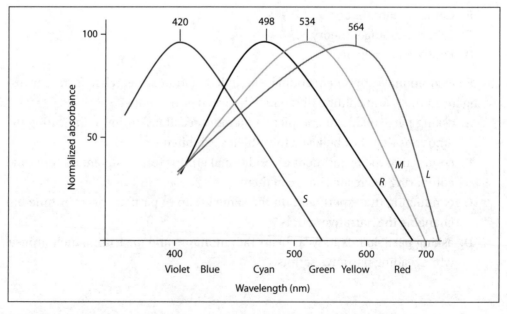

Four photoreceptor absorbance curves for each wavelength of light.

299

SECTION 3:
Psychological,
Social, and
Biological
Foundations
of Behavior

18. The three cone pigment curves shown in the figure are generally used to highlight which historical explanation for color vision?
    A. Hering theory of color vision
    B. opponent-process theory
    C. Young–Helmholtz theory of color vision
    D. Gestalt activation theory

19. A 600-mHz wavelength of light would excite which types of receptors?
    A. only S cones
    B. M and L cones
    C. M and L cones as well as R rods
    D. none of the above

20. Based on the graph and the trichromatic theory of color vision, which of the following statements is TRUE?
    A. Light observed at 475 nm would most likely be perceived as cyan, and each type of receptor would be stimulated, with rods and red-sensitive (L) cones most stimulated.
    B. Light observed at 430 nm would most likely be perceived as blue, and each type of receptor would be stimulated, with rods and blue-sensitive (S) cones most stimulated.
    C. Light observed at 475 nm would most likely be perceived as cyan, and only cones would be stimulated, with blue-sensitive (S) and green-sensitive (M) cones most stimulated.
    D. Light observed at 430 nm would most likely be perceived as blue, and only cones would be stimulated, with blue-sensitive (S) and red-sensitive (L) cones most stimulated.

21. Which of the following statements is TRUE?
    A. A person lacking rod pigment receptors sensitive to red would most likely have red-green color blindness.
    B. A person with red-green color blindness would most likely have a disorder resulting in a lack of color perception at the interneuron level.
    C. A person lacking cone pigment receptors sensitive to blue would most likely have red-green color blindness.
    D. A person lacking cone pigment receptors sensitive to red or green would most likely have red-green color blindness.

22. The wavelength of light and the amplitude of light are associated with what features in perception?
    A. Wavelength primarily characterizes color, and amplitude primarily characterizes brightness.
    B. Wavelength primarily characterizes brightness, and amplitude primarily characterizes color.
    C. Both wavelength and amplitude characterize color equally.
    D. Wavelength characterizes color, but amplitude has no impact on perception.

Question 23 is not based on a passage.

23. Which personality theory characterizes personality as comprised by the interaction between three factors: the id, the ego, and the superego?
   A. psychoanalytic theory
   B. social-cognitive theory
   C. humanistic theory
   D. behaviorism

Questions 24–27 are based on the following passage.

Passage V

Research evaluating human performance under conditions of sleep deprivation has generally found that impaired functioning is observed during specific time intervals. One such study used surveys to determine the characteristics of car accidents to evaluate the relationship between time of day and incidence of car accidents. The following graph shows the number of accidents on the *y*-axis and the time of day on the *x*-axis.

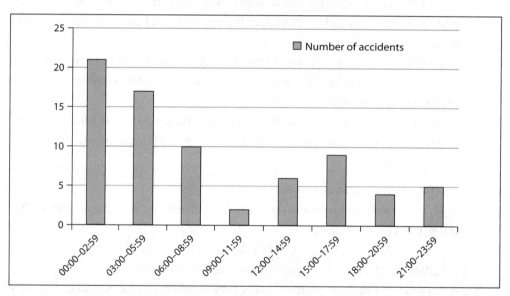

Number of accidents by time of day. *Source*: Adapted with permission from Horne, J. A., & Reyner, L. A. (1995). "Sleep-related vehicle accidents." *British Medical Journal,* 310(6979), 565–567.

24. Based on the graph, which of the following is the MOST accurate statement?
   A. Time of day is not related to the number of accidents.
   B. Sleep deprivation has more impact during the day than at night.
   C. Accidents were more likely during the early morning.
   D. Accidents were more likely in the evening than at midday.

301

SECTION 3:
Psychological,
Social, and
Biological
Foundations
of Behavior

25. What would happen to performance results over time if a similar study was conducted in an artificial environment and in the absence of circadian cues such as light?
    A. The accident peaks would drift to the left on the graph with a slightly shorter circadian cycle.
    B. The accident peaks would drift to the right on the graph with a slightly longer circadian cycle.
    C. There would be no change in the cycle, and the increased risk of accident would occur at roughly the same time.
    D. There would be a breakdown in the cycle, and accidents would be equally likely to occur in any time frame.

26. Why might you expect the results of this study to remain consistent even for people who are time-shifted and consistently work during the early morning hours?
    A. Circadian timing is fixed and therefore cannot be shifted outside normal daytime hours.
    B. Circadian timing is flexible but highly dependent on darkness, which will pressure the circadian cycle toward the nighttime hours.
    C. Circadian timing is flexible but highly dependent on social interaction. The reason the data would remain the same is because people working at night have limited social interaction.
    D. Circadian timing is flexible but highly dependent on light, which will push the circadian cycle toward the daylight hours.

27. Light exposure readjusts the circadian rhythm by acting on which brain structure?
    A. thalamus—lateral geniculate nucleus
    B. midbrain—superior colliculus
    C. brain stem—reticular formation
    D. hypothalamus—suprachiasmatic nucleus

Question 28 is not based on a passage.

28. Which of the following is TRUE about somatoform disorders?
    A. Individuals can experience an exacerbation of symptoms of existing medical conditions.
    B. Individuals are often faking symptoms of existing medical conditions.
    C. Individuals will often explicitly cause harm to themselves to create medical conditions.
    D. Pain can easily be identified as somatoform or real.

Questions 29–31 are based on the following passage.

Passage VI

In a famous series of experiments, the social psychologist Stanley Milgram captured important observations about human compliance. Participants in the experiments were told to play the role of "teachers" and ask "learners" to answer questions. They were not told that the learners were actually actors. Every time a learner gave an incorrect answer, a confederate posing as an authority figure instructed the teacher to administer an electric shock to the learner. The learner would then pretend to suffer pain, even though the "shock" delivered via a realistic-looking apparatus was actually harmless. If a learner continued to provide incorrect answers, the authority figure told the teacher to increase the intensity of the "shock" all the way up to what was said to be a lethal level.

The results from the experiment are depicted in the following graph.

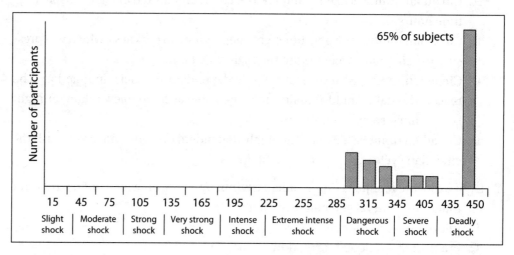

The Milgram experiment. Pretended shock intensity is listed on the *x*-axis and the number of participants who refused to continue past each level is presented on the *y*-axis. *Source*: Adapted with permission from Milgram, S. (1963). "Behavioral study of obedience." *The Journal of Abnormal and Social Psychology*, 67(4), 371–378.

29. Based on the results from this study, which of the following is TRUE?
    A. The majority of participants administered what they believed was a potentially lethal shock.
    B. The majority of participants refused to administer what they believed were lethal shocks.
    C. The data can be interpreted to show that the teachers inadvertently administered what they believed were lethal shocks.
    D. The data can be interpreted to show that the learners inadvertently answered questions that resulted in teachers administering what they believed were lethal shocks.

303

SECTION 3:
Psychological,
Social, and
Biological
Foundations
of Behavior

30. In the Milgram experiment, the participant teacher would typically:
    A. obey the authority figure despite the discomfort or pain exhibited by the learner
    B. resist the authority figure because of the discomfort or pain exhibited by the learner
    C. obey the learner despite protests from the authority figure
    D. obey the learner even when the learner exhibited discomfort or pain

31. The Milgram experiment has been repeated in a number of cultures and with a number of design changes. Based on your knowledge of social psychology, what was shown to reduce the likelihood of the participant teacher administering a perceived lethal shock?
    A. The experiment was completed in a formal lab where the teacher was alone with the authority figure.
    B. The authority figure was dressed in a lab coat and stood close to the teacher when giving the commands.
    C. The participant teachers were recruited from an older population.
    D. The participant teachers took part in a group discussion about the importance of ethics immediately prior to the teaching portion of the experiment.

Questions 32 and 33 are not based on a passage.

32. In social psychology research, what does the term *obedience* represent?
    A. compliance to direct commands
    B. compliance to requests from a group of people
    C. compliance to implied pressure from social norms
    D. compliance with internal morals and beliefs

33. Jack's roommate has offered to pay him one dollar per week for doing the dishes. Jack is reluctant because he doesn't like this chore, but he accepts. After a few days, Jack decides that the chore is somewhat enjoyable. This reaction is consistent with which theory?
    A. groupthink theory
    B. the bystander effect
    C. cognitive dissonance
    D. self-perception theory

Questions 34–37 are based on the following passage.

Passage VII

Classical conditioning is a long-studied and well-documented scientific concept. The Russian physiologist Ivan Pavlov is most associated with this concept and described the conditions necessary for conditioning to occur. Subsequent studies from both comparative and human psychology have supported these initial findings and expanded upon them.

The following graph shows a hypothetical example of conditioning trials for one of Pavlov's dogs over a number of days. During these trials, a bell has been paired with the presentation of food. Trial numbers are displayed on the x-axis and the number of drops of the dog's saliva is displayed on the y-axis.

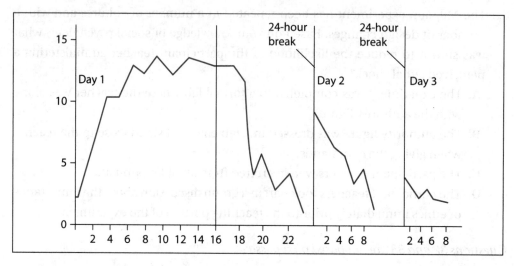

Classical conditioning. The number of drops of a dog's saliva is shown on the y-axis. The number of trials is shown on the x-axis.

34. Based on the saliva responses to stimuli shown in the graph, where would you expect the unconditioned stimulus to be present?
    A. The unconditioned stimulus would be paired with the conditioned stimulus in initial trials on day 2.
    B. The unconditioned stimulus would be paired with the conditioned stimulus in initial trials on day 3.
    C. The unconditioned stimulus would be paired with the conditioned stimulus in initial trials on day 1.
    D. The unconditioned stimulus would be paired with the conditioned stimulus in initial trials over the course of all three days.

35. Based on the saliva responses to stimuli shown in the graph, where would you expect the conditioned stimulus to be present?
    A. The conditioned stimulus would be present only on day 1.
    B. The conditioned stimulus would be present only on day 2.
    C. The conditioned stimulus would be present only on day 3.
    D. The conditioned stimulus would be present on trials over the course of all three days.

305

SECTION 3:
Psychological,
Social, and
Biological
Foundations
of Behavior

36. In the study described in the passage, what is the major difference between the conditioned stimulus and the unconditioned stimulus?
    A. During conditioning trials, the amount of saliva increases in response to the bell but decreases in response to the food.
    B. During extinction, the amount of saliva decreases in response to the food and in response to the bell.
    C. Only the food elicits a response during conditioning.
    D. Only the food elicits a response prior to conditioning.

37. The increase in response to the bell on the initial trials on days 2 and 3 is consistent with which concept?
    A. spontaneous recovery
    B. the presence of the unconditioned stimulus
    C. acquisition
    D. extinction response

Question 38 is not based on a passage.

38. Which of Erik Erikson's stages occurs immediately after an individual is successful at integrating into larger social networks and achieving competence in academics?
    A. identity versus role confusion
    B. industry versus inferiority
    C. ego integrity versus despair
    D. generativity versus stagnation

Questions 39–42 are based on the following passage.

Passage VIII

The psychologist Harry Harlow conducted a series of famous experiments investigating maternal attachment in monkeys, with multiple derivations on his classic study comparing infant attachment to nutrients versus comforting inanimate objects. This research is often referenced to show the development of early attachment and is an example of comparative psychology. The results of Harlow's research present some compelling evidence for the criticality of infant relationships.

The graphs that follow show one of Harlow's later experiments in infant monkey attachment, with hypothetical data representing the behavior captured by Harlow in that study. This data set represents the amount of time (hours per day) that infant monkeys spent with surrogate (artificial) representations of their mothers. The surrogates were either made of wood covered in cloth or made of bare wire. Both the cloth surrogate and the wire surrogate were provided with a rubber nipple that allowed for feeding. Both surrogates were present for all monkeys. The aim of the study was to determine which of the two surrogates the infant monkeys would choose to spend time with. The graph on the left shows the data collected from the group of infant monkeys who took food from the cloth surrogate. The graph on the right shows the data collected from the group of infant monkeys who took food from the wire surrogate. The time spent with the cloth surrogate is represented by the heavy blue line. The time spent with the wire surrogate is represented by the dotted line.

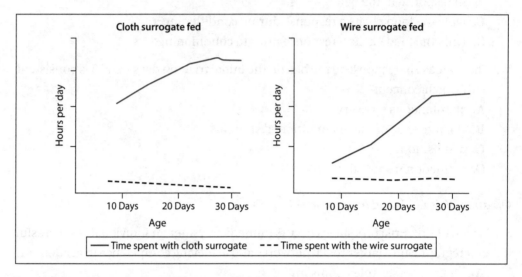

Two graphs representing two different artificial surrogate mothers, both equipped for feeding, and the hours per day that infant monkeys spent with them. *Source*: Data from Harlow, H. F., and Zimmerman, R. R. (1958). "The development of affectional responses in infant monkeys," *Proceedings of the American Philosophical Society*, 102(5), 501–509.

39. Which of the following statements is TRUE?
  A. The infant monkeys preferred to spend more time with the surrogate from which they took food.
  B. The infant monkeys preferred to spend more time with the surrogate that they did not use for feeding.
  C. The infant monkeys preferred to spend more time with the cloth surrogate, regardless of whether they took food from the cloth surrogate or the wire surrogate.
  D. The infant monkeys preferred to spend more time with the wire surrogate, regardless of whether they took food from the cloth surrogate or the wire surrogate.

307

SECTION 3:
Psychological,
Social, and
Biological
Foundations
of Behavior

40. Which of the following statements BEST describes Harlow's findings?
    A. Infant monkeys prefer whichever surrogate they took food from because a nutritive surrogate is of more evolutionary value.
    B. Infant monkeys prefer the cloth surrogate because they were attached to the emotional comfort that the cloth provides.
    C. Infant monkeys do not prefer one surrogate over the other, because both attachment and nutrition are needed equally.
    D. Infant monkeys prefer wire surrogates only when they are being fed by them.

41. Based on Harlow's work and socialization research, which of the following would happen if the infant monkeys were presented with a stimulus (e.g., an unfamiliar object) that caused fear?
    A. The infant monkeys would seek comfort from the cloth surrogate, regardless of which surrogate they took food from.
    B. The infant monkeys would seek comfort from the wire surrogate, regardless of which surrogate they took food from.
    C. The infant monkeys would seek comfort from whichever surrogate they took food from.
    D. The infant monkeys would not seek comfort from either surrogate, because they have already been associated with specific needs.

42. What additional experiment would BEST examine attachment in infant monkeys?
    A. Continue the experiment until the monkeys were more developed in order to test whether they would value nutrition more during a later developmental stage.
    B. Use two wire surrogates and no cloth surrogates to see whether the infant monkeys would attach to the wire surrogate through which they were fed.
    C. Feed adult monkeys from cloth surrogates to see if they develop attachment.
    D. Feed infant monkeys from both the cloth and wire surrogates at the same time.

Question 43 is not based on a passage.

43. Based on self-concept and identity, which of the following is TRUE about low self-esteem?
    A. It results from high self-efficacy and an internal locus of control.
    B. It results from low self-efficacy and an external locus of control.
    C. It results from high self-efficacy and an external locus of control.
    D. It results from low self-efficacy and an internal locus of control.

Questions 44–47 are based on the following passage.

Passage IX

Attribution theory seeks to explain how individuals think about themselves and how they behave toward individuals around them. This theory also examines how an individual views internal and external traits, how he or she acts upon them, and how those views influence self-identity.

The following graphs show hypothetical data regarding last year's academic competition between students from two rival schools. The competition consists of three rounds of quizzes. Last year's competition ended in a tie since each side scored the same number of points.

The first graph shows the percent of questions each team answered correctly in each of the three quiz rounds.

The second graph shows the results from a survey of students who participated in the competition. The survey asked contestants what factors they thought helped them and their opponents pick correct answers. Specifically, they were asked what percent of the correct answers their own team picked and what percent the other team picked were attributable to each of the following two factors:

➤ study and preparation
➤ whether the test questions favored one team over the other

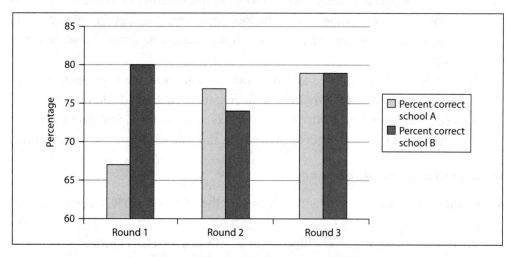

Percent of questions answered correctly by each school team by round.

309

SECTION 3:
Psychological,
Social, and
Biological
Foundations
of Behavior

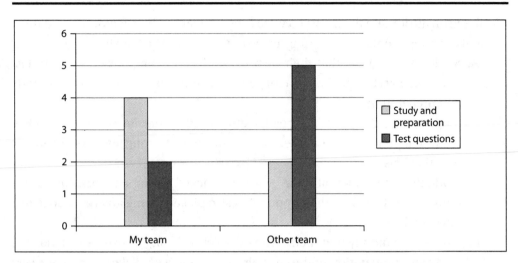

Survey results showing which factor students believed most helped contestants pick correct answers.

44. Based on the passage, which of the following is TRUE about the data set in the second figure?
   A. Students were more likely to attribute correct scores to study and preparation, regardless of whether judging their own team or their opponents.
   B. Students were more likely to attribute correct scores to bias in the test questions, regardless of whether judging their own team or their opponents.
   C. Students were more likely to judge their own team's correct scores as resulting from study and preparation and their opponents' correct scores as resulting from test question bias.
   D. Students were more likely to judge their own team's correct scores as resulting from test question bias and their opponents' correct scores as resulting from test question bias.

45. Based on attribution theory, which statement is MOST likely to be TRUE about the results of the survey?
   A. The results are consistent with the fundamental attribution error.
   B. The results are consistent with a self-effacing bias.
   C. The results are not consistent with the attribution error, but are the result of testing errors.
   D. The results do not show any attribution error, because the overall competition resulted in a tie.

46. Based on attribution theory, if you were to ask students which factors caused them and their opponents to pick wrong answers, what would be the MOST likely result?

    A. Students would say that their own team picked wrong answers due to test question bias, but their opponents picked wrong answers due to lack of study and preparation.

    B. Students would say that their own team picked wrong answers due to lack of study and preparation, but their opponents picked wrong answers due to test question bias.

    C. Students would say that their own team picked wrong answers due to test question bias and that their opponents also picked wrong answers due to test question bias.

    D. Students would say that their own team picked wrong answers due to lack of study and preparation and that their opponents also picked wrong answers due to lack of study and preparation.

47. Which of the following examples BEST represents a self-serving bias?

    A. I didn't do well on a performance evaluation because I didn't put in enough effort on a work project.

    B. I did a great job on my class presentation because of all the help I got from my classmates.

    C. The sound system was great, but my speech really wasn't very good.

    D. I got a terrible performance evaluation because those evaluations never measure actual skill.

Question 48 is not based on a passage.

48. Mental health hospitals and prisons are forms of:

    A. agencies

    B. institutions

    C. functionalism

    D. social cohesion

311

SECTION 3:
Psychological,
Social, and
Biological
Foundations
of Behavior

Questions 49–52 are based on the following passage.

Passage X

Every year, the U.S. Department of Education records how many degrees are awarded based on demographic factors. The following graph shows bachelor's degrees awarded to U.S. students during the school year 2009–2010, categorized by race, ethnicity, and gender.

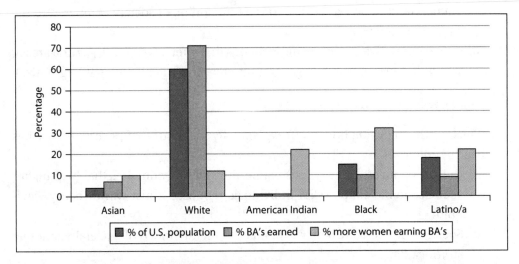

U.S. bachelor's degrees awarded by race/ethnicity and gender. *Source*: Adapted from U.S. Dept. of Education, National Education Statistics 2011.

49. According to the graph, in 2009–2010 which racial/ethnic group(s) earned a higher percentage of bachelor's degrees than their percentage in the U.S. population?
    A. black, Latino/a
    B. American Indian, black
    C. white, Asian
    D. only whites

50. According to the graph, during 2009–2010 in which ethnic or racial group(s) did women earn more bachelor's degrees than men?
    A. none of the racial or ethnic groups
    B. every racial or ethnic group except whites
    C. only whites
    D. every racial or ethnic group

51. What can be concluded from the data in the graph?
    A. Women are more interested than men in pursuing higher educational opportunities.
    B. Financial aid is being offered to greater numbers of women to pursue their education.
    C. Women are completing bachelor's degrees more often than men.
    D. More women than men are pursuing higher-paid careers.

52. Despite their increased education levels, women earn less money than their male counterparts. What sociological phenomenon might explain this?

    A. In the United States, ascribed statuses influence women's master status more strongly than achieved statuses.

    B. Women are more likely to experience sociological role strain because they have more flexible boundaries, which negatively affect their intelligence.

    C. Social functionalism explains the difference because the careers chosen by women tend to be less critical to the functioning of society compared to the careers chosen by men.

    D. More women live in geographic locations that offer lower pay (e.g., rural areas), whereas men tend to live in geographic areas that offer higher pay (e.g., cities).

Questions 53–55 are not based on a passage.

53. Which of the following does NOT explain why the culture of poverty theory has been denounced?

    A. Culture of poverty theory uses blame-the-victim techniques that help higher socioeconomic status (SES) individuals reinforce a just world theory viewpoint.

    B. Social reinforcement better explains the maintenance of societal economic stratification.

    C. Individuals from a lower SES do not have the intellectual ability to merit receiving sufficient financial capital to move out of poverty.

    D. Research has shown that individuals from a lower SES make an equal number of bad choices about their life opportunities compared to individuals from a higher SES.

54. Sandra's family is from a lower socioeconomic stratum. Despite encouragement by her parents, she struggled in her inner-city grade school and did not enjoy learning. A new job required her parents to move to a new town that has better schools. In her new school Sandra was able to improve her grades and consider additional educational opportunities beyond high school. She received a scholarship to attend college. Upon graduating she was offered a position that paid $50,000/year. This scenario is an example of:

    A. social mobility

    B. nepotism

    C. social reproduction

    D. social stratification

313

SECTION 3:
Psychological,
Social, and
Biological
Foundations
of Behavior

55. _____ theory indicates that stratification preserves society's ability to reward those who occupy positions most critical to society.
   A. Functionalist
   B. Meritocracy
   C. Social conflict
   D. Nepotism

Questions 56–59 are based on the following passage.

Passage XI

Greater sleep coherency with fewer awakenings and more consistent sleep is associated with better-quality sleep. However, sleep measurements often require complex electroencephalogram (EEG) sensors that require specific placement and are messy to attach to the head. This makes EEG sleep measurements difficult to perform in a home environment. One distal method to measure sleep coherency is using actigraphy. Lightweight cloth bands (e.g., sweat bands) with sensors in them are placed on the wrists and ankles to measure nighttime movements. More activity can indicate less coherent sleep patterns.

A researcher interested in the effect of noise pollution on those living near the negative amenity of an active airport recruits 100 people to wear actigraphs for one week while they are in bed. The results are shown on the following graph.

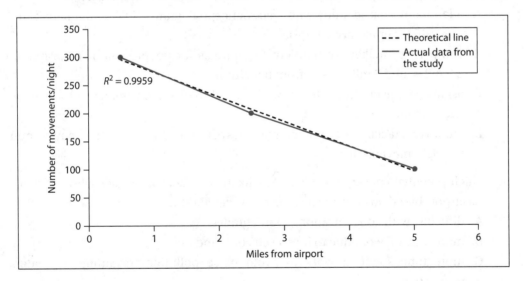

Nighttime actigraphy levels by distance from the airport.

56. What does this graph show?
    A. Living close to an airport has a significant impact on sleep coherency.
    B. There is an inverse correlation between proximity to the airport and sleep quality.
    C. Sleep and nighttime activity are not correlated.
    D. Living close to an airport is related to increased nighttime movements, which suggest poorer sleep quality.

57. Given your knowledge about neighborhoods near negative amenities, what other conditions might be TRUE?
    A. Individuals who work at the airport probably live near the airport and probably have to get up at night to go into work.
    B. Individuals who live near noisy environments eventually adapt, so the people in this study who live close to the airport and have high nighttime activity levels must be new to the area.
    C. The closer a neighborhood is to negative amenities, the cheaper the home prices and the more likely that the neighborhood qualifies as a lower socio-economic status (SES).
    D. Lower SES individuals tend to make poor housing choices and therefore are more likely to experience disrupted sleep.

58. The next logical step to study this phenomenon would MOST likely be:
    A. a laboratory-based study with electroencephalograms (EEGs) in an environment that mimics airport noise
    B. comparing intelligence quotient (IQ) ratings for people who live 0.5 miles, 2.5 miles, and 5 miles away from the airport
    C. asking people how long they have lived in those neighborhoods and why they live near the airport
    D. identifying racial or ethnic characteristics of the neighborhood that may account for night movement

59. Which potential consequence is LEAST likely to affect individuals who live near the airport based on current sociological understanding?
    A. difficulty with concentration; poorer grades
    B. more time off work due to increased colds and flus
    C. more time spent at work to avoid noise pollution, resulting in greater productivity
    D. more car accidents and increased transportation costs

Critical Analysis and Reasoning Skills

53 Questions **Time Limit: 90 Minutes**

Questions 1–4 are based on the following passage.

Passage I

Recent research indicates that our experience of happiness can be self-regulated, regardless of external circumstances. We can actively choose to be happy. It was previously thought that levels of happiness were genetically determined; people were born with a genetic predisposition to cheerfulness or pessimism. However, studies now suggest that such predispositions, although present, are not fixed. Instead, emotion, and indeed the structure of the brain, can be modified through certain practices.

These findings are indebted to the work of psychologist Gordon Watson, who in 1930 conducted a study entitled "Happiness Among Adult Students of Education." Because happiness was considered a highly desired yet elusive and mysterious emotion, Watson's serious endeavor was startling. By the 1970s, the psychological community was researching happiness on a larger scale. Today, it is estimated that over 2000 researchers in 42 countries are actively involved in happiness research.

In that crowded field, the work of a professor of psychology at the University of Wisconsin, Richard Davidson, stands out. Davidson observed patterns of brain activity as they related to a subject's mental and emotional states, using brain science's new technologies, including quantitative electrophysiology, positron emission tomography, and functional magnetic resonance imaging. He discovered what Western science once believed to be impossible: that the brain is not a static organ—it is able to change and develop over time. This capacity is known as neuroplasticity, and it has had a profound effect on the study of happiness.

Davidson's studies found that the functions of the brain's cerebral cortex are not limited to determining intelligence, interpreting sensory impulses, and controlling motor function as once believed. In fact, this area also determines personality, including emotional predispositions. Levels of activity on the right and left sides of the cerebral cortex relate to feelings of happiness and sadness. Specifically, higher levels of activity at the left frontal area of the cerebral cortex coincide with feelings of happiness, whereas activity on the right frontal area corresponds with feelings of sadness. Therefore, activities that generate side-specific activity can enhance those feelings.

For example, meditation has been shown to generate left-brain activity, and studies show that it produces positive emotions. Davidson studied the link between meditation and happiness through a project involving Tibetan Buddhist monks. His research brings together Eastern and Western traditions, and it links together objective reality with internal states of consciousness once thought to be subjective. The connection is made through observable electrical activity in the central nervous system. When the monks in the study meditated, their brain activity was recorded. Increases in left cerebral cortex activity indicate that the practice of meditation can, over time, change the structure of the brain, increasing the size and activity level of the left cerebral cortex.

Another practice that has been shown to stimulate left cerebral cortex activity and enhance feelings of happiness is the altering of conscious thoughts. More specifically, when a subject repeats positive affirmations—thinking optimistic thoughts—activity in the left cerebral cortex increases. As with the practice of meditation, the repetition of positive affirmations can change the structure of the brain over time, creating feelings of happiness and well-being. These findings show that the mind–body connection cannot be denied.

1. In the context of the passage, the word *elusive* means:
   A. prevaricating
   B. deceitful
   C. frank
   D. evasive

2. The author's claim that Watson's scientific study of happiness was startling is supported by:
   A. details about Watson's background and the publicity his study received
   B. the description of the study's subject
   C. the assertion that happiness was, at the time, desired but thought to be elusive and mysterious
   D. the fact that he conducted the study in 1930

3. According to the passage, all of these are TRUE EXCEPT:
   A. The brain is able to change over time, a process known as neuroplasticity.
   B. Science is attempting to prove there is a mind–body connection.
   C. Tibetan monks increase their left-side cerebral cortex activity through meditation.
   D. The right frontal area of the brain corresponds with feelings of sadness.

4. Based on information in the passage, which of these outcomes should someone expect after silently repeating the phrase "I am successful" for 20 minutes?
   A. a feeling of well-being
   B. sadness
   C. a creative impulse
   D. fatigue

Questions 5–11 are based on the following passage.

Passage II

In sharp contrast to the modern, confessional poetry of the 20th century, the oeuvre of Henry Wadsworth Longfellow seems quaint and primly Victorian. During his lifetime, however, he was the most celebrated poet in the country. A closer look at the history of American poetry reveals that, despite his eminence, Longfellow wrote in a mold of both form and content that was already being challenged during his lifetime. But why, a century later, do the artistic works of many of his contemporaries continue to be enjoyed and studied while Longfellow languishes in the tomb of cultural artifacts?

One answer lies in the radical shift that began to take place in poetry in the mid-19th century. Longfellow's themes and steadfast rhymes (and those of John Greenleaf Whittier, Oliver Wendell Holmes, and James Russell Lowell) gave way gradually to confessional verse, whose subjects were more personal and rhymes were looser and less conventional. But to understand this shift, one must first understand the nature of Longfellow's work and his standing in the American literary scene of his time.

Longfellow took as his subject his country's historical imagination, writing on an epic scale about Paul Revere, the Indian Hiawatha, and the pilgrim Miles Standish. He bestowed a mythic dimension on these figures, giving American readers iconic images that helped form a collective consciousness in the new country (indeed, Longfellow was a part of the first generation to be born in the United States). But Longfellow's content went beyond nationalistic pride—it was highly accessible and incredibly popular. Its accessibility is explained by his obvious themes that could be easily understood and embraced by the public. Longfellow did not challenge his readers, but appealed to their desire for stories that expounded an optimistic, sentimental, and moralistic worldview. Those themes were explored in rhyme that allowed readers to commit the poems to memory, much like songs. In 1857, *The Song of Hiawatha*, arguably his best-known poem, sold 50,000 copies, an astounding number at the time. The next year, *The Courtship of Miles Standish* sold 25,000 copies in two months and in London sold 10,000 copies in one day. His success allowed him to give up a professorship at Harvard and focus full time on his writing.

Walt Whitman, Longfellow's contemporary, wrote poetry similar to that of Longfellow—romantic and sentimental, with conventional rhyme and meter. But in the 1850s, indeed two years before *The Song of Hiawatha*, he wrote and published *Leaves of Grass*; a more radical departure from his previous work could not have been imagined. The 12 unnamed poems comprising *Leaves of Grass* are written in free verse—that is, without conventional rhyme and meter. Yet, like Longfellow, he was determined to explore the subject of America and his love for his country.

Whitman looked to the writings of Ralph Waldo Emerson for inspiration. Emerson wrote "America is a poem in our eyes; its ample geography dazzles the imagination, and it will not wait long for metres." Indeed, Whitman paraphrased Emerson in his preface to *Leaves of Grass*, "The United States themselves are essentially the greatest poem." But by that he did not mean he would explore that nation's mythic past. Instead, he took as his subjects the commonplace and the personal, finding beauty everywhere but expressing it in unique ways. He wrote of larger themes such as democracy, slavery and the Civil War, varied occupations and types of work, social change, and the American landscape and the natural world. He also explored more intimate subjects: aging, death and immortality, poverty, romantic love, and spirituality. In his "I Hear America Singing," he brings together these varied subjects to create a vision of America that is as far from Miles Standish as one can fathom. In it, he celebrates the "varied carols" sung by Americans, mechanics, carpenters, masons, boatmen, shoemakers, and mothers in long, unrhymed lines.

Whitman's groundbreaking free verse changed the trajectory of American poetry. The next generation of poets, including Ezra Pound, Hart Crane, Sherwood Anderson, and William Carlos Williams, celebrated their debt to Whitman. Decades later, the influence of Whitman's work on Allen Ginsberg and Langston Hughes, among many others, continues his legacy.

5. According to the passage, what might be the current reputation of poets such as Whittier and Holmes?
   A. They are considered integral writers in the history of American poetry.
   B. They are reviled as part of the Victorian Romantic period of American poetry.
   C. They are regarded as antiquated due to their conventional form and content.
   D. They are viewed as an influence on the Modern movement.

6. The main argument of the passage is that:
   A. Whitman's free verse is superior to Longfellow's rhymes.
   B. Longfellow's standing as an American poet was diminished by a rejection of quaint subjects and conventional rhyme and meter that came in the wake of poets such as Whitman.
   C. Longfellow would be read and studied more today if he had retained his nationalistic subject matter but eschewed the sentimental tone and standard forms of his poems.
   D. Ralph Waldo Emerson aided in the transformation of American poetry from Victorian Romanticism to Modernism.

7. Which of the following statements is NOT presented as evidence that Whitman is responsible for the radical shift in American poetry that occurred in the 19th century?
   A. He used iconic American figures as his subjects.
   B. His poetry was more personal and intimate than that of his predecessors or contemporaries.
   C. He wrote about the common man and commonplace events.
   D. He began writing in free verse rather than conventional rhymes.

8. What does the author mean by "tomb of cultural artifacts"?
   A. a resting place for dead poets
   B. a kind of cemetery in which people can pay their respects to writers of the past
   C. a crypt where culturally significant items are stored
   D. a group of ideas and works of art from the past that are considered to be dead

9. The author apparently believes that:
   A. Poems about iconic American figures can become best-sellers.
   B. Whitman's poems are more popular than Longfellow's because people prefer free verse and more personal poetry.
   C. Ralph Waldo Emerson could be considered the father of Modern American poetry.
   D. Contemporary confessional poetry owes much to the work of Longfellow.

10. One of America's most famous Modern poets, Ezra Pound, said of Walt Whitman, "As for Whitman, I read him (in many parts) with acute pain, but when I write of certain things I find myself using his rhythms." How does this quote affect the author's contention that Pound and his generation of poets celebrated their debt to Whitman?
    A. It repudiates it.
    B. It endorses it.
    C. It denies the contention by showing Pound's distaste for Whitman's work.
    D. It calls into question the author's use of the word *celebrate*.

11. Sales figures for two of Longfellow's poems are cited:
    A. to reinforce the idea that Longfellow's popularity was declining
    B. to compare his sales to those of his contemporaries
    C. because they mark a milestone in American publishing
    D. as evidence of his popularity at the time

Questions 12–17 are based on the following passage.

Passage III

On what basis might it be said that animals have rights? To partisans on either side of the debate, the question itself seems absurd. Supporters of animal rights would reply that animals, as living creatures, have the same type of rights enjoyed by all living beings. Opponents of the cause would rejoin that rights are the product of rationalism and thus are the sole province of humans.

One interesting moral perspective from which to view the debate comes from the philosophy of utilitarianism. Jeremy Bentham, widely credited as the father of utilitarianism, believed that the rightness or wrongness of actions should be judged by the effect they have on all the beings affected by the action. The entire world comprised a closed system to which the actions of any member of the system either added to the sum total of pleasure in the system or to the sum total of pain. To Bentham, the interests and desires of the participants in the system were all equal; Bentham's intellectual disciple Henry Sidgwick famously said, "The good of any one individual is of no more importance, from the point of view of the Universe, than the good of any other."

Bentham himself believed that the good of animals should be taken into consideration in utilitarianism. The issue for him was not whether animals could reason (debatable) or talk (obviously not), but whether they could suffer (absolutely). An animal's capacity for suffering, argued Bentham, implied not necessarily that it should have rights equal to those of man, but that its pain should be given equal consideration when determining exactly what rights it had. It is from this perspective that animal rights can be most justified.

Obviously, it doesn't make sense to say that animals should have the right to free speech or the right to vote, because these are capacities the animal does not and cannot ever possess. But it would be sensible to say that animals have a right to be free from unnecessary pain or suffering. This view of animal rights would preclude many current practices, such as using animals to test new drugs and cosmetics and even perhaps the mass production of animals for food and clothing.

Interestingly, utilitarianism also provides opponents of animal rights with justification for their views. Because utilitarianism is based on calculations of the total good of the system, it is possible to see animal exploitation as adding to, rather than subtracting from, the sum of happiness. For instance, the death of one cow could presumably provide food and clothing for multiple people. This increase of happiness for the many at the expense of the few would satisfy the tenets of utilitarianism. Alternatively, opponents could argue that because utilitarianism operates in a closed system, the negative effect of the death or suffering of one creature can be negated by the birth or pleasure of another creature. Because there are many times more animals that are born and live out their natural lives free from human-inflicted cruelty, the supposed suffering of those animals used for food, clothing, and experimentation is neutralized.

12. The word *province* as used in the passage MOST nearly means:
    A. boundary
    B. subdivision
    C. responsibility
    D. domain

13. A utilitarian who supported animal rights would believe an animal had the right to all of the following EXCEPT:
    A. a right to be free from cruel and unnecessary actions
    B. a right not to be used as a test subject
    C. a right not to be confined in uncomfortable positions
    D. a right to possess a secure habitat

14. The passage implies that Bentham and Sidgwick believe:
    A. There is no privileged frame of reference in the world.
    B. Animal rights are just as important as human rights.
    C. Animals possess the capacity to reason.
    D. Animals possess the capacity to suffer.

15. The author MOST likely included the parenthetical references in order to:
    A. insert his or her personal beliefs into the discussion
    B. emphasize the factors Bentham thought most relevant
    C. present the viewpoint of animal rights supporters
    D. preempt possible objections to Bentham's logic

16. The passage implies that utilitarianism could be used to justify all of the following EXCEPT:
    A. the use of people as means to ends rather than ends in themselves
    B. the death penalty
    C. torture of dangerous criminals
    D. indiscriminate killing

17. The primary purpose of the passage is to:
    A. provide an ethical framework from which to view a controversial issue
    B. explain how utilitarianism can be used to justify animal rights
    C. argue for the end of cruelty to animals
    D. detail Bentham's and Sidgwick's views on animal rights

Questions 18–23 are based on the following passage.

Passage IV

In literature, the period typically referred to as the 20th century actually begins in the previous century. To many, Queen Victoria's Jubilee in 1887 effectively marked the end of a literary epoch. The prevailing aesthetic sensibility, art for art's sake, was dying a slow death, as the gulf between artists and writers and the rest of the public widened, resulting in the widespread idea of the artist as one alienated from the rest of society. This viewpoint was spurred on by the bohemian culture movement, which arose in France and quickly spread. At its core, the bohemian movement scoffed at the limits placed on the individual by polite society and sought to isolate the artist from society as one who both rejects and is rejected by society.

Across the English Channel, developments in England further accentuated the separation of the artist from society at large. The Education Act of 1870 made elementary education mandatory, creating a massive class of literate, though still mostly uneducated, consumers. In response to this new market, new forms of entertainment were created, including the cheap and sensational "yellow press," which focused on scandal, crime, and other base aspects of human nature. Furthermore, publishers now divided up the literature audience into low, high, and middle "brow" members and churned out writing to satisfy the larger proportion of low- and middle-brow consumers. Although certain types of literature have always been directed at specific audiences, the degree and the speed at which these audiences became fragmented occurred at an unprecedented rate in the early 20th century.

The emergence and mass production of such so-called popular literature provided more fodder for the artistic elite's war on the crude and unsophisticated philistines in the public square. Perhaps this divide and the artist's growing awareness of difference led to a prevalence of pessimism and stoicism in the literature of the late Victorian period. Hardy, Housman, and Stevenson all expressed at least some form of overweening negativity or passivity in their prose and poetry.

The end of Victoria's reign brought Edward VII to the throne, and Edwardian England seemed to articulate all those qualities the artistic elite had grown weary of. Edward VII has been described as self-indulgent, and his 10-year regime was a boon to those who had the means to enjoy a life of idle pleasures. Although in the past artists and writers enjoyed the patronage of the royal family and other notables, now they strove to keep their distance from such decadence, perhaps to avoid contaminating their art, perhaps to further their sense of alienation from society.

The Edwardian period lasted a mere decade, with the prevailing cultural mentality changed by the ascendancy of George V to the throne in 1910 and thoroughly extirpated by England's entry into World War I in 1914. With the advantage of hindsight, the Georgian period seems an especially crucial one, a necessary balancing point between the gilded nature of the Edwardian age and the somewhat artificial staidness of the Victorian period. It was in this brief four-year period that English literature held its breath, and when it exhaled, at the end of the Great War, the old order in Europe was no more.

18. In the context of the passage, the word *polite* means:
   A. cultured
   B. nice
   C. affable
   D. deferential

19. According to the passage, a bohemian would likely reject:
   I. current fashion trends
   II. prevailing mores
   III. capitalistic thinking
   A. I only
   B. II only
   C. I and III only
   D. I, II, and III

20. The author implies that the Education Act of 1870:
   A. increased the education level of the English population
   B. led to more people attending secondary school

    C. had mixed results

    D. angered the artistic elite

21. The passage indicates the 20th century differed from earlier artistic periods because:

    A. Artists viewed the public as crude and unsophisticated.

    B. Divisions in society were deeper than before.

    C. The public was just as educated as the artists were.

    D. Artistic works were pessimistic and stoic.

22. The passage implies that Hardy, Housman, and Stevenson were all:

    A. popular writers of the late Victorian period

    B. influenced by the trends of their times

    C. esteemed novelists

    D. writing for low- and middle-brow audiences

23. The author's contention about the Georgian period would MOST be challenged if it were TRUE that:

    A. After World War I, English literature entered a neo-Victorian phase.

    B. Writers in America continued to embrace French bohemianism.

    C. Writers and artists worked to reintegrate themselves into society.

    D. The reign of George V came to an end.

Questions 24–30 are based on the following passage.

Passage V

Engineers and computer scientists are intrigued by the potential power of nanocomputing. Nanocomputers will use atoms and molecules to perform their functions instead of the standard integrated circuits now employed. Theorists believe that the amount of information a nanocomputer could handle is staggering.

A professor at Massachusetts Institute of Technology (MIT) has attempted to calculate the computational limits of a computer with a weight of 1 kilogram and a volume of 1 liter. According to the laws of physics, the potential amount of computational power is a function of the available energy. Basically, each atom and subatomic particle in the computer has an amount of energy attached to it. Furthermore, the energy of each particle or atom is increased by the frequency of its movement. Thus the power of a computer that uses nanotechnology is bounded by the energy available from its atoms.

Specifically, the relationship between the energy of an object and its computation potential is a proportionate one. As Einstein has famously calculated, the energy of an object is equal to its mass times the speed of light squared. Thus, a theoretical computer weighing a mere kilogram has a huge amount of potential energy. To find the total computational power, the minimum amount of energy required to perform an operation is divided by the total amount of energy.

The absolute minimum amount of energy required to perform an operation is determined by Planck's constant, an extremely tiny number. Dividing the total amount of energy possessed by a 1-kilogram computer by Planck's constant yields a tremendously large number, roughly 5×10^{50} operations per second. Using even the most conservative estimates of the computing power of the human brain, such a computer would have the computational power of five trillion trillion human civilizations. The computer would also have a memory capacity, calculated by determining the degrees of freedom allowed by the state of all the particles comprising it, of 10^{31} bits.

These numbers are purely theoretical, however. Were the computer to convert all of its mass to energy, it would be the equivalent of a thermonuclear explosion. And it is unreasonable to expect human technology to ever achieve abilities even close to these limits. However, a project at the University of Oklahoma has succeeded in storing 50 bits of data per atom, albeit on only a limited number of atoms. Given that there are 10^{25} atoms in 1 kilogram of material, it may be possible to fit up to 10^{27} bits of information in the computer. And if scientists are able to exploit the many properties of atoms to store information, including the position, spin, and quantum state of all its particles, it may be possible to exceed even that number.

One interesting consequence of such staggering increases in computing power is that each advance could provide the basis for further evolution. Once technology can achieve, for instance, a level of computation equal to 10^{40} operations per second, it can use that massive power to help bring the theoretical limit ever closer.

24. The central thesis of the passage is:
    A. Computing power is limited only by the laws of physics.
    B. New advances in computer technology allow for staggering levels of memory and computational ability.
    C. It may not be possible to achieve the theoretical limits of computing power.
    D. Computers using nanotechnology have the potential to tap vast quantities of power.

25. The author mentions "thermonuclear explosions" in order to:
    A. indicate that some of the previous discussion is not practical
    B. warn of a potential consequence predicted by Einstein's equation
    C. show a design flaw in the proposed computer
    D. point out an absurd result of the previous discussion

26. The author of the passage indicates that:
    A. The theoretical computer may have even more computational power than described.
    B. Technicians have already built computers that can store 10^{27} bits of data.
    C. 10^{27} bits of data is the theoretical limit of memory capacity in a computer.
    D. The technology exists to create a computer that can perform 10^{40} operations per second.

27. According to the passage, why does the author believe that the theoretical limit of computational power may be approached?
    A. Scientists can exploit many different properties of atoms.
    B. Technological advances engender more advances.
    C. Computers only require a minimal amount of energy.
    D. Recent advances have shown the technology exists to reach the limit.

28. The ideas in this passage would MOST likely be presented in:
    A. an academic journal
    B. a newspaper
    C. a tabloid
    D. a popular science magazine

29. According to the information in the passage, which of the following could increase the computational power of the theoretical computer?
    A. increasing the amount of energy it takes to perform an operation
    B. decreasing the volume of the computer
    C. decreasing the amount of energy it takes to perform an operation
    D. decreasing the mass of the computer

30. The project at the University of Oklahoma indicates:
    A. Current information-storing technology is still in its infancy.
    B. Researchers are close to achieving the predicted memory capacity.
    C. Scientists have learned how to use different aspects of the atom to store information.
    D. Work on reaching the theoretical limits of computation power is now underway.

Questions 31–37 are based on the following passage.

Passage VI

Language consists of three main parts. The first is simply vocabulary, the lexicon of words available to the speaker to describe particular concepts, actions, and states. The second part is morphology, the set of rules that dictates how words and parts of words may be combined to form other words. The final part of language is syntax, the rules that combine words into phrases and sentences. It is morphology that we shall turn our attention to first.

Morphology has two major subdivisions. They are derivation and inflection. Derivation refers to those rules by which new words may be formed out of preexisting words. Inflection, sometimes referred to as conjugation and declension, states how words are changed to indicate their function within a sentence.

Although common mythology holds that English is one of the most difficult languages to learn, many linguists would beg to differ. In fact, when it comes to inflection,

English is almost juvenile in its simplicity when compared to other languages. For example, Spanish verbs have about 50 forms, unique combinations that indicate the first, second, and third person; whether a verb is singular or plural; whether the verb is in the past, present, or future tense; and any number of moods, including the indicative, the conditional, the subjunctive, the imperative, and others. Languages from outside the Indo-European family tree may be even more complex. The Bantu language of Kivunjo has roughly half a million combinations of prefixes and suffixes for a verb. English, however, has a mere four combinations. A verb such as *to walk* is limited to the following forms: *walk, walks, walked,* and *walking.*

Although there are only four basic verb forms, the English language does have more than 13 possible inflections. It just makes do with these four forms for the various functions. English also differs significantly from many other Indo-European languages in that in English, the stem of the word can be pronounced and is in fact part of the language. In Spanish, the stem of the verb *to walk* is *camin-,* but this is not a word in the language. In order to pronounce this word, it must be conjugated and combined with a suffix. English uses the stem form of the verb for four inflections: the present tense (except for the third-person singular), the infinitive, the imperative, and the subjunctive. The verb form ending in *–s* is used in only one case, the third-person singular.

The two possible verb suffixes, *–ing* and *–ed,* are put to use in a variety of ways as well. The *–ing* ending appears in the progressive participle, the present participle, the gerund form, and the verbal adjective form. That leaves the *–ed* form to handle the remaining inflections, including the past tense, the perfect participle, the passive participle, and some verbal adjectives.

Why are there so many different inflections for verb forms that basically sound the same? Simply put, the meanings implied by the various moods are different, even if the words used are fairly similar. Compare the meaning conveyed by the simple past tense (*he walked*) to the meaning inherent in the perfect participle (*he has walked*).

31. The central thesis of the passage is that:
    A. English is easier to learn than many other languages.
    B. Each language is unique in its major forms.
    C. The English language uses a minimum of verb forms in its inflections.
    D. The English language is not as rich in meaning as other languages.

32. The passage suggests that the author MOST likely believes that:
    A. The English language does not suffer from its lack of inflections.
    B. English is the only language in which the verb stem is a word.
    C. English is not as hard to learn as many think.
    D. At one time the English language had more inflections.

33. Which of the following assertions does the author support with an example?
    I. The English language is relatively simple in its inflections.
    II. The English language is not as hard to learn as some believe.
    III. Inflections in the English language can convey a variety of meanings.
    A. I only
    B. III only
    C. I and III only
    D. II and III only

34. The ideas presented in this passage would probably be MOST interesting to:
    A. linguists
    B. language teachers
    C. psychologists
    D. translators

35. The passage indicates that a native Spanish speaker may be puzzled by the verb *to see* in which of the following sentences?
    A. I saw the car.
    B. They want to see the car.
    C. She sees the car.
    D. Seeing is believing.

36. According to the passage, which English inflection can be expressed by two different verb suffixes?
    I. the present tense
    II. the verbal adjective
    III. the present participle
    A. I only
    B. I and II only
    C. III only
    D. I, II, and III

37. The Russian language is similar to the Spanish language in that the verbs have stem forms that are not words unto themselves. From this fact, a linguist might infer that:
    A. Russian verbs have roughly 50 forms.
    B. The Russian language may be of the Indo-European family.
    C. Russian is harder to learn than Spanish.
    D. The Russian language has more inflections than the English language.

Questions 38–44 are based on the following passage.

Passage VII

The man whom Franklin Delano Roosevelt christened "The Happy Warrior" in a nominating speech would later become a thorn in Roosevelt's side. Some thought the switch in loyalties was sour grapes, but others saw Alfred E. Smith as the epitome of William Wordsworth's "happy warrior" and therefore a man who "makes his moral being his prime care"—one who never made a move without consulting his conscience.

Alfred E. Smith was both a successful politician and an unsuccessful one. A four-term governor of New York State, he seemed a sure candidate for president, and indeed he ran three times for that position, only to lose each time.

He had several strikes against him. He was the Catholic son of Irish and Italian-German immigrants, making him anathema to nativists, the xenophobes who underwent a resurgence in the 1920s. He was from New York City, viewed even in the early twentieth century as disconnected from the national character. He was a progressive, which made conservatives of all stripes nervous. And he favored the repeal of Prohibition, a position that lost him the backing of many party leaders.

Who was this unlikely candidate? Born Alfred Emanuel Smith in 1873, Smith grew up on the Lower East Side of Manhattan. His father died when Smith was young, and the boy dropped out of school to take care of the family. At age 21, Smith supported a losing candidate in a local race and came to the attention of New York politicos, who took him under their wing. Nine years later, he ran successfully for the New York State Assembly, where he rapidly rose in the ranks to become Majority Leader and finally Speaker. He played a pivotal role in the revamping of New York's constitution, was elected sheriff of New York County, and then ran for governor in 1918, winning handily. Although he lost a re-election bid two years later, he surged back in 1922 and would remain in the governor's seat for six more years. His terms were marked by unparalleled improvements in labor laws and laws protecting civil liberties, for Smith's goal was to support those he saw as most in need of government's assistance.

In this goal, he was allied with Franklin Roosevelt, and the two were close enough that Roosevelt nominated Smith for president in 1924. The Drys, or Prohibitionists, backed William McAdoo, a son-in-law of former President Woodrow Wilson. Smith's supporters and McAdoo's supporters were so far apart that finally a compromise candidate, John Davis, was nominated and promptly lost the general election to Calvin Coolidge.

In 1928, Smith received his party's nomination on the second ballot, but along with his anti-Prohibition leanings, his religion became a major issue during the campaign, paving the way for Herbert Hoover to win the general election. Meanwhile, Smith had arranged for the nomination of his New York colleague, Franklin Roosevelt, to be governor of New York. Although Smith lost his bid, Roosevelt did not.

Then came the Depression and the election of 1932. Backroom dealings ensured that Franklin Roosevelt won the nominating process, with another would-be presidential candidate in the vice-presidential spot on the ticket. Smith was left out in the cold on his third try for the presidency. Despite his former regard for Roosevelt, he began to work hard, if unsuccessfully, to defeat the New Deal. He supported two Republicans rather than Roosevelt in the 1936 and 1940 elections, and he died in 1944, a man who had never reached his desired goal, yet had inspired many of the changes for which his rival is now known.

38. One important argument of the final paragraph is that:
    A. Roosevelt would have done better with Smith at his side.
    B. The New Deal was anathema to someone with Smith's ideals.
    C. Smith's background made him an improbable candidate.
    D. Smith deserves credit for many of Roosevelt's successes.

39. The passage implies that being from New York City is bad for a national candidate because:
    A. Urban candidates have trouble relating to those in the heartland.
    B. New York is perceived as too different from the rest of the country.
    C. Westerners rarely support or give money to eastern candidates.
    D. New York is the center of liberalism, but candidates must be neutral.

40. The passage suggests that Roosevelt's change of heart toward Smith was influenced by:
    A. ethics
    B. spitefulness
    C. miscommunication
    D. ambition

41. The mention of nativists shows primarily that:
    A. Only those born in the United States are eligible for the presidency.
    B. Bigotry figured into politics in the early twentieth century.
    C. Prohibition was a critical issue for many urban voters.
    D. A candidate for national office must embrace religion.

42. According to the passage, why did John Davis win the Democratic nomination in 1924?
    A. He was not as far to the left as Smith.
    B. He was a Prohibitionist like McAdoo.
    C. He had the support of a former president.
    D. He was acceptable to Smith and McAdoo supporters.

43. The author's claim that Smith was a successful politician is supported by:
    A. the explanation of his sobriquet, "The Happy Warrior"
    B. a review of his work in the assembly and governor's office
    C. descriptions of his three runs for the presidency
    D. a list of the famous names that supported his candidacies

44. If Smith were to run for office today on a platform similar to his original plan, which of the following outcomes would MOST likely occur?

   A. He would be supported by Progressives and union leaders.

   B. He would be opposed by civil libertarians.

   C. He would be supported by those who favor immigration reform.

   D. He would be opposed by those who support social welfare programs.

Questions 45–49 are based on the following passage.

Passage VIII

Fifty years ago, only New Yorkers lived in what is now termed a *megacity*, an agglomeration of more than 10 million people living and working in an urban environment. In contrast, today there are more than 40 megacities, most in less developed countries, and more urban centers are expected to explode in population by the year 2020. Demographers and globalization experts are already referring to the 21st century as "the urban century."

Already, more people on our Earth live in cities than live in rural areas. This is an enormous change in population trends, and it skews the entire planet in ways we haven't begun to analyze.

Although some cities have seen immigration expand their borders, for most megacities, it is migration from within the country that has caused the city to grow. An example is China, where some 150 million rural inhabitants have migrated to cities in just the last 10 years. In many cases, the cities house the only possibilities of employment in this global economy. That is what has grown Mumbai (Bombay), India, from a large city to a megacity of more than 18 million people in just a few years. It's the cause of the explosion of populations in Lagos, Nigeria; Karachi, Pakistan; Dhaka, Bangladesh; and Jakarta, Indonesia.

Whereas just a few years ago, most large cities were in developed nations, now the largest are suddenly in the less developed countries of South America, Africa, and Asia. Imagine the pressure on the infrastructure of these already poor cities as the influx of workers pushes services to the breaking point. Slums and shantytowns spring up around the outskirts of the cities, and government is powerless to affect the disadvantaged workers, leaving them exposed to corrupt local officials or urban gangs. Imagine, too, what happens in the rural areas that these people have abandoned. China faces a desperate shortage of agricultural labor. So do other areas of Asia and Africa.

According to United Nations (UN) statistics, by the year 2030, more than 60 percent of the world population will be urban, up from 30 percent in 1950. Unlike the population growth in developed nations, the birth rate in less developed nations is high, meaning that the cities continue to grow even as migration slows from the rural areas. Megacities such as New York have populations that have leveled off over time. Despite its location in a less developed nation, even a megacity such as Mexico City has a slow rate of growth compared to Asian and African cities such as Mumbai or Lagos.

It is difficult to imagine what the growth of the megacities will mean to the world in the 21st century. Demographers foresee ecological overload, homelessness, uncontrolled traffic, and an infrastructure strained to the breaking point. Despite the notion that industrial jobs improve the lot of the workers, it is already possible to see that megacities are creating a new, even deeper division between rich and poor, as the poor concentrate in the outskirts of town and the rich barricade themselves behind walls and in towers.

45. The main argument of the passage is that:
   A. Megacities are more often found in less developed nations but strain the resources of developed nations.
   B. The growth in population and number of megacities means foreseeable changes, many of them negative.
   C. The movement of population bases from rural to urban locations decimates the countryside and limits our ability to grow food.
   D. We must begin to fight back against the growth of megacities in the less developed nations of the world.

46. The passage suggests that demographers:
   A. have not been able to keep pace with the growth of cities
   B. focus primarily on population trends in the developing world
   C. are observing the growth of the world's cities with concern
   D. work hand in hand with the UN to plan for the future

47. The author's use of UN statistics helps:
   A. strengthen the argument that urbanization is radically changing the world
   B. contradict demographers' claims about megacities and their effects
   C. indicate that the results of urbanization include poverty and crime
   D. complement the assertion that birth rate is the main reason for urban growth

48. According to this passage, why might skyscrapers be a sign of divisiveness?
   A. They cost too much to build.
   B. They are found only in developed nations.
   C. They separate rich from poor.
   D. They house businesses, not people.

49. Which new information, if true, might CHALLENGE the author's contention that cities will continue to grow despite a slowing of migration from the countryside?
   A. Scientists are creating new strains of rice and wheat that require far less in the way of hands-on care.
   B. The number of people living below the poverty level will climb in less developed and developed nations.
   C. Inflationary trends in heating oil and gasoline prices will limit most people's discretionary spending.
   D. New methods of birth control will limit the population explosion in the developing world.

Questions 50–53 are based on the following passage.

Passage IX

Muralism has long been a Mexican tradition, perhaps dating back to the Aztecs, who recorded their history on the walls of their pyramids. The covering of a white wall with political art made the careers of David Alfara Siqueiros, Jose Clemente Orozco, and the best known of them all, Diego Rivera.

Siqueiros, born in Chihuahua, studied art from an early age. He organized a student strike at the age of 15 and later worked to unseat the Mexican dictator Huerta, attaining the rank of captain during the revolution that was taking place. He later brought his tactical knowledge to the world of organized labor, where his activism led to lengthy jail terms. That is where he created some of his finest artworks on canvas. During the 1930s, he went to Spain to join the anti-fascist forces. His life was that of a soldier-artist, and some considered him a dangerous, subversive gangster.

Orozco, too, studied art as a youth and was inspired by the Mexican Revolution. One of his famous murals depicts the Holy Trinity as a worker, a soldier, and a peasant. Later he turned his focus to the dehumanizing effect of large cities on the people who live there. When he wasn't painting vast murals, Orozco was drawing political cartoons.

Rivera, the third of these Mexican Social Realists, *los tres grandes*, remains the most famous through sheer force of personality. His storytelling, his love affairs, his radicalism, and his love–hate relationship with the land of his birth informed his life and his paintings. He incorporated Mexican folklore and cultural icons into his murals in an effort to educate working people in their own history.

In the Chicano neighborhoods of the southwestern United States, political muralism still explodes onto bare walls in the form of graffiti. Edward Seymour's 1949 invention of canned spray paint provided would-be artists with an easy mode of expression, and the graffiti mural took off as an art form in the 1960s and 1970s. It began as outlaw art, which surely would have appealed to an outlaw such as Siqueiros. Despite the new artists' lack of formal training, some members of the outlaw group managed to create something beautiful while making political statements about poverty, injustice, diversity, and racism.

One extraordinary thing about this kind of public art is that it is truly for everyone. You do not need to enter the halls of a museum to see it; it resides on the walls of your local bodega or school or health clinic; you bounce your ball off of it in the basketball or handball court; you cover it over with posters for your favorite band or flyers about your lost pet.

Certainly, many of the graffiti artists were reviled as nuisances, and their art was erased. For some, however, graffiti would prove a launching point into the world of fine art. Today, modern murals in Austin, San Antonio, Los Angeles, and Tucson, among others, attest to the power of the Mexican tradition of the muralist as purveyor of political thought.

50. In the context of the passage, the word *radicalism* means:
    A. extremism
    B. intolerance
    C. discrimination
    D. fanaticism

51. The author probably mentions Orozco's political cartoons as a way of illustrating:
    A. the lack of seriousness in Orozco's art
    B. how multitalented Orozco was
    C. Orozco's intertwining of politics and art
    D. why Orozco's work fell out of favor

52. The author's claim that Siqueiros might approve of Chicano graffiti is supported by:
    A. details about Siqueiros's role in the Spanish Civil War
    B. the description of Siqueiros as an army captain
    C. the fact that Siqueiros moved from Mexico to Spain
    D. information about Siqueiros's gangster past

53. According to this passage, graffiti would BEST be described as:
    A. an attractive way of making a political statement
    B. a pale imitation of the Mexican muralists' work
    C. a nuisance that must be tolerated by urbanites
    D. a way to educate the masses in their own history

STOP. This is the end of Section 4.

ANSWERS AND EXPLANATIONS

Section 1. Biological and Biochemical Foundations of Living Systems

1. **The correct answer is C.** The primary difference between aerobic and anaerobic cellular respiration is the amount of ATP generated. Anaerobic respiration generates far less ATP per glucose molecule than does aerobic respiration.

2. **The correct answer is C.** During semiconservative replication, the DNA helix unwinds so that both strands of DNA can serve as a template. Both strands are copied, producing two double helices. Each one consists of a template strand and a newly synthesized strand.

3. **The correct answer is B.** This question requires a general knowledge of the chemical makeup of the major macromolecules of the cell. Glucose contains only carbon, hydrogen, and oxygen. Generally, lipids contain the same three elements. Proteins always contain C, O, H, and N and perhaps some other elements depending on the amino acids used. Nucleic acids contain C, O, H, N, and phosphorus.

4. **The correct answer is C.** This problem requires a Punnett square to be performed for each generation. For the first generation, the Punnett square for the genetic cross of $TT \times tt$ is:

	T	T
t	Tt	Tt
t	Tt	Tt

In the first generation, the T and t gametes unite to produce individuals with a Tt (heterozygous) genotype. In the second generation, the Punnett square is conducted for the genetic cross of $Tt \times Tt$:

	T	t
T	TT	Tt
t	Tt	tt

The phenotypic results from this cross are that three of the four pea plants will be tall (*TT*, *Tt*, and *Tt*) and one of the four is short (*tt*). Thus, the phenotypic ratio of dominant to recessive pea plants is 3:1, given by choice C.

5. **The correct answer is D.** If a person has cystic fibrosis, his or her *CFTR* gene is mutated and produces a faulty version of the CFTR protein. Increasing the production of the mutated CFTR would not improve the condition. The passage indicates that some mutations of CFTR produce proteins that are misdirected and destroyed instead of being sent to the cell membrane. A drug that stops the destruction of CFTR might sound helpful; but if it doesn't also get the CFTR to the membrane where it is needed, it won't be beneficial. Increasing nutrient absorption in the small intestine would be helpful in countering some of the malnutrition problems that cystic fibrosis patients often have. However, it would lead to an improvement only in that one symptom. Activating an additional chloride channel other than CFTR might help restore ion and water balance to produce mucus of the appropriate consistency.

6. **The correct answer is C.** A codon is a sequence of three nucleotides found on the mRNA that specifies particular amino acids to be added to a protein. The genetic code lists all possible codons. One codon always specifies one amino acid. If the protein is 1480 amino acids long, you might suspect that the mRNA had 1480 codons. However, an additional codon would be present that served as the stop codon. The stop codon does not code for an amino acid, but instead signals the end of translation and the release of the protein. Therefore, 1481 codons would be present on the mRNA.

7. **The correct answer is B.** Carriers are heterozygotes. In the case of recessive inheritance, a carrier will not necessarily know that they are carrying a single allele for the disease. When two heterozygotes are crossed in a Punnett square, the result is that 25% will be homozygous dominant (normal), 50% will be heterozygous carriers, and 25% will be homozygous recessive and will have cystic fibrosis.

8. **The correct answer is A.** Trypsin is a proteinase produced by the pancreas and secreted into the small intestine. It is involved in protein digestion, so if the levels were reduced, proteins would not be well digested. Amylase is the enzyme involved in carbohydrate digestion, and lipases are involved in the digestion of fats.

9. **The correct answer is D.** This question is simply asking about the function of mitochondria in the cell. Mitochondria are involved in aerobic respiration and are the site of the Krebs cycle and the electron transport chain. Aerobic cellular respiration produces large amounts of ATP. Therefore, the more mitochondria a cell has, the more ATP it can produce. Cells with higher ATP demands should have more mitochondria than cells with lower ATP demands.

10. **The correct answer is D.** Men pass on their genetic contribution to the next generation via sperm. Any mitochondria present in sperm typically do not enter the cell.

The passage indicates that all mitochondria in a given cell are derived from those in the egg cell. Because a male does not pass on any of his mitochondria to the next generation, even if he has an mtDNA disease, he could never pass it on to his children. Only when the mtDNA of the egg cell is affected can the disease be passed on.

11. **The correct answer is B.** This question relies on some basic knowledge of endosymbiotic theory. Choice A suggests that this theory is supported because mitochondria are membrane bound. Because cells have many other membrane-bound organelles, this would not provide any compelling evidence for the mitochondria being unique. Choice C indicates that because mitochondria are found in multiple copies within a cell, this would be evidence to support endosymbiosis. Because other organelles are found in multiple copies, this would not be a plausible explanation. The best choice to support the idea that mitochondria were once free-living prokaryotic cells is that they have their own DNA. The passage explains that the mtDNA is circular, which corresponds to the typical DNA conformation in bacteria. Because mitochondria have their own DNA and it resembles that of prokaryotes, choice B would lend the best support to the endosymbiotic theory.

12. **The correct answer is C.** The question explains that mtDNA comes from a single source, which you know is the mother. In the nucleus of diploid cells, each gene is present in duplicate copies that can recombine during crossing over. Because mtDNA comes from a single source, recombination should not occur. The remaining choices listed, such as transcription and translation, should still be able to happen within the mitochondria. Any DNA is subject to spontaneous mutation, including the mtDNA.

13. **The correct answer is A.** Viagra works by increasing NO activity. The NOS enzyme is responsible for the conversion of L-arginine to L-citrulline. Something antagonistic to L-arginine would mean that less would be available to convert to L-citrulline and NO. Decreasing NOS activity would decrease NO. The passage explains that cGMP is needed to modulate the activity of NO. Decreasing cGMP would decrease NO activity. The PDE enzyme degrades cGMP, which in turn decreases NO activity. If the PDE enzyme were to be inhibited, cGMP could work longer and NO activity would increase.

Passage III

14. **The correct answer is C.** Because you know that guanine is a nucleotide, it can be deduced that cyclic guanine monophosphate is some variant of a nucleotide.

15. **The correct answer is B.** Because NO is a gas with a half-life of just a few seconds, it seems impossible for NO to be in these supplements. The PDE enzyme would degrade cGMP and decrease the amount of NO produced. The best explanation is that the supplements contain the precursor to NO, which is L-arginine. Once ingested, the L-arginine could potentially be converted to L-citrulline and NO in the cells.

16. **The correct answer is A.** Nitroglycerin and erectile dysfunction drugs both have similar effects in that they are vasodilators, which increase blood flow to specific areas in the body. Taking both could dilate the vessels to a point where blood pressure drops critically low. With extreme hypotension, tissues and organs become oxygen deprived.

No Passage

17. **The correct answer is A.** Because the 3' end of mRNA aligns with the 5' end of DNA in transcription, the complementary base sequence of the mRNA, reading from the mRNA's 3' end, will be G-U-A. Note that uracil is substituted for thymine in RNA. Because the 5' end of tRNA aligns with the 3' end of mRNA, the tRNA base sequence, from the tRNA's 5' end, will be C-A-U. Except for the substitution of uracil, anticodons are the same as the original DNA triplets they are translating.

18. **The correct answer is C.** Chain growth in DNA replication is initiated by a *primase* and is extended by a *DNA polymerase*. Thus the enzyme acting between Initiation → Elongation is *DNA polymerase*.

19. **The correct answer is A.** *Topoisomerases* are enzymes that cut one of the DNA strands so that it can begin to unwind and serve to relieve pressure in the coil caused by its unwinding. Thus the enzyme acting between Double helix → Nicking of a strand is *topoisomerase*.

20. **The correct answer is D.** Abutting segments of unjoined DNA can be annealed by *ligases*. Thus the enzyme acting between Elongation → Closing of nicks is *DNA ligase*.

No Passage

21. **The correct answer is C.** The majority of the cell cycle is spent in interphase, which consists of three stages: G1, S, and G2. In the G1 stage of interphase, the cell organelles are doubled, and materials required for DNA synthesis are accumulated for the onset of cell division. The S stage of interphase is the stage of the cell cycle where the amount of DNA doubles with the replication of chromosomes. In the G2 stage of interphase, which follows the synthesis of DNA, proteins required for the next cell division are synthesized. Metaphase is the stage in mitosis characterized by the precise lineup of the chromosomes along the equatorial plane.

22. **The correct answer is A.** Osmosis is a specialized form of diffusion, or passive transport. During osmosis, water always moves from the side of the membrane that has more water to the side of the membrane that has less water. The only thing that moves by osmosis is water. This means that choice B can be eliminated because solutes are not moving by osmosis. If there is a concentration difference across the membrane, there will be water movement, which eliminates choice C. When osmosis occurs, water moves from the side of the membrane that has more water to the side that has less water. This means that the side of the membrane with more water has less solute (and is therefore less concentrated) than the side of the membrane with less water and more solute (being more concentrated). Based on the choices provided, choice A is the most appropriate.

23. **The correct answer is D.** Prokaryotic and eukaryotic cells have several structures in common. In order to determine that a cell is eukaryotic, structures that are unique to eukaryotic cells must be identified. Ribosomes perform protein synthesis and can be found in all cells. The cell membrane is the outer boundary of the cell and is also found in all types of cells. DNA serves as the genetic material found in all cell types. Mitochondria (choice D) are true bound organelles that perform the process of cellular respiration. Because they are true organelles, they are found only in eukaryotic cells.

24. **The correct answer is D.** Connective tissues are characterized by cells scattered in a nonliving matrix. This matrix often consists of collagen fibers. Muscle has the ability to contract, whereas epithelial cells are characterized by cells arranged in sheets and a basement membrane.

25. **The correct answer is A.** A bacterial cell performing anaerobic respiration would perform a fermentation step following glycolysis. The Krebs cycle and electron transport chain are associated with aerobic cellular respiration.

Passage IV

26. **The correct answer is C.** This question is asking for a comparison between the organization of DNA in bacteria and eukaryotic cells. Eukaryotic DNA exists in multiple linear pieces termed **chromosomes**. Bacterial DNA consists of a single loop of DNA. Although bacteria can have extra chromosomal DNA known as plasmids, this is not the case for all bacteria. RNA is single stranded, but it is not the primary genetic material of the cells and is only produced during transcription.

27. **The correct answer is A.** Once taken inside a cell, foreign items can be broken down in the lysosomes of the cell. The smooth endoplasmic reticulum is responsible for lipid synthesis, and the rough endoplasmic reticulum deals in protein labeling. The Golgi apparatus sorts and modifies contents from the endoplasmic reticulum.

28. **The correct answer is D.** All of the given choices would give support to the endosymbiotic theory. The subunit sizes of bacterial and eukaryotic ribosomes are known to be different. Bacterial cell membranes have some different properties as compared to their eukaryotic counterparts. Because plasmids are unique to bacteria, finding them in the chloroplasts or mitochondria would support the idea that these structures were once prokaryotic in nature.

Passage V

29. **The correct answer is A.** Retroviruses are unique in that they enter their host as RNA but must convert themselves to DNA to enter the latent phase and insert into the host's chromosomes, which are also DNA. This is indicated by choice A. This conversion of RNA to DNA is carried out by the enzyme reverse transcriptase. The question is asking specifically about retroviruses, so choices B and C can be eliminated, as they are not unique to the retrovirus family. Choice D indicates that the retrovirus needs to recombine with the host chromosomes. Recombination

implies genetic exchange between the two sources. Although the viral genetic material will insert into a proto-oncogene of the host, there will not be an exchange of DNA.

30. **The correct answer is A.** The passage describes the function of the four genes found in RSV. Packaging of viruses for release involves the viral envelope and capsid, which implicates the *gag* gene and the *env* gene. The *pol* gene codes for reverse transcriptase, which converts viral RNA to DNA and is not needed for the packaging viruses. The *src* gene encodes for tyrosine kinase. Kinases phosphorylate other molecules, which would not be part of the viral packaging process.

31. **The correct answer is D.** Oncogenes develop when a proto-oncogene activates. In order for a virus to carry an oncogene into its host, that virus must be derived from a virus that picked up the gene from a former host cell. Spontaneous mutation alone could not account for a virus acquiring an entire proto-oncogene, which eliminates choice A. Viruses do not conjugate, so choice B can be eliminated as well. Transformation occurs when a cell incorporates foreign DNA from its environment into its own genome. This occurs with bacteria but not viruses, meaning that choice C can also be eliminated. This leaves transduction as the only choice. When a virus excises from the host chromosome, it can take with it genes from the host's chromosome. A virus could feasibly acquire an activated oncogene when excising from its host, and this gene could be transferred to a new host.

32. **The correct answer is A.** This question is essentially asking how a cancerous cell could have its cell division halted. Because cancer is characterized by uncontrolled mitosis, the best way to halt the cancer would be to halt mitosis. Disrupting protein synthesis, or aerobic cellular respiration, would not directly affect cell division, so these choices can be eliminated. Introducing additional growth factors to the cell would only increase the rate of cell division, which is the opposite of what this question is asking. The only feasible choice would be to interfere with the microtubules (spindle fibers) and halt mitosis.

Passage VI 33. **The correct answer is B.** For this question, the best strategy is to find the most logical-sounding answer. Choice A suggests that antibiotics cause the mutation rate to increase. You have no evidence to support this assertion; therefore, this choice should be eliminated. Choice C suggests that antibiotics increase the rate of reproduction in bacteria. Again, you have no evidence to support this. Choice D can be eliminated because other choices have already been found incorrect. This leaves choice B as your answer. The antibiotics will kill all but the resistant bacteria, leaving them to multiply and lead to a new generation of resistant bacteria.

34. **The correct answer is D.** This question is asking about a basic knowledge of bacterial conjugation. During conjugation, a bacterial cell copies a plasmid and transfers that plasmid to a recipient that is lacking the plasmid. Because the question tells you that the resistance genes are often passed by conjugation and you know

conjugation passes plasmids, you can assume that the resistance genes are located on plasmids.

35. **The correct answer is B.** This question requires you to locate the most logical explanation as to why antibiotic genes are often purposefully transferred along with a gene of interest in biotechnology procedures. Because the question does not provide information on what type of cells are being transformed, don't assume anything. Choice A suggests that you need resistance genes transferred so the cells can survive in the presence of antibiotics. If the cells transformed are not bacterial, they would survive anyway, as antibiotics would target and kill only bacteria. Choice C suggests that the antibiotic genes are transferred out of convenience because they happen to be near the gene of interest. If the gene of interest is not coming from bacteria, then there could not be any antibiotic resistance genes nearby. Choice D really doesn't offer much in the way of logic, suggesting that antibiotic resistance would be necessary to prevent infection in transformed cells. The only logical explanation is choice B. In order to determine if a cell was transformed with the gene of interest or not, antibiotics could be added. The transformed cells that picked up the gene of interest would also pick up the antibiotic resistance marker and would grow in the presence of antibiotics. The nontransformed cells would not be resistant to the antibiotics and would be killed.

36. **The correct answer is C.** Of the choices listed, only the ribosomes are structurally different between prokaryotic and eukaryotic cells. Although both eukaryotic and prokaryotic ribosomes have a small and large subunit, the sizes of these subunits are different in prokaryotic cells.

37. **The correct answer is A.** The karyotype is the characteristic morphology of a species's chromosome set. The normal karyotype for humans consists of 23 pairs of chromosomes. The 23rd pair constitutes the sex chromosomes, which consist of a pair of X chromosomes in the female or an X and Y chromosome in the male. In Klinefelter's syndrome, males exhibit an altered karyotype in that they possess a third X chromosome.

No Passage

38. **The correct answer is C.** Mitosis is the process during which chromosomes are distributed evenly to two new cells that arise from the parent cell undergoing division. Tetrads, or the formation of four new cells, do not occur during mitosis. Thus the number of tetrads formed during mitosis is 0.

39. **The correct answer is D.** During the S phase of interphase before mitosis proper, each chromosome will have replicated. The two chromosomal strands or chromatids are identical in their genetic material and are joined at a constricted region called the centromere. Within the centromere are one or more rings of protein known as kinetochores, which play a significant role in the attachment of the spindle fibers to the chromosomes.

40. **The correct answer is B.** Diploid organisms have two sets of 23 chromosomes, with one (haploid) set provided by each parent.

41. **The correct answer is D.** This question is asking for a simple understanding of the structures of the peripheral nervous system as compared to the central nervous system. The central nervous system is composed of the brain and spinal cord, and the peripheral nervous system is composed of nerves outside of the brain and spinal cord. Because Guillain-Barré syndrome (GBS) affects only the peripheral nervous system, the neurons in the central nervous system should be unaffected. Of the choices listed, the neurons of the arms and legs, abdominal cavity, and heart are all part of the peripheral nervous system and subject to GBS. The neurons of the spinal cord are part of the central nervous system and should be unaffected by GBS.

42. **The correct answer is A.** The myelin sheath is used to insulate the axons of neurons. Within the myelin sheath there are gaps, known as nodes of Ranvier, where the myelin is absent. Action potentials move down the axon and jump from one node to the next. When the myelin is removed, the gap from one node to the next becomes so large that the action potential can no longer jump the gap. This means that the action potential never reaches the end of the neuron, and the message is not passed to other neurons. Choice A is most indicative of this problem. Choice B suggests that the problem is with the response of muscle cells to the neurotransmitter acetylcholine. If the action potential never reaches the end of the neuron, acetylcholine will not be released to the neuromuscular junction; therefore, the issue is not with the muscle cells' response. The sodium-potassium pumps are used to maintain resting potential in neurons, and there is nothing in the passage or question that would indicate that there is a problem with this. Because GBS is not a problem with the central nervous system, there would be no logical reason to assume that the problem is with the brain.

43. **The correct answer is C.** The passage described Guillain-Barré syndrome (GBS) as a disorder with unknown causes that leads to the production of antibodies from the immune system that attack the peripheral myelin. Because no pattern of inheritance was stated and the disease is unpredictable in terms of who it strikes, there would be no reason to think this is a genetic condition. This allows choices A and B to be eliminated. The passage mentions that GBS can follow an infection in some but not all cases. No other evidence was provided to suggest that GBS is an infection. This leaves choice C as the best answer. Autoimmune diseases are characterized by an immune response to self-structures. Because the immune system is producing antibodies against the peripheral myelin, this would count as an autoimmune condition.

44. **The correct answer is B.** The passage described plasmapheresis as the separation of blood and plasma, where the plasma is discarded and the blood cells are returned to the patient as donated or synthetic plasma. If this helps with the symptoms of GBS, this would indicate that something in the plasma is causing the

problem. The passage indicated that antibodies against myelin cause the demyeli-nation characteristic of GBS. Plasma cells secrete antibodies into fluids of the body, including plasma. By removing the plasma, the antibody concentration is decreased, leading to a reduced level of attack on peripheral myelin.

45. **The correct answer is A.** During a muscle contraction, the sarcomeres contract as the result of myosin heads attaching to actin and pulling the fibers inward. In order for this to occur, ATP and calcium are required. If there were excessive amounts of calcium, you would expect more contractions to occur.

No Passage

46. **The correct answer is A.** Of the hormones listed, the only one that is involved with water levels and the kidneys is antidiuretic hormone. The hormone increases water reabsorption in the nephrons, increasing blood volume and pressure and decreas-ing urine volume. Thyroid-stimulating hormone acts on the thyroid gland to reg-ulate metabolism. Glucagon stimulates the breakdown of glycogen to increase blood sugar levels. Calcitonin is used to decrease blood calcium levels and stimu-late osteoblasts to build new bone matrix.

47. **The correct answer is C.** Pulmonary gas exchange is always based on simple dif-fusion. Diffusion allows for the movement of a substance from an area of high concentration of the substance to an area of low concentration of the substance. Depending on the concentrations, oxygen and carbon dioxide will move in vari-able directions. Choices A, B, and D indicate that the movement of gases always occurs in a fixed direction, which is incorrect.

48. **The correct answer is C.** The hypothalamus is located in the brain, which allows choice D to be eliminated immediately. The cerebrum is the largest portion of the brain that is divided into right and left hemispheres, which are connected by the corpus callosum. The processing of conscious thought and sensory information occurs in the cerebrum. The brain stem consists of the pons (connects the spinal cord to the cerebellum), medulla oblongata (reflex centers for vital functions), and reticular activating system (the activating system for the cerebrum). The hypotha-lamus and thalamus are both located in the diencephalon. The hypothalamus is involved in endocrine regulation as well as regulating conditions such as thirst and hunger.

49. **The correct answer is D.** According to the data, TSH levels are low and T3 and T4 levels are elevated. Choice B suggests that the problem is related to thyroglob-ulin levels. Because this is not mentioned in the data, choice B can be elimi-nated. Choice C directly contradicts the data. The data shows increased levels of T3 (when compared to expected values), and the choice indicates that T3 levels are decreased. The passage indicates an inverse relationship between TSH and T3/T4. When TSH is high, this is in response to low T3 and T4. When TSH is low, this is in response to high levels of T3 and T4. T3 and T4 directly regulate metabolism, so it makes sense that if their levels are elevated, metabolism increases. This is

Passage VIII

characteristic of hyperthyroidism. If T3 and T4 levels were decreased, metabolism should slow, indicating hypothyroidism. As a response to this condition, TSH levels would rise. Based on the data given, choice A should be eliminated because hypothyroidism would cause an increase in TSH levels. This leaves choice D as the only option. The elevated levels of T3 would be characteristic of hyperthyroidism.

50. **The correct answer is A.** To answer this question, you need to be familiar with mechanisms used in the body to maintain calcium homeostasis and bone cell action. The hormones calcitonin and parathyroid hormone both regulate blood calcium levels. Calcitonin, secreted by the thyroid gland, decreases blood calcium by storing excess calcium in bone matrix due to the activity of osteoblasts. Parathyroid hormone, secreted by the parathyroid glands located on top of the thyroid, is antagonistic to calcitonin and increases blood calcium levels. Osteoblasts are bone cells that build bone tissue when there is excess calcium. Their activity is regulated by calcitonin. When active, osteoblasts reduce blood calcium levels. Osteoclasts break down bone tissue and are regulated by parathyroid hormone. When active, osteoclasts increase blood calcium levels. If a patient has had his or her thyroid and parathyroids removed, it would be safe to assume that calcitonin and parathyroid levels would be decreased, making it difficult to regulate blood calcium levels. Choice B suggests that activating osteoblasts would help increase calcium levels. Because osteoblasts build bone and decrease blood calcium, this would actually further decrease the calcium levels in the blood. Taking synthetic calcitonin as suggested by choices C and D would only decrease calcium levels further because calcitonin activates osteoblasts. One potential solution to increase blood calcium levels would be to increase bone matrix breakdown as suggested by choice A. Osteoclasts are the bone cells responsible for this response.

51. **The correct answer is D.** This question relies on your knowledge of the endocrine system. The thyroid gland itself produces T3 and T4 that could be involved with hyperthyroidism, thus eliminating choice C. The thyroid is regulated by thyroid-stimulating hormone (TSH) secreted by the anterior pituitary gland, which eliminates choice B. The anterior pituitary gland is regulated by hormones from the hypothalamus, eliminating choice A. Therefore, the hypothalamus, anterior pituitary, and thyroid gland all could potentially have a role in a thyroid problem. The adrenal glands do not secrete any hormones related to thyroid function, making choice D the correct answer.

52. **The correct answer is D.** This question requires an understanding of the requirements of T3 and T4. Without a certain mineral, neither hormone can function properly. Both T3 and T4 require iodine from the diet to function.

Passage IX 53. **The correct answer is C.** The passage explains that blood doping is used to increase erythrocyte counts in the athlete. Because the function of erythrocytes and hemoglobin is to carry oxygen, it would be expected that an increase in red blood cell count would allow for more oxygen to be transported. This oxygen would be used for electron transport in aerobic cellular respiration, which produces ATP to be used by the athlete.

54. **The correct answer is D.** You know that autologous transfusions come from the athlete's own blood and homologous transfusions come from someone else's blood. Just as is the case with any type of transfusion, there can be problems with incompatibilities or with infectious agents that can be transmitted by infected tissues. Whether the blood transfusion is homologous or autologous, there would be no difference in the ability to carry oxygen by the erythrocytes that would provide an athletic advantage. Autologous transfusions would provide no more erythrocytes than a homologous transfusion. In fact, autologous transfusions often contain fewer cells.

55. **The correct answer is D.** Erythropoietin (EPO) stimulates the cells of the bone marrow to differentiate into new red blood cells. Of the conditions listed, anemia is characterized by a low erythrocyte or hemoglobin count. In this case, additional EPO could stimulate the production of more erythrocytes to correct the condition. Coronary artery disease, hypotension, and renal failure are not associated with erythrocyte deficiencies.

56. **The correct answer is B.** Once the erythrocytes have been collected, the athlete has a low erythrocyte count. His or her own erythropoietin (EPO) is released to stimulate the production of new cells and return the erythrocyte count to normal within a few weeks (similar to what happens to anyone who donates blood). When the erythrocytes are reinfused in the athlete who already has a normal count, they now have extra erythrocytes that can carry more oxygen in the body and perhaps provide an athletic advantage.

57. **The correct answer is B.** The hormones released by the anterior pituitary gland include growth hormone, prolactin, melanocyte-stimulating hormone, endorphins, enkephalins, thyroid-stimulating hormone, adrenocorticotropic hormone, follicle-stimulating hormone, and luteinizing hormone. The hormones released by the posterior pituitary gland include oxytocin and antidiuretic hormone.

No Passage

58. **The correct answer is C.** Acetylcholine is a neurotransmitter found in both the central nervous system (CNS) and the peripheral nervous system (PNS). Because of its presence and function in the CNS and PNS, the impairment of acetylcholine as a direct result of curare exerts a devastating effect on the human body, that is, paralysis.

59. **The correct answer is D.** The pulmonary artery carries deoxygenated blood to the lungs. One would therefore expect it to have the lowest oxygen tension. Blood entering the capillaries around the alveoli from the pulmonary artery does, in fact, have a pO_2 of around 40 mm Hg. Not surprisingly, because it is the source of the O_2

used by the body, inspired air in the alveoli has the highest of the partial pressures: 160 mm Hg. By the time the blood has passed through the capillary beds around the alveoli and into the pulmonary vein, its pO_2 has been raised from 40 mm Hg to 100 mm Hg, which is also the average pO_2 of the air in the alveoli. So the correct values of partial pressures with the corresponding sites are AL: 160 mm Hg, PA: 40 mm Hg; PV: 100 mm Hg.

Section 2. Chemical and Physical Foundations of Biological Systems

1. **The correct answer is B.** Terminal velocity occurs when the drag force exerted on the skydiver becomes equal in magnitude and opposite in direction to the weight of the skydiver. The drag force develops as the air molecules interact with the surface area of the falling skydiver. The greater the surface area of the skydiver that acts perpendicular to the direction of the skydiver's fall, the greater force will be exerted on the skydiver, resulting in a smaller terminal velocity. To the contrary, the smaller the surface area of the skydiver that acts perpendicular to the direction of the skydiver's fall, the smaller force will be exerted on the skydiver, resulting in a larger terminal velocity. From the orientations presented in the options, the one orientation that translates to the smallest surface area and hence the greatest terminal velocity is given by choice B.

2. **The correct answer is C.** Using the relationship

$$\text{density} = \frac{mass}{volume},$$

you can determine the mass of the helium used to inflate the balloon from

$$\text{mass} = (\text{density}) \times (\text{volume})$$

where density $= 0.1785 \, \text{g/cm}^3$ and volume $= 8.5 \times 10^8 \, \text{mL}$, or since $1 \, \text{mL} = 1 \, \text{cm}^3$, volume $= 8.5 \times 10^8 \, \text{cm}^3$. Thus,

$$
\begin{aligned}
\text{mass} &= \left(0.1785 \, \frac{\text{g}}{\text{cm}^3}\right) \times \left(8.5 \times 10^8 \, \text{cm}^3\right) \\
&= 1.52 \times 10^8 \, \text{g} \\
&= 1.52 \times 10^5 \, \text{kg}
\end{aligned}
$$

The weight of the helium used to inflate the balloon can be determined from

$$
\begin{aligned}
\text{weight} &= (\text{mass}) \times (\text{acceleration due to gravity}) \\
&= (1.52 \times 10^5 \, \text{kg}) \times (9.8 \, \text{m/s}^2) \\
&= 14.9 \times 10^5 \, \text{N} \\
&= 1.49 \times 10^6 \, \text{N} \approx 1.5 \times 10^6 \, \text{N}
\end{aligned}
$$

given by choice C.

3. **The correct answer is D.** The initial velocity (v_i) of Felix Baumgartner in the vertical direction is 0, his final velocity (v_f) is 373 m/s, and the acceleration due to gravity is 9.8 m/s² (although in reality it is probably slightly lower because of the significantly

large jumping altitude). The equation of motion that can be used to determine the distance traversed by Baumgartner is:

$$\text{displacement} = \frac{(\text{final velocity})^2 - (\text{initial velocity})^2}{2 \times (\text{acceleration due to gravity})}$$

$$= \frac{\left(373\,\frac{m}{s}\right)^2 - \left(0\,\frac{m}{s}\right)^2}{19.6\,\frac{m}{s^2}}$$

$$= \frac{139{,}129\,\frac{m^2}{s^2} - 0}{19.6\,\frac{m}{s^2}}$$

$$= 7098\,m$$

4. **The correct answer is A.** When an object in free fall reaches terminal velocity, it is in equilibrium. In other words, the drag force acting upward becomes equal in magnitude yet opposite in direction to the object's weight, or:

$$F_d = F_g$$
$$Cv_t^2 = mg$$
$$C = \frac{mg}{v_t^2} = \frac{1{,}156\,N}{\left(373\,\frac{m}{s}\right)^2} = \frac{1{,}156\,N}{139{,}129\,\frac{m^2}{s^2}} = 0.008\,\frac{kg}{m}$$

5. **The correct answer is C.** Terminal velocity occurs for a free-falling object when the drag force (F_d) becomes equal in magnitude yet opposite in direction to the object's weight or force due to gravity (F_g). This is depicted by the free body diagram with the two forces, F_d and F_g, drawn as arrows of equal size in opposite directions, given by choice C.

No Passage

6. **The correct answer is A.** The longest wavelength will have the lowest frequency and the lowest energy. This lowest energy occurs from the transition from $n = 3$ to $n = 2$. The relationship can be found in the equation $E = \frac{hc}{\lambda}$. The energy, E, of a photon is equal to Planck's constant times the speed of light, divided by the wavelength. As the wavelength increases, the value of the denominator increases, decreasing the value of E.

7. **The correct answer is B.** The density of a solution can be determined from $\rho = m/V$, where ρ is the density of the solution (in units of g/cm³), m is the mass of the solution (in units of g), and V is the volume of the solution (in units of cm³). The mass of the solution, m_{sol}, is the total mass of the solution and the syringe, m_{tot}, minus the mass of the syringe, m_{syr}, or

$$m_{tot} = m_{sol} + m_{syr}$$
$$m_{sol} = m_{tot} - m_{syr} = 80\,g - 5\,g = 75\,g$$

The volume of the solution in the syringe is $V_{syr} = 30\,mL = 30\,cm^3$. The density of the solution is:

$$\rho = \frac{m}{V} = \frac{75\,g}{30\,cm^3} = 2.5\,\frac{g}{cm^3}$$

8. **The correct answer is B.** Realizing that the atomic mass is almost at the midpoint value of the two isotopes, you can conclude that the approximate abundance is about 50% for each isotope. This comes closest to choice B. To check, take the relative abundance for each isotope and multiply by the mass number for that isotope. Doing so gives the following: $(0.507)(79) + (0.493)(81) = 40.053 + 39.933 = 79.986$. Considering that there will always be some error in analysis, this is the closest choice to the atomic mass of bromine.

9. **The correct answer is D.** There are four combinations for the bromine atoms: Br-79 and Br-79 (=158), Br-79 and Br-81 (=160), Br-81 and Br-79 (=160), and Br-81 and Br-81 (=162). An m/z ratio of 160 will be detected 50% of the time, whereas the other two m/z ratios occur 25% of the time each.

10. **The correct answer is A.** The electron configuration for bromine is $1s^2 2s^2 2p^6 3s^2 3p^6 4s^2 3d^{10} 4p^5$. Whereas a bromine atom has an unpaired electron, Br_2 does not. Because there are no unpaired electrons, it will be diamagnetic. Br_2 will not be polar because it is diatomic and both atoms have the same electronegativity. Finally, looking at the trend down the halogen family, F_2 will be a gas, as will Cl_2, because of their low atomic masses and low dispersion force attractions. Because I_2 has the greater mass, its dispersion forces allow it to be a solid at room temperature. As per the passage, bromine is a liquid and will be less dense than iodine.

11. **The correct answer is C.** The general trend is that Z_{eff} will increase moving down a family and from left to right across a period. However, because the number of core electrons remains constant while one goes from left to right in a period, the nuclear charge will increase and have a greater effect on the valence electrons. The impact of effective nuclear charge will be greater when moving left to right than from top to bottom on the periodic table.

12. **The correct answer is B.** When $^{80}_{35}Br$ undergoes positron decay, the result is $^{0}_{+1}e + $ $^{80}_{34}Se$. In order to achieve $^{80}_{36}Kr$, two more modes of beta decay need to occur as per the following:

$$^{80}_{34}Se \rightarrow {^{0}_{-1}e} + {^{80}_{35}Br} \quad \text{and} \quad {^{80}_{35}Br} \rightarrow {^{0}_{-1}e} + {^{80}_{36}Kr}$$

13. **The correct answer is B.** This problem can be solved by substituting the results of each scenario into Poiseuille's law and searching for the smallest value. Choice A yields an 8-fold increase in flow. Choice B results in a 32-fold decrease in flow. Choice C yields a 32-fold increase in flow, and choice D results in an 8-fold decrease in flow.

14. **The correct answer is A.** By definition of the two types of lenses, a concave lens increases the focal length of an image, whereas a convex lens reduces the focal

length of an image. Therefore, choices B and C are incorrect and can be immediately excluded. Because myopia results in image formation in front of the retina, the appropriate corrective lens would be a concave lens, which increases the focal length of the image, causing the image to focus past this point and on the retina. Choice A is the correct response. Choice D represents the corrective approach for hyperopia, or farsightedness.

15. **The correct answer is D.** The electrostatic force can be calculated using Coulomb's law:

$$F = k\frac{q_e q_p}{r_{ep}^2} = \left(9 \times 10^9 \, \frac{\text{N} \cdot \text{m}^2}{\text{C}^2}\right) \frac{(-1.6 \times 10^{-19}\,\text{C})(+1.6 \times 10^{-19}\,\text{C})}{(5.3 \times 10^{-11}\text{m})^2}$$

$$= -8.2 \times 10^{-8}\,\text{N}$$

represented by choice D.

Passage III

16. **The correct answer is A.** In single-slit diffraction, light (electromagnetic radiation) passes through a small slit within a diffraction grating and moves toward a screen as wavefronts. As the wavefronts strike the screen, points within the wavefronts will either amplify as a result of constructive interference or cancel each other as a result of destructive interference. The alternating patterns of constructive and destructive interference will result in a pattern of bright and dark fringes on the screen. This observation is indicative of the wavelike behavior of light. Compton scattering involves a two-dimensional elastic collision that can take place only if particles are involved. An electron is a particle, and thus in order to observe the Compton effect, light (electromagnetic radiation) must also behave as a particle.

17. **The correct answer is A.** The interference pattern described in Fraunhofer single-slit diffraction is based on the fact that light behaves as waves. Wavefronts passing through the slit move toward the screen and, depending on the position of the wavefronts, an interference pattern consisting of alternating maxima and minima will result. If the source were composed of particles, the resultant image would depict a linear array of points, consistent with the geometrical constraints of the slit, as illustrated in choice A.

18. **The correct answer is D.** In Compton scattering, a two-dimensional elastic collision occurs between a photon with an incident energy, E_{ph}, and an electron at rest. As the photon collides with the electron, it scatters at some angle θ after transferring a portion of its energy to the electron, which in turn causes it to scatter with an energy, E_{el}, at some angle φ. The energy of the scattered photon, E'_{ph}, is less than the original energy of the photon. From the relation

$$E = hv = h\frac{c}{\lambda},$$

you can see that a reduced energy implies a lower frequency (because energy is directly proportional to frequency) and a longer wavelength (because energy is inversely proportional to wavelength).

19. **The correct answer is A.** This problem requires the application of the conservation of energy:

$$(\text{total energy})_{\text{before collision}} = (\text{total energy})_{\text{after collision}}$$
$$(E_{ph} + E_{el})_{\text{before collision}} = (E'_{ph} + E'_{el})_{\text{after collision}}$$

Although the collision is two-dimensional, only the conservation of energy in the x-direction allows one to develop a relationship between the energy of the Compton-scattered electron and the energy of the incident and scattered photon:

$$(E_{ph} + 0)_{\text{before collision}} = (E'_{ph} \cos(-\theta) + E'_{el} \cos(\phi))_{\text{after collision}}$$

$E_{el} = 0$ because the electron before the collision is at rest. Because cosine is an even function, $\cos(-\theta) = \cos(\theta)$. Therefore,

$$E_{ph} = E'_{ph} \cos(\theta) + E'_{el} \cos(\phi)$$

Solving for E'_{el} yields

$$E'_{el} = \frac{\left[E_{ph} - E'_{ph} \cos(\theta)\right]}{\cos(\phi)}$$

20. **The correct answer is A.** This problem can be solved through the use of unit analysis. The units for Planck's constant, h, are J · s, wavelength, λ, is m, and frequency, v, is 1/s. The question is which combination of these units will yield the units of momentum $\left(\frac{kg \cdot m}{s}\right)$. The term that has units of momentum is h/λ.

21. **The correct answer is A.** The spring constant, k, which is a constant unique to an elastic object that describes the amount of force required to stretch or compress the elastic object by a known distance, can be determined from the data displayed in the first table. Plotting the data with the elastic force, F_{el}, on the y-axis and stretching distance, x_{el}, on the x-axis, the spring constant can be found by taking the slope of the graph. Because the data indicates a linear graph, the slope and thus the spring constant can be found by using the endpoints:

$$k = \text{slope} = \frac{\text{rise}}{\text{run}} = \frac{\Delta F_{el}}{\Delta x_{el}} = \frac{5N - 2N}{0.3m - 0.14m} = \frac{3N}{0.16m} = 18.75\frac{N}{m}$$

Passage IV

22. **The correct answer is D.** The work done in pulling back the slingshot is stored as elastic potential energy, which in turn is transferred to kinetic energy of the moving projectile. Applying the work–kinetic energy theorem:

$$\text{Work} = \text{Elastic Potential Energy} = \text{Change in Kinetic Energy}$$
$$= \frac{1}{2}kx_{el}^2 = \frac{1}{2}mv_f^2 - \frac{1}{2}mv_o^2$$
$$v_f^2 = \frac{k}{m}x_{el}^2 \qquad v_f = \sqrt{\frac{k}{m}}x_{el}$$

23. **The correct answer is C.** The percent error can be found from the following equation and substituting in the appropriate values:

$$\%Error = \left[\frac{\text{Predicted Value} - \text{Observed Value}}{\text{Predicted Value}}\right] \times 100\%$$

$$= \left[\frac{3.94m - 2.64m}{3.94m}\right] \times 100\% = 32.9\% \approx 33\%$$

24. **The correct answer is D.** The horizontal landing distance, Δx, can be determined from the equation:

$$\Delta x = v_x \Delta t$$

From the response to Question 21, the horizontal velocity that the marble leaves the tabletop with is given by:

$$v_f = v_x = \sqrt{\frac{k}{m}} x_{el}$$

The time can be found using the equation for displacement in the y-direction for accelerated motion:

$$\Delta y = \frac{1}{2} g \Delta t^2$$

Solving for Δt yields:

$$\Delta t = \sqrt{\frac{2\Delta y}{g}}$$

Substituting into the previous expression for the horizontal landing distance gives:

$$\Delta x = v_x \, \Delta t = \left[\sqrt{\frac{k}{m}} x_{el}\right]\left[\sqrt{\frac{2\Delta y}{g}}\right]$$

25. **The correct answer is A.** The students are being asked to extrapolate from the data points already collected and displayed in the second table. Performing simple linear regression analysis, the graphed data reveals the following graph of a line:

$$y = 88.3x + 0.895$$

Substituting the value of 10 cm or 0.1 m into the regression line for x, the y-value, or the observed value the students should expect to see when the slingshot is pulled back, to 10 cm is:

$$y = 88.3(0.10) + 0.895 = 9.73 \text{ m}$$

26. **The correct answer is A.** Using the expression for the horizontal landing distance:

$$\Delta x = v_x \, \Delta t = \left[\sqrt{\frac{k}{m}} x_{el}\right]\left[\sqrt{\frac{2\Delta y}{g}}\right]$$

if the mass of the marble were doubled,

$$\Delta x = v_x\,\Delta t = \left[\sqrt{\frac{k}{2m}}\,x_{el}\right]\left[\sqrt{\frac{2\Delta y}{g}}\right]$$

So, in comparison to the original mass of the marble, the horizontal landing distance would decrease by $\sqrt{2}$.

No Passage

27. **The correct answer is C.** The answer choices are best considered as two sets of two: two boat conformations and two chair conformations. Boat conformations in general are almost always of higher energy due to the so-called flagpole interactions shown here:

The distinguishing characteristic between the two chair conformations is that one (choice C) places the chlorine substituent in an equatorial attitude, whereas the other (choice D) forces the substituent to occupy an axial position. An equatorial orientation is almost always energetically preferable.

Passage V

28. **The correct answer is B.** In the decay process of thallium-201, given in the passage as

$$^{201}_{81}\text{Tl} + {}^{0}_{-1}e \rightarrow {}^{201}_{80}\text{Hg} + {}^{0}_{0}\nu$$

it can be seen that the mass number of Tl-201 ($A = 201$) is identical to the mass number of Hg-201 ($A = 201$), the atomic number of Tl-201 ($Z = 81$) is greater than the atomic number of Hg-201 ($Z = 80$), and the neutron number of Tl-201 ($N = 201 - 81 = 120$) is smaller than the neutron number of Hg-201 ($N = 201 - 80 = 121$). Thus, A remains constant, N increases by one, and Z decreases by one. Choice B is the correct choice.

29. **The correct answer is A.** The wavelength of the gamma ray is equal to its energy by the relation:

$$E = hc/\lambda$$

where E is the energy of the electromagnetic radiation (in units of eV), h is Planck's constant ($= 4.15 \times 10^{-15}$ eV $\cdot$ sec), c is the speed of light in a vacuum ($= 3.0 \times 10^8$ m/s), and λ is the wavelength.

$$\lambda = h\frac{c}{E} = (4.15 \times 10^{-15}\ eV \cdot s)\frac{(3.0 \times 10^8\ \text{m/s})}{(167 \times 10^3\ eV)} = 0.074 \times 10^{-10}\ m = 0.074\text{Å}$$

30. **The correct answer is B.** The energy, wavelength, frequency, and speed are related by:

$$E = h\nu = h\frac{c}{\lambda}$$

Because gamma rays have higher energy than x-rays and frequency is linearly proportional to the energy, the frequency is larger as well. Because the wavelength is inversely proportional to energy, the wavelength decreases as the energy increases. The speed of the x-rays, which is the same speed for the gamma ray, is the speed of light in a vacuum and is constant. Thus, choice B is the correct answer.

31. **The correct answer is D.** This problem is solved using the radioactive decay equation:

$$N = N_0 e^{-\left(\frac{0.693}{T_{1/2}}\right) \cdot t}$$

$$\frac{N}{N_0} = e^{-\left(\frac{0.693}{73hr}\right) \cdot 24\,hr} = e^{-0.22} = 0.80$$

Expressed in percentage, the fraction N/N_0 is 80%.

32. **The correct answer is C.** This problem is solved using the radioactive decay equation:

$$N = N_0 e^{-\left(\frac{0.693}{T_{1/2}}\right) \cdot t}$$

$$\frac{N}{N_0} = 0.10 = e^{-\left(\frac{0.693}{73hr}\right) \cdot t} = e^{-(0.0095/hr) \cdot t}$$

Taking the natural logarithm of both sides yields:

$$-2.3 = -(0.0095/hr) \cdot t$$

$$t = \frac{2.3}{0.0095/hr} = 242\ hr \approx 10.1\ days$$

Passage VI   33. **The correct answer is B.** When writing the K_{eq} for a reaction, you need to remember "products over reactants, coefficients become powers." Looking at the reaction in reverse, ammonia is the reactant and the nitrogen and hydrogen gases are the products. This is best demonstrated by choice B.

34. **The correct answer is A.** Because the reaction is exothermic, the addition or presence of heat (a product) will cause more products to be present. More products present will mean that the reaction will shift to produce more reactants. This is why it is vital to cool the ammonia once it is formed. The next two choices favor the reaction to proceed to the right. Choice D, the catalyst, has no effect on the point of equilibrium. However, the catalyst will help equilibrium be achieved faster.

35. **The correct answer is C.** The addition of a catalyst will lower the activation energy by producing an alternative pathway for the reaction to proceed. This makes the potential energy of the activated complex lower. Because the potential energy of the reactants and products does not change, the heat of reaction will not change as well.

36. **The correct answer is D.** The rate-determining step is the slowest of the elementary steps of the reaction. The reaction has to overcome the triple-bonded nitrogen to form nitrogen atoms that need to react. This is why the 79% of the atmosphere that is nitrogen gas is considered inert (for the most part).

37. **The correct answer is D.** Because the reaction is exothermic, the increase in temperature will drive the equilibrium to the left. This causes more reactants to form. A greater concentration of reactants means a greater value in the denominator of the K_{eq} expression and a lower K_{eq} value.

38. **The correct answer is C.** This question touches on four different definitions of acids and bases. Although they do not replace each other, they do enhance each other, depending upon the conditions. Choice A is the classic Arrhenius definition in which H^+ and OH^- neutralize to form water. Choice B shows a proton transfer and demonstrates the Brønsted–Lowry definition. The reaction in choice C shows the ammonia (base) donating a pair of electrons to boron trifluoride (acid), which is indicative of the Lewis definition of an acid–base reaction. The final reaction in choice D shows the less popular Lux–Flood definition in which an O_2^- ion is transferred from the base (CaO) to the acid (SiO_2).

39. **The correct answer is C.** The product shown is the result of a nucleophilic ring opening of an epoxide. Methyl iodide can be discounted because it does not represent a competent nucleophile. Sodium iodide does provide a good nucleophile (iodide), but it would not provide the product shown. The choice then becomes one of base-catalyzed or acid-catalyzed ring opening in methanol. Here the regiochemistry is the deciding factor. Note that the methoxy group ends up at the more substituted position; yet methoxide (Condition A) would attack at the least hindered (less substituted) position. However, under acidic conditions, the protonated epoxide already starts to open, elongating the bond between the oxygen and the more substituted carbon (i.e., more able to sustain positive character). The lone pair on the methanol is then attracted to the developing positive charge at that site, leading to the product shown.

40. **The correct answer is B.** Starting with the chiral center, the priorities can be assigned as follows:

Because the lowest priority is directed away from the observer, and the progression a→b→c describes a clockwise motion, the chiral center is R. The double bond is specified using the same priority rules. Assigning priority to the substituents on either side of the double bond, you have:

Because the two substituents of the same priority are on opposite sides of the double bond, it is given the E(*entgegen*) designation.

41. **The correct answer is C.** Recall that ozonolysis is a type of oxidative cleavage that severs a double bond and, in the case of a reductive workup such as dimethyl sulfide, places a carbonyl at each terminus of the olefin:

Because the total carbon count is the same, choices A and D can be excluded (six carbons and eight carbons, respectively). The decision between choice B and choice C is governed by regiochemistry (the hydroxyl group remains on the three-carbon fragment).

42. **The correct answer is C.** The product of the oxidation is the corresponding ketone, as follows:

The molecular weights of the two compounds are virtually identical; therefore, physical properties are governed primarily by differences in functional groups. Compared to ketones, alcohols can serve as both hydrogen bond donors and acceptors, and thus form more extensive H-bond networks, resulting in higher boiling points (e.g., consider the extraordinarily high boiling point of water). For the same reason, an alcohol tends to bind more tightly to the polar silica gel in chromatography, resulting in lower R_f values.

43. **The correct answer is C.** For the purposes of acidity, the starting material is best classified as a secondary alcohol. A suitable familiar model for such a substrate is 2-propanol (isopropanol), which has a pK_a of about 17.

44. **The correct answer is C.** Aerobic respiration produces far more ATP than does anaerobic respiration. The process of anaerobic respiration produces 2 ATP (both from glycolysis), whereas aerobic respiration produces about 36 ATP from glycolysis, Krebs cycle, and the electron transport chain. The most accurate answer would be choice C.

45. **The correct answer is A.** If the H^+ (proton) gradient were to be destroyed, the electron transport chain would be affected, as it is the only step of cellular respiration that relies on a concentration gradient. You must look for the choice that relates to how a cell performs cellular respiration without an electron transport chain. The only option is to move to anaerobic respiration, which requires fermentation, as indicated by choice A.

46. **The correct answer is D.** S_N2 reactions take place with stronger nucleophiles, leaving groups on primary carbon atoms and at lower temperatures. A polar solvent favors the formation of ions, a characteristic *not* found in S_N2 reactions.

47. **The correct answer is D.** Ethanol has a pK_a of about 16 and, as expected, acetic acid has a pK_a of about 4.8 as the lower pK_a value. Terminal alkynes can give up their terminal hydrogen atoms in a base so as to react and extend the carbon chain when reacted with the proper alkyl halide. A terminal alkyne has a pK_a value of about 25 for its terminal hydrogen atoms. Alkanes are not very acidic at all and have a very high pK_a value of about 50.

48. **The correct answer is C.** This question relies on direct recollection of the steps of aerobic respiration. During the Krebs cycle, CO_2 is released as citric acid, broken down, and rearranged. There is no release of CO_2 in any other steps of aerobic respiration.

49. **The correct answer is D.** The conditions leading to the formation of $N,N,2,2$-tetramethylpropan-1-amine represent reductive amination, which occurs between amines and carbonyl compounds in the presence of a reducing agent such as sodium cyanoborohydride. Because the amine component is given as dimethylamine, consideration of the remaining carbon fragment leads to the conclusion that Compound A is the aldehyde. The conditions leading to Compound B are evocative of the Grignard reaction, which proceeds by nucleophilic addition to a carbonyl.

50. **The correct answer is B.** Sodium cyanoborohydride is a much milder source of hydride than LAH, which allows for its use under the acidic conditions necessary

for iminium formation. If LAH were placed in an environment of pH 5.5, the following reaction would immediately (and violently) ensue:

$$H^- + H^+ \rightarrow H_2(g)$$

51. **The correct answer is C.** Grignard reagents are prepared by the reduction of haloalkanes with magnesium metal, following the mechanism shown here:

52. **The correct answer is D.** Examination of the amine product reveals a methylene group (i.e., two hydrogens) adjacent to the nitrogen. Only one of the hydrogens came from the hydride source (blue); the remaining hydrogen was already attached to the carbonyl carbon, meaning the starting material was an aldehyde.

Passage IX

53. **The correct answer is D.** Choice D shows all correct charges and coefficients for the equation. Five moles of calcium ions contribute +10. Three moles of phosphate ions contribute −9. One mole of hydroxide ions contributes −1. Adding them together results in a net of zero, signifying that the overall charge of the products is equal to the charge of the reactant.

54. **The correct answer is A.** The direction will lie toward the species that is the stronger base. Because hydroxide is a stronger base than fluoride, the equilibrium will lie to the right.

55. **The correct answer is B.** A larger K_{sp} means that the substance is more soluble and that more ions will be produced. Because the ions are the products, a larger K_{sp} means that the products predominate.

56. **The correct answer is B.** A common ion lowers the solubility of the salt. An increase in calcium ion is an increase in the concentration of a product. The equilibrium will then shift to the left so as to consume this increase and make more reactant.

57. **The correct answer is D.** Nine ions are formed when hydroxyapatite dissolves. Because the coefficient of each ion becomes the power of the concentration, you have $[x]^5 \cdot [x]^3 \cdot [x]^1 = [x]^9$.

No Passage

58. **The correct answer is D.** Choice D shows the correct Lewis structure for fluoride ion. A fluorine atom starts with seven valence electrons. Adding one more electron to complete the octet produces an ion with a −1 charge.

59. **The correct answer is** C. Ionic carbonates and hydrogen carbonates (also called bicarbonates) react with acids to form the unstable compound carbonic acid. Carbonic acid rapidly decomposes to carbon dioxide and water. The gas observed is carbon dioxide.

The reaction for carbonates is:

$$CO_3^{2-}(aq) + 2H^+(aq) \rightarrow \text{``}H_2CO_3(aq)\text{''} \rightarrow H_2O(l) + CO_2(g)$$

The reaction for hydrogen carbonates is:

$$HCO_3^-(aq) + H^+(aq) \rightarrow \text{``}H_2CO_3(aq)\text{''} \rightarrow H_2O(l) + CO_2(g)$$

Section 3. Psychological, Social, and Biological Foundations of Behavior

1. **The correct answer is B.** According to frequency theory, pitch perception corresponds to the frequency of vibration of the entire basilar membrane in the inner ear. According to place theory, pitch perception corresponds to the vibration of specific locations along the basilar membrane. Frequency theory cannot account for neurons firing over 1000 times per second, so it is associated only with lower-pitched sounds. The volley theory reconciles the two theories by showing that the neurons work together using the functions described in both place and frequency theories to signal pitch.

2. **The correct answer is C.** If a third tempo of 60 bpm was introduced, it would be in between the *slow* tempo condition (43 bpm) and the *fast* tempo condition (75 bpm). According to Weber's law, a proportional difference in the initial/target and comparison tempos would be necessary for a person to detect a difference. Therefore, the magnitude (number of beats per minute) of the change would need to be greater than the *slow* tempo but less than the *fast* tempo.

3. **The correct answer is D.** If this study used a forced-choice signal detection method, responses could be classified into four categories: miss (failing to identify a changed stimulus), false alarm (identifying an unchanged stimulus as changed), correct rejection (identifying an unchanged comparison as the same as the initial/target stimulus), or hit (correctly identifying a comparison stimulus that differs from the initial/target stimulus). As the magnitude of the comparison tempo increased, the greater would be the likelihood that a participant would perceive a change and the greater the chance that he or she would identify the comparison tempo as different from the initial/target tempo.

4. **The correct answer is A.** According to Weber's law, the JND of a stimulus is in a constant proportion to the intensity/size of the initial/target stimulus. Therefore, the JND must be a constant proportion of the initial/target stimulus. Although the absolute threshold is a similar concept, that term refers to the minimum intensity/size necessary to perceive the existence of a stimulus and does not indicate the amount of change in an existing stimulus necessary to perceive a difference.

5. **The correct answer is A.** The faster the initial/target tempo, the greater the difference needed for detection between the initial and the comparison stimuli. The slower the initial/target tempo, the smaller the difference needed for detection between the initial and the comparison stimuli. The magnitude of the change necessary to perceive differences increases in proportion to the magnitude of the initial/target stimuli. The proportion of difference necessary is constant because the results were consistent with Weber's law.

6. **The correct answer is A.** The occipital lobe is responsible for processing visual images. Further, research examining line orientation has found that specific neurons selectively fire in response to lines of different orientations. This is also consistent with feature integration theory (bottom-up processing).

7. **The correct answer is D.** Janet is displaying an understanding of conservation, whereas Tommy has yet to develop an understanding of conservation. Conservation is characterized by the ability to understand that the amount of a substance within a container remains the same even if the dimensions of the container change. Egocentrism is characterized by difficulty in sharing another person's viewpoint, a problem that is not necessarily represented in the question. Reversibility is not necessary for an understanding of conservation and is associated with a more complex understanding about state changes in objects and numbers. Object permanence is developed earlier, during the sensory motor stage.

8. **The correct answer is A.** The sensory motor stage is associated with the development of motor coordination and a memory of past events. During this stage, children master the concept of object permanence. Object permanence is characterized by the knowledge that an object continues to exist even when out of view of the child.

9. **The correct answer is B.** Assimilation is characterized by the ability to absorb new ideas and experiences and to incorporate them into existing mental structures. Accommodation is the process of modifying previously developed mental structures and behaviors and adapting them to new experiences.

10. **The correct answer is C.** The preoperational stage is characterized by the increased use of mental images and symbols. A key characteristic of the preoperational stage is egocentrism, in which the child is unable to see the world externally. To the child, the world does not exist by itself and only exists to satisfy the child's interests and needs.

11. **The correct answer is C.** Positive psychology is a growing field that examines positive stress and emotions and how positive psychological processes keep humans mentally healthy and resilient.

12. **The correct answer is B.** The Schachter–Singer theory of emotion posits that a stimulus triggers an autonomic arousal in the body (sympathetic nervous system), which causes a person to appraise the environmental context and, based on that appraisal, to interpret the emotion. This is the only theory that requires active appraisal of the environmental context, which is critical because the same autonomic experience in a different context may trigger a different emotion to be identified.

13. **The correct answer is B.** Japanese athletes described fewer self-focused emotions than American athletes. Additionally, Japanese athletes described more self+

other–focused emotions than American athletes. However, Japanese athletes described slightly more self-focused emotions than self+other–focused emotions.

14. **The correct answer is A.** The James–Lange theory posits that a stimulus creates autonomic arousal, causing the individual to identify an emotional state. The Cannon–Bard theory of emotion posits that a physiological arousal can occur without the emotion and that the stimulus simultaneously triggers autonomic arousal by the thalamus and the labeling of the emotion. The Schachter–Singer theory posits that stimuli trigger an autonomic arousal in the body, which causes the individual to appraise the environmental context in order to determine the emotional response.

15. **The correct answer is B.** Conducting the experiment on additional groups from different cultures could yield more information about culture-specific differences in populations. A memory recall task and repeated measures of the same group would most likely not reveal any new information. Likewise, measuring arousal would not be very likely to result in new information.

16. **The correct answer is B.** Episodic memory is characterized as the ability to remember and consciously reexperience past events. Semantic memory is characterized by memory of facts.

No Passage

17. **The correct answer is D.** Interference primarily occurs at the encoding stage of learning information. This is true, regardless of whether it is retroactive or proactive interference. In rare circumstances it can also interfere with retrieval.

18. **The correct answer is C.** The Young–Helmholtz theory of color vision posits that color vision depends on three pigment receptors. Each of these receptors has different spectral sensitivities. Light of a particular wavelength activates the pigment receptors to different degrees, and the pattern of activity represents the perceived color. Ewald Hering proposed the opponent-process theory of color vision. This theory posits that color vision is caused by opposing responses generated by blue and yellow wavelengths and by red or green wavelengths (black and white are also sometimes added).

Passage IV

19. **The correct answer is C.** The photo receptors will all respond to the wavelength of light. However, certain wavelengths will result in increased relative activation compared to others. This relative activation results in the perception of color.

20. **The correct answer is B.** The trichromatic (Young–Helmholtz) theory posits that receptors are stimulated within a range of wavelengths. So although they are preferentially stimulated by certain wavelengths, they respond to many. This is true for both rods and cones. Further, the combination of the three cone pigment receptors creates the perceived color.

21. **The correct answer is D.** A person lacking red- or green-sensitive cone pigment receptors would have red-green color blindness. The photoreceptors' stimulation

curves overlap substantially, and the lack of either can be classified as red-green color blindness.

22. **The correct answer is A.** Wavelength stimulates the cone receptors. The combination of stimulation from the wave creates the perception of color. The perception of brightness results from the amplitude of the wave. The intensity of the stimulation increases, but the relative activation of the cone receptors stays relatively the same.

No Passage

23. **The correct answer is A.** The psychoanalytic theory is characterized by the interaction between the id (basic needs and wants), the ego (based on realistic expectations), and the superego (mediator of both the id and the ego).

Passage V

24. **The correct answer is C.** Accidents were more likely during the early morning. The data collected show two peaks. The first is in the early morning hours. The second, smaller peak is during the late afternoon. However, the early morning peak is the most substantial peak.

25. **The correct answer is B.** The accident peaks would drift to the right on the graph with a slightly longer circadian cycle. In the absence of circadian cues, sleep research has shown that the human circadian cycle has been shown to drift toward 25 hours rather than 24. In this artificial case the main accident peak would continue to occur at the trough of the cycle and so would shift along with it.

26. **The correct answer is D.** Circadian timing is flexible but highly dependent on light, which will push the circadian cycle toward the daylight hours. Research suggests that exposure to light moves the circadian cycle toward the active daylight hours and is a cue that strongly influences behavior.

27. **The correct answer is D.** The suprachiasmatic nucleus located in the hypothalamus is the brain structure that seems to readjust the biological clock based on light exposure. Because some retinal pathways bypass the occipital lobe and project light information directly to the suprachiasmatic nucleus, it is possible for some individuals who are blind but still have this pathway intact to have normal circadian rhythms that respond to light.

No Passage

28. **The correct answer is A.** Individuals can experience an exacerbation of symptoms of existing medical conditions. Somatoform disorders are characterized by the experience of a medical condition that is exacerbated or alleviated by psychological conditions. They are often mistaken for factitious disorders, in which symptoms are intentionally created, or malingering, in which symptoms are reported but not experienced by the individual. True somatoform disorders are not intentional. Pain has multiple psychosocial factors that affect the pain experience, and all pain has a psychosomatic component to it.

Passage VI

29. **The correct answer is A.** The majority of participants (65%) obeyed the authority figure to the point that they administered what they believed were lethal shocks.

30. **The correct answer is A.** The participant teacher would typically obey the authority figure despite discomfort or pain exhibited by the learner. Most participants continued to administer shocks at the insistence of the authority figure until the shocks appeared to be potentially lethal.

31. **The correct answer is D.** The group discussion makes ethics more salient to the participant teachers, and the influence of the group is likely to polarize the individual toward increasing the importance of ethics through groupthink phenomena.

32. **The correct answer is A.** In social psychology research, obedience represents compliance to direct commands from an authority figure.

No Passage

33. **The correct answer is C.** For such a small amount of money, Jack could not justify that he was doing the dishes for the money; therefore, cognitive dissonance theory indicates he will change his attitude about the chore. Cognitive dissonance results when there is a disconnect between an individual's actions and beliefs. When these are at odds, the individual will often change his or her attitudes or beliefs to bring them into line with his or her actions.

34. **The correct answer is C.** The unconditioned stimulus would be paired with the conditioned stimulus in initial trials on day 1. The unconditioned stimulus is paired with the conditioned stimulus during learning trials. In the graph, the saliva is shown to increase only during trials in which the pairing is present (day 1; trials 2–16). The increase between days is typical of spontaneous recovery.

Passage VII

35. **The correct answer is D.** The conditioned stimulus would be present on trials over the course of all three days. The conditioned stimulus would be paired with the unconditioned stimulus on initial trials on day 1 (during pairing/learning). It would also be present during the extinction and spontaneous recovery trials on the remaining day 1 trials, as well as the trials over the next two days.

36. **The correct answer is D.** Only the food elicits a response prior to conditioning. The food is the unconditioned stimulus and will elicit the saliva response without any conditioning. During trials, the bell is paired with the food and will elicit the conditioned response by itself in absence of the unconditioned stimulus. However, the response to the conditioned stimulus will drop over time without any new unconditioned stimulus–conditioned stimulus pairings.

37. **The correct answer is A.** The increase is consistent with the concept of spontaneous recovery. This phenomenon has been noted in certain classical conditioning paradigms. It is characterized by the reappearance of an extinguished response after a period of nonexposure to the conditioned stimulus.

38. **The correct answer is A.** During the industry versus inferiority stage, an individual must successfully integrate into larger social networks and become competent in academics. Once this conflict is resolved, the individual then progresses to the identity versus role confusion stage.

No Passage

39. **The correct answer is** C. The infant monkeys preferred to spend more time with the cloth surrogate, regardless of whether they took food from the cloth surrogate or the wire surrogate. The data indicates that monkeys fed by either surrogate (cloth or wire) spent more time with the cloth surrogate.

40. **The correct answer is** B. Infant monkeys prefer the cloth surrogate because they were more attached to the emotional comfort that the cloth provides. The data shows that regardless of which surrogate fed the infant monkeys, they preferred spending time with the more comforting cloth surrogate.

41. **The correct answer is** A. The infant monkeys would seek comfort from the cloth surrogate, regardless of which surrogate they took food from. The monkeys would seek comfort from the cloth surrogate because they had become emotionally attached to the cloth surrogate. They would prefer the surrogate with which they had formed an attachment if presented with a stimulus-eliciting fear.

42. **The correct answer is** B. This potential design would allow you to see whether attachment could be formed to the wire surrogate if given the right conditions. Using adult monkeys would not help you learn more about attachment in infant monkeys. Feeding monkeys from both surrogate types at the same time would most likely not result in any differences, because the infant monkeys already have shown their preference for the comforting (cloth) surrogate over the wire surrogate.

43. **The correct answer is** B. Low self-esteem results from low self-efficacy and an external locus of control. Low self-efficacy beliefs such as feeling that you cannot succeed and an external locus of control such as feeling that events are outside of your control are associated with low self-esteem.

44. **The correct answer is** C. Based on the data shown in the second figure, students were more likely to judge their own team's correct scores as resulting from study and preparation and their opponents' correct scores as resulting from test question bias.

45. **The correct answer is** A. Participants in the survey believed that correct scores for their team were the result of study and preparation (internal factor) and that correct scores for the other team were the result of test question bias.

46. **The correct answer is** A. Students would say that their own team picked wrong answers due to test question bias, but their opponents picked wrong answers due to lack of study and preparation. This is consistent with attribution theory, which posits that one's own personal successes are attributed to internal characteristics, but others' successes are due to external factors. Conversely, one's own failures (wrong answers) are attributed to external factors (test question bias), whereas others' failures are attributed to internal factors (lack of study and preparation).

47. **The correct answer is D.** Self-serving bias is the tendency to attribute personal successes to personal traits/characteristics and personal failures to external causes. This answer is consistent with self-serving bias.

48. **The correct answer is B.** Both mental health hospitals and prisons are institutions.

No Passage

Passage X

49. **The correct answer is C.** Within each group of three vertical bars, the bar on the left represents the percentage of the U.S. population that identifies as that racial/ethnic group, and the bar in the middle represents the percentage of bachelor's degrees earned by that racial or ethnic group. The bar in the middle is higher than the bar on the left only for the Asian and white populations.

50. **The correct answer is D.** In the graph, the third vertical bar in each group represents the percentage of women earning more bachelor's degrees than men within that racial or ethnic group. In every case, the presence of the bar indicates that women earn more than 50 percent of the bachelor's degrees. If the women in a group were earning fewer bachelor's degrees than men, there would be no vertical bar in that position.

51. **The correct answer is C.** Although choices A, B, and D may be true, interest levels, financial aid, or career choice cannot be extrapolated from this graph. The only conclusion is that women are more successful than men at completing bachelor's degrees.

52. **The correct answer is A.** Research suggests that a woman's ascribed status (mother, wife) may have a greater influence on her overall status in U.S. society than her personal and educational accomplishments. Women's ascribed statuses may also have greater role demands than men's (e.g., for a woman in the United States, being a "parent" and "wife" usually still requires assuming more than 50 percent of child care and household responsibilities, as compared to a man's role demands as a "parent" and "husband").

53. **The correct answer is C.** Intelligence does not differ among SES groups. However, opportunities that allow a person to take advantage of his or her intelligence are rarer among lower SES groups. Individuals who hold a just world theory commonly use blame-the-victim techniques (e.g., claiming that someone is in poverty because he or she deserves it) to explain why they do not experience a negative event (e.g., "I am not in poverty because I work harder"). Social reinforcement is a better explanation of decreased social mobility among established societies. Lower SES individuals encounter greater environmental health risks, fewer economic opportunities, and fewer educational opportunities, all of which maintain the status quo SES. Research has shown that lower and higher SES individuals do not differ in their ability to make good choices about their opportunities. However, individuals from lower SES have fewer opportunities, and any poor decisions that they make have a greater impact on their SES trajectory.

No Passage

54. **The correct answer is A.** Sandra moved from lower SES to middle SES due to an improvement of her educational opportunities and an increase in her human capital. She avoided the social reproduction of maintaining her parents' lower SES. Social stratification does exist in this scenario, but the scenario shows movement across social strata, so social mobility is a better answer. Nepotism does not apply because Sandra's family members were not in a position to provide her with a higher-paying position upon graduation.

55. **The correct answer is A.** Functionalist theory supports societal stratification as a way to reward the best-qualified individuals and lure them into the positions that are the most critical to the functioning of that society.

Passage XI   56. **The correct answer is D.** The graph can tell you *only* the relationship between distance from the airport and nighttime activity. You have to make the cognitive leap that nighttime movements can be a distal measure of sleep coherency. There is a likely association, but because actigraphy is not the most proximal measure of sleep coherency, you cannot make a definitive statement.

57. **The correct answer is C.** Negative amenities tend to decrease housing costs in the affected area, which means that individuals with lower financial resources can afford to live in that area. It is important to note that individuals will report that they "adapt" to noisy environments, but in reality psychology studies show that they continue to have the same level of physiological activation in response to noise disruption and there is no physiological adaptation.

58. **The correct answer is A.** Because actigraphy is a good measure of movement, but is only a distal measure of sleep coherency, the logical next step would be to make sure that sleep coherency is really affected by airport noise using the more proximal measure of direct EEG measurements of sleep.

59. **The correct answer is C.** All of the other answers are known outcomes from living near negative amenities with high levels of noise pollution, but improved productivity is not. Individuals living near airports are more likely to experience disrupted sleep leading to increased illness (due to inefficient immune systems), poorer grades (due to difficulty concentrating and sleep deprivation), and more car accidents (for the same reason as poorer grades).

Section 4. Critical Analysis and Reasoning Skills

1. **The correct answer is D.** This question has to do with interpreting vocabulary. Your first step in answering it is to scan the passage to find the word *elusive*. It appears in paragraph 2, in the context of qualities of happiness. It is not used in a negative connotation, as choices A and B (both synonyms for *lying*) would indicate. Choice C doesn't work with the other quality of happiness, which is mysterious. Something that is frank, or honest and forthright, cannot also be mysterious. Choice D is therefore the best answer.

2. **The correct answer is C.** You need to assess evidence for this question. Because authors ideally use examples to support their statements, you need to find the information that explains why Watson's study was thought to be startling. By scanning paragraph 2 for the exact reference, you will find that the second sentence contains the answer: "Because happiness was considered a highly desired yet elusive and mysterious emotion, Watson's serious endeavor was startling." This is a clear giveaway that choice C is correct.

3. **The correct answer is B.** This question asks you to locate details within the passage. If one statement stands out as false, you can eliminate all other answer choices. But often, it is easier to answer this type of question by eliminating the true statements. The last two sentences of paragraph 3 contain the information in choice A, so you can eliminate it. Paragraph 5 corresponds with choice C, and paragraph 4 corresponds with choice D. Choice B is the correct answer because the passage states that "findings show the mind–body connection cannot be denied," not that science is attempting to prove the connection.

4. **The correct answer is A.** You are asked to identify cause and effect as it is implied in the passage for this question. Note that the example of a subject repeating the phrase, "I am successful" does not appear in the passage. However, the last paragraph notes that repetition of a positive affirmation can lead to an increase in left cerebral cortex activity and increased feelings of happiness and well-being. "I am successful" is such an affirmation, and you could expect choice A, a feeling of well-being, to be the outcome following its repetition.

5. **The correct answer is C.** This question looks at cause and effect, not as directly presented in the essay, but rather as implied by the essay. Whittier and Holmes are mentioned once as contemporaries of Longfellow who also employed similar themes and rhymes. Because Longfellow's reputation is said to suffer because of these very themes and rhymes, it may be implied that the reputations of Whittier and Holmes suffer a similar fate. There is no evidence in the passage to support choice A, so it should be eliminated. Choice B is too negative; neither Longfellow nor Whittier and Holmes are said to be held in contempt or disdain. Choice D is in opposition to the ideas found in the passage. Modern poetry is influenced

by Whitman, not Longfellow, Whittier, and Holmes. Choice C works best, with "antiquated" echoing paragraph 1's "quaint and primly Victorian."

6. **The correct answer is B.** You are asked to find the main idea in this question. This type of question is passage based, meaning you should focus on what is actually said as opposed to what may be implied or suggested. To answer it, ask "What is the author trying to say?" Typically, at least one answer choice is not found within the passage. In this case, choices C and D can be easily eliminated for that reason—neither is stated. Another type of distracter is an answer choice that is too narrow to be the main idea of the passage. Choice A is a good example; the passage encompasses much more than a simple comparison of free verse as opposed to rhymes. You are left with choice B, which is the correct answer.

7. **The correct answer is A.** This question asks you to assess evidence. To answer it, first note the hypothesis as stated in the question stem: Whitman was responsible for the radical shift in American poetry. Then determine which statements support it and which one does not. The one that does not is the correct answer. The fact that his poetry was personal and intimate (choice B) supports the hypothesis, as does his use of free verse (choice D). Choice C, choosing as his subjects the common man and commonplace events, also supports the hypothesis. Nowhere in the passage does it state that Whitman used iconic American figures as his subjects; in fact, that is what Longfellow did, and his poetry was what Whitman's shifted away from. That means choice A is correct.

8. **The correct answer is D.** To answer this question, you need to interpret vocabulary. Find the phrase in the passage and examine it in context. The sentence in paragraph 1 in which it is found reads, "Why do his contemporaries continue to be enjoyed and studied while Longfellow languishes in the tomb of cultural artifacts?" There is a dichotomy set up between continuing to be enjoyed and studied and languishing in the tomb of cultural artifacts. Being in "the tomb of cultural artifacts" is therefore the opposite of being enjoyed and studied. Only one answer choice relates to the idea of this dichotomy; if Longfellow's work is "considered to be dead," it is surely not being enjoyed and studied. Choice D is the best answer.

9. **The correct answer is B.** In this question, you are drawing conclusions about the author's intent, choosing the best or most likely answer. Sales figures for Longfellow's poems about iconic American figures are cited as facts and not implied to be an apparent belief of the author, making choice A incorrect. Although Emerson is revealed to be an influence on Whitman, there is nothing in the passage to suggest that he could be considered by the author to be the Father of American Poetry (in fact, he is not mentioned as being a poet), making choice C incorrect. The passage clearly delineates the vast differences between the work of Longfellow and confessional poetry; therefore, choice D must also be wrong. The terms the

author uses to describe Whitman and his work in the last paragraph ("ground-breaking," "legacy") enforce his view that Whitman's poetry is more popular than Longfellow's (that resides in a "tomb").

10. **The correct answer is D.** This question asks you to apply new evidence to an existing argument. The new evidence is an ambivalent statement by Ezra Pound, in which he both declares his distaste for much of Whitman's work while still admiring it enough to imitate it. The author declares that Pound celebrated his debt to Whitman, which is neither repudiated nor endorsed (choices A and B) by Pound's ambivalence. Similarly, the second part of the statement (regarding imitation) does not deny the author's contention. Choice D is the correct answer because it identifies the passage's use of *celebrate* as too positive a word in light of Pound's "pain" in reading Whitman.

11. **The correct answer is D.** This kind of question asks you to choose an accurate summary. The sales figures are cited to back up the author's assertion that Longfellow's poems were "incredibly popular" (choice D). Choice C is a tricky diversion; although the author does note that sales figures for *The Song of Hiawatha* were "astounding for the time," he does not state or infer that those numbers marked a milestone.

12. **The correct answer is D.** This question asks you to interpret vocabulary. In the context of the passage, the word *province* is used to indicate something that belongs only to humans and to no other living creatures. The answer choice closest in meaning to this is choice D, "domain." Choices A and B are part of the definition of the word *province,* but they are not how the word is used in this context. The passage states that some believe rights are appropriate only for humans, but says nothing about responsibility, as choice C says.

Passage III

13. **The correct answer is D.** For this question, you'll have to use the information in the passage to make predictions. Based on the information in the passage, you need to predict which of the rights in the answer choices a utilitarian would not believe an animal has. The fifth paragraph states that a utilitarian would believe that animals had a right to be free from unnecessary pain and suffering, but that they may not have rights that they don't have the capacity to possess. Choices A, B, and C all indicate actions that would cause the animal pain or suffering. But an animal does not have the right to possess anything, because property is a human concept. This makes choice D the best answer.

14. **The correct answer is A.** You'll have to draw conclusions to answer this question. Look back at the passage to find what Bentham and Sidgwick believe. Bentham states that the interests and desires of the members of a system are all equal; Sidgwick states that the Universe treats all goods as equal. Thus choice A is the best answer. Choice B is unsupported because although the passage states that Bentham believes animals should have equal consideration, it is not clear that

Sidgwick believes that. The passage states that Bentham is unconcerned with the issue of whether animals can reason, so his view on it is unknown, as is Sidgwick's, which eliminates choice C. And it is not clear what Sidgwick believes about whether animals have the capacity to suffer (choice D).

15. **The correct answer is B.** This question asks you to analyze an argument. Remember that everything an author includes in a passage is there for a reason. What role do the parenthetical inserts play in the development of the author's thesis? The discussion of Bentham indicates that Bentham is focusing not on issues of reason or speech—which are unimportant—but on the capacity to suffer, which is the key point. Choice B reflects this sentiment. There is no evidence to support choice A. The views discussed are Bentham's, not those of animal rights supporters (choice C). And the inserts serve to emphasize the important point of Bentham's argument, not to head off possible objections as in choice D.

16. **The correct answer is D.** Again, you'll have to make predictions to answer this question. Use the information the passage provides on utilitarianism to predict which situation could not be justified. Choice A is okay because the passage states that as long as the sum total of happiness increases, the action is okay. Thus in certain circumstances it may be necessary to use an individual in such a way that benefits many others. Choice B can be justified because the death penalty may increase the overall good by ridding the world of a dangerous person. Similarly, torture (choice C) may be justified if it saves the lives of other people. However, indiscriminate killing is not acceptable to a utilitarian. The killing would have to be directed to somehow increasing the good of other people.

17. **The correct answer is A.** This question asks you to find the main idea. The passage states that there is a debate about the validity of animal rights and utilitarianism and provides a framework from which both advocates and opponents of animal rights may view the situation. This is what choice A states. The passage does show how to justify animal rights, as choice B states, but it also shows how to justify not having animal rights. Choice C is wrong because the passage presents arguments for both positions. And choice D is wrong because although Bentham's and Sidgwick's views are mentioned, their ideas form only one part of the larger debate.

Passage IV 18. **The correct answer is A.** You are asked to interpret vocabulary for this question. The sentence states that the bohemian culture rejected limits placed on the society. A cultured person recognizes the standards agreed on by society for certain behaviors, and so a bohemian would reject them. Although the word *polite* could be used to mean the words in choices B, C, and D, this is not how the word is used in this context.

19. **The correct answer is D.** The question asks you to make generalizations. In general, the bohemian is against limits placed on the individual by society. Current fashion

trends represent one way a society may limit an individual by dictating what sort of dress is acceptable. The prevailing mores of a society are the values that the society at large deems appropriate. Capitalism is also a product of the society, and a bohemian would reject thinking in the same way as the rest of the people. Thus all three statements are appropriate, and choice D is the best answer.

20. **The correct answer is C.** For this question, you must draw conclusions. The author does not directly state choice C, but implies it by saying that the Education Act led to a literate, although not necessarily educated, public. This part of the passage also makes choice A incorrect. Choice B is not supported, because the act dealt only with elementary education. Choice D cannot be inferred. It is true that the author believes the act furthered the gulf between artist and public, but it is not clear whether artists were angry about it.

21. **The correct answer is B.** This is a fairly straightforward question asking about supporting details. The answer is found at the end of paragraph 2, where the author states that the degree to which the audiences were fragmented occurred at an unprecedented rate. This supports choice B. There is no support for the other choices in the passage.

22. **The correct answer is B.** This is another question asking you to draw conclusions. The author states that the late Victorian period was marked by pessimism and stoicism and that the authors mentioned all demonstrated such sentiments. Thus it can be concluded that they were influenced by the trends of their time. It is not clear whether they were popular or esteemed, as choices A and C indicate. Nor does the passage state what audience they wrote for, which means choice D is not supported.

23. **The correct answer is A.** This is a question that asks you to modify conclusions. The author contends that after the Georgian period, the old European order was no more. However, if the literature returned to its old Victorian ways, as choice A indicates, the author's conclusion would be incorrect. The developments in America detailed in choice B would be irrelevant to the author's argument. If the artists reintegrated into society as in choice C, it would indicate a change in the prevailing system, not a return to old ways. Choice D also is immaterial to the argument.

24. **The correct answer is C.** This question asks you to find the main idea. This passage explains that theoretically, a massive amount of computational power is available. However, practical considerations make it unlikely that this limit would ever be reached. Thus choice C is the best answer. Choice A is a detail provided in the passage, but it is not the main idea. Choice B is incorrect, because the advances discussed are still primarily theoretical. Choice D is also only partly correct, because it doesn't deal with the practical limits mentioned in the passage.

25. **The correct answer is A.** This question asks you to analyze an argument. The author mentions thermonuclear explosions in the same sentence in which it is

Passage V

stated that the discussion of computing power is purely theoretical. Choice A best reflects this. No other answer choice is supported by the information in the passage.

26. **The correct answer is A.** You are asked to draw a conclusion in order to answer this question. The author indicates that choices B and D are still in the realm of the theoretical. The author also states that the memory limit in choice C may be "exceeded." That leaves choice A, which is supported when the author states that the calculation of the computer's power is based on "the most conservative estimates" of human computational power. Thus the proposed computers can be even more powerful than the author describes.

27. **The correct answer is B.** This question asks about supporting details and evidence. Go back to the passage and find why the author believes technology may reach the theoretical limit discussed. In the last paragraph, the author indicates that each technological advance provides the basis for further evolution, as choice B states. Choice A refers to the author's discussion of memory capacity, not computational power, and indicates a way technicians may exceed the theoretical limits described. Choice C has nothing to do with reaching the theoretical limits of computational power. The technology to reach the limits does not yet exist, as choice D seems to indicate.

28. **The correct answer is D.** This question requires you to combine information. The passage discusses computers, technology, and even physics. However, the information is presented at the level of someone with a casual, rather than expert, knowledge of these fields. Thus choice D would be the best answer. Choice A may be close, but the information in the passage is not written at the level of expertise that a reader would expect in an academic journal.

29. **The correct answer is C.** The question asks you to solve a problem. To answer it, you must first understand how computational power is calculated. The passage states that the power is found by dividing the total energy by the energy required for an operation. Decreasing the amount of energy, as in choice C, would yield a larger quotient. Choice A would do the opposite, and choices B and D would decrease the total energy available.

30. **The correct answer is A.** This question asks you to draw a conclusion. Based on the information in the passage, choice A is the best choice. The passage indicates that thus far, researchers have only been able to store information on a few atoms. Choice B is practically the opposite of what the passage states, whereas the information in choice C is suggested by the author as a way to exceed the theoretical memory limit. The work at the University of Oklahoma relates to memory capacity, not computing power, as choice D indicates.

Passage VI 31. **The correct answer is C.** This question asks you to find the main idea. This passage discusses the basic structure of language and specifically a feature of the English language, namely its paucity of verb forms. Choice C is the best summary of the passage. Choice A is not the main idea of the passage at all. Choice B is too strong. It is not stated that each and every language is unique. Choice D is wrong because the passage states the English language is able to convey a number of meanings even though its verb forms are limited.

32. **The correct answer is A.** This application question asks you to draw conclusions. The author states that the English language makes do with fewer verb forms than other languages, but it still can convey different meanings. This makes choice A correct. Choices B and D are not supported by the passage, and choice C reflects what some linguists believe.

33. **The correct answer is C.** This question involves analyzing an argument. Statement I is supported by the examples of the Spanish language and the Kivunjo language, which have far more forms than the English language. Statement II is unsupported by a specific example. Statement III is supported by the example in the final paragraph of the different meanings of similar-sounding verb forms, which makes choice C the best answer.

34. **The correct answer is B.** In order to answer this question, you'll need to combine information. The passage provides interesting information on language and specifically on the English language. However, it is not directed at linguists (choice A), who presumably would already know much of the information. A language teacher (choice B) would most likely find the information interesting background to a language lesson. It is not clear what psychologists would find interesting in the passage. Translators may find the information interesting, but nothing in the passage pertains specifically to translation, so choice B is a better answer.

35. **The correct answer is B.** This question tests your ability to make predictions. Based on the information in the passage, you need to predict which sentence may strike a Spanish speaker as odd. The passage states that in Spanish, the stem of the verb is not a word. In English, one use of the stem of the verb is in the infinitive form, as used in choice B, "to see." The past tense (choice A), the third-person singular (choice C), and the gerund form (choice D) all involve changing the stem, which is similar to the Spanish language.

36. **The correct answer is B.** This question asks about supporting details. The passage states that the present tense (statement I) is usually expressed using the stem form of the verb, but can also be expressed in the third-person singular by using the -*s* suffix. Similarly, verbal adjectives (statement II) are sometimes expressed using the -*ing* suffix and sometimes with the -*ed* suffix.

37. **The correct answer is B.** This question requires you to draw conclusions. From the information in the passage, what can be concluded about the Russian language? Its lack of pronounceable stems for its verbs makes it similar to Spanish and different

from English. Furthermore, the passage states that English is unlike many Indo-European languages in its use of the stem form as a word. From this information, a linguist may conclude that Russian might (but not necessarily) be part of the Indo-European family. Just because the stem forms are not pronounced gives no information on the number of forms, as choice A states. Choice C is not a valid inference based on the information in the passage. The lack of pronounced stem verbs says nothing about the number of inflections, which are the ways a word changes when taking on different roles in the sentence.

Passage VII

38. **The correct answer is D.** You are asked to find the main idea of the last paragraph. In the last paragraph, the author states that Smith "had inspired many of the changes for which his rival is now known." His rival was Roosevelt, and the implication is that Roosevelt took credit for many ideas that began with Smith. There is no indication that Roosevelt would have done better on a ticket with Smith (choice A), and Smith's background is not a topic of this paragraph (choice C). Contrary to choice B, many of Smith's ideals were those that formed the foundation of the New Deal.

39. **The correct answer is B.** Although choice A may be true, only choice B is alluded to in the passage, allowing you to draw conclusions. New York City, says the author, was "viewed even in the early twentieth century as disconnected from the national character."

40. **The correct answer is D.** Without knowing more about the two rivals, any one of these answers might be possible, but the only one that is supported by the text is choice D. Roosevelt's ambition led to political maneuvering that shut Smith out of the nomination. This is a cause-and-effect question.

41. **The correct answer is B.** The discussion of nativism shows that Smith was not a credible candidate to many because of his Catholic immigrant background. It has nothing to do with his eligibility (choice A); it has to do with the bigotry of the electorate. This is an example of interpreting vocabulary.

42. **The correct answer is D.** Either choice A or choice B might be true, but neither is supported by a cause-and-effect relationship presented in the text. Davis was chosen as a "compromise candidate" when the delegates failed to choose between Smith and McAdoo.

43. **The correct answer is B.** The author presents supporting details about Smith's many successes in the state of New York, from his work as Speaker of the Assembly to his many years as governor. Choice A does not support the claim that he was successful, and choice C actually belies the claim. The list of names mentioned in choice D does not exist in the passage.

44. **The correct answer is A.** Smith was a progressive born of immigrant parents, and he supported both civil liberties and unions, as well as "those he saw as most in

need of government's assistance." Of the answers given, only choice A is likely. This question requires you to combine information.

45. **The correct answer is B.** This is a comprehension question on finding the main idea. This kind of question does not require you to go beyond the boundaries of the passage. You should think, "What is the author trying to say?" In fact, the author never says choice A at all. Although the point is made that megacities are more often found in less developed nations, the second half of that statement does not appear in the passage. Nor does the author discuss decimation of the countryside and limitations in our ability to grow food, as choice C would indicate. And although you might infer choice D, the author never makes any such assertion. The best answer, the one that best conforms simply to the words on the page, is choice B.

46. **The correct answer is C.** This comprehension question has to do with supporting details and evidence. You can answer it easily if you scan the passage for the word *demographer* and then see what information is directly presented. In paragraph 1, demographers "are referring to the 21st century as 'the urban century.'" In paragraph 6, "demographers foresee ecological overload, homelessness, uncontrolled traffic, infrastructure strained to the breaking point." Based on your quick scan of the passage, there is no evidence to support choices A, B, or D. The answer is clearly choice C.

47. **The correct answer is A.** This evaluation question requires you to analyze an argument. Questions like this ask you to explain why an author included certain information. Scan the essay to locate the reference to UN statistics, and you see that those statistics tell us "by the year 2030, more than 60 percent of the world population will be urban, up from 30 percent in 1950." In other words, there has been a dramatic change in the look of the world, thanks to urbanization. This correlates to choice A. It does not contradict demographers' claims (choice B), nor does it say anything about poverty, crime, or birth rate (choices C and D). Notice that this kind of question asks you to think "outside" the passage a bit more than comprehension questions 45 and 46 did.

48. **The correct answer is C.** This application question looks at cause and effect, not as directly presented in the essay, but rather as implied by the essay. In fact, you may have been alarmed to see that the word *skyscraper* never appears in the passage at all, so scanning the passage does not help. Remember that questions get harder within a question set. This question, the fourth one in the set, is harder than the first three. The clue to the answer is in the last line of the essay. "Megacities," the author claims," are creating anew even deeper division between rich and poor, as the poor concentrate in the outskirts of town and the rich barricade themselves behind walls and in towers." Those "towers" are the high-rise apartment buildings

in which the rich dwell, whereas the poor live in shanties on the cities' outskirts. The only answer supported by the text is choice C.

49. **The correct answer is D.** This incorporation of information question asks you to apply new evidence to an existing argument. This kind of question takes you furthest from the passage itself in an effort to get you to recognize its real-world applications. You might begin by scanning to locate the part of the passage that deals with the contention mentioned: that cities will continue to grow despite a slowing of migration from the countryside. It appears in paragraph 5, and its causative link is the notion that "the birth rate in less-developed nations is high." If you take away this cause, as choice D would do, then the author's supposition that cities will continue to grow has no foundation. None of the other answer choices would collapse the argument as well.

Passage IX 50. **The correct answer is A.** This comprehension question has to do with interpreting vocabulary. The first thing to do is to scan the passage and search for the word *radicalism*. It appears in paragraph 4, in the context of qualities that informed Rivera's artwork. It is not used in a negative connotation, as choices B and C would indicate. Choice D is almost right, but again, it has a more negative connotation than the passage implies. Therefore, choice A is the best answer.

51. **The correct answer is C.** This evaluation question asks you to analyze an argument. Authors rarely include information without a reason, and the MCAT often asks you to identify and assess the reasons behind the inclusion of a passage or phrase. Here, Orozco's art is discussed in its relation to politics, from his Holy Trinity of workers to his political cartoons. Although choice B might be correct in a different context, choice C is the better answer.

52. **The correct answer is D.** This evaluation question requires you to assess evidence. Ideally, a writer does not include a statement without adequate support. Here, the statement is that Siqueiros might approve of Chicano graffiti. If you scan to find the exact reference in paragraph 5, you see that the author states, "It began as outlaw art, which surely would have appealed to an outlaw such as Siqueiros." That is a clear giveaway that choice D is the best response; Chicano art was outlaw art, and Siqueiros was considered by many to be an outlaw, or gangster.

53. **The correct answer is A.** This application question calls for making generalizations about a topic—in this case, graffiti. To do this correctly, you must put together the author's statements about the topic and draw a conclusion from the information you are given. Paragraphs on graffiti appear at the end of the passage. Although the author refers to it as "outlaw art" and mentions that some people considered it a nuisance, that is clearly not the author's own impression. Phrases such as "managed to create something beautiful while making political statements about poverty, injustice, diversity, and racism" and "public art ... that ... is truly for

everyone" put a positive spin on the topic. The author does not believe that graffiti is a "pale imitation" (choice B); instead, she indicates that the graffiti artists are following in the muralists' tradition. Choice D appears as a description of Rivera's work and is not relevant to this discussion of graffiti. That makes choice A the most logical answer.

EVALUATION CHART

Use this evaluation chart to analyze your results on the science sections (Sections 1, 2, and 3) of the Practice Test 3. The chart matches each test question to specific content areas that you can review as part of this book's **online resources**. (See page ix, How to Use This Book.) Check the Answers and Explanations section to see which questions you got correct and which ones you missed. For each question that you missed, find the question number in the left column of the following chart. Look in the right column to find the location of the related review material. If you missed questions in a specific content area, you need to pay particular attention to that area as you study for the MCAT.

Item Number	Content Area
Biological and Biochemical Foundations of Living Systems	
1.	Chapter 4: Principles of Bioenergetics and Fuel Molecule Metabolism
2.	Chapter 2: Transmission of Genetic Information from the Gene to the Protein
3.	Chapter 1: Structure and Function of Proteins and Their Constituent Amino Acids
4.	Chapter 3: Transmission of Heritable Information from Generation to Generation and Processes That Increase Genetic Diversity
5.	Chapter 2: Transmission of Genetic Information from the Gene to the Protein
6.	Chapter 2: Transmission of Genetic Information from the Gene to the Protein
7.	Chapter 3: Transmission of Heritable Information from Generation to Generation and Processes That Increase Genetic Diversity
8.	Chapter 1: Structure and Function of Proteins and Their Constituent Amino Acids
9.	Chapter 2: Transmission of Genetic Information from the Gene to the Protein
10.	Chapter 2: Transmission of Genetic Information from the Gene to the Protein
11.	Chapter 2: Transmission of Genetic Information from the Gene to the Protein
12.	Chapter 2: Transmission of Genetic Information from the Gene to the Protein
13.	Chapter 1: Structure and Function of Proteins and Their Constituent Amino Acids
14.	Chapter 1: Structure and Function of Proteins and Their Constituent Amino Acids
15.	Chapter 1: Structure and Function of Proteins and Their Constituent Amino Acids
16.	Chapter 1: Structure and Function of Proteins and Their Constituent Amino Acids
17.	Chapter 2: Transmission of Genetic Information from the Gene to the Protein
18.	Chapter 2: Transmission of Genetic Information from the Gene to the Protein
19.	Chapter 2: Transmission of Genetic Information from the Gene to the Protein
20.	Chapter 2: Transmission of Genetic Information from the Gene to the Protein
21.	Chapter 7: Processes of Cell Division, Differentiation, and Specialization

(Continued)

Item Number	Content Area
22.	Chapter 5: Assemblies of Molecules, Cells, and Groups of Cells Within Multicellular Organisms
23.	Chapter 5: Assemblies of Molecules, Cells, and Groups of Cells Within Multicellular Organisms
24.	Chapter 5: Assemblies of Molecules, Cells, and Groups of Cells Within Multicellular Organisms
25.	Chapter 5: Assemblies of Molecules, Cells, and Groups of Cells Within Multicellular Organisms
26.	Chapter 5: Assemblies of Molecules, Cells, and Groups of Cells Within Multicellular Organisms
27.	Chapter 5: Assemblies of Molecules, Cells, and Groups of Cells Within Multicellular Organisms
28.	Chapter 5: Assemblies of Molecules, Cells, and Groups of Cells Within Multicellular Organisms
29.	Chapter 6: Structure, Growth, Physiology, and Genetics of Prokaryotes and Viruses
30.	Chapter 6: Structure, Growth, Physiology, and Genetics of Prokaryotes and Viruses
31.	Chapter 6: Structure, Growth, Physiology, and Genetics of Prokaryotes and Viruses
32.	Chapter 6: Structure, Growth, Physiology, and Genetics of Prokaryotes and Viruses
33.	Chapter 6: Structure, Growth, Physiology, and Genetics of Prokaryotes and Viruses
34.	Chapter 6: Structure, Growth, Physiology, and Genetics of Prokaryotes and Viruses
35.	Chapter 6: Structure, Growth, Physiology, and Genetics of Prokaryotes and Viruses
36.	Chapter 6: Structure, Growth, Physiology, and Genetics of Prokaryotes and Viruses
37.	Chapter 7: Processes of Cell Division, Differentiation, and Specialization
38.	Chapter 7: Processes of Cell Division, Differentiation, and Specialization
39.	Chapter 7: Processes of Cell Division, Differentiation, and Specialization
40.	Chapter 7: Processes of Cell Division, Differentiation, and Specialization
41.	Chapter 5: Assemblies of Molecules, Cells, and Groups of Cells Within Multicellular Organisms
42.	Chapter 5: Assemblies of Molecules, Cells, and Groups of Cells Within Multicellular Organisms
43.	Chapter 5: Assemblies of Molecules, Cells, and Groups of Cells Within Multicellular Organisms
44.	Chapter 5: Assemblies of Molecules, Cells, and Groups of Cells Within Multicellular Organisms
45.	Chapter 9: Structure and Integrative Functions of the Main Organ Systems
46.	Chapter 8: Structure and Function of the Nervous and Endocrine Systems and Ways in Which These Systems Coordinate the Organ Systems
47.	Chapter 9: Structure and Integrative Functions of the Main Organ Systems
48.	Chapter 8: Structure and Function of the Nervous and Endocrine Systems and Ways in Which These Systems Coordinate the Organ Systems
49.	Chapter 8: Structure and Function of the Nervous and Endocrine Systems and Ways in Which These Systems Coordinate the Organ Systems
50.	Chapter 8: Structure and Function of the Nervous and Endocrine Systems and Ways in Which These Systems Coordinate the Organ Systems

Item Number	Content Area
51.	Chapter 8: Structure and Function of the Nervous and Endocrine Systems and Ways in Which These Systems Coordinate the Organ Systems
52.	Chapter 8: Structure and Function of the Nervous and Endocrine Systems and Ways in Which These Systems Coordinate the Organ Systems
53.	Chapter 9: Structure and Integrative Functions of the Main Organ Systems
54.	Chapter 9: Structure and Integrative Functions of the Main Organ Systems
55.	Chapter 9: Structure and Integrative Functions of the Main Organ Systems
56.	Chapter 9: Structure and Integrative Functions of the Main Organ Systems
57.	Chapter 8: Structure and Function of the Nervous and Endocrine Systems and Ways in Which These Systems Coordinate the Organ Systems
58.	Chapter 8: Structure and Function of the Nervous and Endocrine Systems and Ways in Which These Systems Coordinate the Organ Systems
59.	Chapter 9: Structure and Integrative Functions of the Main Organ Systems

Chemical and Physical Foundations of Biological Systems

Item Number	Content Area
1.	Chapter 1: Translational Motion, Forces, Work, Energy, and Equilibrium in Living Systems
2.	Chapter 1: Translational Motion, Forces, Work, Energy, and Equilibrium in Living Systems
3.	Chapter 1: Translational Motion, Forces, Work, Energy, and Equilibrium in Living Systems
4.	Chapter 1: Translational Motion, Forces, Work, Energy, and Equilibrium in Living Systems
5.	Chapter 1: Translational Motion, Forces, Work, Energy, and Equilibrium in Living Systems
6.	Chapter 5: Atoms, Nuclear Decay, Electronic Structure, and Atomic Chemical Behavior
7.	Chapter 2: Importance of Fluids for the Circulation of Blood, Gas Movement, and Gas Exchange
8.	Chapter 5: Atoms, Nuclear Decay, Electronic Structure, and Atomic Chemical Behavior
9.	Chapter 5: Atoms, Nuclear Decay, Electronic Structure, and Atomic Chemical Behavior
10.	Chapter 5: Atoms, Nuclear Decay, Electronic Structure, and Atomic Chemical Behavior
11.	Chapter 5: Atoms, Nuclear Decay, Electronic Structure, and Atomic Chemical Behavior
12.	Chapter 5: Atoms, Nuclear Decay, Electronic Structure, and Atomic Chemical Behavior
13.	Chapter 2: Importance of Fluids for the Circulation of Blood, Gas Movement, and Gas Exchange
14.	Chapter 4: How Light and Sound Interact with Matter
15.	Chapter 3: Electrochemistry and Electrical Circuits and Their Elements
16.	Chapter 4: How Light and Sound Interact with Matter
17.	Chapter 4: How Light and Sound Interact with Matter
18.	Chapter 4: How Light and Sound Interact with Matter
19.	Chapter 4: How Light and Sound Interact with Matter
20.	Chapter 4: How Light and Sound Interact with Matter
21.	Chapter 1: Translational Motion, Forces, Work, Energy, and Equilibrium in Living Systems
22.	Chapter 1: Translational Motion, Forces, Work, Energy, and Equilibrium in Living Systems

(*Continued*)

Item Number	Content Area
23.	Chapter 1: Translational Motion, Forces, Work, Energy, and Equilibrium in Living Systems
24.	Chapter 1: Translational Motion, Forces, Work, Energy, and Equilibrium in Living Systems
25.	Chapter 1: Translational Motion, Forces, Work, Energy, and Equilibrium in Living Systems
26.	Chapter 1: Translational Motion, Forces, Work, Energy, and Equilibrium in Living Systems
27.	Chapter 7: The Nature of Molecules and Intermolecular Interactions
28.	Chapter 5: Atoms, Nuclear Decay, Electronic Structure, and Atomic Chemical Behavior
29.	Chapter 5: Atoms, Nuclear Decay, Electronic Structure, and Atomic Chemical Behavior
30.	Chapter 5: Atoms, Nuclear Decay, Electronic Structure, and Atomic Chemical Behavior
31.	Chapter 5: Atoms, Nuclear Decay, Electronic Structure, and Atomic Chemical Behavior
32.	Chapter 5: Atoms, Nuclear Decay, Electronic Structure, and Atomic Chemical Behavior
33.	Chapter 6: The Unique Nature of Water and Its Solutions
34.	Chapter 6: The Unique Nature of Water and Its Solutions
35.	Chapter 6: The Unique Nature of Water and Its Solutions
36.	Chapter 6: The Unique Nature of Water and Its Solutions
37.	Chapter 6: The Unique Nature of Water and Its Solutions
38.	Chapter 6: The Unique Nature of Water and Its Solutions
39.	Chapter 9: Structure, Function, and Reactivity of Biologically Relevant Molecules
40.	Chapter 9: Structure, Function, and Reactivity of Biologically Relevant Molecules
41.	Chapter 9: Structure, Function, and Reactivity of Biologically Relevant Molecules
42.	Chapter 9: Structure, Function, and Reactivity of Biologically Relevant Molecules
43.	Chapter 9: Structure, Function, and Reactivity of Biologically Relevant Molecules
44.	Chapter 10: Principles of Chemical Thermodynamics and Kinetics
45.	Chapter 10: Principles of Chemical Thermodynamics and Kinetics
46.	Chapter 9: Structure, Function, and Reactivity of Biologically Relevant Molecules
47.	Chapter 9: Structure, Function, and Reactivity of Biologically Relevant Molecules
48.	Chapter 10: Principles of Chemical Thermodynamics and Kinetics
49.	Chapter 9: Structure, Function, and Reactivity of Biologically Relevant Molecules
50.	Chapter 9: Structure, Function, and Reactivity of Biologically Relevant Molecules
51.	Chapter 9: Structure, Function, and Reactivity of Biologically Relevant Molecules
52.	Chapter 9: Structure, Function, and Reactivity of Biologically Relevant Molecules

Item Number	Content Area
53.	Chapter 6: The Unique Nature of Water and Its Solutions
54.	Chapter 6: The Unique Nature of Water and Its Solutions
55.	Chapter 6: The Unique Nature of Water and Its Solutions
56.	Chapter 6: The Unique Nature of Water and Its Solutions
57.	Chapter 6: The Unique Nature of Water and Its Solutions
58.	Chapter 7: The Nature of Molecules and Intermolecular Interactions
59.	Chapter 6: The Unique Nature of Water and Its Solutions

Psychological, Social, and Biological Foundations of Behavior

1.	Chapter 1: Sensing the Environment
2.	Chapter 1: Sensing the Environment
3.	Chapter 1: Sensing the Environment
4.	Chapter 1: Sensing the Environment
5.	Chapter 1: Sensing the Environment
6.	Chapter 1: Sensing the Environment
7.	Chapter 2: Making Sense of the Environment
8.	Chapter 2: Making Sense of the Environment
9.	Chapter 2: Making Sense of the Environment
10.	Chapter 2: Making Sense of the Environment
11.	Chapter 3: Responding to the World
12.	Chapter 3: Responding to the World
13.	Chapter 3: Responding to the World
14.	Chapter 3: Responding to the World
15.	Chapter 3: Responding to the World
16.	Chapter 2: Making Sense of the Environment
17.	Chapter 2: Making Sense of the Environment
18.	Chapter 1: Sensing the Environment
19.	Chapter 1: Sensing the Environment
20.	Chapter 1: Sensing the Environment
21.	Chapter 1: Sensing the Environment
22.	Chapter 1: Sensing the Environment
23.	Chapter 4: Individual Influences on Behavior
24.	Chapter 4: Individual Influences on Behavior
25.	Chapter 4: Individual Influences on Behavior
26.	Chapter 4: Individual Influences on Behavior
27.	Chapter 4: Individual Influences on Behavior
28.	Chapter 4: Individual Influences on Behavior
29.	Chapter 5: Social Processes That Influence Human Behavior
30.	Chapter 5: Social Processes That Influence Human Behavior
31.	Chapter 5: Social Processes That Influence Human Behavior
32.	Chapter 5: Social Processes That Influence Human Behavior
33.	Chapter 5: Social Processes That Influence Human Behavior
34.	Chapter 6: Attitude and Behavior Change
35.	Chapter 6: Attitude and Behavior Change
36.	Chapter 6: Attitude and Behavior Change
37.	Chapter 6: Attitude and Behavior Change
38.	Chapter 7: Self-Identity
39.	Chapter 7: Self-Identity
40.	Chapter 7: Self-Identity
41.	Chapter 7: Self-Identity
42.	Chapter 7: Self-Identity

(*Continued*)

Item Number	Content Area
43.	Chapter 7: Self-Identity
44.	Chapter 8: Social Thinking
45.	Chapter 8: Social Thinking
46.	Chapter 8: Social Thinking
47.	Chapter 8: Social Thinking
48.	Chapter 10: Understanding Social Structure
49.	Chapter 11: Demographic Characteristics and Processes
50.	Chapter 11: Demographic Characteristics and Processes
51.	Chapter 11: Demographic Characteristics and Processes
52.	Chapter 11: Demographic Characteristics and Processes
53.	Chapter 12: Social Inequality
54.	Chapter 12: Social Inequality
55.	Chapter 12: Social Inequality
56.	Chapter 12: Social Inequality
57.	Chapter 12: Social Inequality
58.	Chapter 12: Social Inequality
59.	Chapter 12: Social Inequality